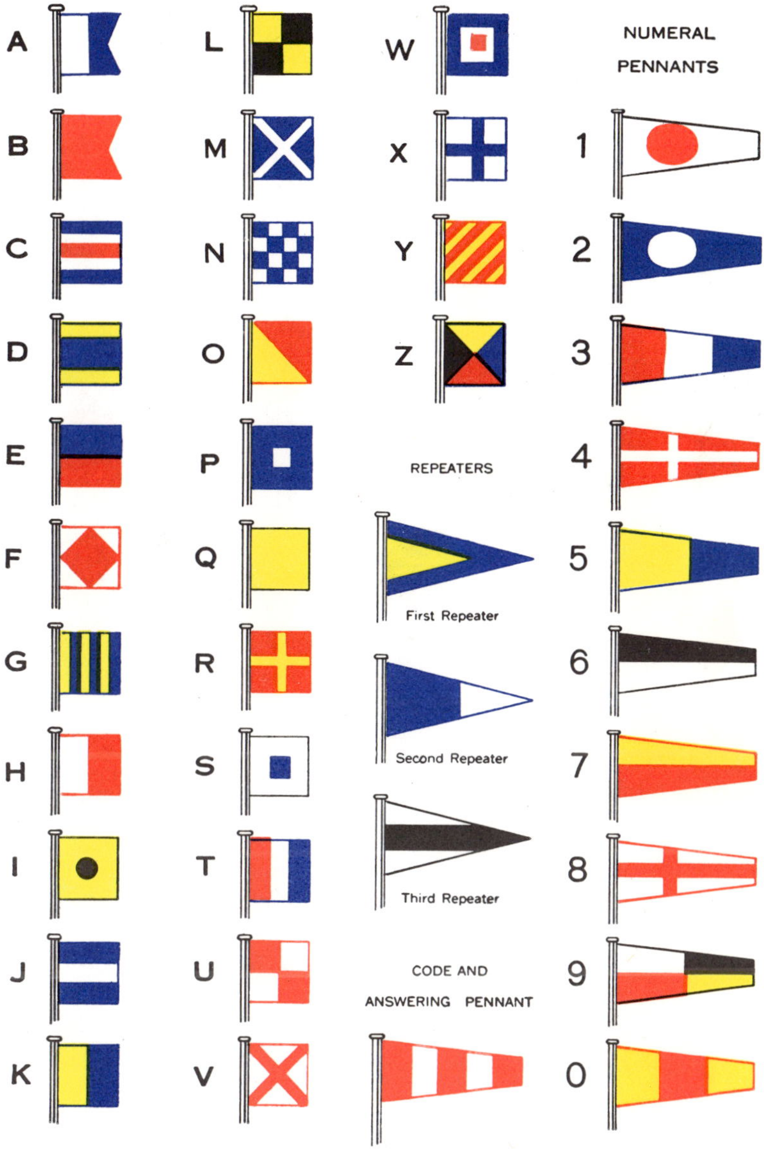

International Code Flags and Pennants.

THE VNR DICTIONARY OF SHIPS & The SEA

John V. Noel
Captain, USN (ret.)

 VAN NOSTRAND REINHOLD COMPANY
NEW YORK   CINCINNATI   ATLANTA   DALLAS   SAN FRANCISCO
LONDON   TORONTO   MELBOURNE

Van Nostrand Reinhold Company Regional Offices:
New York Cincinnati Atlanta Dallas San Francisco

Van Nostrand Reinhold Company International Offices:
London Toronto Melbourne

Copyright © 1981 by Litton Educational Publishing, Inc.

Library of Congress Catalog Card Number: 80-15276
ISBN: 0-442-25631-0

All rights reserved. No part of this work covered by the copyright hereon may be reproduced or used in any form or by any means—graphic, electronic, or mechanical, including photocopying, recording, taping, or information storage and retrieval systems—without permission of the publisher.

Manufactured in the United States of America

Published by Van Nostrand Reinhold Company
135 West 50th Street, New York, N.Y. 10020

Published simultaneously in Canada by Van Nostrand Reinhold Ltd.

15 14 13 12 11 10 9 8 7 6 5 4 3 2 1

Library of Congress Cataloging in Publication Data

Noel, John Vavasour, 1912-
   The VNR dictionary of ships and the sea.

   1. Naval art and science—Dictionaries. I. Title.
V23.N63   359'.003'21   80-15276
ISBN 0-442-25631-0

*This book is dedicated
with respect and admiration
to*

Jacques-Yves Cousteau

Preface

This is the first, new, general maritime dictionary in over 30 years and thus, it reflects the world of the ocean and its ships as we are interested in them today. Man's new appreciation of the sea and its environmental, as well as its economic importance to his welfare, are recognized. The age of sail has not been forgotten, particularly as it is reflected in modern sailing for recreation and adventure, but the major emphasis is on the world's shipping as it develops technically. Some ancient nautical terms, old even in the latest days of sail, dealing with building and rigging sailing ships have been omitted unless they have survived in modern usage.

All major activities and disciplines of the sea have been considered in the selection of the words to define; including oceanography, ocean engineering, familiar sea mammals, fish and plants, weather, ships and shipping, seamanship along with operating in ice, cargo handling, commercial maritime terms, marine insurance, ships and gear used in ocean fishing, yachting under power and sail, and the sport of surfing. Whaling, fortunately nearly finished due to the disappearance of most whales, is not treated in depth. In selecting words from this broad spectrum, an effort has been made to choose those of interest to the layman and generalist.

This book is truly a dictionary in that it defines words and terms but does not explain how. Familiar words with a great many general meanings are defined only in regard to their maritime use, such as the word overhaul. Compound terms are usually listed under the noun, unless the adjective is the distinctive word, as for example, in naval stores. Whenever possible, words are defined according to their legal sense, such as vessel or short blast. Guidance to the pronounciation is provided only when radical differences exist, such as for the words tompion and tackle. Only naval terms of general interest are included. Acronyms relevant to the ocean are given but the term itself is only defined when its meaning is not obvious. Words, peculiar to the sea that are used in definitions, are not identified; it can be assumed that they are defined elsewhere in the book.

British words, so often different in meaning from their American counterpart, are noted but no claim is made that all have been included. Many British terms, particularly in yachting and marine insurance, seem to have moved across the Atlantic and these are defined.

I acknowledge with gratitude the assistance of Commander George W. Loveridge USN (ret.) whose review of the manuscript was most constructive.

The language of the sea, like so many others, is always growing and changing, and there are often legitimate differences of opinion among literate mariners as to current meaning. Words often have a regional meaning — a scow in San Francisco may be called a barge or lighter in Baltimore. Comments and criticism will be most attentively and appreciatively received and will be incorporated to improve future revision.

Captain John V. Noel, USN (ret.)

A

A. International signal code alphabet burgee. When hoisted singly means: "I have a diver down; keep well clear at slow speed." Spoken: "alpha."

A#1. An insurance rating given by Lloyds of London for the highest quality equipment on a ship.

A-60 bulkhead. A fire and flame resistant bulkhead insulated to meet certain temperature requirements for 60 minutes.

AA. Always Afloat. *See* always safely afloat.

AAR. Against All Risks.

AB. Able Bodied. *See* able bodied seamen.

aback. A sail is aback when sheeted to windward causing a braking effect on the ship's motion or when the wind strikes it on what has been the lee side. A ship is thus taken aback and may be forced astern.

abaft. Back of, towards the stern; used by a seaman instead of aft of.

abaft the beam. Behind a horizontal line drawn at the center of, and perpendicular to, the fore and aft axis of the ship.

abalone. A large edible marine snail or gastropod with a single protective shell and a muscular foot used for locomotion and firm attachment to submerged rocks near the shore. Found along the rocky coasts of all continents and many islands. Called abs (plural) for short in California; ormer, omar or Venus Ears in the United Kingdom.

abandonment. A marine insurance term used to designate damage to a ship equivalent to total loss.

abeam. Said of something that is to the side of a ship, midway between dead ahead and dead astern.

able. In seamen's language means capable, seaworthy, and well equipped in describing a ship.

able bodied seaman (AB). An experienced deck hand, superior to an ordinary seaman; one who can "reef, hand and steer."

aboard. In or on any ship or station. A sailor properly serves in a ship.

about. To go or come about is to tack in a sailboat, i.e. to steer the bow into and then across the wind in order to have the wind blow against the other side of the sail.

abreast. By the side of. A ship may lie abreast or alongside of another.

ABS. American Bureau of Shipping. *See* classification. Also Acrylic Butadiene Styrene, a plastic used to mold small boats.

absence flag or indicator. A flag that indicates the absence of the ship's owner, master, or commanding officer. Also called an absentee. In a yacht, it is a small, rectangular blue flag during the day and a blue light at night.

absentee. *See* absence indicator.

aburton. A cargo stowage word describing cargo stowed athwartships instead of fore-and-aft.

abyss. A modern word for ocean deep. The abyssal zone extends from the four degree isotherm (1000-3000 meters) to the ocean bottom. *See* benthic division, hadal, bathal.

abyssal hill. A small topographic feature of the deep ocean floor; 2000 to 3000 feet high and a few miles wide.

abyssal plain. A nearly flat, large area of very deep ocean floor with a slope of less than five degrees per mile. Term now used instead of deep to denote the ocean bottom.

abyssobenthic. A term describing sea life on the ocean floor or abyssal plain. *See* bathybenthic, bathypelagic.

abyssopelagic. A term describing fish and other animals living in ocean depths over 6000 feet deep. *See* bathypelagic, bathybenthic.

acanthaster. A coral-eating starfish that destroys coral reefs. Also called crown-of-thorns.

acceleration of the tide. *See* tide.

accommodation ladder. Portable steps from the gangway (access to the ship) to the water with platforms at the top and bottom. Sometimes called a gangway ladder but term should never refer to a gangway. *See* gangway, ladder.

accommodations. Old word for the living quarters aboard ship.

acey deucey. A nautical version of backgammon, popular in the Navy.

acorn. Small ornamental conical or global piece of wood that once retained the windvane on top of the masthead of a square-rigger.

acropora. A variety of green, mauve, and blue hard coral attaining heights up to eight feet in shapes of branches or umbrellas.

"Act of God." An expression used in marine insurance and chartering to indicate a misfortune or loss which could not have been prevented by reasonable precaution. Same as force majeure.

address commission. A chartering term. A percentage of the freight sometimes paid to charterers upon the signing of the bills of lading. If none is due, the vessel is free of address.

adjustable pitch propeller. Adjustable blades that increase, decrease, or reverse the angle at which they push the water; permits the use of a constant speed motor or engine. *See* variable pitch propeller.

admeasurement, certificate of. Certificate issued by the U.S. Customs listing exempted spaces in computing the registered tonnage of the ship.

admeasurer. Person who measures the inside of a ship for registry purposes.

admiral. The highest ranking naval officer of flag rank. Also among North Sea fishermen, the senior captain who directs operations when several vessels are fishing together. In sailing ship days, a long wooden fid used to open the eyes of hemp rigging.

admiralty. The system of jurisprudence relating to both civil and criminal maritime law. Admiralty courts have jurisdiction over all matters relating to the sea. In the U.S., the Constitution grants it to all navigable waters; in other countries, it usually extends only to the sea below the low water mark in tidal waters.

adrift. Free upon the waters; neither moored nor anchored in any way nor under any propulsive power. In naval usage, means not properly stowed.

advance. Distance a ship continues to travel on the original course while undergoing a turning maneuver; measured from the point at which the rudder was put over to the point where the ship has arrived on her new course. *See* transfer.

advance staysail. A light, four-sided staysail set above the main staysail in schooner-rigged yachts.

advantage. A tackle is rigged or rove to advantage when the moving block holds the hauling part. If the hauling part leads to the fixed block, there is less mechanical advantage and thus the tackle is rigged to disadvantage.

advection fog. Fog formed at sea by warm humid air over cold water.

adventure. A commercial venture. In marine insurance, a period or risk, whether or not insured. *See* frustration of the adventure.

adze. A hand wood-working tool with the cutting edge set at right angle to the handle; used by shipwrights for trimming planks and timbers.

aeolian dust. Fine sand blown off deserts combined with cosmic dust, organic debris, salt, and man-made pollution to form sea haze.

afloat. Supported by water; not aground.

afore. Archaic word for forward of.

A frame. A triangular metal tubular frame used to support a latteen sail in a catamaran. Also called bipod spars.

aft. Towards the ship's stern as in "go aft." A seaman says "abaft," not "aft of."

after. An adjective meaning towards the stern as in the after engineroom or the after mast.

afterbody. The after part of a ship's hull, abaft the middle or midships.

after bow (quarter) spring. A mooring line at the bow (quarter) that leads aft from the ship to the pier. *See* mooring line.

aftercastle. Old word for poop, the aftermost structure on deck; no longer used.

afterguard. The officers who traditionally lived aft. Now a yachting term for the owner and his guests. The officers of a yacht club.

afterguy. A line controlling the fore-and-aft trim of the spinnaker pole.

afterhoods. In wooden ship construction, all the after ends of the planking fitted into the sternpost.

afterpeak. *See* peak.

after perpendicular. The frame station farthest aft, usually at the intersection of the waterline and the after end of the sternpost.

afterrake. Part of the stern that overhangs the keel.

afterspring. *See* spring.

agar. A jelly (colloid) made from an algae known as agarophyte and used principally for bacteria culture, the food industry, and the production of beer, wine, and cosmetics. *See* algin.

age of the moon. The time since the last new moon.

age of the tide. The interval between the time of new or full moon and the maximum effect of these phases upon the range of tide or the speed of tidal currents.

Ageton's. A navigational method that starts with the Dead Reckoning position; devised by Adm. Arthur Ageton who is also known for his sight reduction table, a government publication, H.O. 211.

agonic line. A line that joins points on the earth's surface which do not have magnetic variation.

aground. A ship resting on the ocean floor. When put aground or allowed to take ground deliberately, a ship is said to take ground. If done accidently, she is run aground. *See* grounding, stranding.

Aguaje. The extensive discoloration of water off the coast of Peru caused by the sudden death of plankton due to sudden changes in the temperature of the sea.

Agulhas current. A strong branch of the South Indian Ocean Equatorial current that flows south through the Mozambique Channel along the east coast of Africa and deflected eastward by the Agulhas Bank.

ahead. Forward of the bow. Also a ship may go ahead showly but when she backs, she goes astern.

Ahoy. A traditional nautical hail, still used in the Navy but usually replaced elsewhere, these days, by "Hello" or "Hi there."

ahull. A vessel that spreads no canvas nor uses engines in very heavy weather is lying ahull as it drifts; sometimes a sound tactic. Also called hulling. *See* heave to.

Air Almanac. Similar to the Nautical Almanac but designed for celestial navigating in aircraft instead of surface ships and thus arranged somewhat differently; published by the Naval Observatory. *See* Nautical Almanac.

air ejector. In a steam power plant, a device that removes air from a condenser thereby increasing its efficiency.

airfoil. In the maritime sense, the curve of a sail over its whole area.

air lift. A suction pump used to draw up sand and debris from a wreck to recover artifacts and other treasures. Also a spraytight fitting or opening on deck used for the escape of ventilating air in a ship.

airlock. A double door that preserves the air pressure in a ship's fireroom or any other pressurized space and that lets people come and go.

airport. A round opening in a ship's side fitted with a hinged glass cover (portlight) and a metal cover (deadlight or Navy term, battleport). A ventilating deadlight as well as a windscoop may be inserted. British term: scuttle or sidescuttle.

air register. An air regulating device in the casing of a boiler.

airscoop. Same as windscoop.

Alaska current. The north flowing branch of the Aleutian current carrying relatively warm water. It flows into the Gulf of Alaska where it circulates counterclockwise.

albacore. Part of the tuna and mackerel family, distinguished by its very long pectoral fins, white meat and fighting spirit when hooked. *Thunnus alalunga* is found worldwide, grows to 90 pounds and is important commercially.

albatross. A large bird of the petrel family with a wing span of up to 20 feet. The wandering albatross follows ships far at sea for months.

alcyonian. A form of soft coral in pink, green and blue. It swells up at night to large dimensions and then shrinks with the arrival of day.

Aldis lamp. A portable light used for signaling by ships and aircraft.

alee. On or toward the sheltered side of a ship or boat, away from the wind. Except for the expression hard alee, concerning the tiller of a sailboat when tacking, the word is seldom heard today. Common usage is to leeward.

Aleutian current. The northern extension of the Japan current or Kuroshio. Flowing east between 40 and 50 degrees north latitude, it divides into the Alaska current that flows north into the Gulf of Alaska and a southward branch that becomes the California current.

alewife. A small baitfish of the herring family.

algae. Marine plants ranging from very small (single cell phytoplankton) to large kelp and other seaweed.

algin. The generic name of a water-soluble gum extracted from brown seaweed such as kelp. It is used to stabilize and thicken food, drugs, etc.

alidade. Aboard ship, a bearing circle equipped with a telescopic sight for taking bearings and azimuths. It is usually fitted over a pelorus or dumb compass with unobstructed vision. *See* pelorus, bearing circle.

All Hands. All those aboard ship except those on watch. Also a call made on a boatswain's pipe.

all hatch ship. A modern cargo ship having a maximum number of holds divided into compartments, each of which has its own hatch serviced by a crane instead of a boom.

allowance list. List of machinery spare parts and tools needed for ship operations. Other allowance lists include electronic spares or weapons spares.

all standing. Literally describes a ship with all her sails up or set. A sailing ship may run aground or jibe all standing, usually with unfortunate results. Officers and men on duty but not actually on their feet, such as the anchor watch, may turn in all standing which means fully dressed.

all time. Surfer's slang for great, fantastic, wonderful.

all told. A chartering term describing deadweight capacity that includes bunkers, water, provisions, dunnage, stores and spare parts.

almanac. *See* Air Almanac, Nautical Almanac.

Almanac for Computers. An almanac that provides equations and numerical constants from which celestial navigation calculations can be done by computers; published by the Naval Observatory—first edition 1979.

aloft. Up above, topside, opposite of below or alow.

alow. Old word meaning below; the opposite of aloft. Rarely used.

altars. Steps on the side of a graving dock extending virtually all the way around; used to support shores.

altitude. In celestial navigation, the vertical angle between the horizon and a celestial body, measured with a sextant. This observed altitude, when corrected for the sextant's index error, is apparant altitude and when also corrected for dip and semi-diameter (sun and moon) becomes rectified or corrected altitude.

alto cumulus, altostratus. *See* clouds.

Aluminaut. An aluminum hull research submarine, 50 feet long, designed to reach a depth of 15,000 feet.

Alusna. Official abbreviation for U.S. Naval Attache. An officer stationed in most U.S. embassies to advise the ambassador on naval and shipping matters and to collect intelligence.

always safely afloat. A clause in a charter party that prevents the loaded ship from being sent to a port where she may have to take the ground at low water.

ama. The sea women of Japan who dive, for example, for oysters or seaweed. Also an outrigger or additional hull of a multihull boat.

ambergris. A fatty substance sometimes found in the intestines of a male sperm whale or floating on the sea; used in making perfume and was, at one time, extremely valuable.

American Bureau of Shipping. The U.S. classification society that provides information and establishes design, construction and operating standards for U.S. ships; issues annually The Record and, monthly, The Bulletin which contain matters of interest to those involved with shipping.

American Ephemeris. An astronomical almanac containing the coordinates of sun, moon, planets, certain stars, and other data useful to astronomers and those doing celestial navigation; published by the U.S. Naval Observatory. *See* Nautical Almanac.

American Institute of Marine Underwriters. The trade association for companies, American and foreign, who handle marine insurance in the U.S.

America's Cup. A trophy first won in England by the U.S. schooner America in 1851 and held since by the New York Yacht Club despite periodic challenges by foreign 12-meters.

amidships or midships. In the center or middle of a vessel. "Rudder amidships" is an order to the helmsman to bring the rudder in line with the keel.

amphibious. At home both on land and at sea, such as a turtle or an amphibious tank.

amphibious operation or landing. An operation or landing carried out by combined naval, land and air forces against an enemy coastal objective.

amphipod. A small crustacean found in polar waters and that feeds on plankton.

amphitrite. A 65 foot, six ton, shallow draft, inflatable boat used as a tender for diving operations.

amphora. A clay pot or urn, often with a pointed bottom, used in the ancient world to carry oil, wheat, wine, etc; found in most old wrecks and often recovered intact by divers or by fishermen trawling the bottom.

amplitude. In celestial navigation, the angle at the zenith between the prime vertical and the vertical circle passing through the observed body.

AMVER. Automatic Merchant Vessel Report System.

anadromous. A salt water fish such as a salmon or shad that lives at sea but enters fresh water to spawn. *See* catadromous.

anal fin. *See* fin.

anchor. A device that is lowered to the bottom of the sea by means of a chain or rope and that holds a vessel in place. Originally a lump of stone. Old fashioned or stock anchors have been largely replaced by stockless (patent) anchors that can conveniently be stowed in the hawsepipe, and anchors for special attachment such as screw anchors and those that can be forced into the ground by explosives, hammers, gravity, or by water jet. *See* mushroom anchor. stockless anchor, old-fashioned anchor, Danforth anchor, fisherman's anchor, plow anchor, Meon anchor, Baldt anchor, Bruce anchors, kedge, yachtsman's, Herreshoff.

anchorage. A place or area with good holding ground and protected from the sea where ships anchor; often marked by anchorage buoys.

anchor and chain certificate. A ship's document, issued by a classification society or government agency, stating that the anchors and chains have passed the required tests and inspections.

anchor and chain clause. A statement in some marine insurance policies that exempts the underwriters from the cost of recovering the anchor and chain if lost while the ship is afloat.

anchor ball. A visual indication that the vessel is at anchor. In inland U.S. waters, a black ball shown forward in the rigging. International Rules of the Road only require a ball displayed where it can be best seen.

anchor bar. A wooden hand spike once used to dislodge an old-fashioned anchor from the billboard.

anchor bed. Same as billboard.

anchor bells. Signals from the forecastle to the ship's bridge that are used to report the progress in heaving in the anchor. No longer used; now replaced by sound-powered telephones. The term is not to be confused with the ship's bells used to sound fog signals when the ship is anchored in the fog.

anchoring bolt. Bolt used to fasten down or secure a fitting, a piece of machinery or whatever.

anchor buoy. A small float, attached by a light line, that is used to mark the location of the anchor on the bottom; not to be confused with anchorage buoy.

anchor cable, chain. *See* chain.

anchor chock. A fitting on deck near the bow of a boat to hold the anchor in place when it is stowed on deck.

anchor crane. Crane installed on the centerline forward of the windlass for hoisting a stock or old-fashioned anchor on deck. It replaces the anchor davit or fish davit used previously.

anchor hoy. A lighter for carrying ground tackle around a harbor. Also called a chain boat.

anchor ice. Submerged sea ice attached to the bottom of the ocean. Also called bottom ice, depth ice, ground ice, and underwater ice.

anchoring expressions. 1. To back an anchor is to make fast a second anchor or a weight to its rode or anchor cable to increase the holding power. 2. To break out an anchor is to dislodge it from its partially submerged position before hauling it up. 3. To bring home an anchor is to pull the ship up to it when heaving in. 4. To cast an anchor is to drop it. 5. To fish an anchor is to bring an old-fashioned anchor aboard for securing. 6. To house an anchor is to bring it up snugly into the hawsepipe. 7. To gimlet an anchor is to rotate it at the hawse. 8. To sight an anchor is to heave it in far enough to see whether it is foul or clear. 9. To swallow the anchor is to retire from the sea and live ashore. 10. To shoe an anchor. *See* shoe. 11. To cat an anchor. *See* cat. *See* anchor's aweigh.

anchor knot. A fisherman's bend.

anchor lights. Lights required by the International or Inland Rules of the Road to be displayed by a ship at anchor or moored. Also called riding lights.

anchor lining. Sheathing on the bows of a vessel to prevent damage to the hull when hauling in the anchor.

anchor pocket. Recess at lower end of hawsepipe into which a stockless anchor is secured.

anchor ring. The ring fastened to the upper end of the shank of an anchor and to which the chain is shackled.

anchor rocket. Rocket with an anchor-shaped head for firing at a stranded vessel in order to make fast a rescue line.

anchor's aweigh. When hauling in the anchor before getting an anchored ship underway, the Boatswain on the forecastle reports to the bridge as appropriate: anchor at short stay, anchor up and down, anchor is aweigh, anchor in sight, clear (or foul) anchor, and finally, anchor secured for sea.

anchor shackle. A heavy shackle, a roughly U-shaped connecting link, by which the anchor is connected to its cable. Also any shackle whose center section is wider than its mouth. *See* shackle, bending shackle.

anchor shoe. A flat block of hardwood fastened to the hull to prevent damage by the bill of the anchor as it is brought aboard or when lowering. Also a broad triangular piece of wood fastened to the fluke of an anchor to improve its holding power when the bottom is soft.

anchor watch. A small group of men kept on duty when the ship is anchored at night or in heavy weather to handle emergencies. The anchor watch is usually permitted to sleep near the forecastle.

anchor windlass. *See* windlass.

anchovy. Very numerous, small (4 to 6 inches) fish of the family Engraulidae. They feed on plankton and are fed upon by larger fish, whales, seabirds, and humans.

anemone. A solitary, flower-like primitive sea animal, an invertebrate that lives attached to rocks or to a reef. It is cylindrical, muscular and crowned by a number of tentacles armed with stinging barbs with which it captures its food. An anemone fish, immune to these barbs, lives within the tentacles in a relationship of mutualism.

anemometer. An instrument that measures wind velocity and direction, usually indicated on a dial on the bridge or in the charthouse.

aneroid barometer. *See* barometer.

angary, right of. The claim by a belligerent power of the right to seize the ships of a neutral country for its own use if necessary.

angel. A light sail carried aloft in a square-rigger. *See* kites.

angelfish. A medium size, disc-shaped, flat tropical reef fish noted for its bright colors. The young are orange or yellow; the adults striped in black and white. Grows to two feet, is edible and lives in schools.

angle of attack. In a hydrofoil vessel, the angle between the foil (measured along the line joining its leading and trailing edges) and the direction of apparent movement of the oncoming water.

angle of incidence. In a hydrofoil vessel, the angle between the foil (measured along the line joining its leading and trailing edges) and the horizontal axis of the vessel.

angle of repose. The maximum angle of roll of a ship at which the bulk cargo will maintain its form. For grain, it is 25-35 degrees; for coal, 30-45 degrees. At greater angles the cargo, if unrestricted, will flow downhill like a liquid.

animal sling. Same as web sling.

annelid. An extensive family of wormlike animals, some of which build tubelike homes on the submerged portion of boats.

Annie Oakley. A yacht's spinnaker pierced with small holes for better control.

anniversary winds. Winds of local origin or on a larger scale, as the monsoon, that recur each year.

annunciator. Same as engine order telegraph.

answering pennant. One of the international signal code flags which, when hoisted singly at the dip means "your signal understood"; and when two-blocked, "your signal read but not understood."

Antarctic Circle. The geographic parrallel having a south latitude equal to the complement of the declination of the summer solstice (about 66 degrees and 33 minutes S).

Antarctic Circumpolar Current. The ocean current with the largest volume transport and swiftest current, flowing east around the Antarctic continent through all oceans. Also known as the West Wind Drift.

anti-cyclone. A high pressure weather mass around which the winds blow clockwise in the Northern Hemisphere (counter clockwise in the Southern); generally indicates fair weather. *See* cyclone.

anti-fouling paint. A special toxic composition applied to the ship's bottom to prevent marine growth, such as barnacles, that interferes with propulsion.

Antilles Current. An ocean current (the northern branch of the North Equatorial Current) flowing northwest along the northern side of the Greater Antilles (Cuba and Haiti). It eventually joins the Florida Current north of Florida Straits, thus joining the Gulf Stream System.

antipodes. Any place on the earth's surface opposite or opposed to another geographically, such as Australia and New Zealand because they are opposite to the United Kingdom.

antipodean day. The day gained in crossing the 180th meridian going west.

anti-rolling fins. Long, shallow steel blades running fore-and-aft along the turn of the bilge to provide resistance to the rolling of the ship. *See* bilge keel.

anti-rolling tanks. Tanks fitted into each side of a ship into which water can be pumped and transferred in order to reduce the rolling.

antitrades. A deep layer of westerly winds in the troposphere above the surface trade winds of the tropics. They are best developed in the winter.

apeak. In a vertical or nearly vertical position. Same as up and down when referring to an anchor being hauled in. Term rarely used.

aphelion. The point in the orbit of a heavenly body when it is farthest from the sun.

aphotic zone. Portion of the ocean with sufficient sunlight for photosynthesis; in contrast to the euphotic zone.

apnea. The suspension of breathing for a variable length of time that is characteristic of most sea mammals, such as whales.

apogee. The position of an earth satellite, such as the moon, when it is farthest in its orbit from the earth, as opposed to perigee.

apostle. Same as knighthead.

apparel. In chartering terms, describes the equipment of a vessel such as anchors, chains, or lifeboats. In old sailing days it was the collective name for the rigging used to support the masts.

apparent. In reference to celestial navigation means true or actual as opposed to mean. Since the earth moves in an elliptical orbit around the sun, its speed relative to the sun varies with its position in the orbit; thus the time for a complete rotation of the earth varies and the length of a day varies. Therefore a mean or average sun is conceived about which the earth rotates in exactly 24 hours. Apparent noon, sun, or time are real and true whereas mean describes the theoretical or average.

apparent wind. The wind felt by a person on a moving ship. It is the geometric sum of the true wind and the ship's course and speed.

appendage. Referring to a ship, a fitting that extends beyond the main hull, such as struts, rudder, shafting, or bilge keels.

apple stern. Describes a round convex stern, common in old Dutch sailing ships.

appurtenances. According to Admiralty law, all the tackle, furniture, and other gear necessary for the proper and designed operation of the ship.

apron 1. A curved timber inside a wooden ship above the forward end of her keel that is used to strengthen and join various parts of her stem. Also called a stemson or stomach-piece. 2. Part of a drydock on which the sill is fastened. 3. The area on a wharf or pier where cargo is unloaded.

aquaculture. Sea farming.

Aqua-lung. Trade name for the first self-contained underwater breathing apparatus (SCUBA) of the demand or open-circuit type, permitting free dives to considerable depths. Invented by Cousteau and Gagnan.

arcform. A type of steel ship construction in which the bilges are curved.

archipelagic apron. A gentle, smooth, fan-shaped slope on the floor of the ocean, found around groups of islands (archipelagoes) or seamounts.

arch knee. Curved timber fitted between the propeller post and the rudder post in a wooden ship.

Arctic Circle. The geographic parallel having a north latitude equal to the complement of the declination of the winter solstice (about 66 degrees and 33 minutes N).

Arctic Current. Same as Labrador Current.

Arctic tern. A graceful white seabird with a black cap that travels each year 25,000 miles from Alaska to the Antarctic and back.

ardent. A sailing ship that tends to come into the wind, thus requiring a weather helm. Contrary tendency is for the ship to fall away from the wind and to be slack. An ardent ship shows ardency.

argonaut. A small cephalopod living in warm and temperate oceans, usually found floating near the water's surface. The female is 20 times bigger than the male, whose only purpose is to impregnate her by losing his hectocotylus. Also called paper nautilus.

argosy. A large medieval trading carrack that sailed the Mediterranean, especially the Adriatic.

argument. The numerical value used in entering a navigational table.

arm. To fill the cavity at the bottom of a sounding lead with tallow or soap in order to learn the nature of the bottom. Also part of an old-fashioned anchor that branches out from the crown and becomes a palm or fluke. A timber knee is said to have two arms.

arm cleat. A cleat with one arm or horn. Also called a horn cleat.

armed guard. Naval gun crew aboard an armed merchant ship during wartime.

armed mast. Mast made of two timbers fastened together.

armored rope. Wire rope used mostly in salvage, that has a hemp or other fiber core and a flat wire wound around each wire strand.

armor rock. The very large pieces of stone that provide the facing for a groin.

arrest. A ship may be detained because of some violation of regulations. She is arrested if a maritime lien is to be served upon her.

Arret de Prince. An old term under International law that means the right of a belligerent to detain neutral vessels whose departure might result in revealing military information. The detainee supposedly pays for any consequent loss of trade.

arse. The lower opening in a block, opposite the swallow through which the rope or wire passes. Also called breech.

artemon. A forward raking spar on an ancient Roman vessel (forerunner of the bowsprit) upon which a spritsail was set as a headsail. The use of the artemon disappeared with the fall of Rome but reappeared in northern Europe in the fourteenth century.

Articles of Agreement. A merchant seamen's contract of employment applying to a specific voyage. Short and common term is Articles.

ascension. The elevation of a celestial body above the celestial horizon. Right ascension is the arc along the celestial equator measured eastward from the vernal equinox to an hour circle passing through the celestial body; one of the coordinates for locating a celestial point.

ascidian. A small animal, either free swimming or attached to anything underwater, that has a saclike body covered with a sort of tunic. Also called a sea squirt and is known to foul ship's hulls.

ASDIC. *See* SONAR.

ash breeze. Sailor's slang for rowing.

ash bucket. A tool for ridding a coal burning ship of ash; other tools include ash chute, ejector, hoist, and whip.

ashore. On the shore, land or beach. A sailor goes ashore on liberty in the U.S. Navy and on shore leave in the Merchant Service.

ASNE. American Society of Naval Engineers

aspect ratio. In nautical terms, the relationship between the length of a sail or rudder and its width or height. Also a short boom and a high mast in a sailboat produce a high aspect ratio rig.

astern. Back, towards the stern or beyond; behind the ship.

astigmatizer. A simple optical device fitted to the telescope of a sextant that elongates the image of a star from a dot of light to a line, thus making an accurate measurement of the star's altitude easier.

astro. Short for astro-navigation; the British word for celestial navigation.

astrolabe. A simple and primitive instrument first used in the thirteenth century for measuring the altitude of celestial bodies.

ASW. Anti-Submarine Warfare.

athwart, athwartships. Across, at right angles to the fore-and-aft axis of the ship; from side to side.

Atlantic Ocean. Named by the Greeks as the sea beyond the Atlas mountains (near the Straits of Gibralter).

Atlantic Ridge. A long undersea mountain range or ridge from Iceland south to Bouvet Island in the South Atlantic that separates the Atlantic into two large basins.

atoll. A ring-shaped island or belt of islands formed by the skeletons of coral polyps enclosing a lagoon; common to the Pacific near the equator.

atrip. An old term seldom used today meaning ready for completed action as in an anchor on the bottom ready for hoisting or a sail hoisted ready for trimming.

atry. Said of a ship hove to in a gale; seldom heard today.

at sea. Legally, for insurance purposes, a ship is at sea when it has cast off all lines from its berth or is underway at its anchorage.

augmentor. A device or mechanism for improving the efficiency of an air pump as part of a ship's steam power plant.

Aurora. A luminous phenomenon appearing in high latitudes in the form of rays, bands, and arcs of light; modified by Borealis for the northern hemisphere and Australis for the southern. Also called polar Aurora.

Automatic Merchant Vessel Report (AMVER) system. Computer' report for the U.S. Coast Guard that plots all of the world's merchant shipping. Largely used for search and rescue information.

auxiliary machinery. Machinery aboard ship other than the main propulsion, includes generators, winches, and emergency pumps.

auxiliary ship. Ship used in the Navy to assist warships. *See* warship.

auxiliary yacht. A sailboat with an engine.

availability. A period assigned to a ship for repairs and maintenance. May be restricted in time and purpose to technical, regular overhaul, voyage repairs, or upkeep.

avast. A command to stop or cease as in avast heaving which means stop pulling. Not recommended for those who are not genuine sailors.

average. A marine insurance term for a partial loss. An average adjuster is an expert in loss determination and there are average agents, bonds, clauses, or warranties. *See* particular average and general average.

avoidance. In marine insurance to avoid a contract is to cancel or nullify it; sometimes done by the insurer for cause.

avulsion. Rapid erosion of shoreland by waves during a storm.

awash. Just above sea level, as a reef is awash. Also covered with water as the deck of a ship may be awash.

away. Expression used in passing the word as in "away the rescue and assistance party" or "away the liberty party." A man on watch may be directed by the commanding officer to "call away the gig" which means to summon the crew, man the gig, and have it come alongside. *See* call away.

aweigh. Said of an anchor when it has just broken ground when being hauled in. *See* weigh.

aye aye. The traditional nautical affirmative reply to a request, suggestion, or command.

azimuth. The great circle direction of any place or object (such as the sun) from a given point, usually referred to true north and expressed in degrees. Azimuth is generally used in regard to celestial bodies and bearings when terrestrial objects are involved.

azimuth circle. A simple ring fitted with open sight vanes over a compass bowl and by which azimuth or bearing of something may be read. It is fitted with a prism mirror in order to observe the azimuth of the sun. Without this mirror, the instrument is called a bearing circle. *See* alidade.

B

B. International signal code alphabet burgee. When hoisted singly means: "I am taking in, or discharging, or carrying dangerous goods." Spoken. "bravo."

baboon watch. In the days of sail, the man left on watch on board ship in port while the rest of the crew goes ashore.

baby stay. Another name for an inner forestay.

BACAT. Barge Aboard CATamaran. A Danish designed system for carrying barges or lighters aboard a twin-hulled vessel. LASH-size barges are carried and hoisted between the catamaran hulls and special, smaller barges are carried on deck by means of lifting elevators in the stern. *See* LASH.

back 1. To cause a ship to go astern; to reverse engines. **2.** The wind backs when its direction shifts counterclockwise; hauls or veers when the shift is clockwise. By international agreement these definitions hold in both hemispheres. **3.** To back an anchor is to attach another or a weight to an anchor's cable. **4.** To back a sail is to hold it out to windward. **5.** To back oars is to row backwards. *See* anchoring expressions.

back and fill. An old expression describing the alternate backing and then the filling of the sails of a square-rigger working its way up a channel too narrow to permit tacking.

backbeach. Same as backshore.

back freight. Undeliverable freight returned to the shipper.

backhanded. A rope made by twisting each strand in the same direction as the yarns and then laying the strands left-handed.

backlaid rope. Same as backhanded; compared to plain-laid rope.

back letter. Letter that supplements the terms of a charter party after the latter has been signed.

back-off. A wave that has broken and then reformed into an advancing wall of solid water is said by a surfer to have backed off.

back out. *See* walk out.

backrope. A small line on the hook of a cat block or fish block by which it is swung out and hooked to the anchor. Also one of the stays leading from the lower end of the martingale of a sailing ship.

backrush. The seaward return of water following the uprush of waves on a beach.

backshore. Part of a beach or shore that is usually dry, reached only by the highest tides. Also called backbeach.

backsplice. A method of finishing off the end of a rope by making a crown knot and then tucking the strands back two or three times each.

backstaff. A primitive instrument, following the cross-staff, for measuring the altitude of a heavenly body. The observer stood with his back to the celestial body.

backstay. A supporting rope or wire stay that runs aft from aloft on a mast to the deck. A shifting backstay is one that can be set taut or slacked, depending on which tack the boat is on and thus which side of the mast suffers the most strain. Backstays are led aft to both sides of the deck aft, port, and starboard. A shifting backstay is also known as a running backstay, a runner, or a preventer.

backstay stool. Planking or light plating projecting from the sides of a sailing ship to which the ends of backstays can be made fast.

backstrap. A short length of chain connecting the upper and lower bridles of a fishing trawl. British spelling is backstrop.

backwash. Water or waves thrown back by an obstruction such as a ship, breakwater or cliff. Also called backrush.

backwater. *n* 1. Water created by an eddy, obstruction, or opposing current, remote and away from the main stream. 2. An arm of the sea, usually parallel to the coast behind a narrow strip of land. *vb* To backwater is to row backwards.

backweight. A cargo handling rig aboard ship that uses a weight (deadman) as the balance for a light boom. Also called a deadman rig.

backwind. Air flowing aft off one sail onto the lee side of another. The receiving sail is said to be backwinded.

badge. In old sailing days, a carved wooden ornament on the stern. Now an insignia on the bow of a boat or a protective piece of wood on a boat's quarter where the side planking meets the transom.

baggywrinkle. Old bits and pieces of used line wrapped around a stay as antichafing gear on a sailboat.

baguio. Local name in the Philippines for a typhoon.

bail. To dip out, as removing water from a boat. A bow-shaped fitting supporting an accommodation ladder over the side of a ship or the awning in a launch. A spreader for holding the lines of a bridle apart. A bail shackle is the slip ring holding the hook down on a pelican hook and is released by pulling out the bail pin. The metal straps around a spar to which blocks are shackled are bails. Sometimes spelled bale.

bait. *n* 1. Any substance, animal, or small fish attached to a hook to attract fish. 2. If cast on the water, it is called chum. 3. Another name for small fish. *vb* To bait fish is to offer them bait.

baitboat. A fishing boat that uses bait (small fish) to catch fish in contrast to those that net fish.

balanced rudder. A rudder in which part of the blade is forward of the pivot point or axis; less energy is needed to turn it.

balanced lug. A lugsail whose boom and lug both project forward of the mast thus providing a reasonably balanced sail.

balancing ring. Ring fitted to the shank of an anchor by which it can be hoisted with a crane.

baldheaded. Said of a square-rigged ship on which no sails are set above the topgallants, and of a schooner having no topmasts.

Baldt anchor. A trade name for a modern stockless anchor.

bale. *See* bail.

bale capacity. The usable cubic capacity of a ship's cargo spaces below decks, usually in cubic feet. If cargo is loaded into containers, barges or lighters, the interior volume of these containers is used as bale capacity. Same as bale cubic, bale measure, bale space. *See* grain cubic.

baleen. The horny material (whalebone) growing down from the upper jaw of large, plankton-feeding whales with which they strain out their food. The baleen whales are the Mystacoceti, a suborder that includes right whales, gray whales, and rorquals.

bale shackle. *See* bail.

ballao. *See* ballyhoo.

ballast. 1. Any heavy material carried aboard ship to ensure her stability. Water is often used and is carried in ballast tanks which can be emptied and filled as needed. Submarines are partly controlled in depth by ballast tanks. 2. To ballast a ship is to replace the fuel oil, as used, by water. 3. A merchant ship is in ballast when not carrying cargo whereas a yacht is always considered legally to be in ballast.

ballast keel. The keel of a yacht made and shaped from the lead or iron ballast she needs for stability under sail.

ballistic error. An error induced by a change in course or in speed, as seen on a gyro compass.

balloon sail. A light sail used by yachts when reaching or running in light to moderate weather; may be a balloon jib, foresail, spinnaker or topsail. Also called a ballooner or a kite.

ball stopper. A plastic ball fastened to the end of a halyard to keep it from unreeving and going adrift.

ballyhoo. Game fishermen's slang for ballao; a small, thin fish used widely as a skipping bait for billfish.

balsa. A very light tropical wood used in life rafts and floats. Also the name of a sea-going sailing raft found on the west coast of South America.

Baltic bow. Describes the stem or bow of early ice-breakers.

Baltic Exchange. The association of ship's brokers in London who arrange world wide charters for tramp shipping, representing either ship owners or those who have freight to move.

banca. General word for small craft of the Philippines.

banded humbug. An Indo-Pacific species of damselfish associated with coral.

bank. A moderately flat topped elevation of the ocean bottom, shallow but with enough water for safe navigation in fair weather; may be a shifting bank of mud, sand, or the margin of a river. Also a tier of oars as in old rowing vessels.

bank cushion. The repelling force close to the bow of a moving ship as it passes close to the bank of a waterway or to the side of a ship. It is caused by the ship's bow wave striking the bank or the other ship and causing the bow to be deflected away. *See* bank suction, bank effect.

bank effect. The lateral movement or deflection of the bow or stern of a moving ship in a narrow waterway or when close to another ship as when going alongside underway. The bow wave causes the bow to move away and the stern is attracted or pulled in. *See* bank suction, bank cushion.

banker. Old name for a fishing vessel employed on the Grand Banks off Newfoundland.

bank suction. The attracting force upon the stern of a moving ship as she passes close to the bank of a waterway or to the side of a ship. It is caused by the propeller current along which pressure is reduced. *See* bank cushion, bank effect.

bar. A bank or shoal, usually at the mouth of a river, which obstructs navigation and causes breaking, dangerous surf in heavy weather. Also a unit of atmospheric pressure under the metric system. *See* millibar.

Baralyme. Trade name for diver's CO_2 (carbon dioxide) absorbent.

barbel. The filament-like appendage under the lower jaw of a fish.

barber. A severe storm at sea during which spray and snow freeze on the ship's decks, rigging, and superstructure. In the Gulf of St. Lawrence, a local blizzard in which wind-carried ice particles cut exposed human skin.

barber haul. *vb* To attach a short line and a block to a headsail sheet to improve its angle of lead and thus the efficiency of the sail. *n* The control line is sometimes called a barber hauler and the barber haul is the block used.

barbette. The round, fixed armor plate structure in a warship in which the gun turret rotates.

barca, barco. A small fishing craft working in the Mediterranean and off Portugal.

bar draft. Amount of water required of a fully loaded ship to pass over a bar to reach or depart from a port upriver. It is usually less than normal full load draft.

bareboat charter. *See* charter.

bare poles. A sailing vessel without sails set on the masts; a rather common condition in very heavy weather.

bare sailing. Sailing a yacht with the sheets hauled in too far; termed pinching her, a common error of beginners.

barge. *n* A general term for a heavy, flat bottomed, often rectangular vessel used to carry cargo, usually in sheltered and inland waters but also, sometimes at sea; usually pushed or towed by tug. By U.S. Government definition, barges are any non-self propelled vessels other than houseboats and dredges. In Europe, barges are smaller, powered frieght carriers with conventional bows and often living quarters aft for the master and his family. Also a ceremonial boat used by officials and dignitaries. In naval usage, it is an admiral's boat. The words lighter, barge, and scow are often used interchangeably according to local usage although, in general, barges make voyages while lighters are used locally. *vb* To barge in a sailing race is to force your opponents to give you room to windward at the start or when rounding a mark.

barge carrier. A ship specially designed to load, transport and unload cargo-filled barges. *See* LASH, BACAT, Seabee.

Barge Cluster Pushtowing System. An American method of securing barges rigidly together in 2 to 5 rows of 2 to 5 barges each and pushing this cluster through inland and sheltered water with a pushboat.

bark. A sailing ship having as many as five masts with all of them square-rigged except the aftermost one which has fore-and-aft sails; once called a shipentine. British spelling is barque.

bar keel. A continuous, heavy steel bar, oblong in section, extending along the bottom at the centerline built into small vessels. Also called a hanging keel as it is outside the hull.

barkentine. A three or four-masted sailing ship having all masts fore-and-aft rigged except the foremast which is square-rigged. Also spelled barquentine.

barnacle. A salt water crustacean, of the order Cirripedia, enclosed in a shell and permanently attached to something underwater, quite often a ship's hull. Barnacles are separated into two types: acorn and stalked (also known as gooseneck or goose barnacle).

barney post. Post in the cockpit of a sailboat on which fairleads and jam cleats are fitted to control sails and rigging.

barogram. *See* barometer.

barograph. *See* barometer.

barometer. An instrument for measuring atmospheric pressure. An aneroid barometer has a thin, metallic, partially exhausted, sealed chamber which senses pressure changes and transfers them by mechanical linkage to a dial pointer or a recording pen on a moving cylinder of paper (barograph). This recording on a barograph is called a barogram. A mercurial barometer is a column of mercury set in a bowl of mercury whose height indicates atmospheric pressure. A marine version is designed to damp out the oscillations caused by ship movement.

bar port. A harbor that can be entered only at high tide when there is sufficient water to permit ships to pass over the bar.

barracuda. A pike-like, warm water fish of the genus *Sphyraena*. It is a voracious, steel-colored fish with prominent teeth that is sometimes dangerous to swimmers and grows to 6 feet; edible in the Pacific, sometimes poisonous in the Caribbean.

barratry. Any illegal act willfully committed by the master or crew of a vessel to the detriment of the owners or the charters; includes scuttling with malicious intent, smuggling, deliberate violation of the rules of safe navigation, running a blockade, etc., but does not cover negligence. A barrator is the person who commits barratry.

barrel. 1. The drum, roller, or cylinder of a crane, winch, or steering gear, upon which ropes or chains are wound. 2. A quantity measure, varying according to cargo or liquid, i.e. for petroleum, 42 gallons at 60°F. 3. The lookout station aloft in old sealing ships; the trained man was called the barrelman.

barrico. British spelling of breaker, a container used for water, traditionally of wood but now often of plastic. *See* breaker.

barrier reef. Reef separated from the shore by water too deep to have coral growth; distinct from the closer fringing reef.

bar warning sign. At sea, a flashing light activated by the Coast Guard to warn mariners that heavy seas are breaking over the bar and that it should not be crossed.

base line plane. In ship construction, an imaginary plane used as reference for all vertical dimensions; near the base of the ship, usually through the upper edge of the flat plate keel and parallel to the water planes.

basin. 1. A depression in the sea bottom, roughly circular in shape. 2. Any enclosed or sheltered cargo handling or anchoring area which protects ships from tide and weather.

basin, model. A large indoor pool that is used for model ship testing and evaluation.

basking shark. *See* shark.

basnig. A type of lift fish net developed and used in the Philippines.

bass. Striped bass, *Morowe saxatilis,* is a popular gamefish of up to 60 pounds found close to shore in North America; also called rockfish, linesider, and squidhound. Channel bass is really a drum. Sea bass is a common name for a small, bottom food fish of our eastern coast, *Centropristes striatus,* that grows to five pounds and is locally known as black fish, black perch, rock fish and rock bass.

bast. The inner bark of certain trees such as lime and linden that was once used for ship cordage and matting.

bateau. In North America, one of the various small, scow-like craft that range from rowing boats to Chesapeake Bay crabbing boats. *See* scow. Also spelled batteau.

bathal zone. The top layer of the ocean, above the 4°C isotherm down to 1300 meters, marked by warm water and rich marine life. Below this isotherm is the abyssal zone, marked by cold water, less light and consequently less abundant marine life. *See* abyss.

bathometer. Any instrument used to measure depth of water.

bathybenthic. A term describing sea life on the bottom of the ocean in depths of 2000–6000 feet. *See* abyssobenthic, mesobenthic, littoralbenthic, bathypelagic.

bathycurrent. A deep ocean current that does not reach the surface.

bathymetric. Pertaining to depth of water.

bathymetric map or chart. Map that shows, by continuous depth contour lines, the ocean bottom. Produced by the National Ocean Survey, these maps permit accurate piloting using an echo sounder.

bathypelagic. A term that describes fish and other life in ocean water 2000 – 6000 feet deep. *See* bathybenthic, abyssopelagic, mesopelagic, epipelagic.

bathyscaph. A free-diving, self-contained, deep sea research vessel with a flotation hull to which is secured a manned observation capsule.

bathysphere. A round, steel, non-propelled vessel designed by Charles Beebe in which he was lowered to record depths in 1934.

bathythermograph. An instrument for recording temperature at various depths of water, thus revealing the temperature gradient. BT for short.

batten. A narrow, usually thin piece of wood or plastic that is used to stiffen the leech of a yacht's sail (inserted in pockets), to secure tarpaulins over old-fashioned hatch covers, for fairing in the lines of a ship design in a mold loft, as interior planking in wooden boat building, and as a timber used in cargo stowage. *See* cargo batten.

batten cleat. A bracket fastened to the hatch coaming for holding the tarpaulin battens as they are wedged into place to hold the tarpaulin.

batten down. An expression meaning to make secure or to fasten in place as in "batten down all hatch covers, secure for heavy weather".

battle port. Naval word for a deadlight; the hinged steel cover for an airport.

battleship. Classically, the largest and most heavily armed and armored warship.

bay. A wide indentation in the coast, smaller that a gulf and larger than a cove.

bayam. A violent squall with thunder and lightning along the South Coast of Cuba.

bay ice. Level fast ice of more than one winter's growth, up to two meters above sea level; thicker than two meters above sea level, an ice shelf.

bayou. A small sluggish stream, generally tidal, which wanders through marsh and swamp. Most common to Louisiana; sometimes called a slough in other states.

beach. *n* 1. The shore, including foreshore and backshore. Technically, a sandy area from low water up to any marked change such as the start of vegetation. 2. Slang for waterfront. 3. To go ashore for a sailor is to hit the beach. *vb* To run a boat or ship ashore is to beach it.

beach break. Waves that break on a sandy bottom or a beach rather than on rocks or a reef.

beachcomber. Literally one who made his living picking up things on the beach. Now describes a man along the coast who does not seem to have a steady job. Also a long, curling wave that breaks on the beach, a comber.

beach gear. The varied equipment used by salvage crews in assisting a stranded vessel that includes anchors and wire rope sheaves and blocks.

beach seine. *See* seine.

beach wagon. A heavy cart or truck used to carry surf boats.

beacon. Any structure marked by lights and/or distinctive shapes, placed ashore or in shallow water to serve as an aid to navigation. Chart symbol is Bn.

beadle. A large mallet used in making wooden boats.

beak. A metal point or ram fitted on the forefoot of ancient warships.

beakhead. In a sailing warship, the space forward of the forecastle. In old ships, it was open to the sea and used as the crew's toilet or head.

beam. The width of a ship. Also a transverse structural member of a ship's framing. *See* beam ends. Objects outside of the ship may be reported as abeam (90 degrees relative on either side), abaft the beam or forward of the beam.

beam ends. A ship is on her beam ends when she has rolled over 90 degrees and lies on her side. In more general terms, describes someone in trouble.

beam trawl. An old-fashioned triangular purse-shaped fishing net whose mouth is held open by a beam; once used by sailing fishermen.

bear. *n* A block of wood or a weighted mat that is used to sour wooden decks. *vb* 1. To lie in a certain direction, as a distant ship is reported as bearing just abaft the beam. 2. To bear off means to turn away; to bear down means to sail towards. 3. To bear away or to bear up means to sail away from or towards the wind.

"bear a hand". An expression meaning to hurry as in "bear a hand and secure that boat".

bearding. The line of intersection between the keel, stem, and sternpost of a ship with the framing timbers or beams. Also called bearding line or stepping point.

bearing. The direction or point of the compass in which an object is seen or sensed; expressed in general terms as "off the port bow", or in degrees true, magnetic, or relative. A danger bearing is a limiting one that indicates a danger to the ship. Bearings are for terrestrial objects; azimuths for celestial.

bearing circle. A ring, fitted over a compass or compass repeater, with which bearings can be taken by sighting through vanes fitted on the ring. If a reflecting device permits bearings of celestial bodies, it is an azimuth circle. If a telescope is fitted instead of vanes, it is an alidade. Bearing finder was an old collective term for all such devices.

beat. In a sailing vessel, to advance against the wind by sailing close-hauled on alternate tacks; doing so can result in a long beat.

beat to quarters. Old sailing warship term for general quarters which is the command for all hands to prepare themselves and the ship for battle. British now use action stations.

Beaufort Scale. A universally adopted wind velocity scale.

Force		State of Sea	Knots
0	calm	smooth	0-1
1	light airs	small wavelets	1-3
2	slight breeze	short waves, cresting	4-6
3	gentle breeze	small waves, breaking	7-10
4	moderate breeze	definite whitecaps	11-16
5	fresh breeze	moderate waves	17-21
6	strong breeze	larger waves	22-27
7	moderate gale	spindrift formed	28-33
8	fresh gale	much spindrift	34-40
9	strong gale	seas start to roll	41-47
10	whole gale	seas roll, break heavily	48-55
11	storm	surface all white, big seas	56-65
12	hurricane	enormous seas	above 65

becalmed. A sailing vessel unable to move for lack of wind.

beche de mer. *See* sea cucumber.

becket. 1. Any of various small ropes, lines, loops, or grommets common to sailing ships and named after their purpose. 2. Most commonly a short line with a knot at one end and eye at the other; used for temporarily holding ropes or small spars. 3. A type of knot or bend. 4. An eye in the tail of a block.

becket rowlock. A rowlock formed by a piece of line made fast to a thole pin.

becue. To rig an anchor for use on foul ground by bending the warp or rode to the crown instead of the ring. The rode is stopped to the ring with light line so that a normal pull on the shank is possible unless the anchor is caught on rocks. In that case, the stops part and the anchor comes up crown first. This was also called scowing an anchor.

bed. The bottom of the ocean; also called the seabed.

bedplate. The foundation in a ship on which a large piece of machinery rests and is secured. Also called a soleplate.

bee. Traditionally in the days of sail, a rounded block of wood or iron through which a stay's lower end was rove before it was set up and made fast. A modern bee block is used on the boom of a sailboat to bring the cringle down to its proper position for reefing.

beetle. A large mallet used in driving pegs or wedges in ship building.

before the mast. Formerly indicated service; a sailor traditionally lived forward in a ship in contrast to the officers who lived aft.

Belat. A strong northerly wind blowing along the south coast of Arabia between December and March.

belay. To make fast or secure a rope or line to a cleat or other fitting. Also to cancel or annul a command as in "belay that last word".

belaying pin. In the days of sail, a wooden or metal rod around which a rope or line was secured. Pins were usully fitted into fife rails around the masts or inside the bulwarks and were a handy weapon for casual disputes. Now persists on the edge of a flag bag to which the signal halyards are made fast.

bell book. An official record, kept in a ship's engine room of all orders to the engines passed down from the bridge.

bell buoy. Buoy fitted with a bell whose clappers are activated by the movement of the sea. A common aid to navigation.

bellmouth. A ship's ventilating air supply terminal that delivers large volumes of fresh air to hot compartments such as machinery spaces. Also called a cowl vent. *See* ventilator.

bell pull. A wire, usually from the bridge to the engine room, once used to transmit orders to the engines. Still found in old tugs and boats. Engine order telegraphs are now used.

bell purchase. A tackle consisting of two fixed blocks and two movable ones.

bell rope. The piece of line, often braided, used to swing the clapper in a ship's bell.

bell, ship's. Traditionally carried to strike the hours (*See* ship's time) and to sound fog signals when at anchor as well as certain emergency signals such as fire. Some naval boats carry bells which the coxswain sounds to control the speed and direction of the boat's engine to the boat engineer.

belly. The part of a sail that bulges out under the wind pressure.

bellyboard. A short surfboard used to ride in on a breaking wave while prone.

belly guy. A rope or wire supporting the middle part of a sheer leg or spar.

bellyline. A line used in large otter trawls to strengthen the after part of the net.

bellyrobber. Traditional slang for a ship's steward or cook.

belly strap. Strap slung under a boat to carry out an anchor.

below. Nautical word for downstairs. Below decks is the part of the ship below the maindeck, not topside.

belship. A word of British origin for a heavy lift ship designed for big loads. It would normally have jumbo booms with a 200 ton capacity.

belt gripe. A piece of matting or canvas holding a boat in its davits against the strongback.

beluga. A whale growing to about 10 feet and normally white in color. Also the great sturgeon of southeastern Europe and the Caspian from which beluga caviar comes.

benchmark. A permanent metal marker located by official measurement that indicates datum level for tide observations, reference for survey, or other references as the alignment of guns and missile launchers.

bend. *n* **1.** A special form of knot used in the joining of two lines. **2.** The making fast of a line to an eye, ring, or spar that can be cast off easily when necessary. *See* knot. **3.** The curved or rounded part of a fishhook. *vb* **1.** To fasten or secure by means of a knot as in bending the rode to the anchor. **2.** To bend on three knots is to increase the ship's speed by that amount.

bender. Old nautical word for a drinking party or celebration.

bending shackle. A U-shaped connecting link with the curved end aft connecting the anchor cable to the anchor shackle. Sometimes called the end shackle.

bends. The dreaded diver's affliction usually caused by too rapid ascent which releases nitrogen bubbles into the blood. The cure is quick recompression followed by gradual decompression.

beneaped. Same as neaped.

Benguela Current. A strong northerly ocean current off the coast of Africa. It is a continuation of the South Atlantic Current and turns west to join the South Equatorial Current.

benthic division. A classification of the ocean environment; a primary division which includes the ocean floor. It is divided into the littoral and the deep sea systems which are further classified in accordance to depth. Benthic, in describing marine life, means living on the bottom.

bergy bit. Medium size pieces of glacial ice afloat, a hazard to navigation. They are generally less than five meters above sea level and about 100-300 square meters in area. *See* growlers.

bergy water. An area of freely navigable waters without sea ice but which contains ice from land origins.

berm. A narrow, raised embankment along a stream or beach; may be formed by material deposited at high water and thus marks the tidal limit.

Bermudian rig. Rig recognized by triangular, fore-and-aft sails having a foot, luff, and a leech without gaff. Also called a Marconi rig or jib-headed rig.

Berne List. List consisting of international call signs, and radio stations; published by the International Union of Telecommunications in Geneva.

berries. The eggs of crustaceans such as lobsters.

berth. 1. Anchorage, mooring space, or the space alongside a pier assigned to a ship. 2. A sleeping space for a man aboard ship. He is said to berth in that compartment. 3. To give somthing a wide berth is to pass it at a distance.

berthing hawser. British word for mooring line.

between wind and water. Part of the ship's hull along the water line and thus the most vulnerable to cannon fire.

B/H. Bill of Health.

bibbs. Pieces of wood bolted to the hounds of a mast giving additional support to the trestletrees.

bible. Same as holystone.

bigboy. *See* blooper.

big gun. An extra large surfboard designed for very big waves.

bight. 1. The loop of a rope. 2. The doubled-over part of a rope when folded. 3. A recess or indented area in a sea coast or ice edge. 4. Caught in the bight is to be entrapped or snared.

biglet. The bight of a cargo or rope sling through which the long end is passed when hooking on.

bilge. *n* 1. The lower inside hull of a vessel up to the point where the sides become vertical, the turn of the bilge. A sharply curved bilge as in flat-floored hulls is a hard or sharp bilge. If there is an angle instead of a curve, it is called a chine. 2. In cargo ships with double bottom tanks, the triangular channels on both sides of the ship formed by the margin plate, the curved shell plating and the bilge ceiling. 3. The area where the bilge water collects requiring a bilge pump to pump the bilges. 4. Often slang for rubbish or nonsense. *vb* To bilge a ship is to damage its lower hull; to cause it to leak.

bilge and cantline. A method of stowing barrels or casks with bilges or bottoms of the casks of the upper tier over the cantlines (empty spaces between rows) of the lower tiers.

bilge block. A wooden piece used to support a ship in drydock. Sometimes called bridge cribbing.

bilgeboard. A board projecting out and down from each bilge as in a shallow-draft inland lake racing scow or sailboat. It reduces leeway in the same manner as a centerboard and is similarly housed in a case or trunk.

bilgeboard scow. Same as inland lake scow.

bilge keel. Another term for a docking keel; a protruding structural member on each side of the keel along the ship's bottom, parallel to the keel. Also a fin fitted to the outside of the hull on each side of the keel at the turn of the bilge to reduce rolling of the ship. Also called a rolling chock or anti-rolling keel.

bilge keelson. A fore-and-aft girder, log, timber, or plank placed across the frames inside the ship at the turn of the bilge.

bilge pump. Used aboard ship to remove either casual water or flooding due to holing, grounding, or burst pipes. An important safety measure for yachts that automatically turns on when rising water activates a switch.

bilge rail. Fore-and-aft hand rail fitted outside the hull of a lifeboat at the turn of the bilge so that if the boat capsizes people can hold on.

bilge strake. Strake along the turn of the bilge.

bilge water. Water that accumulates in the bilges and that must not be pumped overboard if it contains oil.

bilge well. A collector for bilge water in some ships whose tank tops extend to the sides of the ship. Same as drain well.

bill. Point of the flukes of an anchor; also called the pea. A list of the crew of a naval ship with assignments for watch, berthing spaces, battle stations, etc. Also the sword, spike or spear of a billfish.

billboard. In the days of the old-fashioned or stock anchor, the sloping platform close to the bow on which the anchor was stowed. Also called an anchor bed.

billet. Space assigned to a seaman as his living quarters. In U.S. Navy usage, a man's duties and responsibilities.

billethead. *See* fiddlehead.

billfish. Any of the gamefish marked by a long bill such as marlin.

bill of health. A certificate needed by a ship entering port attesting to its freedom from disease or recent exposure. It is the basis for granting pratique. British term is jerque note.

bill of lading. A list of the cargo of a freighter, signed by the person (the master) or his agent who contracts to transport it and stating the terms on which the cargo is to be delivered, as well as received aboard; a receipt for goods shipped as well as a transferable, quasi-negotiable document of title. Normally prepared by the shipping agent and unless qualified by the carrier who signs, it is a clean bill of lading. If qualified (goods unsound or badly packed), it is a foul or dirty bill of lading. Also called blading or B/L.

bill of store. A license granted by the customs authorities to a ship by which it is allowed to carry voyage stores and provisions duty free.

billow. A large ocean wave. A word, like prow, more often used by poets than by seamen.

Bimini belt. A harness with a gimballed socket on a metal plate into which the butt of the fishing rod fits as the angler, wearing the belt, plays a large game fish.

Bimini top. A light, collapsible fabric sun protector rigged over the flying bridge or open cockpit of a yacht. Also called a Navy top.

binder. In marine insurance, an agreement to insure; used before a final policy is written. British word is slip.

binnacle. The covered, non-magnetic, lighted stand or receptacle for the ship's magnetic compass, equipped with compensating balls and bars as well as gimbals to keep the compass level.

binnacle list. Daily sick list on a naval ship, so called because it was once stowed in the binnacle.

binoculars. A hand-held pair of telescopes, always an important tool for the conning officer, lookouts, and navigator.

bioluminescence. Light seen on the surface of the sea on a dark night; generated by living organisms, most commonly plankton. Also called seafire.

bipod spars. *See* A frame.

bird's nest. *See* crow's nest.

bireme. An ancient gally having two banks of oars.

bite. An anchor bites when it digs itself into the ground or bottom as it is designed to do, and thus holds the ship in place.

bitter. Traditionally a turn of the hawser or cable around the bitts.

bitter end. The end of any line, rope, or cable on board; originally it was the last link in the anchor chain in the chain locker.

bittern. The liquid remaining after sea water has been evaporated to the point where salt crystals form. Also a wading marsh bird with a deep resonant cry.

bitts. Short, heavy steel posts, usually in pairs, located on deck and used for securing lines and ropes. According to usage and location, they include towing bitts, mooring bitts, and quarter bitts. Bollards are corresponding fittings found on docks, piers, and wharfs.

bivalve. A mollusk, clam, or oyster with two shells; distinct from a univalve.

B/L. Bill of lading.

blackbird. Old sea slang for an African slave, thus blackbirding was slave trading.

Black Current. Another name for the Kuroshio or Japan Current.

blackfish. **1.** Common name for almost any dark-colored fish, large or small. **2.** Local name for sea bass. *See* bass. **3.** Local name for tautog. **4.** Another name for a pilot whale.

black gang. The engineer personnel aboard ship; in the Navy, they are also called snipes.

black jack. The flag traditionally flown by pirates. Alleged by fiction writers to have been a skull and crossbones on a black field, there is no real evidence that such a flag was ever used.

Black Sea mooring. A 10 inch manila or equivalent synthetic rope, approximately 180 feet long spliced to a 60 foot wire rope with a five inch eye at the end.

blackwall hitch. A knot used for fastening a line to a steel hook.

blade. The main flat portion of a rudder; also called the rudder body. *See* propeller.

blading. Abbreviation for bill of lading, as is B/L.

Blake slip. *See* cable stopper.

blanket. In a sail boat race, to come between another boat and the wind. A whaling term for a strip of blubber.

blanket net. *See* lift net.

blast. Signal on a ship's whistle; short, 1 second, prolonged 4-6 seconds, and long over 6 seconds; defined by the International Rules of the Road.

bleeder. Describes a small cock, valve or plug used to drain off fluid. A bleeder plug is a semi-permanent closure or tank or compartment drains in a hull of a ship that are used only when the ship is in drydock. To bleed a system is to remove the fluid.

blinder. *See* blind rollers.

blind rollers. Long, high sea swells that peak but do not break as they pass over shoal water. They may break in heavy weather as they become larger. Also called blind seas or blinders.

blink. The reflected glare or light from sunlight shining on ice, snow, or white sand as seen in the sky above it; called ice, snow, or lagoon blink.

blinker. A set of lights aloft on a yardarm activated by a telegraph key on the bridge; used to signal between ships at night, particularly in the Navy. Also called yardarm blinker.

blinker tube or gun. A hand-held directional light that is used to signal between ships.

blister. A built-in bulge, an additional outer skin used in ships to improve stability and in warships as protection against mines or torpedoes.

blobbing. *See* bobbing.

block. A temporary support or shore such as a building block, used to support a ship's hull under construction or a solid permanent piece of wood or metal used for any purpose such as a thrust block or sole block. *See* block, pulley.

blockade. A naval operation barring foreign ships from a port or an ocean area. Ending the operation is called raising the blockade.

block and tackle. Two blocks with the necessary line rove between them.

block coefficient. A ship design term; the ratio between the volume of a ship and that of a block of wood from which the ship theoretically could have been carved. It is about the ratio of the immersed volume to the product of the ship's length, beam, and draft.

blocking. Collective name for the shores and blocks used to support a ship in drydock. Also called cribbing.

blocking off. Wedging cargo tightly in a ship's hold so that it will not shift.

block, power. A large steel block used to haul fishing trawls; incorporates a power driven, usually hydraulic, sheave as part of the block. It is rigged at the end of a boom or crane.

block, pulley. A wooden, plastic, or metal shell in which one or more sheaves rotate. Rope or wire travels on these sheaves either to gain a mechanical advantage, especially with multiple blocks, or to attain a fairlead. The sheaves of modern blocks rotate on plastic bearings or, for heavy loads, on steel bearings. The shell of the block is fitted with a hook or an eye at the top and a line or becket at the other end. The space over the sheave nearest the hook is the swallow and the other end is the breech or arse.

blocks (for modern sailing yachts). *See* snatch block, fiddle block, twin-sheet lead block, reacher block, tweaker block, traveller block, cheek block, turning block, fairlead block, mainsheet swivel block, ratchet block, bullet block, jamming fiddle block, spreacher block, and exit block.

block ship. An old hulk once used to obstruct a channel or harbor entrance or as a receiving ship or store facility in a shipyard.

block span. A light wire stretched between the purchase blocks of a lifeboat falls to prevent twisting while the boat is hoisted.

block stopper. *See* stopper.

blocks, traditional. *See* bee, cat block, cheek block, clump block, dasher block, differential block, fiddle block, fly block, gin block, heel block, jack block, jewel block, monkey block, patent block, purchase block, rouseabout block, running block secret block, shoulder block, standing block, sister block, swivel block, tackle block, telegraph block, thick-and-thin block, three-fold block, and wrecking block.

bloomer. *See* buckler.

blooper. A lightweight, very full, overlapping headsail set on racing sailboats when running before the wind. Also called a bigboy.

blow. *n.* A gale or storm. *vb* **1.** To blow a tank is to expel its contents by air pressure. **2.** To blow great guns describes very strong winds.

blowfish. A small tropical reef fish, family Tetraodontidae, that inflates itself when threatened. Also called a puffer or sweller.

blowhole. A whale's nostril through which it breathes and periodically emits a jet of air and vapor. Also a hole in the rocks of a shoreline where the surge of the surf often produces a jet of water. Also a hole in the sea ice that seals keep open in order to have a place to breathe.

blow tubes. To clean boiler tubes with steam under pressure, a periodic operation to maintain water tubes of a marine boiler free of soot.

blubber. The thick layer of body fat found on most pelagic sea mammals and the source of whale oil.

bluefin tuna. Also known as horse mackerel. *See* tuna, mackerel.

bluefish. *Pomatomus saltatrix,* a popular food and game fish weighing up to 25 pounds; found worldwide in temperate waters.

bluejacket. Traditional American and British name for a naval enlisted man. He is also called a tar, white hat and swabbie and, improperly, a gob.

bluenose. Person who has crossed the Arctic or Antarctic Circle.

blue peter. Slang for the alphabet flag P. A blue rectangular flag with a white square in the center, traditionally hoisted at the foremast of a vessel on the day of her departure from port.

blue pigeon. Traditional term for the lead weight in a leadline or sounding lead.

blue whale. The largest of the rorquals or baleen whales up to 100 feet in length. Gentle and intelligent, it is now nearly extinct due to relentless and now often illegal hunting.

board. To go on or into a vessel. Boarding parties are organized to assault a ship. The men are called boarders and respond to the ancient cry: "away boarders." Also the distance covered in one tack when beating to windward; same as leg or tack.

boardboat. A small, inexpensive sailboat such as a Windsurfer or Sailfish whose hull resembles a surfboard. Also called a sailboard, a word more often applied to the surfboard used in windsurfing or boardsailing.

boarding call. Official visit by a Naval officer upon another warship, usually foreign. Honors are rendered and greetings exchanged. Precedes but does not replace the exchange of calls by senior officers concerned, i.e. the two commanding officers.

boardsailing. Same as windsurfing.

boat. A small craft, open or decked, propelled by oars, sail, or motor and made of wood, fabric, metal, cement, or plastic in various shapes. Generally any craft capable of being carried aboard ship. A powerboat is one driven by engine alone; a sailboat uses sails but may have auxilliary power. A submarine may be called properly a boat in accordance to old customs but it is not common usage today. A yacht is always referred to as a boat by her owner. Boats is the traditional short title for Boatswain.

boat ahoy. A hail or call used to address a boat in the Navy as it approaches the ship at night in order to learn the rank of the passengers. Response may be a shout: "hello" meaning there are enlisted men aboard or as another example, if the response is the name of the ship, it means that the commanding officer is embarked.

boat boom. A spar swung out from the side of a ship to which boats are hauled out. It is provided with securing lines and rope ladders for the boat's crew. Also called a riding boom and a guess-warp boom.

boat box. Container in a boat for first aid supplies and emergency signaling equipment.

boat call. A flag signal used by a warship to communicate with her boats.

boat cloak. A cloak made of heavy navy blue wool once used by Naval officers over their full dress or evening dress uniforms.

boat cloth. A dark blue woolen seat cover used in the stern sheets of a Naval boat that carried officers.

boat deck. A partial deck of a ship above the main deck, usually where boats are stowed.

boat drill. The required exercise aboard any ship, especially one carrying passengers, in manning and sometimes partly lowering the lifeboats; should take place as soon as practicable after leaving port.

boat falls. The ropes by which a boat is lowered and hoisted in its davits.

boat gong. A signal used to indicate the departure of officers as well as their boats. Also indicates the arrival of senior officers and visitors.

boat hails. Naval ships at anchor or moored at night hail approaching boats to learn the identity of passengers. *See* Ahoy.

boat hook. A metal hook at the end of a wooden pole used by the bowhook or sternhook of a warship's boat to pick up a mooring line, for making fast, or in fending off when going alongside a ship or a pier.

boat lead. A lighter, shorter and differently marked hand lead once used for taking soundings from a boat.

boat painter. *See* painter.

boat skids. *See* skids.

boat stations. The allotted places for each person aboard ship when ordered to abandon ship.

boatswain. The petty or warrant officer aboard ship responsible for deck seamanship and in charge of the deck force. He is in charge of boats, anchors, etc. and is familiarly known as Boats.

boatswain's call. The sounds or piping made by the boatswain's pipe or whistle, used as a specific signal or command, such as hoist away. Not to be confused with the boatswain's pipe which is the instrument itself according to U. S. usage, particularly in the navy. British usage often refers to the call as being the instrument.

boatswain's chair. A wooden or metal seat used when sending a man aloft.

boatswain's locker. A compartment aboard ship for stowing deck gear.

boatswain's pipe. The hand-held silver instrument used to sound the calls or signals. *See* boatswain's call.

bobbin. A wooden, plastic, or metal sphere or roller fitted on the bottom or footrope of a trawl net to reduce friction over a rough bottom.

bobbing. A primitive form of fishing, using a hookless handline, in which the fish, crab, or eel holds on to the bait when it is pulled up. Also called blobbing.

bobbing a light. When a light is first seen on the horizon at sea, it will disappear if the observer moves his eyes down several feet and it will reappear when the observer returns to his original position. This procedure will establish whether or not the light is really on the horizon and, if so, the approximate range to the light.

bobstay. A rope, chain, or iron rod that extends from the bowsprit end down to the stem and counteracts the lifting strain of the forestay of a sailing ship.

body. The hull of a ship, as in afterbody (after part of the hull).

body plan. An end view of a ship's hull showing curves of the sides of the transverse frame lines; part of the series of drawings making up the sheer draft.

body surf. To ride in, down, and across a breaking wave without the aid of a mat or board. The quick-breaking, moderate to big surf is best suited to this sport.

boggin line. A length of chain secured to either side of the rudder as a safety device in the event of a steering control casualty. Also called a rudder pendant; not common today.

boiler. A steel chamber used to generate steam for ship propulsion; may be firetube, scotch (which is rare), or watertube and the source of heat may be coal, oil, or nuclear energy. In a firetube boiler, the flame is contained in tubes which pass through water; in a watertube system, the steam is generated in the tubes above the flames.

boiler casing. The protective, insulating outer metal covering for a boiler.

boiler scale. A hard coating, mostly of calcium and magnesium, deposited on the surface of the tubes and plates in contact with the water in a steam watertube boiler.

bollards. Heavy steel, short posts, usually in pairs on a dock, pier, or wharf that accommodate a ship's mooring lines. Similar fittings on board ship are bitts.

bolo. A light, weighted line which can be twirled and propelled to a greater distance than a heaving line but has not the reach of a line-throwing gun.

bolster. A general term for anti-chafing or supporting wood or metal pieces, i.e., the bolster plate sometimes is welded near the hawse hole as protection from the wear of the anchor chain.

bolt. A roll of canvas of specific length and width.

boltrope. A line or wire sewn around the endge to strengthen a sail, awning, or tarpaulin. Also called roping. *See* luffrope.

bommie. A small coral reef or coral head.

bonaventure mizzen. The lateen sail set on the aftermost mast of a caravel or similar sixteenth century ship.

bond. British term for the hoisting and lowering wire on a ship's crane.

bone. White water at the bow of a ship that is underway. She has a bone in her teeth means that the ship is obviously making good speed.

bonito. Any of several food and game fish of the mackerel family, 2 or 3 feet long, found in the Atlantic and Pacific. Also called skipjack. *See* tuna, mackerel.

Bonjean's curves. Sectional area curves drawn at each frame station of a ship and used in calculating ship displacement in any condition of trim.

bonnet. An additional strip of canvas fastened to a fore-and-aft sail, especially a jib, to increase its power in moderate weather. Also called a studsail. An additional piece of canvas was sometimes laced to the foot of the bonnet and was called a drabbler. Also any metal, canvas or wooden cover placed over the engine in an open boat.

booby. A dark brown, diving seabird, smaller than a gannet, with similar feeding habits. Boobies live along the coast and are often a major source of guano.

booby hatch. 1. A raised shelter over a ladder entrance or companionway leading below decks from a weather deck. Also called a companion or a dog house. *See* companionway. 2. An additional opening in a hatchway leading to the hold. *See* bridge deck.

book. A whaler's term for a slice of blubber cut on the mincing horse before being cast into the try pot.

boom. 1. Any pole, spar, or timber that projects over the side, supports a sail, and protects the ship's side when alongside a pier. Most are described by their names such as a boat boom. A cargo boom is a hinged spar used to handle weights. Floating plastic barriers rigged to contain oil spills are containment booms; log booms hold logs together into log rafts. 2. A wooden spar along the foot of a sail. 3. To lower the boom is slang for giving maximum punishment.

boom crutch. The support for a mainsail boom when the sail is lowered or for a cargo boom when it is down and secured. Also called boom rest, boom saddle, boom cradle, or boom gallows.

boom guy. Same as lazy jack.

boom horse. A semi-circular iron bar at the end of a boom of a sail for the sheet block to travel on. Also called a boom traveler.

boom jack. Same as boom vang.

boomkin. *See* bumkin.

boom table. A structure built around the foot of a mast to support the heel bearings of the various cargo booms rigged from that mast.

boom traveler. *See* boom horse.

boom vang. A line used in a sailboat to steady the boom Same as boom jack.

boot. U.S. Navy slang for a new sailor or marine; a recruit.

boot camp. The training center ashore to which a sailor reports when enlisted.

boot iron. A caulking tool with a long blade used to reach difficult corners.

boot topping. The surface of the outside hull plating of a ship between light and load waterlines. Also the special paint used in this area to resist wear and to mark the ship's waterline.

Bora. A cold, very gusty and strong northeast wind blowing off the coast of Yugoslavia in the Adriatic Sea; similar to a williwaw.

bordereau. A marine insurance word meaning list or schedule.

bore. A steep moving wall of water caused by the piling up of the advancing flood tidal wave as it is constricted in the mouth of a bay or river. The current of the river increases the severity of the bore. Also called an eagre, mascarat or pororoca.

borer, marine. Any organism that feeds on a ship's wooden bottom. May be a shipworm, toredo, gribble, or martesia.

bosom. A supporting piece, an inner recess or a short piece of angle bar (bosom piece) in steel ship construction. Also the middle part of the curve formed by the foot rope of a fishing trawl net.

boss. 1. The center piece of a magnetic compass card, supported by the pivot. 2. The central part of the propeller to which the blades are attached. 3. Any protuberance on a shaft, a raised rim or a projecting structural member, especially the rounded protuberance of the hull plating containing a propeller shaft's tail end tube. Also called a shell bossing or shaft bossing.

bottlenose whale. A toothed whale of the family Ziphiidae; 20-30 feet long, common to the north Atlantic.

bottle paper. A printed form supplied by the U.S. government on which latitude, longitude, and date are entered by the recording ship before sealing it in a bottle and throwing it overboard. Those recovering the bottles are asked to report place and date; thus information is gathered on ocean currents.

bottlescrew. Same as turnbuckle or rigging screw. Bottlescrew and rigging screw are common British usage; turnbuckle is more common in the U.S.

bottom. 1. The floor of the sea or the bottom of a ship. 2. Sometimes refers to an entire ship. 3. Technically refers to the part of the ship between the keel and the turn of the bilge; and more generally, to the part of the hull below the light load line.

bottom blow valve. A device at the bottom of a marine boiler that is used periodically to blow out sediment.

bottom contour chart. *See* bathymetric.

bottom fishing. A type of fishing that harvests groundfish such as sole.

bottom paint. A special, poisonous compound that inhibits marine growth on the submerged part of the hull.

bottom plating. The steel plates of a ship's bottom from the keel to the turn of the bilge. The remainder of the plates are the side plating.

bottomry. A mortgage or lien upon a ship and her cargo arranged for by a master who needed funds to complete a voyage. Also called respondentia. Not common today with improved communications.

bottom, smelling of. A ship smells the bottom when she handles poorly and is difficult to steer because of shallow water.

bound. A ship may be bound for a certain port, be homeward bound, or be fog bound.

boundary layer. The thin layer of water dragged along from the friction of any object, such as the hull of a ship moving through the water.

boundary waves. Same as internal waves.

bounty ship. In the days of sail, a merchant ship, usually French, that was partly supported in its operations by a government bounty or subsidy.

bouse. To pull strongly on a tackle, to tighten standing rigging or a lashing by passing a line or swifter around it; as in bouse down the shrouds. Also spelled bowse.

bow. The forward part of a ship above the waterline. Archaic term was prow. Stem is the most forward part or leading edge of the bow. *See* stem, bow shapes.

bower anchor. Traditionally a principal anchor; either the port or starboard bower. If unequal in size, the largest is called the best bower; the other, the small

bower. In modern ships with two anchors, they are usually called the port and starboard anchors. The word bower is not used in the U.S. Navy and seldom in the Merchant Service.

bowhead whale. The Greenland right whale or polar whale, a baleen or whalebone whale of moderate size, now endangered and completely protected except for a small quota for Alaskan natives who have always depended on the bowhead for their winter supply of food.

bowhook. U.S. Navy term for man in a boat crew who handles lines forward when coming alongside; usually uses a boathook. The sternhook handles lines aft.

bowl. Surfer's name for a shallow area on the bottom in the path of a breaking wave that causes the wave to break harder and faster, and often higher on that spot.

bowline. 1. A rope attached to the leech of a square sail, leading forward to steady it. **2.** Commonly, a knot that cannot slip. **3.** A bowline on a bight or a french bowline is a special knot used to support a man sent aloft. Pronounced bolin. *See* sailing on a bowline.

bowman. The man in the crew of a sailboat who handles headsails and thus works on the bow, the forward part of the deck.

bowpicker. A gillnet fishing boat in which the net is handled over the bow.

bowse. Same as bouse.

bowser boat. Used to refuel seaplanes, boats, and vehicles during an amphibious operation.

bow shapes. A plumb bow is straight and vertical; a raked bow slants forward; a spoon bow has a convex curve; a clipper bow has a concave curve; and a Meirform bow has a bulbous shape below the waterline. Bows may have flare or overhang; others may have a projecting underwater stem or ram.

bowsprit. A built-in spar projecting forward and slightly up from the bow of a sailing vessel. It extends the headsails and is a major support of the masts because of the headstays that are fastened to it. A bowsprit is fitted inside the bowsprit bed or pillow chock and stepped into a bowsprit bitt.

bowthruster. *See* thruster.

bow wave. The moving bulge or mass of water pushed forward by a ship that is underway; the cause of bank cushion.

box gauge. A tide gauge operated by a float in a long vertical box to which the tide is admitted through an opening in the bottom.

box hook. A sharp pointed steel hook with a short shank and thick handle used by stevedores; shorter and heavier than a cotton hook. Also called a cargo hook.

box keel. Two longitudinal vertical plate girders fastened to the edges of a flat-plate keel with its upper or fourth side common with the double bottom plating or plated over. The duct thus formed houses the ships piping and wiring, and is also called the duct keel.

box the compass. To name all the 32 points of the compass from north through east and back to north. It starts by N, N by E, NNE, NE by N, NE, NE by E, ENE, E by N, E, E by S, and so on.

brace. *n* A rope used in a square-rigged ship to control the horizontal movement of the various sails and yards. Fore and main braces lead aft; mizzen braces lead forward. *vb* 1. To brace the yards is to move them in various directions. 2. To brace up is to bring the yard nearer to the centerline by hauling on the lee braces, thus sailing closer to the wind.

brackish. Part salt and part fresh water; maximum salinity ratio at 17 parts of salt per thousand.

braid. Modern fiber line made by braiding instead of twisting. Braided filament lines, called braid-on-braid are the latest and most expensive.

Braidline. Trade name for a special type of fexible rope for small boats. It has a braided sheath over a core.

brail. *n* 1. The lines or ropes by which sails are gathered to the mast for furling and stowing. They are secured to the after leech and passed through blocks made fast to the mast. 2. Various pieces of fishing gear such as dip nets and purse lines are known as brails or brailers. *vb* To brail up is to haul in by means of the brails.

brail net. A scoop net used to remove fish from a purse seine; now often replaced by a fish pump.

branch. A British word for a certificate of competence issued to certain pilots by Trinity House.

branch line. Same as a snood or a dropper line. *See* snood.

brash ice. Small fragments of floating ice, not more than two meters across.

brave west winds. A sailor's term for the strong and persistent westerly winds over the ocean in the middle latitudes, 35° to 65°; strongest in the Roaring Forties, 40° S to 50° S.

Brazil Current. The portion of the westerly South Atlantic Equatorial Current that turns south along the coast of Brazil; near the Rio de la Plata, it turns east.

breach. Said of a whale or large fish that jumps clear of the water. This may be done in play or to rid itself of parasites.

breadth. The width of a ship, same as beam.

break. *n* 1. The point at which an area of deck or superstructure of a ship changes level. 2. The after end of the forecastle, if above the main deck, is known as the break of the forecastle. *vb* 1. To break a flag is to unfurl it suddenly when it is two-blocked by a smart pull on the halyard that parts the light line with which it has been stopped. 2. An anchor breaks ground as it starts away from where it has dug in. 3. A man breaks out stores from a storeroom; a line never breaks for a seaman, it parts.

breakage. The space lost in stowing cargo; the difference between the measurement of a hold and the actual space occupied by the cargo. Also an allowance made for loss because of destruction of merchandise. In bills of lading, this means loss due to Acts of God.

break bulk. *adj* Describes loose packages, boxes, bales, but not pallet or container loaded. Describes a cargo vessel that loads its cargo in that manner; also called a bulker. *vb* To break bulk is to start discharging cargo.

breakdown light. *See* not-under-command.

breaker. A small cask or barrel, traditionally made of wood, that contains water for a boat, often a lifeboat. British term: barrico.

breaker, bread. A container used to carry emergency food in a boat, although not a cask.

breaker, ship. A firm that breaks up old ships for scrap.

breaker (wave). A wave or swell breaking on shore and forming surf; may curl over and break suddenly with a crash (plunging breaker), or crest and break slowly over a considerable distance (spilling breaker) or peak up without breaking (surging breaker). The above behavior is a result of the different contours and gradients of the bottom.

breakwater. Any heavy structure of stone or concrete built to protect a harbor or anchorage from the sea. *See* jetty. Also a small V-shaped or straight coaming abaft the hawse holes on the forecastle to prevent water from moving aft. Also called a spurnwater.

bream. To clean a ship's bottom by means of a blowtorch. *See* grave. Also an important food fish of the Sparidae family, related to snappers and grunts.

breast. To breast a ship in or out is to move it laterally towards or away from the pier or dock or another ship.

breast band. A strap secured around the man heaving the lead from the chains; it keeps him from falling overboard as he uses both hands on the lead line.

breasthook. A triangular steel plate bracket that joins the port and starboard side stringers at the stem of a ship. Also called a forehook. *See* knee.

breast line. 1. A line perpendicular to the ship, usually rigged only amidships. Also called a breast fast or breast rope. 2. The vertical line of a seine net.

breast shore. *See* shore.

breech. The outer angle of a knee timber opposite the inner angle or throat. Also the end of a block away from the hook, opposite to the end the line passing through the swallow. Also called arse.

breeches buoy. A device for transferring people suspended from a line or wire, the jackstay, passed between two ships alongside or between a stranded vessel and the shore. Traditional design, now improved, was a shallow canvas bag with leg holes for the passenger, hung from a block that traveled on the jackstay.

breeze. *n* A light, moderate, or strong wind, up to 27 knots; short of a gale. *See* Beaufort Scale. Land and sea breezes are caused by the difference between the land's and sea's warming to the sun as well as retaining the sun's heat. In the morning, the land heats faster, warm air rises and the sea breeze moves in to replace the rising warm air. The reverse occurs at night with the sea retaining the heat longer than the land and causing an off-shore or land breeze to blow towards the sea. These are known as solar winds. *vb* To shoot the breeze is to have a conversation.

breeze, ash. The act of rowing.

brickfielder. Same as southerly buster.

bridge. A ship's structure, topside, containing control and conning stations in a pilot house or wheel house. There may be a special navigating and/or signal bridge and, at the highest level, a flying bridge which may be used for piloting, navigating, or signaling. Bridges may be amidships, forward as in some tugs, or aft as in large tankers and container ships.

bridge deck. The topside structure or island of a ship amidships on the main deck housing for example the bridge and chart house. Also called the mast house in older ships. In a sailboat, the decked-over structure between the cockpit and the cabin to prevent water from going below. Also called a booby hatch.

bridge gauge. An instrument used to measure the vertical and lateral clearances of a journal in a sleeve bearing made in halves. Most common use is in measuring propeller shaft clearances.

bridle. Any span of rope, wire, or chain with both ends secured and the strain taken on the middle that is used in such activities as towing, moving cargo, or mooring.

brigantine. A two-masted sailing vessel with square sails forward and fore-and-aft rig aft, on the mainmast. Old name was hermaphrodite brig since it evolved from the brig.

brightwork. Unpainted brass, copper, chromium, or stainless steel kept clean and shining. Unfinished wood, not painted, such as teak, is referred to as bright. It may be oiled or varnished. British limit word bright to wood and exclude metal.

brine cock. Same as scum cock.

bring. When combined with another word or phrase means to accomplish something. A rope is brought to a winch; a ship is brought up all standing by sudden anchoring or stranding. A rope is brought up with a round turn when its motion is stopped by passing it around a cleat. A ship is brought about on the opposite tack. A boom being rigged in is said to be brought home.

broach. A ship, when running before a heavy sea may accidentally swing parallel to the sea and broach which may include dismasting, rolling over and capsizing. A hydrofoil broaches when its foils come out of the water in heavy weather and thus lose lift which results in the hull dropping sharply.

broadbill. *See* swordfish.

broad command pennant. Pennant used in warships as the flag of an officer below flag rank who commands a unit of several ships as a destroyer division commander.

broad on the bow (quarter). A relative bearing midway between the beam of a ship and dead ahead (astern) either port or starboard. Broad on the port quarter is the same as 225 degrees relative.

broad reach. *See* reach. In British usage, broad is an expanse of inland waterways.

broadside. Simultaneous firing of all assigned guns on one side of a man-of-war. Modern term is salvo fire which normally changes to rapid fire when a hitting gun range has been established.

broad strake. One of the three rows of planking or plating next to the garboard strake. *See* strake.

brogan. A decked version of the Chesapeake sailing log canoe.

broken stowage. The space wasted in a ship's hold when stowing general cargo.

broken water. An area of disturbed, moving water in an otherwise calm or stable sea.

brought. *See* bring.

brow. A ramp or long and wide plank sometimes fitted with rollers used for passage between ships moored alongside or between a ship and the pier. It may rest aboard ship on a platform called a brow landing and the rollers are fitted to a brow truck. Sometimes a brow is called a gangplank or gangboard and, quite incorrectly, a gangway. Also a small ramp used to allow passage of wheels, as in a forklift, over hatch coamings or door sills in a ship.

Bruce anchor. A modern British-designed anchor with three curved flukes or palms extending from a single arm.

brushing. Testing a racing sailboat, being tuned against a similar boat that maintains a constant trim.

bubble sextant or octant. Sextant or octant using a bubble to establish an artificial horizon in measuring the altitude of a celestial body.

buccaneers. Freebooters and privateers of the Caribbean and Pacific in the 17th century; differed from pirates as they usually did not prey on ships of their own country. Some fought against the Spanish under Henry Morgan; others made remarkable voyages of exploration.

bucket dredge. A device for removing material such as soil, sand, or mud from the bottom by means of buckets that move on a continuous chain; usually mounted on a barge.

buckeye. A distinctive Chesapeake Bay centerboard schooner up to 80 feet long with sharply raked masts, used as a market and fishing boat; now built or converted as yachts. Also called a bugeye.

buckler. A general term for a device that prevents the leakage of water through hawse holes, chain pipes and around the barrels of large turret guns. In the latter case, they are called bloomers.

bucko. A term commonly used to describe the tough and often brutal mates of the clipper ships.

bucktail. A game fishing lure traditionally made of dyed deer hair.

buffalo. 1. In old wooden ships, the bulwarks on each side of the bow near the stem. Also called a buffalo rail. 2. A block of wood upon which the fluke of an old-fashioned stock anchor might rest on deck.

bugeye. Same as buckeye.

builders model. The traditional half model of a wooden ship made by the builder to show the lines of the ship; often made of alternate strips of light and dark wood.

bulk. The hold space in a ship; also the cargo. Also described the type of cargo not stowed in containers such as wheat or coal.

bulk carrier. A ship designed to carry cargo in bulk. Also called a bulker.

bulker. Same as a bulk carrier.

bulkhead. *n* 1. Any vertical partition or wall in a ship; may be watertight, fireproof, or structural. 2. A structure along the shore that separates land and water, primarily designed to resist earth pressure not water pressure. *See* jetty. *vb* In naval terms, to bulkhead is to complain so that a superior will hear the complaint; the man complaining is bulkheading.

bulkhead deck. The uppermost deck up to which the transverse watertight bulkheads and shell plating are carried.

bulkhead stop. Any ship's valve in a bulkhead that serves to isolate a system of liquids within a major compartment.

bullboat. A willow framed boat covered with hide that was once used by the American Indians.

bulldog clip. A shackle or clamp closed with two bolts, used to join two pieces of wire together in a bulldog splice. Several clips are used for one splice. British term: bulldog grip.

bulldogging. A gamefisherman's term for the rapid swinging of a hooked fish's head from side to side.

bull earring. An earring or ring for hauling out taut the edge of an awning.

bullet block. Block with aluminum sheaves to use with wire for heavy loads such as vangs, outhauls, or halyards on large sailboats. Originally bullet blocks were streamlined and used aloft in the square-riggers when it was necessary to avoid fouling other gear.

bull gear. Any large gear, especially a low gear mounted on the forward end of the main shaft of a turbine driven ship.

bullnose. A closed chock, usually amidships, at the bow of a ship; used as a fairlead for the anchor chain when mooring to a buoy or for a tow rope or cable. British term: bullring.

bull rail. A large timber set along the edge of a wharf or pier.

bullring. British word for bullnose.

bullring vang. *See* vang.

bull riveting. Riveting that uses compressed air or hydraulic machinery to drive and expand rivets.

bullrope. Originally a rope used for hoisting a topmast in a square-rigger. Now any line used to steady, secure, or move cargo. Also a line led to a mooring buoy from the bowspirit of a sailboat or other small craft to keep it from touching the buoy.

bullseye. Same as decklight, a fixed piece of heavy glass set into a deck, bulkhead, or door to admit light; also called a deadlight. Also the name of a sheaveless block with a hole bored in it to take a line as a fairlead.

bullseye squall. Squall that forms in fair weather; found off South Africa. Identified by the small isolated cloud that forms the center of the invisible vortex of the storm.

bull trawl. Same as pair trawl.

bulwark port. Same as a freeing port.

bulwarks. The raised wood fence or steel plating along the side of a ship above the deck used as protection for people and for cargo.

bumbershoot policy. A marine protection and indemnity policy that takes effect after the limits of the basic policy have been reached; same as the ordinary insurance term umbrella cover.

bumboat. Any small harbor craft selling goods to ships in the harbor.

bumkin. Originally a short projecting spar from the bows or quarters of a square-rigger. Now the short outrigger or spar projecting aft over the stern of a yawl to which the mizzen sheet block is secured. Also spelled boomkin.

bummock. From a submariner's point of view, a downward projection of ice from the underside of the ice canopy; the counterpart of an ice hummock.

bumper. *See* fender.

bumper bobbin. Same as bobbin.

bund. Oriental term for harbor, pier, or landing place or an embankment.

bung. The plug set flush in a wooden deck over a deck bolt.

bungee. Same as shock cord; elastic cord that has many uses in a boat.

bunk. Traditionally, a built-in wooden bed in a ship but now includes cots and pipe berths. In general, the nautical word for bed.

bunkboard. A wooden board used either to protect the sleeper from a sweaty steel hull or to keep him in when the ship rolls.

bunk bottoms. The removable canvas strips under the mattress of a pipe berth.

bunker. *n* **1.** The compartment in a ship where fuel, originally coal, is stored. **2.** In general, fuel or the act of fueling. **3.** A slang word for menhaden, short for mossbunker. *See* menhaden. *vb* **1.** A ship enters port to bunker or for bunkers. **2.** Bunkering is the technique of fueling a ship in such a manner that it can carry maximum cargo.

bunkroom. Room used mainly for sleeping.

bunt. 1. Traditionally the middle part of a sail or seine. **2.** In modern sailboats the lower part between reef points and the foot of the sail.

buntline. A rope used in furling a squaresail. Also another word for codend.

bunting. The signal flags of a ship. Originally the special woolen cloth used to make the signal flags.

buoy. A floating, anchored, unmanned device used to mark a channel, danger, or obstruction; may be a nun, spar, can, lighted, bell, whistle or other buoy. An anchor buoy is used to mark the location of an anchor. A mooring buoy provides something for a ship or boat to make fast to. A sea buoy is the one farthest at sea; the first to be passed when a ship approaches a port or a channel. There are dozens of special purpose buoys.

buoyage. The U.S. and Canada use the lateral system of buoyage. Other countries, including European ones, use the cardinal system. Progress is being made by the International Association of Lighthouse Authorities to agree on two universal standards. *See* System A, B.

buoyancy. The upward force exerted by a liquid on a floating and immersed object; equal to the weight of the liquid displaced by the floating object. The weight of the water depends on its density.

buoyancy compensator (BC). A brightly colored life vest worn by some scuba divers.

buoy raft. A inflatable raft that can be ballasted with water after launching and thereby improve its stability in a seaway.

burden. Technically, the cargo capacity of a ship; the difference in tons between her light and loaded displacement. By common usage, it is the same as net registered tonnage. An old spelling is burthen.

burdened vessel. *See* give-way vessel.

Bureau Veritas International (B.V.). The French national classification society in Paris. *See* classification.

burgee. A swallow-tailed pennant used as a distinguishing flag by yachts and some merchant ships.

burgoo. Seamen's slang for porridge.

burton. A common and small, general purpose tackle or purchase, usually formed by two blocks with a hook block in the bight of the running part. Variations are single Spanish and double Spanish burtons.

burton or burtoning rig. A system for moving cargo ashore or to another ship alongside (sometimes underway) in which two ship's cranes or booms are used with a single hook. One boom plumbs the hatch; the second swings the draft outboard. Also called union gear purchase or double fall rig.

bush. The mass of spray or dense water vapor marking the base of a waterspout.

buster. A heavy southerly squall encountered on the south coast of Australia.

bustle. An underwater bulge in the after part of the hull of a sailboat.

butt. The ends of two planks or plates which meet exactly. They are said to butt one another and thus form a butt joint. Also the lower end of a fishing rod below the reel.

butterfly fish. A somewhat imprecise term for any of numerous small tropical reef fish. One, a chaetodon, appears to have four eyes since it has a large dark spot rimmed in white on each side of its tail. *See* sergeant major.

butterfly net. Oval, scoop fishing nets, shaped like butterfly wings, used by Mexicans on lakes and in sheltered waters.

Butterworth. A patented cover for a compartment or tank opening that is air and water tight.

buttock. The intersection of the molded surface of a ship's hull with the vertical plane at a given distance from the center longitudinal plane of the ship and parallel to it. Also the rounded overhang of the lower stern forward of the ruddder.

buttock planes. The vertical planes passing through the buttocks of a ship.

button. A projecting ring on an oar, above the leather that keeps it from sliding through the oarlock.

B.V. Bureau Veritas International located in Paris; the French classification society.

Buys Ballot's Law. Facing the wind, the center of low pressure will normally be 8 to 12 points (100 to 130 degrees) on your right in the northern hemisphere and on your left in the southern hemisphere.

by. **1.** In nautical terminology means near, toward, or in position as in N.E. by N. (one point north of northeast). **2.** Down by the bow or stern describes a ship whose draft is greater at the bow or stern. **3.** If a mast goes by the board, it goes overboard. **4.** A ship sailing by the wind is sailing close hauled. **5.** A ship sailing by the lee is sailing free and downwind. **6.** By and large describes a sailing ship that could sail close hauled as well as large (free); thus by and large has come to its present general meaning. **7.** By the run describes a line or tackle that is fully released and allowed to run free.

C

C. International signal code alphabet flag. When hoisted singly means: "yes, affirmative". Spoken: "charlie".

C-1, C-2, etc. *See* C-type ships.

casing whale. A type of blackfish or grumpus, common to the North Atlantic and closely related to the ocra or killer whale.

cab. The covered portion of the outboard ends of the bridge wings in a ship.

CAB. Captive Air Bubble vessel; a type of air cushion or ground effect machine partially supported above the water by an air bubble enclosed on both sides by shallow draft hulls.

cabin. Any room or apartment aboard ship used by officers and passengers. On warships, the Commanding Officer also has a sea cabin where he sleeps while underway. In small boats, the major space below deck.

cabin top. A built-on structure over a boat's cabin to permit greater headroom. Also called a coach roof or a trunk cabin.

cable. Any heavy rope, wire, or chain used for anchoring, towing, salvage or for transmitting electricity (wire). Most anchor cables are steel chains unless used for boats and yachts where they may be of synthetic rope and are called rodes. Also a traditional, little-used nautical measure of length or distance now universally accepted as being one tenth of a nautical mile, 608 feet, 200 yards or meters, or 100 fathoms.

cable holder. Same as wildcat.

cable hook. A long handled tool used in the past to stow chain cable by hand in the chain locker. All modern ships are designed so the anchor chain is automatically arranged in tiers as it falls down the chain pipe.

cable jack. A heavy bar and fulcrum used for lifting the anchor chain off the deck so that a pelican hook or similar device can be made fast.

cable-laid rope. Three or four plain-laid, three-stranded ropes twisted together in the opposite direction to the twists of the individual ropes. Also known as a water-laid rope; it was superior to plain-laid rope when used as an anchor cable.

cable lifter. *See* wildcat.

cable markings. Turns of wire around the studs of chain cable links to show amount of cable paid out. At every 15 fathoms on a link painted white a turn of wire shows the number of 15 fathom shots from the anchor.

cable ship. Ship designed to lay and repair telegraph and telephone cables laid on the bottom of the sea.

cable stopper. A device to hold an anchor chain on deck commonly called in the U.S. a pelican hook; British call them slips. There are Blake slips, screw slips, Senhouse slips, and devils claws, all serving the same purpose by engaging one of the links of the chain. Also called a chain stopper and a slip hook.

cable wheel. *See* wildcat.

caboose. A small structure topside on a ship once used as the galley.

cabotage. The limitation of domestic shipping to those vessels documented under the flag of that country.

cachalot. A sperm whale.

CAD. Cash Against Documents or Cash After Delivery; a method of shipping.

caique. A small, originally Turkish coasting vessel of the eastern Mediterranean used for commerce and fishing. Its traditional, simple design and sturdy construction have appealed to yachtsmen.

caisson. Any watertight structure, usually pressurized, that is used in underwater repair and construction. Also the floating gate of a drydock.

calamary. A squid.

calashee watch. An old square-rigger term for all hands on deck to handle the sails in an emergency.

Calderata. A strong hot wind blowing off the mountains of the north coast of Venezuela.

calendar. A device composed of two rollers that is used to apply heat and pressure to sailcloth as part of the finishing process after weaving. This process is called calendering.

calf. *See* calving.

California Current. An ocean current flowing south along the west coast of North America to about latitude 23°N where it moves westward to join the North Equatorial Current. It originates as the southern branch of the Aleutian Current between 40° and 50°N.

calk. *See* caulk.

call. Various sounds made on a boatswain's pipe such as call away the gig or pipe to dinner. In British usage, it refers to the silver pipe used by the petty officers.

Callao rope. A mooring line used to secure lighters working cargo in an open roadstead. It is 15 feet long made of 12 inch manila or equivalent synthetic material spliced to a wire pendant at each end.

call away. A naval term passed by voice or pipe meaning assemble and report for duty, as in call away boarders or call away the anchor detail. *See* away.

call sign. In maritime communications, the identifying letters and/or numerals of a station or ship.

calm. A state of sea and weather marked by little or no wind.

calving. The breaking away of ice from a berg, shelf, or glacier into the sea. The resultant piece of ice is a calf.

camber. The athwartships, convex, curve of a ship's deck, higher in the center than at the sides. Also the fore-and-aft curvature in a sail, sometimes called flow. British name for a small basin within a harbor.

cam cleat. A quick release fitting for holding a line or sheet of a sailboat between the teeth of two adjacent discs or cams.

camel. A heavy spar, timber, or a number of them bolted together, used to keep a ship away from the pier or from another ship. Also sometimes a buoyant device used in salvage as a lifting pontoon.

cam stopper. A holding device built into modern blocks so that the line passing through the block may be stopped and held.

canal. An excavated, man-made waterway. Also a long, natural arm of the sea.

canard. A hydrofoil configuration or design in which the main lifting struts and foils are aft.

Canary Current. An ocean current, part of the north Atlantic clockwise circulation, that flows southwest past Portugal and the northwest coast of Africa from the Canary to the Cape Verde Islands where it divides to move west with the North Equatorial Current and southeast and east to become the Guinea Current.

can buoy. A cylindrical, flat-topped, navigational buoy, usually painted black in U.S. waters. It carries odd numbers and is left to port when entering a harbor or a channel from seaward. *See* nun buoy.

candela. The International Standard Candle; the unit of light or candle power used to express the power of navigational lights worldwide, particularly those in the Light List.

C & F. Cost and Freight. The seller sends goods to the agreed destination paying the freight charges. The buyer must pay insurance and any other transit and unloading costs. The seller only pays the unloading costs if the terms are C & F landed.

candle-fish. A kind of smelt common to the Pacific coast of North America; very fat and highly valued for food.

can do. Nautical, particularily U.S. Navy slang for able, efficient and willing.

can hooks. A special gear or sling used for handling casks and having hooks that fasten to the ends of the cask.

canoe. A general term for a narrow, usually double-ended, open boat of simple design such as the Polynesian sea-going canoes fitted with outriggers and capable of making very long voyages in the Pacific.

canoe stern. A sharp rear end of a boat built much like a spoon bow.

canopy. A metal or fabric cover or hood providing protection from the weather for the people or the machinery of a boat.

cant. *n* A piece of wood (cant timber) laid on deck to support something under construction. *vb* To cant is to place at an angle instead of perpendicular or parallel.

cant beam. A deck beam at the stern of a ship extending radially abaft the transom beam.

cant frames. Frames that are not perpendicular to the keel as shown in the plans of a ship as the cant body.

cant hook. A piece of wood having a curved, movable part that is used to turn logs. Also called cant dog.

cantline. The groove between strands on the outside of a rope. Also the unused space along the bilges of casks laid in tiers. Same as guntline.

cant spar. A spar movable as a boom, mast, or yard.

cant tackle. The gear used for turning over a whale while flensing. Also called a cant purchase.

canvas. Classically a double warp, single weft fabric made of hemp used for sails, awnings and tarpaulins; classified as to thickness and strength by numbers 0–12, 0 being the strongest. Modern canvas is made from cotton or cotton and synthetic fiber mixtures. Also canvas is used as a collective term for sails, i.e. the boat needs new canvas.

cap. 1. A metal band or collar at the end of a spar. 2. The center piece or fitting on a compass card supported by a pivot. 3. A piece of leather over the end of a rope. 4. Sometimes the name for the top of a mast. *See* cravat.

cap stay. A stay between the tops of adjacent masts; sometimes called a triatic stay or signal stay.

capacity plan. A scale drawing showing in detail for example the spaces for carrying cargo in a ship and the size of hatches.

cap block. One of the pieces of wood used at times under the keel in a building dock or drydock as a leveling device.

cape. An area of land projecting into the sea; more prominent than a point. Cape Stiff is sailor's slang for Cape Horn. Cape Flyaway in old sailing days was sailor's slang for imagined and falsely reported land.

Cape Ann oar. An oar with a square loom or shaft.

Cape Horn fever. A malady ascribed to those who avoided a Cape Horn passage.

capel. An end connection for wire rope made with a metal cap instead of an eye splice.

capelin. A small food fish of the smelt family abundant in the north Atlantic and Pacific.

cap log. The major horizontal timber on a quay or pier, designed to take the impact of a ship coming alongside. Also called a cap wale.

capping. A strip of wood fitted to the top of the gunwale of a wooden boat to strengthen it.

cap scuttle. A small hatchway closed by a cap or lid fitted over the outside of the coaming.

capsize. To turn over; to turn upside down.

capstan. Originally a vertical, revolving concave barrel usually ridged with whelps and powered by men turning wooden capstan bars set into pigeon holes in the capstanhead, drumhead or trundlehead. In modern ships, it is usually called an anchor windlass or winch, both of which may have horizontal or vertical drums. *See* winch.

capstan bar. The stout wooden stick or pole set into the square pigeon hole of a capstanhead which the men pushed in order to turn the capstan.

capstanhead. Same as a drumhead or trundlehead; the top circular part of a capstan.

captain. 1. Technically and nautically a grade or rank in the Navy, Coast Guard, and other U.S. government services. 2. The title by which a ship's master or anyone having master's papers not serving under a master or the commanding officer of any rank of a naval ship should be addressed. *See* Master, Commanding Officer. 3. The chief of the paid hands of a yacht is the captain; the owner or other amateur in charge is the skipper. 4. In naval ships, the man in charge of the washroom and toilet is known informally but properly as Captain of the Head.

captain's protest. A formal statement made in writing by the master of cargo ship that has suffered damage to ship or cargo.

car. A container aboard a vessel to keep fish alive. Also called a fish car or a fish box.

caravel. A small Mediterranean trading vessel of the 14th through 17th centuries. Originally lateen rigged on two masts, it came to be square-rigged on two masts and lateen rigged on a third, the mizzen. The ships for Columbus' first voyage were caravels.

carboy. A container for corrosive liquids and chemicals aboard ship.

cardinal point. The four principal points of the compass, north, east, south, and west.

cardinal system of buoyage. System using buoys and other marks to indicate the mark's direction from the danger being buoyed. Since the buoy or mark tells the navigator the direction, north, south, east, or west that the buoy lies from the danger, he can steer accordingly. *See* buoyage. The cardinal system is used abroad, the lateral system in the U.S. *See* lateral system of buoyage, system A.

careen. To move a ship over on its side; afloat or on a sandy beach, for cleaning the bottom and repairs. Careening gear or tackle leading ashore is sometimes used.

carfloat. A deck barge equipped with rails that carries railroad cars over water.

cargo. All merchandise, goods, or material transported by ship; may be containerized, palletized, dry, bulk, general, heavy lift, deck, dangerous, liquid, refrigerated, or frozen cargo. There are special falls, hatches, hoists, mats, pumps, slings, skids, and winches used in cargo handling. There is also the associated supervision and paperwork involving bills of lading, cargo lists, sheets, and clerks.

cargo batten. Wooden planks, usually 2 by 6 fir, fitted into clips welded to the frames of a cargo hold to keep cargo from contact with the condensed moisture or sweating found on steel plating. *See* sparring.

cargo block. A term applied in general to all single and multiple blocks used for cargo handling aboard ship.

cargo boat. *See* tramp.

Cargocaire. Trade name for a popular dehumidification system for cargo ships.

cargo cluster. Lights used when working cargo at night. Also called a cargo reflector or a cargo light.

cargo hook. A special steel hook fitted with a swivel, at the end of a cargo whip used for lifting cargo. If fitted with a hinged piece to prevent the escape of the sling, it is a safety hook or a snap hook. Also the hand-held steel hook or handhook (called as well a box or cotton hook), used by stevedores in handling cargo.

cargo jack. A screw device used by stevedores to force cargo, such as cotton bales, into small spaces.

cargo manifest. A summary of all relevant bills of lading grouped by ports of discharge.

cargo net. A square piece of heavy rope netting used to lift freight or catch it before it goes overboard (save-all); used in emergencies to recover people from the water, or to facilitate disembarking of troops when rigged over the side with the top secured to the rail.

cargo pallet. *See* pallet.

cargo plan. A list giving quantities, description, and location in the ship of cargo after loading is complete.

cargo port. A large door or opening in a ship's side primarily used for loading and unloading cargo. Also called a side port.

cargo ship. A merchant ship carrying cargo or freight; may be a liner (scheduled) or a tramp (unscheduled), a dry general cargo vessel (roll on – roll off, containership, barge carrier, pallet ship, refrigerator ship, or reefer), a dry bulk carrier (cement, grain, coal, ore), a specialized dry cargo ship (lumber, paper, vehicles), or a liquid bulk carrier (crude oil, gasoline, chemical or liquid gas tanker). *See* carrier.

cargo whip. A chain or rope used in connection with a boom, derrick or mast for handling cargo. Also called a cargo hoist or cargo rope.

Caribbean Current. An ocean current flowing westward into the Caribbean through the Yucatan Channel and north past Florida as the beginning of the Gulf Stream System. It originates at the joining of the North Equatorial and Guiana currents.

Carley float. A ship-carried life raft made of an oval buoyant ring enclosing a wooden grid; has been largely replaced by self-inflating rubber life rafts.

carling. A short fore-and-aft timber or steel beam placed under a deck to strengthen it where mooring bitts, winches, and hatchways impose an extra load. Also carlin.

carpenter. At sea, a specialist in damage control and upkeep of boats, some deck machinery and wooden fittings or gear such as hatch covers, and spars. In the Navy, the carpenter reports to the First Lieutenant.

carpenter's stopper. A device used in salvage work to hold fast and prevent movement of rope and wire under heavy strain.

carrack. A 14th to 17th century European merchant ship similar to a three-masted caravel but generally larger and stronger. They were square-rigged on main and foremast, lateen rigged on the mizzen.

carrageenin. A derivative of red algae similar to agar used to stabilize emulsions and suspend solids in food and chemicals. *See* algin, agar, irish moss.

carriage. A sliding fitting on a track or traveler to which a sheet block or vang block is attached.

carrick bend. A kind of knot used mostly in fastening two hawsers or large ropes together. Also called a sailor's knot or anchor knot.

carrick bitts. Vertical heavy wood timbers in wooden ships that supported the windlass. It was topped with carrick heads to which lines were made fast.

carrier. A general word for ships that carry cargo such as grain carrier or ore carrier. Private carriers move only their owner's or company's freight; common carriers can move anyone's cargo. Contract carriers make special agreements with one or more companies. The person or firm who owns or charters ships and who transports freight as a common carrier has certain legal responsibilities. Aircraft carriers are naval warships from which aircraft are flown and recovered.

carrier bearing. The main supporting bearing on the part of the ship's structure (rudder post) that holds the rudder.

carry away. To break, part, give way, or wash overboard.

carry on. A naval command meaning to continue previous activity; usually after men have been called to attention.

cartography. The science of chart-making in which a projection of the earth's surface is described on a flat sheet of paper.

carvel. A type of boat construction using wooden planks meeting flush; giving a smooth surface in contrast to clinker, in which the planks overlap.

casco. Philippine word for a barge or lighter used in moving cargo ashore.

case. The cavity in the head of a sperm whale in which a case bucket was used to bail out the oil (spermaceti) stored there. Now a word seldom heard.

casing. Any covering or shielding for machinery made from light metal such as a boiler casing.

cask. A barrel, hogshead, pipe, butt, tun, or keg normally made of wood and used to carry liquid. In modern ships, most liquids are carried in bulk in tanks.

cast. *n* British word for the leader used to fasten a line to a fishhook. *vb* 1. Heaving the lead to measure depth of water is to cast the lead. 2. To move a ship's bow as in to cast to starboard upon leaving an anchorage is to swing the ship to the right. 3. To cast off means to throw off, as a mooring line is cast off the bollard.

castaway. *n* Someone put ashore or shipwrecked on a lonely island or coast. *vb* To cast away a ship means to wreck her, usually intentionally.

casting. The act of throwing a bait or lure with a casting rod.

cast net. Net that is weighted on its periphery and thrown out by hand from the shore or from a boat to encircle and trap small fish.

cast off. A command given in a ship when leaving a pier meaning to throw off all lines, or the one indicated, from the bollards ashore.

cat. 1. To hoist and secure an old-fashioned stock anchor to the cathead. The tackle used included cat blocks, a cat beam, a cat chain, a cat back, cat stoppers, cat pendants, etc. 2. An 18th century sailing collier. 3. Short for catamaran, cat-o'-nine tails.

catadromous. A fish that lives in fresh water, such as the eel, then goes to sea to spawn; opposed to salmon which is anadromous.

catamaran. A twin-hulled vessel powered by sail or engines but most common as sailing yachts for racing and cruising as well as small sailboats used for day sailing. British word for a raft used in painting a ship's side.

cat block. Block used to hoist an old-fashioned stock anchor aboard.

catboat. An eastern U.S. coastal pleasure and fishing sailing boat that has a single unstayed mast stepped forward and no headsail. It is very beamy and stable, has a centerboard, and is often called a cat for short.

catch a crab. Said of an oarsman when, on his recovery stroke, he strikes the water accidentally thus breaking the rhythm of the rowing.

catcher boat. Any size boat that hunts and fishes for the mother or factory ship which collects the catch. Also called a killer boat, a whale killer, or a whale catcher.

catenary. The dip or slack in a rope, cable, chain, or fishing line when suspended between two supports. It often provides an important spring effect in anchoring, mooring to a buoy or when towing.

cathead. Formerly a projecting structure on the bow of a ship using the old-fashioned or stock anchor. Not used on modern ships and now usually refers to a fixed crane projecting from the upper floor of a warehouse.

cathole. An opening in the quarter of an old sailing ship for passing mooring lines, etc.

cat ketch. A ketch-rigged sailboat with the mainmast stepped all the way forward. There are no headsails and the jigger or mizzenmast is about the same height as the mainmast.

cat-o'-nine tails. Nine lengths of knotted cord fixed to a handle with which sailors were once flogged. The practice ended in the late 19th century. *See* room to swing a cat.

catoptric, catadioptric. *See* lighthouse.

catspaw. A light, passing breeze and the ruffled surface of the water that results; sometimes called a catskin. *See* flaw. Also a twisting hitch made in the bight of a rope, forming two eyes through which the hook of a tackle can be passed.

catting. Hoisting aboard and securing an old-fashioned stock anchor.

catty. *See* water monkey.

catwalk. Any walkway aboard ship over or around an obstruction.

caudal. Pertaining to the tail, as the caudal fin of a fish.

caulk. To seal a joint between steel plates or wooden planks. For the latter, various materials such as oakum are used, hammered in with caulking tools. Also spelled calk.

caulk off. Slang meaning to nap, doze, or sleep. Spoken: "Cork off."

cavil. Same as kevel.

cavitation. A physical phenomenon around rotating propeller blades and struts that involves the collapse of transient air bubbles associated with the flow of water. It produces increased corrosion and reduces efficiency.

cay. A low insular bank of coral and sand; a small, low island. Also key.

ceiling. The inside planking, sheathing or plating of a ship, including the flooring of a ship's cargo hold. It has nothing to do with a ceiling ashore; *see* deckhead, overhead. Also the height of clouds above sea level.

ceilometer. An instrument for measuring the height of clouds.

celestial. Pertaining to the heavens. Celestial navigation uses the observation of heavenly bodies such as the sun, moon, stars, and planets. The British term for celestial navigation is astro-navigation.

celestial sphere. With the use of celestial coordinates, an imaginary globe on which the heavenly bodies are located and the earth in the center.

cellar. A watertight control and repair room built over the top of an oil producing well on the ocean floor. Men are carried and supported there by a service capsule lowered by a support ship on the surface.

centerboard. A hinged metal or wooden fin which can be raised and lowered beneath a sailboat to improve its resistance to lateral movement or leeway when sailing. It is housed in a centerboard trunk. Also called a center keel, centerplate, or sliding keel and somewhat inaccurately, a drop keel. See dagger board.

center keel. Same as centerboard.

centerline. An imaginary line from bow to stern down the middle of the ship.

centerline plane. In ship design and construction, an imaginary longitudinal plane perpendicular to the base line plane and parallel to the buttock planes, port and starboard.

centerplate. Same as centerboard.

centerplate keel. Similar to a bar keel but built up by extending a center, vertical member below the ship's bottom and stiffening it on each side by continuous narrow plates called keel slabs. Also called a sidekeel.

centerplate rudder. Rudder made of a single heavy plate fastened to the rudder stock or main piece by steel arms.

center of buoyancy. A point through which passes the resultant of all upward forces and by which a floating ship is supported.

center of effort. In a sailing ship, the theoretical point at which the resultant of the wind force on all sails may be calculated to act.

center of gravity. The point at which all factors that comprise a ship's weight may be considered as concentrated; where the sum of all moments of weight are zero. In surface ships, the center of buoyancy is usually below the center of gravity.

center of lateral resistance. The theoretical point through which the resultant of resistance of the ship's hull to lateral motion passes.

centipede. A strong rope running below the length of the bowsprit of a large sailing ship, fitted every 3 or 4 feet with small loops to assist the crew in stowing headsails.

CEPEX. Controlled Ecosystem Pollution EXperiment.

cephalopod. A mollusk with 8 or 10 legs, a beaked head, sometimes an internal shell and prehensile tentacles. Those with eight legs (octopods) include the octopus; those with ten (decapods) include cuttlefish, common squid, and the giant squid upon whom the sperm whale feeds.

certificate. An official paper testifying to some condition or fact regarding the ship, crew, passengers, or cargo such as certificate of discharge, disinfection, identification, of origin, of ownership, of registry, of record, or of survey.

certificate of protection. Certificate granted by the U.S. government to a foreign built yacht purchased by a U.S. citizen giving it protection as the property of a U.S. national.

certificate of registry. A document issued by a government establishing the nationality and ownership of a vessel. Short term is registry.

cesser clause. Part of a charter party that relieves the charterer of any liability once cargo is loaded and gives the owners a lien on the cargo for payment of freight, demurrage, or average.

cetacea. The scientific name for whales and porpoises.

chafing gear. Any material or device that is used to prevent or reduce wear of ropes, cables, or canvas; may be chafing mats, battens, chains, strips of leather, plastic, canvas, or baggywrinkle.

chafing plate. A rounded plate that minimizes the wear on lines such as at a hatch coaming.

chain. Connected iron or steel links principally used as anchor and mooring cable; also used in early steering mechanisms for ships and is sometimes used in securing cargo. Anchor chain links are normally fitted with cross-pieces or studs for increased strength and to prevent kinking.

chain grab. *See* wildcat.

chain hoist. Lifting gear using an endless chain, several blocks, and certain gears; used to lift heavy weights aboard ship especially in machinery spaces or in dry-dock. The special chain hoist blocks used are usually differential blocks having two or more sheaves of different diameters.

chain hook. A heavy steel hook attached to a short handle used by men for handling anchor chain links, as in putting on a stopper.

chain locker. A compartment below decks where the anchor chain is stowed aboard ship as it falls down the chain pipe.

chain pipe. A heavy vertical steel tube just forward of the anchor windlass or wildcat through which the anchor chain falls down into the locker below. Also called a chain locker pipe, chain taker pipe, spurling, spilling or spill pipe, deck pipe, or monkey pipe. British term: naval pipe.

chain plate. A flat piece of steel bolted to the side of a sailing vessel to which the lower ends of the shrouds are secured.

chains. The platform or station, traditionally near the chain plates from which the leadsman heaves his lead while taking soundings.

chain shot. A short length of chain or two balls connected by chain, fired by an ancient cannon to damage the rigging.

chain sling. A length of short link chain used in handling some types of cargo, usually fitted with a ring at one end and a hook on the other.

chain stopper. A device for holding a heavy anchor chain on deck, using a short length of chain, one end made fast to the deck, a turnbuckle for adjusting tension, and a pelican hook for holding and releasing the cable. Also called a dog stopper or a cable stopper.

chandler. A merchant or a maritime retailer. A ship or yacht chandler sells all the gear and supplies needed to outfit a ship for sea. In the Far East, a ship's chandler is a comprador.

chank shell. A sacred conch that is revered by certain religious sects in India and that has been collected for over 2000 years.

channel. 1. The deeper, navigable, and usually marked, buoyed part of a river, bay, harbor, or other body of water. **2.** A large strait such as the English Channel. **3.** A timber fastened to the side of the hull of an old wooden sailing ship that is used to spread the shrouds outboard away from the ship. **4.** A radio frequency.

channel bar. A bar of rolled steel that has a U-shaped cross section.

channel net. A trawl net with wings on each side used for catching shrimp in tidal water of the eastern U.S.

chantey. A sailor's song, traditionally sung in unison to expedite some heavy hauling chore such as hoisting the anchor. Seldom heard at sea now. British spelling shantey.

chapel. *n* The grooves in a built-up wooden mast. *vb* A square-rigged ship is said to be chapelled when taken aback or losing her way in light airs; she is brought around to her original tack and heading by the use of the rudder alone. The ship is swung stern first in a complete circle.

chaplain. Priest, rabbi, or minister of any faith serving aboard ship. In the Navy, he is a commissioned officer. Slang is sky pilot or padre.

chariot. A manned torpedo used by both sides in World War II.

Charlie Noble. Slang for the smokestack or visible exhaust funnel of the ship's galley.

chart. Nautical word for map, showing the coast line with its major geographic features, aids to navigation, depths of water, nature of bottom, and so on. Charts for U.S. waters are produced by the National Ocean Survey and for the rest of the world by the Defense Mapping Agency Hydrographic Center. Standard charts are made for ships; special folding charts for small craft. *See* pilot chart, bathymetric map, Marine Weather Services Charts.

chart datum. The plane of reference for all depth of U.S. water data, including tide tables. In the U.S., it is mean lower low water or mean low water. In the United Kingdom, it is the lowest astronomical tide; the lowest water predictable.

charter party (c/p). A formal agreement to hire, rent, or lease a ship or yacht. A bareboat or demise charter is one in which the charterer provides crew and equipment, stores fuel, etc. A time charter is for a fixed period; a voyage charter is for a specified voyage. In an open charter, neither the nature of the cargo nor its destination need be specified. There are two standard forms used: gencon and warshipvoy.

chart house. The compartment near the bridge where charts are stowed and where the navigation is done. Also called chart room.

chartlet correction. A paste-over as a partial chart correction provided in Notices to Mariners.

chase. *n* A ship being pursued.

chase, bow. Guns fixed to fire directly forward. Those fixed to fire aft were called stern chase (guns).

chase guns. Guns temporarily moved from their broadside position.

cheater. Another term for a spinnaker staysail.

check. To slack or ease a line or rope, maintaining tension but not parting the line or permitting it to run away. Snub is a stronger term for holding a line or wire just short of parting.

checker. One of the portable wood divisions or planks that form the sides of the fish pond on the deck of a fishing vessel. British term: pound board.

checking bollard. A bollard used for warping ships through the entrance of a drydock. Also called a warping bollard or deadhead.

checkman. Man in the fireroom of a ship who controls the water level in the boilers.

check the helm. When changing course, an order to the helmsman to slow the swing of the ship and not pass the desired final heading. Often spoken as "check her."

check valve. Valve that permits a fluid to pass through only in one direction. Also those used for overboard discharge are also called clack or clapper valves.

cheek. 1. One of the projections on the lower mast of a wooden ship that supports the trestle-trees and framing. Also called the mast cheek and, in steel construction, cheek plates. The cheeks on the upper masts were called hounds. 2. One of the sides of a block or the jaw of a gaff. 3. The curve or turn of the bilge of a ship.

cheek block. Block used for sheets and halyards; usually a fixed block, attached to a convenient boom, deck cabin top, or coaming. Plastic sheaves are for use with rope while blocks with aluminum sheaves are used with wire and wire-rope combination. Somtimes called a clamp.

cheek knee. One of the side knee pieces by which the cutwater was secured to the bow of a wooden ship.

cheese. British word for a coil of line which has been cheesed down. U.S. usage is coil and coiled down or flemished down. *See* coil, fake.

chesstree. A piece of wood with holes, later fitted with sheaves, that was fastened topside in a square-rigger as a fairlead for the bowlines and tacks.

chest. Any container, trunk, or box for a specific purpose, i.e. chronometer chest, mess chest, or steam chest.

Chief. Short for the Chief Officer, Chief Engineer, Chief Petty Officer (Navy) etc. The Chief Officer is the second in authority in a merchant ship, corresponding to the Executive Officer of a warship.

chine. The line of intersection between the sides and the bottom of a flat or V-bottom hull. Since an angle exists between the side and the bottom, the ship can be said to have a hard chine. *See* bilge.

Chinese landing. Bringing a boat or a ship alongside another, bow to stern or down stream. Sometimes necessary but usually more complicated.

chinse. To caulk lightly or temporarily.

chip. Surfers' slang for a modern surfboard.

chip log. An historic and obsolete method of measuring the ship's speed by using a measured and marked line attached to a chip or piece of wood. When cast overboard, the chip carried the line a certain distance in a measured time interval thereby permitting a calculation of the ship's speed. *See* log.

chipping. Removing rust and old paint by repeated blows with a hammer or scraper.

chipping hammer. A small hammer with a sharp peen and face set at right angles to each other, used aboard ship for chipping and scaling. Also called a scaling hammer or a boiler pick.

Chips. Familiar name for the ship's Carpenter; comparable to Boats for the Boatswain.

chilton. Member of the flat mollusks class; they are protected either by calcareous spicules (spines) or plates.

chock. *n* 1. A heavy metal fitting through which a rope, wire, or chain has a fairlead on the deck of a ship or on a pier; may be an open or closed chock, or may be fitted with a roller to reduce friction (a roller chock). British term: fairlead. 2. Any shaped block of wood or metal used to prevent cargo, a boat, or a vehicle from leaving or moving from its stowed position inside a rolling ship or on deck. *vb* To chock is to secure somthing with dunnage.

chock-a-block. Two blocks close together; full or no room to go further or no more room to store cargo. *See* two blocked.

chock, boom. A fitting shaped to receive the head of a boom when it has been lowered.

chocolate gale. A strong northwest wind blowing in the West Indies.

choke. To foul or jam, as the hauling part of a tackle is thrust into the block in order to stop movement, thus choking it. This is also called choking the luff.

chop. *n* 1. Slang for signature, initials, or any official seal or stamp on a document. 2. In Naval usage, a change in operational control. *vb* A Naval ship passing from one ocean or area to another is said to chop in or chop out.

chop chop. Pigeon English and nautical slang for hurry.

chops of the channel. British term for the western approaches to the English Channel.

choppy. Describes a short sea in a moderate wind.

chow. Slang for food.

chow down. Means the meal is ready.

chow line. The mess line in naval usage.

Christ disturber. A light sail carried aloft in a square-rigger. *See* kites.

christmas tree. Any control panel using colored lights, such as those now common on the bridge of ships that indicate the status of important machinery.

christmas tree worm. A salt water tropical worm whose feathery plumes, extended above the coral of the reef, look like a tiny christmas tree. When the worm feels threatened its plumes are retracted into its body.

chronometer. An accurate clock or watch used for celestial navigation. Modern cheap and very accurate watches, with or without radio time ticks, now serve yachtsmen as adequate time pieces. In the Merchant Service, chronometers are usually wound up at 0800; in the Navy, before noon.

chronometer error. The difference from Greenwich Mean Time; a rate of error can be determined and applied to learn GMT at any time.

chronometer record book. A record book where all data, including temperature, are recorded daily.

Chubasco. A violent rain and wind squall met in the rainy season along the west coast of Central America and Mexico.

chuck. A narrow passage or strait swept by tidal currents. Also the current itself.

chum. Ground bait thrown overboard to attract fish. The procedure is called chumming as well as tolling.

church pennant. Pennant having a blue cross on a white background; flown at sea on a Navy ship when church services are held. The only flag that may be flown above the colors.

chute. Slang for spinnaker.

CIF. Cost, Insurance, Freight. The same as C&F except that the seller now pays for insurance.

ciguatera. Food poisoning resulting from eating various tropical reef and inshore fishes such as groupers, baracuda, and jacks which for some reason at certain places and at certain times become poisonous. Not usually fatal but often seriously disabling for a boat or ship's crew.

Cinque Ports. Five ports on the English coast: Dover, Sandwich, Romney, Hastings, and Hythe who joined together in mutual defense in 1278.

circle sheet. Sheets prepared for and employed in hydrographic surveys for plotting navigational fixes.

cirriped. A crustacean having hooked appendages with which it can attach itself parasitically to other organisms, on rocks, or ship bottoms.

cirro-cumulus or stratus. *See* cloud.

cirrus. In general, cirrus clouds are above 20,000 feet; often thin wisps or a thin haze producing a halo around the moon. They accompany good weather. *See* cloud. Also one of the appendages of a barnacle.

clack valve. *See* check valve.

clam. An edible bivalve mollusk that lives mostly just submerged in mud and sand off the coast. More popular in the U.S. than abroad, the soft-shelled surf, razor, and ocean quahog are all important as food and bait; harvested by hand digging or by powered clam dredges.

clam, giant. *See* giant clam.

clamp. 1. In wooden ships, a heavy timber fastened to the inside of the frame timbers to support the shelves and the ends of deck beams. **2.** A cheek block. **3.** Any device used to hold something together.

clamp down. To sprinkle a deck with water and then dry it with a swab. Not the same as swabbing which involves the use of a wet swab periodically rinsed and wrung out.

clamshell snapper. A steel device for taking small, disturbed sediment samples of the ocean bottom.

clap on. 1. To take hold and haul as in "clap on the halyard." **2.** To clap on a stopper means to put it on and use it. **3.** To clap on sail means to set more canvas.

clapotis. Waves reflected from a seawall, bulkhead, or steep beach.

clasp hook. Same as sister hook.

classification. In its maritime sense means placing a vessel in a certain category with regards to size, material condition, strength of construction, and equipment, as specified by a government or private organization. This is mostly for insurance purposes. *See* classification society.

classification society. The private or public organization that establishes standards of safety and sound construction for ships. There are 13 societies comprising all the major maritime countries patterned after Lloyd's Register of Shipping in the United Kingdom. The American Bureau of Shipping is the U.S. society.

claw off. Said of a sailing vessel when close hauled in a gale trying to sail away from a lee shore.

cleading. The wooden or metal casing along the inside of a lifeboat behind which buoyancy tanks are fitted. Plastic foam is now used instead of tanks.

clean. 1. Sharp, neat, as in the clean lines of a ship. **2.** Free of obstruction, as in a clean anchorage; opposed to foul. **3.** Free of any unfavorable or qualifying clause as a clean bill of health or bill of lading. **4.** A clean charter is one free of commission or agency fees. **5.** Clean full refers to sails kept drawing steadily; also called rap full. **6.** A clean run describes the fine afterbody of a ship that causes little disturbance of the water or wake when underway, in contrast to full run.

clean slate. Originally the slate used as a rough log during a watch on the deck of a sailing ship. It recorded such items as courses, distance run, and ship's position. It was wiped clean, ready for the next officer after the officer going off watch had written in his log.

clear. *n* A rope free to run is clear. *adj* A clear anchor is, on being hoisted aboard, free of entanglement in contrast to a foul anchor. *vb* **1.** To free from legal detention, as in clearing a cargo or to free from entaglement, as in clearing a tackle. **2.** To clear the forecastle means to remove all personnel promptly. **3.** Clear for action means to get ready for battle. **4.** Clearing the harbor, a cape, or obstruction means departing and passing safely.

clearance. Official permission, often in writing, for a ship to enter or leave port in regard to customs, health, or immigration.

clear days. In a charter party, refers to days not to be considered lay days. *See* lay days. Clear days are usually the first and last days of the charter as well as Sundays and holidays.

clear hawse. Two anchor chains out in a moor and no chain entanglement.

clear hawse pendant. A length of chain or wire used in mooring or when clearing a foul anchor.

clearing iron. A caulking tool, same as ripping iron.

clear-view screen. A circular revolving glass disc set into the window of a ship's bridge that provides a clear view through rain, snow and spray.

cleat. *n* **1.** Any piece of wood or metal aboard ship designed to hold rope, wire, or to provide fairleads; usually anvil-shaped and fastened to bulwarks, decks, or spars. For examples of the older types, *see* comb cleat, batten cleat, mooring cleat, snatch cleat, thumb cleat, reefing cleat. Modern sailing yachts use a variety of mechanical cleats, some with hinged wedges or teeth that are designed to hold a line and release it quickly if necessary; these include jam cleat, cam cleat, and clam cleat. **2.** A transverse piece of wood or metal used to prevent slipping on a sloping brow or plank. **3.** Metal clips on a ship's frame that hold cargo battens. *vb* To cleat a line is to make it fast on a cleat.

clevis. Same as shackle but not as commonly used at sea.

clevis pin. A short rod or bolt fitted with a cotter pin or ring that is used to close a shackle or clevis.

clew. *n* The after lower corner of a fore-and-aft sail and one of the two lower corners of a squaresail or spinnaker. There are clew cringles, jiggers, ropes, lines, patches, rings, and traveling rings, all associated with the clews of sails and their handling. *vb* To clew up is to haul a squaresail up to its yard; to clew down means to haul on the clew lines and thus force a sail down.

clew cringle. A loop or eye formed in the boltrope at the clew of a sail.

clew jigger. A light tackle used in clewing up.

clinch. A method of securing a heavy rope to a ring by seizing the rope after taking several turns around the ring. Also to burr or bend over the end of a bolt or a nail after driving it in.

clinch knot. An effective way to attach a fishhook to a monofilament leader. Several inches of mono are passed through the eye of the hook and then 5 or 6 turns are made around the standing part with the free end. This end is then passed back through the open space between the eye of the hook and the start of the first turn.

clinker built. A method of boat construction in which the lower edge of each plank overlaps the upper edge of the plank below it. Planks were traditionally fastened with copper boat nails. Also known as lapstrake construction. Clinker plating refers to the same construction using steel plates. Older British spelling was clencher or clincher. *See* carvel.

clinometer. An instrument for measuring the amount of roll of a ship. Same as inclinometer, it may use a pendulum or a bubble.

clip. A short piece of angle iron used in shipbuilding to connect various structural parts. Also called a lug or lugpiece. *See* bulldog clip, slide, hank.

clip hook. Same as sister hook.

clipper. American built, the fastest sailing ship of the 19th century. Initially schooner-rigged as in the Baltimore clipper, and later between 1840 and 1870, square-rigged. Their importance declined rapidly with the advent of the steam engine and the opening of the Suez Canal.

clipper bow. A distinctive concave curve of the bow and bowsprit.

clog. An attachment to the sole of an otter board that reduces wear on a rocky bottom. Also called a shoe.

close. Approach near to; in strict Naval usage, about 600 yards for a ship and 400 yards for a boat when either is directed to close something or to go close aboard. A vessel closes the range when the range markers (day beacons) marking the channel seem to draw together as the ship nears the center of the channel; the range opens when the vessel strays from the channel.

close hauled. Sailing on the wind, as near to the wind as practicable. *See* reach.

close-out. A surfer's description for large waves breaking solidly all the way across a beach with no wave faces forming across which a person could slide; thus the surf is unrideable.

close-reefed. Describes a sail or a sailing ship with all reefs taken in.

close up. A signal flag or group of flags hoisted all the way up, instead of being at the dip. Same as two-blocked which is no longer the correct term.

cloth. According to sailmaker's usage, a length of canvas or material sewn up with others to make a sail. *See* miter.

cloth, boat. A blue woolen seat cover used on a Naval barge or gig.

clothes stops. Small bits of string used to fasten washed clothing to a drying line or to tie up rolled clothing to be stowed in a seabag.

cloth, hammock. Cloth once used to cover stowed hammocks.

clothing. Insulating material for pipes such as steam lines or water pipes, covered by lagging. Also the old word for the various pieces of rigging which held a bowsprit in position.

cloud. Visible moisture and/or ice in the sky. High clouds are cirrus, feathery and indicating fair weather; cirro-cumulus, mackerel sky indicating possible foul weather; cirro-stratus, thin, hazy and halo producing. Intermediate clouds are altostratus, dark, usually containing rain or snow and altocumulus, layers or rolls or castles. Low clouds are cumulus, puffs of wool that indicate fair weather, cumulus-stratus, low, dark—if low enough are fog, and cumulonimbus, thunderheads and full of storm, some of which can also be much higher. Nimbus and nimbo-stratus are low dark rain clouds which when broken up in stormy weather become fracto-nimbus or scud.

cloud tickler. A light sail carried aloft in a square-rigger. *See* kites.

clove hitch. A knot consisting of two half hitches in opposite directions put around a rope or spar.

clove hook. Same as sister hook.

club. *vb* 1. An emergency method of coming about or tacking a square-rigger by dropping an anchor from the lee bow after leading its cable aft to be made fast to the lee quarter. When the bow is thus forced through the wind and the sails are filled on the new tack, the anchor cable is cut. 2. To club haul a ship at anchor is to use a line led from a quarter to her anchor chain and haul on this line to reach the desired headings. Any spar that extends along the foot of a fore-and-aft sail, i.e. a club-footed jib.

club burgee. Burgee that carries a yacht club insignia.

club foot. A form of bow construction in which most of the displacement is at the forefoot, near the keel; a bulbous bow. Also the broadened after end of the stem near the plate keel.

club-footed jib. Jib with a boom along its foot that can be rigged to a traveler thus not requiring handling when the boat is tacked.

clubbing. Drifting downstream with anchor down and dragging at short stay. Rarely used today.

clumbungay. A British word for an old yacht that is well preserved and maintained.

clump. 1. A fitting welded near the bottom of a ship's stem for securing paravane gear. 2. The heavy mass or weight that anchors a mooring buoy.

clump block. A strong, thick, single block of various sizes with a wide sheave and swallow.

clupeids. Herring and related small fish.

cluster. *See* Barge Cluster Pushtowing System.

clutter. Radar reflections of waves, snow, or rain, that interfere with a clear visual radar presentation. Also called sea return.

coach roof. *See* cabin top.

coach whipping. Nautical decorative fancy work done with cord on for example stanchions and bellropes and on the end of manropes. Similar to coxscombing in purpose but not in design.

coak. A small piece of hardwood used as additional security in scarfing two pieces of wood together.

coalfish. Same as cobia.

coaling bags. Large canvas bags, once used in coaling ship, now used to transfer loose freight and mail between ships who go alongside underway.

coaming. The raised borders around hatches and doors aboard ship and around open cockpits of boats to prevent easy entry of water.

coast. The land that borders the sea.

Coast and Geodetic Survey. Now the National Ocean Survey, part of the National Oceanic and Atmospheric Administration of the U.S. Department of Commerce.

coaster. A ship or a person engaged in maritime business along a coast.

Coast Guard. In general terms, a governmental, para-military organization charged with enforcing safety of sea laws, customs regulations and other laws that apply to mariners. It provides assistance to mariners in distress. The U.S. Coast Guard is under the Treasury Department except in time of war when it comes under the jurisdiction of the Navy.

coasting lead. A heavier hand lead, 14-28 pounds, than normally used around a harbor. It was used in water of 20-60 fathoms but has been replaced by the echo sounder.

Coast Pilot. A publication issued by the National Ocean Survey giving detailed information concerning the nature of the U.S. coast and inland waters, particularly the hazards, aids to navigation, and other local data useful to ships and yachts. *See* Sailing Directions.

coat. Traditionally a piece of tarred, painted canvas, or leather fitted around a mast or rudder casing, to prevent the entry of water below decks; now replaced by modern sealing devices and techniques.

cobia. A worldwide, migratory, schooling gamefish, *Rachycentron anadus*, that grows up to 100 pounds; in Australia called a black kingfish, in the Caribbean, a lemonfish or ling, and in Chesapeake Bay, a crab-eater, coalfish, or sergeant fish.

coble. A small clinker built open fishing boat, once common on the East coast of England.

cock. A valve, faucet, or tap used in controlling the flow of liquid or steam; may be a petcock, draincock, oilcock, indicator cock or steam cock. *See* seacock.

cockbill. 1. To top the yards of a square-rigger unevenly, one end high, as a sign of mourning. 2. Cockbilled means uneven, cockeyed, drunk. 3. To cockbill an old-fashioned anchor was to suspend it from the cathead before dropping.

cockboat. Old name for a ship's boat.

cocked hat. British slang for the triangle often resulting from plotting 3 lines of position or bearings that do not meet in the ideal point. U.S. sailors usually call it a triangle.

cockpit. The well or sunken space in the after part of a boat for the crew.

cockscomb. A notched cleat on the yardarm of a square-rigger to facilitate hauling out the reef earings.

cod, codfish. Any one of several bottom-dwelling fish of the family Gadidae. For centuries, an important North Atlantic commercial fish; over-fishing has deprived many of a basic staple, particularly the Portugese.

code. In the maritime sense an international system of ship-to-ship and ship-to-shore communications by flag, flashing light, or radio. Involving a code book and various code flags.

codend. The round, aftermost end section of a trawl where the fish are collected; often called cod for short or bunt.

codline. The line used to close off the codend.

codling. A young cod.

coelacanth. A rare, ancient fish rediscovered in 1938. It is an evolutionary link between fish and amphibians and was discovered off South Africa by Miss Courtenay-Latimer.

coelenterate. An organism that exists in the ocean either fixed in place as a coral polyp or free swimming as a medusa or jellyfish. All have stinging cells and may show bioluminescence.

coffee grinder. Yachtsmen's slang for the expensive hand-cranked deck winches used topside in racing sailboats to haul taut sheets for example.

cofferdam. The empty space between compartments aboard ship. Also the watertight wall built around a damaged area of the hull; same as caisson.

coffin plate. A shell plate used on the propeller bossing of a twinscrew vessel.

cog. A north European merchant ship of the 13-15th centuries, clinker built, very broad in the beam and bluff in the bows.

COGSA. Carriage of Goods by Sea Act; a U.S. law that specifies certain precedence for handling ocean shipping by U.S. flag vessels.

coil. *n* Rope made up in a series of adjacent rings, usually 200 fathoms long. *vb* To coil a line is to lay it down in a circular pattern on deck, with each loop on top of the other; if it is to be run out, it should be faked down in long bights or loops so that it does not kink. British word for a coil is a cheese and line that is coiled or flemished down is said to be cheesed down. *See* flemish, fake.

coir. A weak, elastic, and buoyant fiber from coconut husks. Now little used for rope making but still used as oakum for native boats in the South Pacific.

co-latitude. The complement of the latitude of a celestial body; the difference between the latitude and 90 degrees.

cold. A ship is referred to as cold if she has no crew aboard and fires are not lit. The men who periodically inspect the interior of a cold ship, especially the engineering spaces, are the cold iron watch.

collar. The eye or loop at the end of a stay or shroud that goes over the masthead and holds the mast; seen today mostly in sailboats.

collier. Any ship used to carry coal.

collier's patch. The result of the archaic practice of tarring a worn place in a sail.

collision bulkhead. Bulkhead that is watertight and athwartships to limit flooding in the event of a collision.

collision mat. Mat made of canvas thrummed with rope yarns close together, used over the side to slow the entrance of water if the ship is holed. Yachting term is fothering blanket.

colors. The national flag or ensign. Also the ceremony aboard a warship not underway, of raising the flag and the Union Jack at 0800 and lowering at sunset. At 0800, the national anthem is played. *See* ensign.

Colregs, 72. The International Regulations for Preventing Collisions at Sea, 1972.

colt. In old sailing ship days, a short knotted rope used by petty officers to reinforce their orders to the men. Also called a starter because it was used to encourage or start men going aloft.

combatant ship. *See* warship.

comb cleat. A piece of hard wood with holes bored through to serve as fairleads for various parts of the running rigging in old sailing ships.

comber. Short for beachcomber, a long curling wave that breaks on a beach. Also a deep water wave whose crest is pushed over by the wind, much larger than a whitecap. A long-period spilling breaker, lines of which form surf. *See* beachcomber.

combination buoy. Buoy fitted with both light and sound signals.

combination lantern. Lantern having both red and green sections; used as sidelights in a small boat.

combination rope. Fiber rope that incorporates some wire strands.

come about. To tack a sailboat; to bring the wind on the other side of the sails. Also come around or come round is sometimes used in the same sense.

come along. A fitting flush with the deck that can be used as a cleat in securing for example cargo, airplanes, or vehicles. Also a device used in bringing steel plates together accurately for welding.

come home. Said of an anchor when it drags or when it is heaved in. Anything that approaches its normal stowed position comes home.

come up behind. Command to slack or ease a line being hauled so it can be belayed; usually shortened to up behind.

Commander. 1. A senior naval officer below the rank of Captain. 2. In the days of sail, a wooden mallet as well as a large spike or fid used in wire splicing.

Commanding Officer. The official and specific title for the master or captain of a ship in the Navy, Coast Guard, or other maritime government service. He may be of any grade below flag officer but is addressed as captain when in command. *See* Master, captain.

commission. To place a ship or yacht in active service. In the Navy when a commanding officer does so, he breaks his commission pennant.

commission pennant. A narrow red, white and blue pennant with seven stars, flown at the mainmast of a naval ship in commission under the command of a commissioned officer. Also called a long, narrow or whip pennant. The British commissioning pennant is white with a red cross.

committee boat. Boat used by the race committee in officiating at a yacht race.

Commodore. A senior captain (master) in a passenger ship company; also the president of a yacht club. In the U.S. Navy, the grade between Captain and/Rear Admiral, not used in peacetime except as a courtesy title for the commander of a unit of small ships such as destroyers. *See* broad command pennant.

common carrier. *See* carrier.

companion. Usually a structure such as a booby hatch or long dog house that is built over a companionway (ladder). Sometimes refers to the ladder itself.

companion hatchway. An opening in the deck.

companionway. Usually a ladder or staircase aboard ship. Sometimes companion for short and thus the confusion with the structure built over the companionway as protection against the weather.

company. 1. The crew of a ship, all hands; often called the ship's company. **2.** Ships steaming or sailing together are in company. **3.** The once powerful East India Company was referred to as the Company.

compass. An instrument that indicates direction on the earth's surface. Originally it was magnetic in which a floating magnet pointed towards the earth's magnetic pole. Ships now use a gyroscopic compass in which a rapidly spinning wheel seeks to align itself with the earth's axis and thus points to true north. A standard compass is the one to which all others, such as the steering compass, are referred. Also a simple drafting and plotting tool used to describe circles.

compass card. The circular card on which directions are marked attached to the magnetic needles of a magnetic compass.

compass error. The algebraic sum of deviation and variation; essentially the difference between the magnetic course or bearing and the true course or bearing.

compass range. A pair of markers, beacons or other seamarks that, when placed in line indicate a true compass direction against which the ship's compass can be compared. British word is transit.

compass rose. Outer and inner graduated concentric circles on a nautical chart used for laying out courses and bearings. One circle, the outer one, represents the true heading; the other the magnetic heading. The difference is the variation in that vicinity.

composite sailing. A combination of great circle courses and a latitude line which meets these circles tangentially.

comprador. A term used in the Far East for a ship chandler.

compressor. A device for holding chain cable from running out by jamming it against the chain pipe; now rarely seen. Also the brake band on an anchor windlass for checking and temporarily holding the anchor chain.

computer, navigation. *See* navigation computer.

conch. A large gastropod mollusk or marine snail found mostly in tropical waters; has a brightly colored shell and edible flesh. Also known as a whelk, periwinkle, or winkle depending on local custom although the latter ones generally refer to smaller animals found further north. Sometimes pronounced conk.

concluding line. A small rope down the middle of a side ladder that is made fast to each step.

condenser. A device for turning steam (water vapor) into water; a necessary part of any steam system of propulsion in order to conserve boiler water.

cone. A fabric or metal shape, often yellow, once used as a visual speed signal by naval ships in formation and as gale warnings when hoisted ashore. Cones, either singly or in pairs end to end are used as dayshapes under the Rules of the Road.

cone shell. A tropical marine snail of the family Conidae that can inject venom into its prey. People have died as a result of a skin puncture by a cone shell.

conference, shipping. An organization of shipping companies who establish uniform rates as they are theorectically competing in the same ocean area. Nonconference ships who attempt rate cutting are countered by conference "fighting ships" who offer lower rates. The resultant losses are borne by the conference.

conger eel. A large, up to 10 foot, voracious salt water eel of the family Congridae, related to the moray eel; found off Europe and North America.

conjunction. The position of 2 celestial bodies when they are in the same longitude or right ascension.

conn. The control of a ship underway; a person is said to have the conn when he is responsible for the ship and her movements. He is also said to be conning the ship. British spelling is con but the word is not widely used abroad.

connecting shackle. Shackle used in joining lengths or shots of anchor chain. Also called a joiner shackle or Kenter shackle.

conshelf. Short for the continental shelf.

consignor. Same as the shipper of cargo or freight.

Consol. A medium range navigation system developed in Europe for ships and aircraft. Accuracy is moderate and no special radio is needed. The U.S. version was Consolan and is now obsolete.

consort. A vessel in company with another is her consort. They are said to be in company.

Consul. An officer of the U.S. Foreign Service who in a foreign port represents U.S. ships and people and who performs the necessary legal, commercial, and humanitarian services. A Consul General serves in a large seaport while in some small ones part-time Consular Agents represent U.S. interests.

consular invoice. Invoice signed by the Consulate of the exporting country located in the importing country showing that the goods have met regulations. This is required before certain goods can pass customs.

container. A standard rectangular metal box in which cargo and freight are moved today, both at sea and over land; usually built to International Standards Organization (CISO) specifications with a capacity of up to 30 tons, a cross section of 8 by 8 feet and a length of 10, 20, 30, 35, or 40 feet. Short term is box.

containership. Ship converted or designed specially to carry containers below decks and topside. Semi-containerships carry boxes topside and any other cargo below decks. British word is vanship.

continental shelf. The ocean zone extending from the line of permanent immersion on the coast to depths of usually 120 meters. At this point, the descent is steep towards greater depth. The shelf can be over 100 miles wide although the average is about 30 miles.

continental slope. The declivity from the edge of the continental shelf, usually at 120 meters in depth towards the bottom.

continuous voyage. Under International Law, a doctrine in which the cargo consigned to a neutral port may be condemned as a prize if it can be shown that its ultimate destination was a belligerent port.

contline. The space between the strands of a rope filled with worming when the rope was served. A Victorian version of the old word cunting.

contra-guide rudder. Rudder having an upper and a lower section somewhat offset to improve the thrust and the efficiency of the propeller.

contra preferentum. The principle that holds that any ambiguity in a marine insurance policy must be construed against the party who drafted it.

contra-propeller. The arrangement of vertical or horizontal pieces of steel plates attached to the rudder post or struts of a ship in order to divert the propeller stream into a more efficient shape and improve propeller thrust.

contra-rotating propellers. Two propellers that revolve on the same composite shaft in opposite directions to balance torque, such as in torpedoes.

controlled port. Port in which all activities from entry to departure are directed by military authority.

controller. Same as chain stopper, *see* stopper. Also called cable or bow stopper.

control ship. Ship that directs the landing craft during an amphibious assault. It is normally stationed on the line of departure of the assault boats.

convoy. *n* Merchant ships steaming together for mutual protection in time of war, directed and protected by a Naval escort. *vb* To convoy is to escort and protect.

convoy commodore. The officer from the U.S. Navy or Merchant Marine that is appointed to command the convoy. He is usually a subordinate to the escort commander.

cooperage. A charge made by the cargo carrier to the consignee for repair of damaged or defective packaging. Originally it involved the frequent replacement of hoops on casks done by a cooper.

Coordinated Universal Time (UTC). *See* universal time.

copepod. Very small, primitive crustaceans, some zooplankton, some parasites, some living on the bottom. An important link in the food chain of the sea.

copper bottom. The copper sheathing of wooden ships used as a protection against worms or torpedoes; no longer needed with the perfection of toxic bottom paint.

copper fastened. A wooden ship whose hull was fastened together with copper or bronze nails or bolts. This avoided galvanic action with copper sheathing and iron nails.

copra. The albumin of the coconut which, when dried, produces coconut oil.

copy. To maintain a continuous radio watch, including a record of what is heard.

coracle. A small primitive, paddled river boat of Ireland and Wales that was made of lath and covered with fabric. *See* currach.

coral. A colony of sea animals known as polyps; jelly-like bodies enclosed in calcium carbonate. One type forms the red jewelry coral of the Mediterranean, another forms tropic reefs. Fire coral is a smooth, dull yellow, plant-like organism resembling moose horns whose stinging cells inflict painful welts and rash upon contact. Coral is also called madrepores. *See* reef, geographic. Also the unfertilized eggs of lobsters.

coral head. A massive mushroom or pillar of coral growth.

corange lines. Lines on a chart passing through all points having the same tidal range.

cord. Small twisted rope used, for example, for fishing or netting.

cordage. The collective term for rope, line, or cord.

cordonazo. Mexican word for hurricane.

cordwood. Small pieces of wood used as dunnage aboard ship.

core rock. The fill in a groin, composed of relatively small pieces of rock.

Corinthian. A yachting word for an amateur sailor as distinct from a paid crew member or one who makes his living by yachting.

Coriolis Force. The effect of the earth's rotation on all moving bodies particularly on air and water masses. It is the force that deflects the trade winds from a south or north direction.

cork light. Describes a ship having no cargo aboard.

corkline. The buoyant top line of a seine, gill, or trammel net supported by cork, plastic wood, or glass floats. Also called a floatline. In a trawl, the topmost line is a headline.

cork paint. An insulating paint containing cork particles used to combat condensation or sweating on steel bulkheads aboard ship.

cormorant. A large, fish-eating, diving bird; some, such as the ones in the Galapagos, are not capable of flight. They are a major source of guano.

corposant. Ball or streak of light or flame sometimes seen on the rigging of a ship at sea, caused by atmospheric electrical and magnetic forces. Also called St. Elmo's Fire or Light.

corsair. A Mediterranean privateer who was usually licensed by the government of Turkey and who operated from North Africa and preyed on European (Christian) shipping as late as 1825. Also the man who manned the privateer.

corvette. Ocean going warship smaller than a destroyer or frigate.

coryphaena. *See* dolphin fish.

Coston light. An obsolete chemical shipboard signaling device.

cothon. Historically an inner walled and defensible harbor or port inside an anchorage; a favorite defense of the Phoenicians, such as at Carthage.

cotidal. Pertaining to the same high water level at various places. Indicated by cotidal lines, the basis for a cotidal chart is to connect all points having high water at the same time.

cotton hook. A sharp, pointed hook with a short handle used by longshoremen in handling such items as boxes or bales of cotton. Also called a box or cargo hook.

counter. The aftermost part of the stern of a ship that overhangs the rudder and is above the waterline. Also called the fantail except that by naval usage, the fantail is usually the space on deck aft.

counter current. Current running in the opposite direction, either below or adjacent to the principal current.

country. Area of a ship's interior designated for specific people as, for example, officer's country, Admiral's country, or passenger's country.

coupling. A connecting device used on the end of a fire hose or fuel hose aboard ship.

course. The direction in which a ship is steered, measured in modern ships from north (000 degrees) clockwise in a circle of 360 degrees. Also the lowest sail on each mast of a square-rigger.

course made good (CMG). The single resultant direction from one point to another of a ship underway that steers a number of different courses.

course over the ground (COG). The actual path of a ship with respect to the earth.

cove. A small indentation in a coastline, smaller than a bay, that might afford shelter to a boat.

cover. A standard tactic in sail racing, when leading, to tack at the same time as your opponent does behind you, thereby staying between him, the mark, and the wind; thus you cover him.

cover pot. A primitive device of wood, wicker, reed, or metal dropped by hand to capture small fish in shallow water.

cove stripe. A decorative stripe painted on a yacht running fore and aft on the hull topside just below the rail.

cowfish. A small colorful tropical reef fish that has spines or horns growing from the top of his head like cow's horns.

cow hitch. Same as lark's head. Also a term for any unusual or ineffective knot.

cowl. *See* ventilators, ship's.

cowry. A tropical marine mollusk with a smooth, colorful, gloosy shell, highly prized by collectors and at times used as money in the South Pacific. Also spelled cowrie.

cow's tail. Nautical term for the unsightly, frayed end of a rope.

coxcomb. In old sailing ships, a piece of wood bolted to the yardarm to keep turns of the reef earing from slipping.

coxcombing. Decorative lashing or winding usually done with white cord around boathooks or tillers; similar to coachwhipping in its purpose but not its design.

coxswain. A petty officer or leading seaman in charge of a boat. Pronounced coxun.

c/p. Charter Party.

CPA. In piloting, the closest point of approach to, for example, a hazard, buoy or point of land.

CQR anchor. An anchor shaped like a plow. Also called a ploughshare anchor by the British and a plow anchor or a spade anchor in the U.S.

crab. A marine crustacean of the order Decopoda (10 legs) and related to hermit or king crabs. Also an old-fashioned and obsolete capstan having no drumhead.

crabbing. Moving sideways in a sailboat; making leeway.

crab-eater. *See* cobia.

cradle. The framework upon which a ship rests in a marine railway or in launching ways. Also the support for a boat or a particular piece of cargo carried on deck. *See* skids, launching cradle.

craft. A collective term for small boats, lighters and barges.

cran. A measure of liquid volume used by Scottish fishermen and equal to 45 gallons.

crank. A ship with low stability, easily inclined and with a long slow roll is said to be crank. Opposite is stiff which describes a ship having a short, quick, uncomfortable roll. An excessively crank ship may capsize. Often termed tender or cranky as well as crank.

cranse. An iron hoop or band with eyes, fitted to a spar to which, for example, shrouds stays or blocks are fastened. The iron band securing the jibboom to the bowsprit was known as a cranse iron. Also spelled crance.

cravat. A shield plate attached to the top of the inner smokestack to keep rain and spray out of the space between the stack and the casing. Also called cap.

crawdad. *See* crayfish.

crawfish. *See* crayfish.

crayfish. A freshwater crustacean locally called a crawfish or crawdad, resembling a lobster but much smaller. A popular but inaccurate name for the ocean spiny lobster. *See* spiny lobster.

creek. A small stream sometimes tidal. By British usage, it is a narrow sheltered inlet, deeper than a cove.

creeper. British word for grapnel.

crest. A narrow rise of irregular profile forming an elevation above the sea bottom. Also the top of a wave, above the trough.

crevalle. *See* pompano.

crew. The men who man a ship and form its complement. Also the sport of competitive rowing using special lightweight shells.

crewboat. Any boat used to transport men and light freight between an oil rig or platform at sea and the shore.

crib. A structure filled with stones or rubble forming part of a temporary breakwater, harbor blockage, or bridge support. Also a cradle.

cribbing. *See* blocking.

cribbing ram. A battering ram used to knock away the wooden supports called blocking or cribbing under a ship about to be launched.

crimp. *n* 1. Originally a man who lured others aboard ship and was paid for this criminal act of shanghaiing. 2. One who defrauds sailors ashore. *vb* In shipbuilding, to crimp a plate or bar is to shape it for better fitting. This is also called joggling.

cringle. Formerly limited to a rope eye or a metal ring in the edge of a sail but now a word used almost interchangeably with grommet.

crinoid. A class of echinoderms (bottom living marine animals) normally attached by a long stalk to the bottom of the sea; known as sea lily, feather star, or sea feather.

crinoline. In cable-laying ships, a framework fitted in each cable tank to prevent kinking when paying out cable.

Cromwell Current. An easterly flowing, subsurface current moving along the Equator in the Pacific. In other oceans, its counterparts exist and are called Equatorial undercurrents.

crook. Any naturally grown curved wooden piece once used in shipbuilding and now used by hobbyists in making wooden boats.

cropping. In rope making, to comb out short fibers. In ship repair, to cut away damaged parts before repairing.

cross. Across, athwartships, from side to side, unfavorable, as in cross bearings, cross planking, cross seas, or cross signals.

cross cut. Describes a headsail when all of the panels of canvas are roughly horizontal.

cross hawse. When, in a ship moored with two anchors, the cables lie across each other just outside the hawsepipes.

crossing the line. A traditional ceremony aboard ship involving the initiation of all who have not crossed the Equator. Pollywogs are made shellbacks after suffering various indignities under the supervision of King Neptune.

crossjack. The squaresail extending below the lowest yard on the mizzenmast of a square-rigger. Pronounced: krojek.

crosspointing. Line or strips of leather or canvas braided around a stanchion, boathook handle, or whatever for decoration. Originally it was a method of finishing off the end of a rope by cutting away the inner yarns and braiding the outer yarns.

cross signal. An illegal practice under the Rules of the Road of responding to a one blast whistle signal with two blasts, or vice versa.

cross spall. *See* spall.

crosstree. An athwartship wood or steel spreader on the mast over which the shrouds are led in a sailboat. Crosstrees are one continuous piece, whereas spreaders may be a fitting on one side only of the mast. *See* spreader.

crow. A handspike or crowbar. Slang for the device, an eagle, worn on the uniform sleeve to distinguish a petty officer in the Navy.

crowfoot. An end of an iron beam bent to form a knee. The small lines rove through a euphroe or led to a single rope to support an awning.

crowfoot bar. A bottom-fishing device made up of barbless hooks attached to an iron bar that is dragged over the bottom.

crown. Part of an old-fashioned stock anchor where the arms and the shank join. In stockless anchors, the part between the arms where they pivot on the shank.

crowning. *See* becue.

crown-of-thorns. A starfish. *See* acanthaster.

crow's eyes. Seeds of the plant, *Nux vomica,* used to stupify fish.

crow's nest. A lookout station aloft in a ship. Originally it was a cask secured to the foremast. Sometimes a lower station, as far up towards the masthead as practicable, was assigned and called a bird's nest although the two terms were often used interchangeably.

CRP. Controllable Reversible Propeller. *See* pitch.

cruise. A journey or trip by sea that is more than a voyage and involves a number of visits or stops over a length of time. To yachtsmen, a cruise means more than one day underway in a non-racing boat.

cruiser. A warship, traditionally larger than a destroyer and smaller than a battleship, battle cruiser, or aircraft carrier. Any pleasure boat capable of feeding and sleeping its crew is called a cruiser or cabin cruiser.

cruiser stern. Stern that is broad and nearly flat below the water line becoming conical, rounded and slanting forward as it emerges from the waterline to meet the deck.

crushing strips. Soft wood under the cradle of a ship being launched, designed to splinter and thus distribute the load during launch.

crustacean. Pertains to the large class of commercially important aquatic animals with a hard exoskeleton, such as lobsters, crabs, shrimps, and barnacles. All breathe by means of gills or similar organs.

crutch. Any forked device used to support a spar, boom, or steering oar.

Crux. The constellation commonly known as the Southern Cross.

cryology. The study of ice and snow, particularly sea ice.

CSD. Closed Shelter Deck ship, in contrast to one with an open shelter deck.

C-type ships. The various Maritime Commission (now the Maritime Administration) designed cargo ships classified as C-1, C-2, C-3, and so on. These were built just before and during World War II; not included in this classification are the emergency designs such as Liberty and Victory ships.

cuckold's knot. A hitch by which a rope is secured to a spar. The two parts of the rope cross each other and are seized together.

cuddy. A small room or cabin below decks; a locker forward in a small open boat, too small to be a cabin but providing some shelter.

cucumber, sea. An echinoderm that lies on the bottom of the sea. Its soft cylindrical body sometimes ejects its intestines. It is considered to be an aphrodisiac by the Chinese who relish them as food.

cufa. As described by Herodotus, a wooden frame, skin-covered boat that is roughly circular in shape and similar to the ancient Irish coracle or currach.

culmination. The greatest and least altitude of a celestial body as it crosses the meridian; makes a transit.

cumshaw. A present, a gift or a tip. In the U.S. Navy, something obtained for the ship without official payment. A cumshaw artist is a person gifted in obtaining extra work done in return for favors or friendship; unofficial but usually honest.

cumulonimbus. A massive towering cloud with vertical development; its summits rise in towers or mountaneous shapes. Also called a thundercloud or thunderhead. *See* cloud.

cumulus. A cloud with the appearance of a mass of cottom wool billowing up into the sky. It is most often a low cloud reaching up to 7 000 feet and usually a feature of good weather. *See* cloud.

Cunningham hole or eye. An opening in a sail for a loop of line by which the sail can be flattened or eased. The line is often called a cunningham. There may be a line to flatten the foot and another one for the luff called a luff puller.

cunt splice. The original version of cut splice.

curl. Excessive curvative in the luff or leech of a spinnaker or in the leech of a mainsail or jib, or in the foot of a jib.

currach or curragh. A primitive wooden frame and canvas boat found on the coast of Ireland; usually rowed by four men. *See* coracle, basket boat.

current. A moving horizontal stream of water as in nearshore currents, tidal currents, and ocean currents. A current's velocity is its drift and the direction towards which the current flows is its set. *See* nearshore current system, tidal current, ocean current.

Current Charts. The short and usual name for Tidal Current Charts issued by the National Ocean Survey on which tidal current data are graphically shown for a number of important waterways (such as San Francisco Harbor). Tidal Current Chart Diagrams, one for each month, are also published by the NOS and are to be used with the Current Charts.

Current Tables. Short and common name for the Tidal Current Tables published by the National Ocean Survey that give daily predictions of the times and velocities of tidal currents.

curtain plate. A fore-and-aft vertical piece of steel plate connecting the outboard ends of deck beams in steel ship construction.

cusk. An edible North Atlantic food fish of the family Brosme.

cusp. Sand or mud deposited along the shore by wave action in the form of points or bars pointing seaward.

custom of the port. Usage which, by common consent and long practice, has the force of law at the place or concerning the subject to which it relates; specifically it is the port speed, rate of unloading or loading at a particular port.

customs. The government officials charged with collecting import and export taxes, tolls, and so on, known as duties. Thus there are, for example, customs bills of entry, customs bonds, brokers, and agents.

cut. *n* Appearance, style as in "cut of her jib." *See* mitre cut, vertical cut. *vb* **1.** Cut out in old Naval usage was to capture and take away a ship in an enemy harbor or anchorage. **2.** Cut and run meant literally to cut one's anchor hawser and perhaps the rope-yarn with which the sails were lightly furled and sail away quickly.

cutlass or cutlas. A short sword once used by boarders, now ceremonial.

cut splice. Two rope ends spliced together so as to form a slit or an eye in a rope. Originally and at sea it was called a cunt splice.

cutter. In modern U.S. usage, a Coast Guard patrol ship, a square stern pulling boat, or a single masted sailboat whose mast is set farther aft than a sloop. It is a sailboat (sloop) with more than one headsail.

cutting. Part of an open ship's railing that is portable and can be removed to produce a gangway or to admit a brow or the top of an accommodation ladder.

cuttle-bone. The internal shell of a cuttlefish used as its organ of buoyancy and valued by caged bird owners as a source of calcium for their birds.

cuttlefish. An oval, edible, invertebrate sea animal, a mollusk and a decapod equipped with suction disks. Closely related to the squid, it lives in shallow coastal waters, moves by jet propulsion, and feeds mostly on shrimp. It ejects a dark ink in self defense and can grow to five ft.

cuttyhunk. A traditionally tough, braided linen fishing line, now largely replaced by synthetic line that resists rot.

cutwater. Originally a strengthening and protective timber bolted to the outside of the stem; now describes the leading edge of the stem near the waterline or the stem itself.

cyclone. A closed atmospheric circulation, rotating counterclockwise in the northern hemisphere (and clockwise in the southern); also called a low. If of tropical origin with a warm center and strong winds to 64 knots, it becomes a tropical storm. If winds are higher, it becomes a hurricane or, in the Indian Ocean, a cyclone or in the western Pacific, a typhoon or Baguio. *See* anti-cyclone.

D

D. International signal code alphabet flag. When hoisted singly means: "keep clear of me, I am maneuvering with difficulty." Spoken: "delta."

Dacron. A trade name for a modern synthetic fiber used for sails and ropes; Terylene in the United Kingdom, Tergal in France, Tetoron in Japan, and Lavsan in Russia.

Dagger. Any structural member placed diagonally as the fore-and-aft bracing in a launching-poppet.

dagger board. A sliding keel moving vertically in a trunk but not hinged as a centerboard, yet having the same purpose.

Daily Memorandum. Provides the synopsis of the latest information on navigational aids as well as dangers to mariners and advance information on the more important items that will be published in Notices to Mariners; issued by the Defense Mapping Agency Hydrographic Center in two editions, Atlantic and Pacific.

damper. A device inserted in a ship's stack, flue, or chimney to regulate air flow.

damselfish. *See* sergeant major.

dan buoy. A small floating device used to temporarily mark obstructions or dangers to navigation, such as mine fields or fishing gear. Also marks concentrations of fish.

dandy. 1. An archaic British rig similar to a yawl. Sometimes also describes a mizzensail or jigger. 2. A herring fishing line used off the coast of Scotland.

dandyfunk. In old square-rigger days, a holiday dish made of sea biscuit pounded in a canvas bag and mixed with water and molasses.

Danforth anchor. A popular boat anchor with long pointed flukes close to the shank and a sort of stock or rod passed perpendicular to the flukes and to the shank at their junction. This prevents the flukes from rolling out of the ground and at the same time permits the anchor to be housed in a hawsepipe. Also known as a lightweight or LWT anchor.

danger angle, bearing. In coastal piloting, the angle or bearing marking a hazard; one that establishes a limit for safe navigation.

danger buoy. Buoy that marks a shoal, rock, or other hazard to navigation. In U.S. waters, it has red and black stripes; in Europe, it is usually green.

dangerous semicircle. Area in the direction of advance and movement of a hurricane or typhoon subject to winds of greater velocity. The opposite side is the navigable semicircle. Also called the dangerous quadrant.

danger signal. Under Rules of the Road, the five or more short and rapid blasts of a ship's whistle required, when approaching another ship; if there is a failure to understand the other's intention or doubt about the action being taken. Also called a signal of doubt.

dangles. Series of iron rings joined by loops of chain through which the ground rope of a beam or otter trawl is rove in a fishing trawl net.

danleno, dan leno. Part of a trawl net that holds the upper and lower wings of the net and to which the warps are attached.

Danube rudder. *See* salmon tail.

dap. The groove or notch cut in the outside of wood ship frame timbers to receive and hold steel strapping.

dasher block. Block rigged at the end of a spar or gaff for the ensign halyard.

data logger. Device used to scan a ship's power plant instrument panel rapidly and automatically.

date line. Meridian of longitude separating east and west, generally following 180 degrees but by international agreement shifts to include all the islands of the same group. This expression helps easier recall, "When eastward bound, add a day, when westward bound drop a day." Also called the international date line.

datum. A level or plane of reference from which the height of the tide is measured; usually in the U.S. it means low water or lower low water. Now marked in meters on most navigational charts and called chart datum.

Davidson Current. An ocean current flowing northward along the west coast of North America as a counter current to the California Current. It is normally detectable only in November-January when the upwelling has ceased.

davit. A small derrick or crane, often in pairs, used for handling, for example, boats, ladders, or stores. Most common boat davits are gravity, crescent, quadrental, and radial. Mechanical davits, other than the simple radial or gravity types, are known to the British as luffing davits.

davit head. The top part of the davit on which boat falls or span wires are attached.

Davy Jones. Traditional among sailors referring to the spirit of the sea, usually considered evil. Davy Jones locker is on the ocean bottom and is thus overboard.

daybeacon. A large brightly painted sign; may be lighted or numbered. In U.S. waters, usually has a triangular or rectangular shape outlined by reflecting tape; used to mark a channel and when in pairs, to mark the line or range of the center of the channel. It is set on posts driven into the bottom or on small structures ashore. Also called a daymark or leading mark. *See* dayshape.

dayboat. *See* day sailor.

dayman. British word for idler; a crew member who never stands night watches.

daymark. *See* daybeacon, dayshape.

day, nautical. From noon to noon, using mean civil time.

day sailor. A small sailing boat, usually open but may have a cuddy forward; used for short sails or for racing. British word is dayboat which also may apply to a small power boat if not used for racing or overnight cruising.

day signal. Same as day shape.

dayshape. The black ball, cone, or diamond required to be shown by a ship towing, being towed, fishing, or not under command. Also inaccurately called daymark although this applies to a daybeacon or other similar aid to navigation which is unlighted and not afloat. *See* daybeacon.

days work. Twenty-four hours of navigation from noon to noon, including sun lines, morning, noon and afternoon, and morning and evening star sights, if possible.

dead. Absolute, as dead calm, dead low water, and dead ahead (000° relative).

deadeye. A disc of wood pierced with holes for lanyards and attached to the ends of shrouds or stays; used in the days of sail to tighten the shrouds by setting up on the lanyards.

dead freight. The difference between the capacity in tons of a chartered ship and the amount actually loaded.

deadhead. 1. A floating log, most of which is submerged; sometimes called a sleeper. **2.** Any heavy post on a pier or dock used for making lines fast. *See* checking bollard. **3.** A block of wood or a log used as an anchor or mooring buoy. **4.** A yacht sailing with a minimum crew to meet the owner or a charter group is deadheading.

dead horse. U.S. Navy slang for an advance in pay.

dead in the water. Said of a ship that is stopped with no way on.

deadlight. A hinged metal cover for an airport; also called a battleport in the Navy. A ventilating deadlight is one fitted with vanes and metal strips that admit air but no light. Also a heavy, fixed round glass set into a deck, bulkhead, or door; synonymous to bullseye and decklight.

deadman. 1. A log or timber ashore or in ice as a temporary mooring for a ship or boat. 2. The weight used to retrieve the gear in a backweight or deadman rig after the load or draft has been swung over the side. 3. An old word for Irish pennant.

dead reckoning. Short term DR. The ancient and still important technique in navigation using only a ship's speed and course to estimate her position. In modern ships this is done mechanically by the dead reckoning tracer which receives courses and speeds automatically from ship's compass and log.

deadrise. 1. The vertical distance between a ship's keel and the turn of the bilge. Also expressed in terms of the angle that the underbody makes with the horizontal in an athwartships section. 2. The name of a small power boat with a V-bottom, an engine aft, and a cuddy forward used on the eastern coast of the U.S. The deadrise launch of North Carolina waters has a round stern.

dead rope. Rope that does not pass through a block or other fairlead.

dead water. Water drawn along with a moving ship by friction. Also a phenomenon reported by sailing ships and slow moving steamers, especially where a layer of fresh water is above the salt water. At the boundary, the energy of forward motion of the ship may be partially absorbed by the generation of small internal waves, thus causing the ship to be retarded. An increase of speed quickly overcomes this slowing force. Also known as the boundary layer phenomenon. *See* internal waves.

deadweight, tonnage. Essentially the difference between a fully loaded ship and her light displacement. Total deadweight is the carrying capacity of a ship; for cargo deadweight substract fuel, water, stores, and so on. A merchant vessel is described in terms of her deadweight tonnage.

deadwood. In modern ships, the structure between the keel line and the stern post.

deboner. A gamefisherman's tool; a hollow tube with saw teeth at one end; used to remove the backbone of bait fish.

decapod. A sea animal with 10 legs, either a crustacean (crab, shrimp, lobster) or a cephalopod (squid).

Decca. Medium frequency hyperbolic continuous wave radio navigation system; is accurate, has relatively short range and is used in coastal waters of the U.S. and Europe.

deck. The floor of a ship. *See* floor, sole. Decks are numbered and named according to use as boats, bridge, berth, and mess. A weather deck has no cover; a shelter deck is partly covered. *See* shelter deck. Partial decks are sometimes called flats. There are water-tight decks and armored decks. A Naval officer on watch, the Officer of the Deck, may be said to have the deck.

deckhand. A sailor who works topside.

deckhead. The inner bottom surface of a deck as seen from below; the ceiling of a compartment as the word ceiling is used ashore. Also called the overhead. *See* overhead, ceiling.

deckhorse. A bar placed athwartships on deck on which the sheet block of a fore-and-aft sail can travel.

deck iron. A wood caulking tool with a broad straight edge; also called a dumb iron.

decklight. A heavy piece of glass fixed in a deck to provide light below. Also called a bullseye or deadlight.

deck log. A full, daily record of a ship's activities, written by the officer on watch (Officer of the Watch or Deck in the Navy). Usually based on a rough log written by a petty officer who records courses, speeds, and other items as sightings, accidents, and casualties. The rough log is a legal record and should contain no erasures.

deck officer. Officer distinguished from an engineer officer, commissary officer, etc.; one concerned with, for example, operations, navigation, seamanship, and cargo handling. In the Navy, a deck officer is a line officer.

deck pillar. Same as stanchion.

deck pipe. Same as chain pipe.

deck ponds. Flat portable wooden dividers on the deck of a fishing vessel used in sorting fish. Also called checkers; sometimes spelled pounds.

deck stopper. *See* stopper.

deck stringer. Strake or line of deck plating that runs along the outboard edge of a ship's deck, adjacent to the hull plating.

declination. The angular distance of a heavenly body from the celestial equator measured on the hour circle of the body, north or south of the equinoctial. Magnetic declination was an old term for variation.

decompression. A diver's word for the gradual return from the high pressure of deep water to normal pressure at the surface; done either by gradual ascent or by entering a decompression chamber in which the pressure can be gradually reduced. *See* bends.

deep. An indicator, in fathoms, on a leadline. The expression "by the deep 6" means six fathoms which falls between the marks of 5 and 7. Also a very deep part of the ocean, usually over 6 000 meters, was labeled a deep but is now called an abyss.

deeping. A light fishing net used for fishing herring and other fish.

deep scattering layer. A layer of ocean water composed of marine animals such as jellyfish and copepods who rise near the surface at night and sink during the day; causes confusion of sonar operations.

deep-sea lead. A heavy sounding lead for measuring depths of water over 60 fathoms. Also called a dipsey lead; now replaced by echo sounders. Pronounced led. *See* watch-ho-watch and lead.

deep six. To give something the deep six is to throw it overboard or to throw it away. Also used as a verb "deep six it."

Deep Submergence Rescue Vessel. A small naval rescue submarine designed to assist people in a damaged submarine lying on the bottom.

deeptanks. Tanks in some cargo ships used to increase water ballast capacity. They extend from the double bottom tank tops to the 'tweendecks and extend the full width of the ship.

Defense Mapping Agency Hydrographic Center (DMAHC). Current name for the Naval Oceanographic Office which was formerly the Navy Hydrographic Office; produces charts and publications relating to navigation and hydrography. Works with the National Ocean Survey (NOS) which is under the National Oceanic and Atmospheric Administration (NOAA) of the Department of Commerce.

degaussing. Reducing the effect of a ship upon the earth's magnetic field by wrapping it with cables carrying direct electric current. This protects the ship from magnetic mines and torpedoes. *See* deperming, flashing.

delta. The deposited silt known as deltal deposits composed mostly of topsoil and left in a fan-shaped mound at the mouth of a river.

demersal fish. Fish who live and reproduce on the bottom, i.e. cod, turbot, and flounder. Also called groundfish.

demise charter. Same as a bareboat charter. *See* charter party.

demurrage. Money paid by the charterer to the owner of the ship for delay in loading and unloading in accordance with the terms of the charter party. Also a sum charged consignees for late picking up of their cargo.

denticle. A tooth-like scale on the skin of sharks.

departure. Position on a chart from which a ship leaves an anchorage or harbor when setting out on a voyage. Also the distance, expressed in miles, a ship makes good east or west along a parallel.

deperming. Reducing a ship's permanent magnetism by energizing with electric current temporary coils placed vertically around the ship for protection against magnetic weapons. *See* degaussing, flashing.

deploy. In naval terminology, warships to change from a cruising or approach formation to a combatant one for battle or for an amphibious asault. Also to send ships or aircraft units abroad for duty is to deploy them. The duration of their stay abroad is a deployment.

depth. The vertical distance amidships from a ship's keel to her upper or main deck or to the deck to which it is referred. Depth of the ocean is now measured by echo sounders and is to be expressed in meters. *See* draft.

depth charge, bomb. An explosive anti-submarine weapon dropped from a ship or aircraft.

depth finder. Same as echo sounder or depth sounder.

depth recorder. An instrument that shows and records the depth of water as measured by echo sounding.

depth sounder. Same as depth finder or echo sounder.

derelict. Goods, cargo, or a ship abandoned by the owner at sea and large enough to be a menace to navigation.

derrick. A fixed structure on a ship, barge, drilling rig, or platform used to handle material, loading or unloading. Heavy lift derricks aboard ship can handle hundreds of tons.

desertion. The unauthorized absence of a person from his ship or station and without intention to return.

despatch. *See* dispatch.

destroyer. A relatively small (less than 10,000 tons), fast, well-armed multipurpose warship larger than a patrol or escort ship and smaller than a cruiser.

detach. In naval usage, an officer is detached from his duty station but an enlisted person is transferred. A detachment of men or ships is a temporary unit.

detachable link. A link of anchor chain that can be taken apart, opened, and reassembled.

detail. *n* A group organized for a special purpose such as travel, cleaning, or recreation. *vb* In naval usage, to detail people is to assign them to duty.

detent. Mine release gear on a minelayer.

Det Norske Veritas (NV). The Norwegian national ship classification society located in Oslo. *See* classification.

deviation. Magnetic compass error (the angle between the compass needle and the magnetic meridian) caused by the magnetic properties of the ship. It varies with the ship's heading. Together with variation, a terrestrial force, it makes up magnetic compass error. Semi-circular deviation varies as the ship changes course. Also a marine insurance term meaning the departure without lawful reason or excuse of a merchant ship from her scheduled route.

deviation table. A record of magnetic compass deviation kept handy by the navigator where deviation can be combined with variation shown on the chart to obtain compass error and thus a true course when steering by magnetic compass.

devil. Old name for any very difficult seam to reach when caulking wooden planking. Thus the expression "the devil to pay." To pay is to apply pitch to a caulked seam.

devil fish. A large ray or manta. *See* manta.

devil's claw. A very strong steel hook used to hold a link of chain cable in a cable stopper or slip. *See* pelican hook.

dhow. An Arabic and African small trading vessel, originally lateen rigged and now often diesel powered; trades in the Red Sea, Persian Gulf, Indian Ocean and African coast.

dew point. *See* point.

diamond shape. When required to be displayed by the Rules of the Road, a shape consisting of two cones having a common base, thus forming a diamond. *See* shape.

diamond stays. A pair of stays, one on each side of a mast, held out by spreaders, forming a diamond shape. They start together on the mast and finish together higher up on the mast providing lateral rigidity and strength. A long diamond stay is sometimes called a diamond shroud, particularly if there is no conventional shroud.

diaphone. A sound signal device used as a coastal aid to navigation in low visibility or fog, usually powered by compressed air giving a low-pitched strong blast ending in a sharply descending note called a grunt. *See* nautiphone.

diatom. Tiny phytoplankton of various shapes and colors that form a major part of the foundation of the food chain of the sea. Their skeletal remains on the sea bottom form diatomaceous earth or ooze.

die lock chain. Modern anchor chain in which links are made in two sections forged together.

diesel electric. A system of ship propulsion in which a diesel engine drives a generator that provides electricity for an electric motor geared to the propeller(s).

differential block. Block fitted with two or more sheaves of different diameters. *See* chain hoist.

ding. Surfer's word for a hole or break in a surfboard.

dinghy. A small, square stern boat used with oars or with sail for racing, general utility, or as a yacht's tender for getting ashore when anchored.

dinky. An auxilliary diesel generator.

dinoflagellates. Highly developed, very small, mostly unicellular, mobile organisms forming a major part of the phytoplankton or plants that are the basic unit upon which the ocean food chain is based. *See* red tide.

dioptric light. Light in which the major beam of a navigational lighthouse is concentrated and directed horizontally by means of prisms and lenses.

dip. Short for dip of the horizon or height of eye correction of a sextant altitude of a celestial body. The sun or moon is said to have dipped when its lower limb or bottom of observed curvature touches the horizon.

dip, at the. A signal flag or the colors is at the dip when it is hoisted halfway up. When all the way up, it is close up or two-blocked.

dip colors. As a salute, merchant vessels dip their colors to a warship by lowering the ensign halfway and then running up to the top again. The warship responds by the same gesture. This traditional and customary courtesy is a survival of the ancient practice of a merchant ship striking (furling) her top sails as a gesture of identification and implied submission to a passing man-of-war.

dip, magnetic. The dip of a compass needle due to the attraction of the earth's magnetic field.

dip net. Net used to scoop or dip fish out of the water. It is made of a mesh bag hung on a frame. Large ones are power-operated and sometimes called kill devils.

dipper. The Big Dipper or Ursa Major, a constellation of seven stars in the northern hemisphere, important to seamen because the two end stars point to Polaris, the North Star. Polaris is at the end of the handle of the Little Dipper or Ursa Minor of lesser magnitude.

dipper dredge. A barge carrying a powered excavating shovel.

dipping lug. *See* lugsail.

dip rope. The control line of a collision mat that passes under the hull. Also the line used in clearing a fouled hawse.

dipsey. Same as deep-sea lead. Also an old word for a float on a fishing line.

dip the eye. To arrange the loops (eyes) of two mooring lines on the same bollard so that either one can be cast off without removing the other.

direct drive. Any ship's main propulsion system in which there are no gears between the main engine and the propeller. Otherwise, it is geared drive.

direction finder. Same as radio compass.

dirk. A small ceremonial sword or dagger worn by midshipmen in the Royal Navy.

dirty ship. Describes a tanker equipped to handle so-called dirty oils such as crude and fuel oil in contrast to clean oils such as gasoline. Many, if not most, commercial tankers are dirty ships in the sense that they pollute the sea despite laws to the contrary.

disadvantage. *See* advantage.

disc area. Area of circle described and enclosed by the revolving tips of propeller blades.

dismasted. Said of a ship with mast(s) carried away by the force of the wind, sea, collision, stranding, and other.

dispatch. The total time allowed by the charter party for the loading and discharging of the ship. Sometimes considered to be the rate specified in the c/p, earned by the charterer for each day he returns the ship to the owner in advance of the termination date specifed.

displacement. Weight of a ship in tons equal to the weight of water she displaces. Warships are described in terms of displacement tonnage. *See* tonnage.

displacement hull. In a powerboat, as distinct from a sailboat, a hull that is relatively narrow, round-bottomed and easily driven. It has a built-in maximum or hull speed. A displacement boat is one wholly supported by the volume of water she displaces in contrast to a hydroplane. *See* hydroplane.

disrate. To reduce an enlisted person in the Navy in rating (rank).

distance line. A line marked in feet used between ships passing freight, fuel, or passengers while underway and alongside one another. It assists in maintaining a desired distance. Also one of the lines fastened to the corners of a collision mat.

distance made good. Number of miles along her intended course that a ship travels.

distance, tactical. The space in yards between foremasts of adjacent warships in formation.

distress signal. To seamen, any recognized action that indicates an emergency and requests assistance; may be a gun fired at intervals of about one minute, a continuous sounding of any fog signal, rockets or shells showing red stars, SOS and Mayday by any method, the international code signal NC by flag or light, flames as from a burning barrel of oil, the national flag flown upside down, flying a square flag having above and below anything resembling a ball, a smoke signal giving off orange smoke, slowly and repeatedly raising and lowering outstretched arms, or the bright flashing light of a strobe light.

ditty bag or box. Small container for a sailor's personal gear.

diurnal. Daily, happening every day, as a diurnal tide occurs once a day with one high water and one low. British term: single day tide.

diurnal inequality. The difference in height and/or time of the two high waters or of the two low waters of the tide each day. Also the difference in velocity of either the flood or ebb currents each day.

diurnal range. The difference in height between mean higher high water and mean lower low water in those places where the tide is mainly diurnal.

dividers. A pair of small, hand-held metal rods with sharp points at one end and hinged at the other; used to measure or step off distances on a chart.

diving bells. Modern and sophisticated pressurized containers for men working deep underwater on oil rigs, oil and gas lines, salvage, or research.

diving saucer. A mini-submarine, disk shaped, used for underwater research and first designed and used by Jacques Cousteau.

division. The basic administrative unit in both the U.S. and Royal Navy in which men and women are organized. Also a tactical unit of naval ships and aircraft.

DMAHC. Defense Mapping Agency Hydrographic Center, the Department of Defense office that produces charts of the world (other than those for U.S. waters published by the National Ocean Survey) as well as related publications. *See* Defense Mapping Agency Hydrographic Center.

dock. *n* A large basin, either permanently filled with water, a wet dock, or one that can be drained and filled, a drydock or graving dock. Word now often used interchangeably with pier and wharf. *vb* To dock a ship is to put her inside or alongside a dock.

dockage. Charges against a ship using dock or wharf facilities for any purpose.

docker. Old term for longshoreman.

docking keel. Doubling strips of steel plate attached to ship's bottom parallel to the keel and about halfway up towards the turn of the bilge to assist the hull to withstand the stress of docking. Also called a bilge keel.

docking plan. Plan that shows in detail the blocking or supports required by a particular ship when being docked, as well as other information needed by docking personnel.

dockman. *See* longshoreman.

dockmaster. The engineer in charge of docking and undocking a ship in a graving dock or floating drydock.

dock sill. The structure along the bottom of the dock entrance against which the gates or doors of a drydock are shut.

dock trials. Testing of the ship's propulsion machinery system while alongside a dock or pier; done before getting underway for sea trials that follow.

dockyard. A ship repair facility.

dodger. A weather cloth on the bridge or elsewhere rigged as protection from the weather.

dodging. A word used by powerboat sailors when they run into heavy seas and maneuver at minimum speed to avoid damage.

dog. Any one of the many simple devices or handles used for fastening down or closing a door, hatch, or port. Also called a snib or staple. A dog or dog iron is a bar bent at 90° at both ends and used to fasten dock timbers together.

dog curtain. A flap on a canvas binnacle cover.

dogging. To whip together adjoining strands of a fiber rope when splicing.

doghouse. The short deckhouse, usually over the main hatchway which is raised above the level of the cabin top of a yacht. Also called a booby hatch or a companion.

dog shores. Short timbers used for holding a ship in a launching way and prevent her from launching when the keel blocks are removed. British term: dog shapes.

dog stopper. An old name for chain stopper.

dog-vane. An auxilliary wind vane rigged on the weather side of the quarterdeck of a square-rigger, in the shrouds, or set on a staff since the sails usually obstructed the view of the vane aloft.

dog watch. One of the two hour watches into which the 1600-2000 watch is divided; the first dog watch is 1600-1800, the second, 1800-2000. In a three section watch, this permits each section to share the different watches.

doldrums. An ocean area, the equatorial trough, of calm or light winds lying near the equator between the trade winds of the two hemispheres. Also known as the intertropic convergence zone, the origin of tropical storms.

dolly, dollie. 1. A small bollard to fasten rope on a dock wall from barges and other crafts. **2.** A strong frame on small wheels used for moving heavy weights. **3.** A steel bar that supports a rivet being hammered closed.

dolly bar. Any heavy bar or tool used for moving weights.

dolly winch. A small hand-powered winch used on sailing yachts.

dolphin. 1. A cluster of piles, piling, or a single pile. Also called a rack. *See* pile. **2.** A heavy mooring post on a dock or pier. **3.** A pudding fender. **4.** An ocean mammal of the family Delphinidae. *See* porpoise.

dolphin fish. A brightly colored game and food fish of tropical waters that lives in schools. They normally weigh under 20 pounds but lone males are found to weigh as much as 60 pounds. Of the family Coryphaenidae, also known as dorado, mahimahi, coryphene; should not be confused with the mammal dolphin.

dolphin striker. A short spar hanging down from the bowsprit of a large sailing ship that is used to spread the martingale stays. Also called a martingale boom.

DOMES. Deep Ocean Mining Environmental Study.

donkey engine. Any small auxilliary power source used on board a ship, on a pier, or dock.

donkeyman. British term for the man who operates the winch or donkey engine aboard ship. American word: winchman.

donkey's breakfast. Traditional slang for a sailor's straw mattress.

door, trawl. *See* otter board.

doppler navigation system. System that uses the doppler principle of a change in the frequency of sound or radio waves caused by motion. By measuring the frequency shift, the speed can be calculated and thus the distance recorded.

dorade ventilator. A specially designed wind scoop or ventilator on the deck of a boat (yacht) through which air passes below but spray and rain are trapped and drained off.

dorado. A prized game and food fish. *See* dolphin fish.

dorsal. Refers to the back or upper part, as the dorsal fin of a fish.

dory. A small double-ended fishing and pleasure boat, originally made of wood, and used for hand lining of bottom fish or setting out trawls when carried by large fishing vessels. Thwarts of working dories could be removed so that the dories could be nested on deck.

dory gaff. A gaff or gaff hook used to land a hooked fish.

doryman. The man who fishes from a dory. Also the ship that carried the dories nested on deck.

DOTTO. Department Of Transportation Trans Oceanic classification code, used in the compilation of maritime trade data.

double. To double a point of land, such as a cape, is to go around it by water.

double-banked. A rowboat in which two opposite oars are pulled by two rowers on the same seat or thwart. If only one-man, the boat is single-banked.

double bottom. The space in a ship between the hull at the bottom and the watertight plating immediately above; always compartmented and sometimes used for storage.

double ended. Craft, such as canoes, whose stern comes to a point like their bow.

double luff. A tackle in which the blocks have two sheaves each. *See* double purchase.

double purchase. A tackle consisting of two single-sheaved blocks, the standing part being fastened to one of them. Also called a double whip and a gun tackle.

"double up." An order used to double the mooring lines from a ship to the pier when the ship is in position. *See* single up.

Douglas Scale. A series of numbers, 0-9, denoting sea state from calm through rough to confused. Now replaced by the World Meteorological Organization (WMO) Code 75. Not to be confused with the Beaufort Scale of wind force.

douse. 1. To put out as "douse that light" or to pull down and stow as "douse the jib." 2. To cease or to quit or to drench with water. Also spelled dowse.

down below. Downstairs aboard ship; upstairs in proper nautical language is topside. The word stairs is not used aboard a ship.

down by the head or stern. Describes a ship or boat that lies deeper in the water than normal forward or aft. Down by the bow is the same as down by the head. Trimmed by the head or stern is also used. *See* trim.

downhaul. Any line aboard ship, usually on a sailboat, used to pull something down such as a sail. *See* inhaul, outhaul.

DR. Dead Reckoning.

DRA. Dead Reckoning Analyzer.

drabler. *See* bonnet.

dracone. A large flexible container or bag for transporting certain liquids by water. It is usually towed by a tug.

draft. 1. The depth to which a freely floating ship is submerged as indicated by the draft marks at bow and stern in feet. 2. A sailmaker's word for the curve or belly sewn into a sail. 3. A single sling or pallet load of cargo is a draft, hoist, set, or sling. 4. In the Navy, a draft is a group of new men traveling together officially. British spelling is draught.

drafting. A sailboat riding the stern wave on the quarter of another perhaps faster and larger boat in a race. The boat astern tries to ride the slope of the second wave created by the moving stern of the boat ahead.

drafting machine. Mechanical parallel rulers used in navigation and piloting to lay down, for example, courses and bearings.

drag. *n* 1. The force opposing a ship's forward motion caused by skin friction, rudder action, a protuberance from the hull, or the effect of shallow water. 2. The amount that a ship's draft aft is greater than that forward. 3. Any device that impedes or reduces movement such as a sea anchor or drogue. *vb* A ship and her anchor are said to drag when the anchor no longer is holding.

dragger. A small trawler common to the eastern coast of North America. It can be rigged as a side trawler for ground fish or as a dredger for scallops and other shellfish.

draggerman. A fisherman who drags his trawl over the bottom, as well as his boat.

dragonfish. A small colorful tropical reef fish, one of the *Pterois*, with 18 striped and spotted dorsal spines; all dangerously venomous.

drag sail. Same as sea anchor.

drag seine or net. A net used mostly in shallow water placed or dragged around a school of fish and then hauled in. Some are fitted with a bunt or bag of heavier twine to hold the catch. When used to close off the mouth of a bay or river, a drag seine is called a stop seine or stop net. A drag seine is also known as a sweep seine, haul seine, beach seine, or shore seine.

drail. A game fisherman's special trolling sinker shaped like a torpedo but with an offset towing neck.

drain well. A small tank projecting down from the inner bottom of a ship into the double bottom to permit pumping out if necessary. Also called a bilge well.

drakar. The Danish version of the Viking longship with which the Danes raided the British Isles in the 8th and 9th centuries.

draught. British spelling of draft.

draw. In describing a ship's draft, the ship is said to draw so many feet, forward and aft.

drawback. Money refunded by Customs to an importer who later exports the goods upon which he paid duty.

dreading. In chartering terminology, the charterers may ship general cargo at a loading port.

dredge. *n* 1. A weighted net or trawl dragged on the bottom. 2. Any device used to remove and bring up, for example, sand or mud to deepen a channel or an anchorage. It may be a grab, bucket, or suction dredge. *vb* To operate a dredge is to dredge.

dredge, bucket. Dredge used to remove the soil such as mud or sand by means of an endless chain equipped with buckets that work over an adjustable arm. Spoil is raised by buckets and then tipped out as the chain revolves.

dredge, grab. Dredge that removes spoil by means of a crane that raises and lowers a grab; a toothed scoop that seizes the spoil on the bottom and deposits it into the hopper barge.

dredger. A barge or boat carrying a dredge. Also one who dredges.

dredge, suction. Dredge that uses a suction pump to suck up spoil from the bottom and discharge it into a barge or, by means of portable pipe, on to the adjacent shore.

dredging. Using an anchor at short stay, dragged over the bottom, to hold the bow up against the wind while bringing a ship alongside a pier.

Dreisonstock. A modern method of celestial navigation devised by Comdr. Dreisonstock, USN. His compact sight reduction tables are H.O. 208, a government publication.

dress. Once used as a synonym for decorate or rig as well as to coat or cover with preservative. Now used in term dress ship meaning decorate with flags, bunting, or pennants. On festive occasions, ships may be dressed with large national ensigns or fully dressed. Also displaying signal flags on standing rigging; at night, lights may be used instead of flags.

drift. 1. The speed of a current or of moving ice, in knots or miles per day. 2. The movement of anything on the surface of the sea as a result of wind and current. 3. Length of rope or chain roused out on deck for mooring. 4. The difference in diameter between any pin, spar, or fitting and the hole in which it is secured or placed. 5. A pin or long bolt used in riveting or bolting. 6. Leeway or set in a boat sailing and being moved sideways by the wind. 7. In oceanography, a wide and slow moving ocean current. 8. To a naval architect, any break in the sheer line.

drift current. Any broad and shallow, slow ocean current in which only Coriolis force and wind frictional forces are significant as generating factors. Also called wind drift. *See* ocean current.

drifter. 1. Yachtsman's word for the lightest possible headsail, jib used for racing in very light airs. Also called a ghoster and a windseeker. 2. A fishing vessel drifting with nets out to windward.

drift ice. A large mass of floating sea ice consisting of floes, pressure ridges, and openings or leads, all presenting an extensive obstacle to navigation. Drift ice often requires an icebreaker to ensure passage. Also called pack ice.

drift lead. A weight fastened to a line dropped over the side of an anchored ship and watched in order to detect possible dragging of the anchor.

drift lines. Fishing lines that are baited and buoyed, and allowed to drift during the night.

drift sail. A sea anchor.

driftweed, driftwood. Matter afloat, often cast up on a beach.

drill. Exercise or training involving crew and/or passengers to prepare for an emergency such as fire drill or lifeboat drill.

drilling rig, mobile or sea-going. A movable structure for oil and gas drilling, either submersible, floating, semi-submersible, or temporarily fixed to the bottom with legs, spuds, or piles. Jack-up rigs raise the legs when underway and then lower them again to the bottom when on new location. Rigs may be single hull, catamaran, outrigger, anchor, or spar.

driver. The fifth or sixth mast from forward on a multi-masted schooner.

driving face. *See* face.

drogue. A prepared or improvised device, or even a long rope or warp streamed astern by a ship in very heavy weather, running before the gale. This is a preventative measure for a ship to avoid being pooped by slowing down. A drogue, such as a canvas cone towed by its open end, can be used as a sea anchor to hold the ship's head up to the sea, but the two terms are not at all synonymous. Sometimes spelled drag. *See* sea anchor, Fenger anchor, Voss drogue.

dromond. A large Mediterranean sailing ship of the 9th-15th centuries fitted with many oars and a single mast supporting a squaresail.

drop. In the nautical sense for a ship to drop astern or drop aft means that it goes or passes astern. Also the depth of a sail from head to foot measured in the middle.

drop keel. Originally the detachable keel of an early submarine, now somewhat inaccurately used instead of centerboard.

dropper. *See* snood.

dropper line. Same as branch line. Also, in a gillnet the line from the corkline to the net.

dropping moor. A method of mooring in which a ship drops one anchor, veering chain while still moving slowly ahead to drop the second anchor. While veering chain to this second anchor some of the first chain is hauled in, thus mooring the ship between the two. Also called a flying moor.

dropsonde. A weather recording and transmitting device dropped by weather reconnaissance aircraft to get data at different altitudes.

DRT. Dead Reckoning Tracer.

drum. A revolving steel cylinder mounted horizontally on a windlass or capstan and used for handling rope or wire. Sometimes called a capstan head, drumhead, or trundlehead (archaic). A steam drum is part of a marine boiler. Also a popular surf fish, *Sciaenops ocellatus*, native of eastern North America and weighing up to 20 pounds; often called red drum or channel bass.

drumfish. A round North Atlantic food fish that makes a loud drumming noise and belongs to the family Sciaenidae.

drumhead. The round top of an old-fashioned sailing ship capstan with pigeon holes into which the capstan bars are fitted. Men push on these bars to actuate the capstan. Also called capstan head or trundlehead.

drum seiner. Seiner that stores its net on a large reel or drum aft.

drydock. A structure into which a ship can be floated, blocks and shores having been set up to receive her, the dock emptied and repair work accomplished. A large gate opens and closes to handle this ship's movement. A floating, mobile drydock is one that can be moved. It may be a continuous wingwall floating dock or a sectional dock. Both are ballasted to permit a ship to float in, then pumped out and thus raised so that the client's hull is exposed for repairs. A drydock is also called a graving dock. *See* dock.

dryrot. A fungus decay that attacks wood. It is common and destructive in all wooden ships and boats and often difficult to find.

D shackle. Shackle shaped like the letter D, having a screw pin as the straight side.

DSL. *See* Deep Scattering Layer.

DSRV. Deep Submergence Rescue Vessel.

dub. To cut and smooth a wooden timber or plank by hand.

duck. A light cotton material, finer than canvas, traditionally used for sailors clothes but now replaced by synthetic mixtures.

ducktail stern. Stern that slants forward.

duct. A layer in the atmosphere or in the ocean whose characteristics are different in regard to temperature, density, and so on. Thus sound and electro-magnetic waves may be refracted, distorted or channeled. The phenomenon is known as ducting and extraordinary radio, radar, and, in the ocean, sound reception may result.

duct keel. Same as box keel.

duff. A traditional sailor's dessert in olden days of sail; a stiff flour pudding containing fruit, as in plum duff.

dugong. An aquatic mammal, related to the manatee, found in the South Pacific; lives on vegetation along the coast and in rivers. Also called sea cow.

dugout. A native boat or canoe made from a single log, hollowed by fire or tools.

Dukw. A naval amphibious boat and vehicle combined, used also by the Coast Guard for rescue.

dumb. Having no means of propulsion as a dumb barge.

dumb chalder. A metal cleat or block bolted to the after side of the wooden sternpost of a boat for the end of the rudder pintle to rest on.

dumb iron. A type of caulking iron used in wooden boat building.

dumb sheave. A groove for a rope in the end of a spar or as part of a bulwark.

dumbo. A seaplane used for search and rescue at sea in World War II.

dummy gantline. *See* gantline.

dumper. Surfer's word for a fast-spilling wave whose face is too steep to ride, throws him forward, down, and then falls on him.

dump, fastening. A bolt used in fastening wood that does not pass all the way through at one end.

dunderfunk. Same as dandyfunk.

dungarees. The blue cotton work clothing traditionally worn by sailors and now popular ashore worldwide as jeans.

dunnage. Loose wood or other material used in a ship to secure cargo. Also a sailor's personal gear or baggage.

Dunn's anchor. A trade name for a modern stockless anchor.

duplex pressure proportioner. A portable foam fire-fighting device.

Dusty Jack. Same as Jack-of-the-Dust.

dutchman. A piece of material that is used to fill a void such as a spacer piece in a ventilation duct to replace a heating unit. A patch of any kind or a piece of steel fitted or driven into an opening, often to conceal poor workmanship.

dutchmen's log. Another term for chip log.

duties. *See* customs.

DWT. Dead Weight Tonnage. *See* tonnage.

dyce. The archaic command to a helmsman meaning "keep her steady," or "steady as you go." The latter is now common usage.

dynaship. A new modern design for a square-rigged ship using Dacron sails, mechanically trimmed and reefed, on steel masts having no shrouds.

E

E. International signal code alphabet flag. When hoisted singly means: "I am altering my course to starboard." Spoken: "echo."

eagre. Same as bore. Also spelled eager.

earing. A short line secured to the cringle, ring, or grommet in a sail or awning to pull it into place.

ease. To take the pressure off. To ease the rudder is to reduce the amount of rudder angle. To ease a line is to slack it, to reduce tension.

easing out line. Any line used to slack off something or ease it out, as on a mooring chain, collision mat, etc.

East Australian Current. A South Pacific ocean current setting southward along the east coast of Australia.

East Greenland Current. A North Atlantic ocean current setting south and then southwest along the east coast of Greenland.

East India Company. Established towards the end of the 16th century as a private monopoly by the British government for trade with the Far East. It was powerful and prosperous until dissolved in 1858; similar companies were formed by other countries, particularly the Netherlands.

easting. The distance a ship makes good towards the east, as in "running her easting down to Australia after rounding the Cape of Good Hope."

easy. Carefully, as in "lower that draft easy".

eat to windward. To take advantage of every puff and flaw of wind to gain distance to windward.

ebb. The falling tide ebbs and is called the ebb. The rising tide floods. There are ebb tide, ebb current, and ebb stream.

echinoderm. A classification of benthic (bottom living) marine animals including star fish, sea urchins, and sea cucumbers.

echograph. A fish finder that uses the echoes from sound waves to delineate schools of fish underwater. Also called a fishfinder.

echo ranging. *See* SONAR.

echo sounder. An electronic device aboard a ship or boat that generates sound waves and measures the time it takes them to be reflected from the bottom. This interval is translated into depth of water since the velocity of sound in water is known and shown on a depth recorder. A depth alarm can be set to ring at a pre-set depth. Also called a depth finder, Fathometer (a trade name), or sonic depth finder. *See* SONAR.

ecliptic. The great circle on the celestial sphere that the sun seems to describe in one year around the earth from east to west, as the earth revolves around the sun.

economizer. Any device that uses wasted energy, for example, the tubes in the boiler uptake used for preheating the feed water with stack gas heat.

ED. On a chart means existence doubtful.

eddy. A circular movement of water or air usually formed where currents pass obstructions, or between adjacent currents flowing in opposite directions, or along the boundary of a permanent current. Mesoscale eddies are large, slow patterns of oceanic rotation which are the chief mechanism for the storage and transport of midocean energy. They are being studied by a U.S.-Russian project known as Polymode.

Edo. Trade name for a popular echo sounder.

eductor. A type of pump used to empty tanks or spaces aboard ship.

eel. A snake-like fish of the order Anguilliformes which includes salt water species (moray and conger) and freshwater species. The latter ones are highly prized as food by many non-Americans. The moray and conger can reach 13 feet in length, are predatory and sometimes dangerous to unwary swimmers. All eels breed in salt water; the freshwater eels of Europe and North America spawn in or near the Sargasso Sea. Larva are known as elvers or glass eels. *See* electric eel.

eel comb. An eel-spearing device having a series of barbed points arranged on a bar in a comb-like fashion.

eelgrass. An important salt water weed that provides food for water fowl, invertebrates, and fish. The largest extent of eelgrass is in Izembek Lagoon near the tip of the Alaskan Peninsula.

Eell's anchor. A patented stockless anchor with long flukes used in salvage work.

elasmobranch. Any cartilaginous fish-like vertebrates such as sharks, skates, and rays.

electric eel. A large South American freshwater, snake-like fish, not a true eel, that can generate electricity to stun its prey.

electromagnetic log. Log that uses a retractable rodmeter fitted with an induction device to produce voltage that varies with the speed of the ship.

elephant seal. A sea elephant, the largest of the seals reaching 20 feet in length.

Elephanta. A southerly gale that blows along the coast of Malabar in September and October marking the end of the southwest monsoon.

elliott eye. Eye worked over a thimble at the end of a hawser.

El Niño A warm ocean current setting south off the coast of Ecuador. In some years the current extends south to the coast of Peru where the normal upwelling of cold, nutritious, deeper water is interrupted. This has a disastrous effect on the fish and consequently seabird life, resulting in an economic crisis as anchovy and guano diminish.

Elokomin rig. A particular arrangement of blocks, lines, hoses and related tackle used in fueling ships underway at sea.

elver. A young eel, also called a glass eel.

embargo. A law or international agreement prohibiting commerce with a certain country in all or some goods. An embargo can also be imposed by force.

embarkation. Going aboard a ship.

Emergency Position Indicating Radio Beacon (EPIRB). A small battery-powered radio transmitter, automatically started by water immersion, that floats on the surface and transmits distress signals on frequencies normally guarded by ocean crossing commercial aircraft or by the Coast Guard. Now carried by many prudent yachtsmen, fishermen, and by aircraft that venture out to sea.

end-door ship. British term for a roll on/roll off ship.

end for end. To reverse the ends of a line, such as a boat falls, in order to equalize the wear.

engine-order telegraph. Instrument on a ship's bridge by which orders are passed to the engines. Duplicate instruments for acknowledgement and information are located in the engineroom and in the firerooms. Also called an annunciator.

engine room. The compartment in a ship where the main propulsion machinery is located.

enlisted man or woman. A crew member in the U.S. Navy who is not an officer or warrant officer.

ensign. 1. The national flag or colors of a country flown from the gaff, on a mast, underway and from a flagstaff on the stern in port. The British merchant marine and most private boats fly the red ensign, the British Navy and the Royal Yacht Squadron fly the white ensign, and some yachts may fly the blue ensign. *See* colors. 2. The most junior commissioned in the U.S. Navy.

entrance. The part of a ship's immersed hull forward of amidships. Also known as the forebody.

entrepot. A place or warehouse in a seaport where transshipment of cargo takes place or where goods are held pending reshipment. Also used as an adjective to describe the trade of a port as being one of transshipping or reexport.

entry. The shape of a ship's hull at the stem, usually described as fine or sharp, or full and rounded.

EP. Estimated Position.

epeiric seas. Shallow inland bodies of water, such as Hudson Bay, with restricted outlet to the open ocean and having depths less than 250 meters.

Ephemeris. *See* American Ephemeris.

epipelagic. A term describing fish and other life living in ocean water up to 600 feet deep. *See* bathypelagic, bathybenthic.

epiplankton. Plankton found in the ocean in water less than 600 feet deep.

EPIRB. Emergency Position Indicating Radio Beacon.

equation of time. The difference between mean or average time and apparent or sundial time; can be found for each day in the Nautical Almanac and is important in the calculations of celestial navigation. *See* time.

equator. A circle around the earth, equidistant between the poles, that separates it into two hemispheres, north and south. A point of reference for latitude measurements.

Equatorial Counter Current. An easterly flow along the equator between, and opposite in direction to the North and South Equatorial Currents.

Equatorial Undercurrent. An easterly flowing sub-surface stream that is thin, relatively narrow, and fast; it follows the equator and in the Pacific, called the Cromwell Current.

equator, oceanographic. The zone of maximum sea surface temperature lying generally along the geographic equator. Specifically, that area where the surface water temperature is over 28° Celsius.

equinoctial. The celestial equator; pertains to the equinox.

equinox. The time at which the days and the nights are the same length; March 21st and September 21st when the sun's apparent path intersects the equinoctial equator.

equipment number. Number assigned to a merchant ship by a classification society such as the American Bureau of Shipping to designate or identify the number and type of anchors, anchor chains, and other particulars.

equipment tonnage. *See* tonnage.

ERTS. Earth Resources Technology Satellite; reveals important information about the oceans.

escarpment. A long, steep face of rock underwater; a long submarine cliff.

escolar. A North Atlantic food fish similar to a mackerel; grows to about 3 feet.

escort. An escort vessel is a warship, usually small, that does escort and convoy duty.

essential oils. In cargo handling these include almond, attar of roses, clove, wintergreen, and lavender; all oils that require special stowage.

establishment of a port. *See* lunitidal interval. Also known as high water full and change.

estuary. The mouth of a river where the tide meets the stream and where seawater and freshwater have mutual influence in regard to movement, salinity, and temperature. The adjective is estuarine.

ETA, ETD. Estimated Time of Arrival; Estimated Time of Departure.

etesian winds. Northerly winds blowing in summer over the eastern Mediterranean. Also called meltemi.

euphausiid. *See* krill.

euphotic zone. The top layer of a body of water that receives enough sunlight for the process of photosynthesis; in contrast to the aphotic zone.

euphroe. A sort of deadeye, a block of wood or metal with multiple holes, used to hold the small lines of a crowfoot for spreading an awning or the many parts of the main sheet of a fully-battened Chinese junk sail. Also spelled uphroe.

eustatism. Fluctuations of sea level due to glacial growth or melting, deposit of sediment, or sub-surface earth movements.

evaporator. The machine aboard ship that makes freshwater from salt water.

even keel. Describes a ship having no list, either to port or starboard, and no uneven trim, not down by the bow or by the stern.

Executive Officer. The second in command of a ship or station in the Navy responsible for administration; corresponds to a Chief Officer in the Merchant Marine.

exit block. Block designed for internal halyards, those inside a mast, and for the control lines that pass through a bulkhead.

exit plate. An exit block that has no sheave.

exposure suit. *See* survival suits.

extra. Australian yachting word for a headsail.

ex-works, ex-factory, ex-warehouse, etc. A selling arrangement in which the seller only packs goods to be sold and makes them available at the facility referred to.

eye. Traditionally the loop in a shroud or stay that fits over the top of the mast.

eye, anchor. The hole at the end of the shank of an anchor through which the anchor ring or shackle is passed.

eye block. A rope-strapped block with a thimble secured to the strap.

eyebrow. Elliptical metal ridge over an airport or porthole to shed water; known in the United Kingdom as a rigol, now often spelled wriggle.

eye of a cyclone, typhoon. The center of relative calm about which the storm revolves.

eye of the wind. The exact direction from which the wind blows.

eyes of the ship. Part of the ship's bow, near the hawsehole; topside, all the way forward, the traditional station for a fog lookout.

eye splice. A loop spliced at the end of a rope. A metal oval or thimble is normally inserted; if not inserted, it is called a soft splice.

F

F. International signal code alphabet flag. When hoisted singly means: "I am disabled; communicate with me." Spoken: "foxtrot".

FAA. Free of All Average; a marine insurance term meaning that coverage is for total loss only. *See* average.

fabricated ship. A ship mass-produced of parts made by distant suppliers, assembled in large units and then fitted together.

face. The after, driving surface or side of a propeller blade. Also called thrust surface or driving face.

face plate. A narrow stiffener or piece of steel fitted along the inner edge of web frames or stringers to form a flange in steel ship building.

facing. Any wooden or metal bar or plate superimposed on or fitted to another to increase strength or rigidity. Examples include face bar, face piece, and face plate.

factory ship. A floating fish or whale processing plant which usually has its own fleet of fishing craft, catcher boats.

fag end. Untidy loose end of a rope that has become untwisted or an unravelled edge of canvas. The process of becoming untwisted is fagging. *See* cow's tail.

fair. Favorable, as a fair wind, or smooth and matching as in fairing a timber in wooden boat construction. Free and unhindered, as a rope may be said to have a fair lead aft.

fairbody draft. Same as molded draft.

fair in place. Ship repair term for restoring to nearly original shape any of the damaged structure not needing replacement.

fairlead. A ringbolt, eye, loop, chock or a device with holes used to guide a rope easily in the required direction. Also called a fairleader. Fairlead means chock in the United Kingdom.

fairlead block. Block used to provide a clear and easy lead for genoa sheets and halyards, usually mounted on a slide.

fair maid. Same as porgy.

fairwater. Any plating, casting, or other material used to reduce water resistance on the hull or exterior fittings of a ship, such as a strut.

fairwater cap or cone. Cap or cone fitted at the extreme after end of the propeller shaft.

fairway. The navigable and thus safe part of a harbor or river which includes the main ship channel.

fairway buoy. A buoy that marks a fairway or channel.

fake. *n* One of the circles or windings of a line as it lies in a coil. Also called flake. *See* coil. *vb* To fake down is to lay out a line in long bights so that it can run without twisting, an impossibility from a circular coil. *See* coil.

falbot. A popular, small folding boat with a fabric-covered frame that is used mostly on lakes and rivers. Also folbot.

Falkland Current. An ocean current flowing northward along the coast of Argentina. Originating as part of the westwind drift, it joins the Brazil Current at about 35°S where both turn east across the Atlantic.

fall(s). *n* A line passed through one or more blocks; used as a hoisting tackle as in boat falls. The fixed end is the standing part and the pulling, movable end is the hauling part. *vb* **1.** To move or go as in fall astern or fall in. **2.** To fall afoul of is to collide with, and more generally, to have a dispute with. **3.** To fall in with at sea is to meet. **4.** A sailing ship falls off (away) from the wind or from a desired heading.

fall cover. A fabric covering fitted over the boat falls as protection against snow and ice.

false colors. A flag which is not one's own. Showing false colors is a legitimate ruse at sea and not contrary to international usage.

false keel. In wooden ships, the shoe or facing of heavy planking lightly fastened under the main keel to bear the possible chafing and rough usage in drydocking or when grounded. Also called false keel shoe.

fan, sea. Related to the jellyfish, a colony of polyps or coral that looks like a large, colorful mound or fan sometimes 4 to 5 feet high.

fancy line. Line running through a block under the gaff at the jaws and used as a downhaul for the fore-and-aft sail.

fancy work. Decorative knots and pieces of canvas used aboard ship, particularly in gigs and barges of the Navy; includes crosspointing, McNamara lace, and whiplashing.

fanning. Describes a sailboat making a little headway in light airs. A more modern word is ghosting.

fantail. The aftermost deck area on the weather deck of a naval ship; on a merchant ship, the overhanging stern section or counter.

farewell whistle. Traditionally, three prolonged blasts by a departing ship; may be answered by the same signal after which the departing ship responds with a short blast. Not common today.

farm. 1. Open storage area near a pier or wharf. 2. The commanding officer of a Naval ship who faces disciplinary action after a collision is said to have bought the farm.

farm, bird. Naval slang for an aircraft carrier.

faro. A small atoll-shaped reef or coral knoll with shallow lagoons, part of a barrier or atoll rim.

FAS. Free Alongside Ship. Seller delivers packaged goods at the specified port alongside the ship so that the cargo may be loaded with ship's tackle. The buyer accepts custody when cargo is alongside.

fashion. To shape steel without heat, such as a fashion plate.

fashion board. British term for splash board.

fashion piece. A shaped timber worked into the counter of a wooden ship.

fashion plate stem. A cold rolled steel stem piece. Also called a soft nose stem.

fast. *n* Old name for a mooring line, still used in stern fast, the line used to secure the stern of a boat while the bow painter secures the bow. *vb* Tight, secure as a line is made fast to a cleat.

fast boat. Boat made fast to a whale by harpoon, in contrast to a loose boat.

fast ice. Accumulation of sea ice attached to the shore; ice foot, if frozen to the shore; shore ice, if cast up or beached.

Fata Morgana. A mirage commonly observed in the Straits of Messina, marked by multiple distortions, generally in the vertical which produces fantastic images.

fathom. Traditional measure of depth of water or of length, 6 feet. Charts are marked in fathoms, feet, and meters; it is important to know which, although meters are used on all new charts. A cable is 100 fathoms but is rarely used.

Fathometer. Trade name for an electronic echo sounder.

fay. To fit together as two planks. The meeting surfaces are faying surfaces.

FCL. Full Container Load. *See* LCL.

feather. *n* **1.** The curve, if there is one, in the blade of an oar. **2.** A bit of spray as in the periscope feather of a submerged submarine running at periscope depth. *vb* **1.** To feather oars when rowing is to turn them 90 degrees on the return stroke. **2.** To feather a sail is to allow some of the wind to spill out.

feathering propeller. A propeller whose blades can be turned to a neutral or feathering position; used on sailing yachts while under sail alone.

feaze. To unwind strands at a rope's end to produce feazing, a ragged end.

feed. The water used in a boiler to produce steam, short for feed water.

feeders. Wooden or metal structures erected when loading grain in bulk in a ship in order to divert the grain into all the free space available and thus prevent shifting of the grain while underway in a seaway.

feed cock. A control valve used for feed water or any other liquid.

feed heater. A device used for preheating boiler feed water supplied by a feed pump. *See* economizer.

feel. A ship feels her way along a channel by frequent soundings or she may feel the wind, the sea, or a current.

felucca. The ancient lateen rigged, twin-masted trading and fishing craft of the Mediterranean; now rare except on the Nile.

fend off. To push away or hold off, as the bowhook of an approaching boat fends off to avoid hard contact.

fender. Any device made of, for example, wood, wicker, or plastic that is used between ships alongside or between a ship and the pier as a bumper or buffer to prevent damaging contact. Common yachting word is bumper, although some old salts do not approve.

fender rail. A timber bolted horizontally along the ship's side above the waterline to act as a fender. Also called a fender guard, guard rail, or sheer rail.

fenger drogue. Drogue made of two planks fastened together along their lengths at an angle to each other and streamed by means of a bridle made fast at all four corners.

ferrocement. Boat and small ship construction method using steel frames, wire mesh, and cement; widely used in China for fishing craft.

ferrule. The male and female metal parts that form a joint in a fishing rod.

ferry. A ship designed to carry passengers, freight, and usually vehicles for relatively short passages. Some have comfortable overnight accommodations.

fetch. The distance a wind blows over the sea without appreciable interference from land; an important factor in the size of the waves thus generated. Other uses of the word, rarely heard now, include fetch (reach) the harbor, or fetch up on the port tack or fetch (set) a compass course, fetch up with a round turn or fetch up all standing. Fetch the mark meant to reach it without another tack. A point of sailing between close hauled and a reach was sometimes known as a fetch.

fiber-clad rope. A combination of wire and fiber in which each strand of wire is wrapped in fiber. Also called marline-clad rope.

fiberglass. Tiny glass fibers set in plastic, usually a synthetic polyester resin, used widely for boat hulls up to about 100 feet in length. Fiberglas is a trade name. British term is glass reinforced plastic, GRP.

fiber rope. Rope made up of fibers, yarns, and strands in that order; traditionally made of natural fibers such as manila, hemp, and cotton but now usually made of synthetic fibers that are stronger, more elastic, and rot resistant. Examples are Dacron, polypropylene, polyethylene, Nylon. Fiber rope over five inches in circumference is a hawser. Synthetic fiber rope is often pre-stretched.

fid. 1. A round, tapered and pointed hand tool used for opening the strands of rope for splicing. A very large fid was sometimes called a commander. **2.** A fixed sailmaker's tool for making eyes and cringles in canvas; also called a cringle fid. *See* marline spike. **3.** A square and wedge-shaped piece of wood or iron once used to support a topmast.

fiddle. Portable fence around a ship's table or galley range top installed in rough weather to keep dishes and pots from sliding off. Also called a rack.

fiddle block. Block having two or more sheaves of different diameters arranged one above the other in the same plane, similar to a sister block; used in sailing yachts, most commonly with mainsheet rigs and boom vangs.

fiddle-head. Instead of a figurehead, a carved wooden scroll at the upper end or top of the stem with the carving turning outward from the ship. If the carving of the scroll turns inboard, it is a billethead.

Fiddler's Green. The traditional, mythical sailor's paradise.

fidley. 1. A large trunkway or opening above the firerooms through which uptakes, ventilators, and ladders are led. **2.** The steel guardrail around the ladder of a deck hatch. Sometimes spelled fiddley.

fidley deck. A platform over the machinery spaces.

fidley gratings. Steel bars fitted over some machinery space hatches.

field day. In the Navy, a day of general cleaning or, more generally, any sustained effort to clean spaces or equipment.

field glasses. Same as binoculars; often shortened to glasses.

field ice. Ice resulting from the freezing of the surface of the sea.

fife rail. Rail traditionally arranged in a semicircle around the foot of a sailing ship's mast. It is fitted with holes for belaying pins to which various lines can be made fast. Also called a pin rail and sometimes fitted along a bulwark as well.

fighting chair. A sturdy, swiveling seat equipped with a rod butt gimbal, foot, and arm rests and arranged in the stern of a gamefishing boat. The angler uses the chair to play and land his fish. A lighter version, without a foot rest is known as a fishing chair.

fighting fish. Small aggressive fish *(Betta pugnax)* of Southeast Asia which provide amusement and gambling when matched against each other.

fighting ship. In the naval usage, a warship or combatant ship. In merchant marine shipping terms, a ship that offers low rates to combat non-conference competition. *See* conference.

figure-eight fake. Coiling rope to produce a series or overlapping figure eights which advance one or two rope diameters with each turn. Often drapped over the lifelines to dry out natural fiber rope.

figurehead. An ornamental carved wooden statue or bust fitted forward on a sailing ship over the cutwater and under the bowsprit. Now being revived in modern materials on some merchant ships, particularly those of the Fred Olsen Line.

fike net. Same as pound net. Also spelled fyke.

fin. An appendage of a fish used for guidance and propulsion; dorsal fin, on the back, ventral or pelvic fin, on the deeper part of the belly, pectoral fin, on each side near the head, anal fin, below and just forward of the tail, and caudal fin, tail. The fin of a whale is called a flipper and is more than an appendage; it is a vestigal limb.

finan haddie. Smoked haddock, a popular food fish of the North Atlantic.

final diameter. A circle made by a ship turning with a constant rudder angle.

finback. One of the rorqual whales.

fine. Long and sharp, as in the fine lines of a ship. Also means close or near as in the expression fine on the bow which means nearly dead ahead.

finger pier or slip. A pier or floating structure projecting at right angles to a larger pier or float to provide dock space.

fin keel. A deep short yacht keel with a larger, cylindrical bottom that constitutes most of the ballast.

finning fish. A fisherman's term for fish that swim near the surface with dorsal or tail fin showing.

fins, anti-rolling. *See* anti-rolling fins.

fire bill. A posted list of the stations and responsibilities assigned to ship's officers and men in case of fire. It includes the gear that they are required to bring to the fire and how to operate it.

fireboat. A harbor vessel, usually a tug, fitted with such items as high pressure pumps, hoses, and nozzles to fight fires afloat and on the waterfront.

firebox. Part of a marine boiler where combustion takes place.

fire bulkhead. A fire resistant transverse bulkhead required by law to be built into all ships at specified intervals from bow to stern.

firemain. The saltwater line that provides firefighting and flushing water throughout the ship.

fire point. Temperature at which fuel if ignited will continue to burn. *See* flash point.

fireroom. The compartment where combustion takes place to provide steam for the ship's engines; same as boiler room. In coal burning ships, it was called a stokehold.

fireship. In the days of fighting sailing ships, a ship filled with combustible material set on fire and drifted down without a crew upon the anchored enemy ships.

fire-tube boiler. An obsolete marine boiler in which the gases of combustion pass in tubes through the water which is thus heated to produce steam. Also called a Scotch boiler. Modern boilers are watertube in which steam is produced in rows of boiler tubes over which flow the hot gases of combustion.

fire warp. A flexible wire rope led from a ship alongside a pier or to a buoy or anchor so that, in case of fire either on board ship or ashore, the ship may be swung away from its berth.

firing aisle. The area in-between the ship's boiler fronts in a fireroom. From this area, the fuel oil atomizers are fired and tended.

firn. Old snow which has recrystallized into a denser material; often found on sea ice.

first dog watch. 4 pm (1600) to 6 pm (1800). The first watch is 8 pm (2000) to 12 midnight (2400 or 0000). *See* dog watch.

fish. *n* **1.** A cold-blooded aquatic vertebrate having fins, gills, and a streamlined body. **2.** A tapered piece of wood, spliced to a spar to strengthen it. *vb* **1.** To repair a spar or mast by strengthening it is to fish it. **2.** To fish an anchor was to stow an old-fashioned stock anchor on its billboard.

fish box. Box kept in a fishing boat to hold the catch; may be fixed or portable and is usually insulated and fitted with drains to hold ice. Modern fishing craft now have refrigeration.

fish davit. Same as anchor davit.

fisherman's anchor. A small, one-piece boat anchor similar to a mushroom anchor. Also the British term for an old-fashioned stock anchor.

fisherman's bend. Two half hitches on two round turns around the anchor ring. Also called an anchor knot.

fisherman's paravane. Same as a flopper stopper.

fisherman's staysail. Staysail set between masts of a schooner; now used mostly in large yachts.

fish factory. Same as factory ship.

fishfinder. Same as echograph.

fishhook. Hook made by early man out of wood or shell, now fashioned from steel with a barbed point. The straight shaft fitted with an eye for securing the fishline is called the shank and the curved portion is the bend. The gap between the shank and the point and the throat (horizontal distance between the end of the point and the top of the bend) are important dimensions. The size of a fishhook is given as the width of the gap. Also a small broken strand on wire rigging.

fishing belt. Belt that supports a leather or metal cup into which the butt of the rod is thrust by the sport fisherman who is playing his fish.

fishing chair. *See* fighting chair.

fish ladder. A passage for migrating and spawning fish, such as salmon, around and over an obstruction such as a dam.

fish pump. A motor-driven suction device used, for example, to transfer small fish out of a closed purse seine into a fishing vessel.

fishweir. *See* weir.

fish well. A large water tank or compartment in a fishing vessel used to keep the fish or the bait alive.

fish wheel. A device similar to a water wheel that rotates with the current and scoops up the fish moving up stream. If rigged on a barge, it is called a sow.

fitting. General word for any part, piece of machinery, or equipment not having a more specific name.

fitting out. Act of completing and equipping a newly built or overhauled ship.

fitting out basin or berth. Place where the newly built ships are fitted with, for example, their machinery, upper hull structure, and anchors.

fix. A ship's position as determined by any means of piloting or navigation.

fixed light. A navigational aid that shows a constant light instead of flashing or occulting.

fixing letter. A letter of agreement stating the terms of a charter accepted by all parties concerned; drawn up before the formal charter party.

fixture. A report of vessel charters published in shipping journals.

fjord. A narrow bay or deep inlet with high mountainous sides that is found in Norway, Alaska, New Zealand, and other places.

flag. A piece of cloth, usually rectangular but sometimes a burgee or a pennant, used to denote nationality, to signal with or to show rank. Flags are flown anywhere on halyards and often on flagstaffs. *See* luff.

flag of convenience. Flag under which shipping companies worldwide register and operate their ships to avoid taxes and regulations of their own countries. Panama and Liberia are popular countries for this purpose.

flag officer. In the Navy, an admiral or commodore who flies his personal flag showing 1 to 5 stars. His staff may include a flag lieutenant, a flag secretary, and his ship is commanded by his flag captain. In yachting circles, an officer of a yacht club, commodore, vice-commodore, rear-commodore, flag captain, may fly his flag on his own yacht.

flagship. Ship carrying a flag officer and flying his flag; includes the commodore of a merchant convoy. The newest and largest ship of a shipping line is often called the flagship.

flagstaff. The small spar on which the national flag is displayed.

flake. Same as fake. Also a small stage or platform rigged over the side.

flake out. Slang for to lie down, to take a rest, or to take an equal strain on all parts.

flam. *See* flare.

flange. The turned up edge of a steel plate or structure, or the ring at the end of a pipe for connecting to a similar ring at the end of another pipe.

flanging. Cold bending of the edge of a steel plate.

flank speed. Naval term for the maximum speed of a ship; greater than full speed.

flapper. A small tapered section of net inside the trawl at the beginning of the codend designed to prevent the escape of fish.

flapper valve. Valve that permits flow in one direction only, closing a swinging hinged plate if the liquid starts to flow in the wrong direction. The British merchant service term is non-return valve.

flare. A pyrotechnic used to attract attention, using in an emergency at sea. In naval architecture, the flare of a ship's side is the spreading outward from the waterline to the main deck, a concave curve; the opposite of tumblehome. Flam refers particularly to the upper part of the flare and is useful in keeping spray off the deck.

flare gun. A hand-held device, such as a Very pistol, used to fire pyrotechnics by a ship in distress.

flare-up light. An intermittent white light with a maximum interval of 15 minutes required by the Inland Rules of the Road to be shown by a pilot vessel underway.

FLASH. Feeder Lighter Aboard SHip, a system of barge transport in which a partly submerged mother barge loads smaller barges, rises again to her normal waterline, and is then towed off.

flashing. Reducing the permanent magnetism in a ship (as protection against magnetic mines and torpedoes) by energizing temporarily coils of wire placed horizontally around the ship. *See* deperming, degaussing.

flashing light. Communication by means of code sent by blinker or searchlight between ships. Also a navigational aid, a light whose period of illumination is less than its period of darkness. A flashing light aboard ship, as required by 72 Colregs, has at least 120 flashes per minute. *See* quick-flashing light and light, occulting.

flash plate. Metal plate on the forecastle on which the anchor chain rests and from which sparks are visible when the chain runs out. British word is Scotchman.

flash point. The temperature at which fuel gives off explosive vapors; seldom the same as the fire point.

flat. 1. A partial deck of a ship. 2. Areas of shallow, nonnavigable water. 3. Short for flatboat.

flatboat. A scow, barge, or lighter with square ends and a flat bottom.

flatfish. Any flounder, fluke, sole, or halibut; fish that lie and swim on one side instead of upright. Also referred to as ground fish since they live on the bottom.

flat-plate keel. A heavy plate forming a central strake in the ship's bottom and to which the center girder is fastened.

flatline. A trolling line used without an outrigger or a kite.

flattie. A small flat-bottomed rowing or sailing boat.

flattop. U.S. Navy slang for an aircraft carrier.

flaw. A sudden, violent gust of wind; a temporary increase in wind velocity. *See* catspaw, squall. Also a narrow separation zone between pack ice and fast ice. If navigable, this is a flaw lead.

fleet. *n* A group of ships organized for any purpose under an administrative or operational head such as a fleet of tanks, a fishing fleet, or a naval fleet. *vb* 1. In an old-fashioned and rarely heard sense, it means to change, move, or shift the position of any rope, line, or hawser. 2. To fleet up is to move up or be promoted.

Fleet Guides. Detailed information about ports, organized and published for the use of naval ships by the Defense Mapping Agency Hydrographic Center.

flemish down. To lay down a line in concentric rings, each loop on deck. *See* coil, fake.

flemish eye. Eye made at the end of a line or halyard, usually to prevent the line from passing through a block and going adrift.

flemish horse. A short additional footrope at the end of a yard on a square-rigger.

flense. To cut away the blubber or fat from a whale's carcass. The procedure, now happily infrequent, is known as flensing.

Flettner rudder. Ship that uses a small auxilliary rudder which, when turned, exerts pressure to turn the main rudder.

flexible rope. Wire rope with fiber core(s) making it easier to use for mooring lines and other uses requiring some flexibility.

flight deck. The top operational deck of an aircraft carrier, just above the hanger deck, where the planes are stowed and serviced.

flinders bar. A bundle of soft iron bars placed in the binnacle of a magnetic compass to compensate for the deviation caused by the ship's vertical iron.

flip. A traditional British Navy drink of the days of sail made of beer, spirits and sugar, heated with a red hot iron.

flipper. The pectoral fin of a whale. X-ray reveals five finger bones, a wrist and an arm, evidence of the cetacean's land origin.

float. An article or device used to sustain fishing nets or people in the water (life floats). A car float is a harbor craft used to carry railroad cars.

floatline. Braided polyethylene line with a core of foam; a very buoyant line used by gillnet fishermen. Also called a corkline.

floe. An area of sea ice, other than fast ice, whose limits are visible; distinct from an ice field; may be light (thin) or heavy (thick) and may be vast if over 10 kilometers across, big if from 1-10 kilometers, medium if 200-1000 meters across, and small if 10-200 meters across. *See* ice field.

floeberg. A massive, hummocked piece of sea ice, resembling an iceberg or a bergy bit.

flog. 1. To beat with a cat-o'-nine tails; no longer done. **2.** Slang for sell or promote. **3.** A sail or awning flogs when it shakes or flaps heavily.

flood. *n* The inflow of tide in contrast to ebb. *vb* To flood a compartment or tank is to fill it with water.

floodable length. Part of a ship's hull, measured along the waterline that may be flooded with the ship remaining afloat. A ship's compartment may also have a floodable length. *See* margin line.

floodgate. The door of a drydock or tidal basin that controls the entrance of water.

flood tide. Tide that forms flood currents and a general rise in the water level.

floor. *n* **1.** The transverse steel plate immediately above the bottom shell plating of a ship; often located at every frame and extending from bilge to bilge. **2.** In yachts, it refers to the structure supporting the sole. *vb* Stevedores floor off when they level a tier of cargo.

floor boards. The removable pieces of the sole.

floor plates. The removable steel decking in a ship's machinery spaces.

flopperstopper. 1. An anti-rolling system used by some powerboats when fishing off-shore. Delta-shaped metal plates suspended under water, parallel to the surface on each quarter and suspended by booms. Also called a fisherman's paravane.

Florida Current. Part of the Gulf Stream System that passes through the Florida Straits and along the coast of Florida up to Cape Hatteras.

flotation gear. Anything designed to keep something afloat as, for example, the buoyancy tanks or the foam built into a lifeboat.

flotilla. A group of small vessels, as a flotilla of patrol craft, usually composed of two or more squadrons.

flotsam. *See* jettison.

flounder. Any of several large, flat groundfish that swim on their side and have both eyes on the top side. An excellent food fish that grows to 200 pounds.

flow. *n* **1.** Flood or rise of the tide. **2.** Same as camber, the fore-and-aft curvature in a sail. *vb* To ease or slack the sheet of a sail.

flowing sheet. An eased sheet; a rarely used term today.

fluke. 1. The palm or flat part of an anchor that goes into the ground when an anchor is dropped and set. **2.** A flatfish or flounder. **3.** The barb on the end of a harpoon. **4.** The lobe of a whale's tail. **5.** An accident or a stroke of good or bad luck.

fluke bar. A British device of hooks attached to a bar, used to impale groundfish as it was dragged over the bottom.

flush deck. Describes a ship having a flat, unbroken main or weather deck from bow to stern, such as the flush deck destroyers or flush-deckers, the American four-pipers of World War I and World War II.

fly. *n* **1.** The length of a flag measured from its hoist near the staff to the end that flutters in the wind. The end is also called the fly. **2.** A small pennant set at the top of a mast to indicate wind direction. *vb* **1.** A sailing ship may fly up into the wind, means to turn quickly to windward. **2.** To let fly is to let go quickly. **3.** A ship flies her national ensign as well as a personal flag although in the United Kingdom, she wears the personal flag.

fly block. The moving block in a Spanish burton purchase that supports the hauling part of the fall.

flybridge. Same as flying bridge. A recent commercial term not altogether acceptable to old hands.

fly-by-night. A small squaresail once used only by sailing craft when running before the wind.

flying. A sail sent aloft and set from the deck below was said, in old sailing days, to be set flying, in contrast to one set by men sent aloft.

flying bridge. The topmost bridge of a ship or of a boat, usually above the navigating bridge and in some old ships, the location of the magnetic compass.

Flying Dutchman. A legendary nautical ghost, a ship whose appearance was believed to be frequent in the waters near the Cape of Good Hope.

flying gaff. A large steel hook with a detachable head to which a stout line or wire is made fast; used in landing very large game fish.

flying fish. Any one of several small, edible, tropical fish that launch themselves into the air and then glide for long distances to escape predators.

flying fish sailor. A sailor who delights in calm seas and mild weather.

flying foresail. A square foresail sometimes used on yachts, especially when running before the Trades.

flying jib. The sail set on the fore topgallant royal stay in old square-riggers.

flying kites. The general term for light sails in square-riggers and in yachts; usually shortened to kites.

flying light. Said of a ship that is unloaded and floating high in the water.

flying moor. To moor with two anchors, dropping them in succession a certain distance apart while underway and then adjusting the cable to rest between them. Same as a dropping moor.

flying studding sail. A sail set between the masts of a square-rigger.

foam. A chemically produced, smothering suds or foam blanket used in fighting oil, electric, and other fires aboard ship. British say froth.

foaming. The formation of bubbles on the surface of the water in the steam drum of a ship's boiler; caused by excessive dissolved solids.

FOB. Free On Board. Seller must deliver goods aboard ship where the buyer accepts all subsequent charges.

Föehn wind. A warm dry wind blowing offshore, such as the Southeasters off Cape Town or the Santa Ana off southern California.

fog. A cloud touching the sea; a mass of tiny water droplets causing a reduction of visibility to less than 1000 meters. *See* mist. When mixed with polluted air, it is smog. A ship stopped because of fog is said to be fogbound, common before radar. *See* ice fog, steam fog, advection fog.

fog bow. A rainbow seen in the fog or cloud.

fog eye. A spot of sunlight showing through fog.

fog buoy. *See* towing spar.

fog lookouts. Special lookouts required by the Rules of the Road to be stationed either in the eyes of the ship or aloft if the fog only exists near the water. They must report such encounters as ships, boats, and buoys.

fog nozzle. A fire fighting device that produces a fine, smothering spray or mist of water; used for most fires aboard ship.

fog signal. Any horn, whistle, bell, gun, diaphone, nautiphone, or other device used to produce warning signals when in low visibility, either at a shore station, other aid to navigation, or aboard ship. Latter usages, governed by the Rules of the Road, specify the nature of the sound signal required, its duration, and frequency.

fog spar. Same as a towing spar.

fogy. Naval slang for an increase in pay based on length of service. Pronounced fohgy.

folbot. *See* falbot.

following. Going in the same direction, as a following sea or wind. A propeller blade has a following edge and a leading edge.

foot. *n* The bottom or lower edge of any sail. *vb* A sailboat is said to foot well when she makes good progress to windward.

footband. The strengthening band of canvas along the foot or bottom of a squaresail on the after side.

foot boat. An old term for a ferry that carries only people.

footing. Fore-and-aft fixed strips of wood in the bottom of an open boat.

footline. The bottom line of the three lifelines installed topside on warships and some merchant ships.

foot locks. Wood or metal strips on a gangplank or inside a ship.

foot rope. Pieces of served wire rope rigged under the yard of a square-rigger on which the men stand who furl and reef the sails. Also rigged under a boom or under the bowsprit of a sailing ship. Foot ropes are supported every few feet by stirrups.

foraminifera. Numerous and widespread, shelled marine protozoans of various shapes. Unicellular organisms that form an important base for the food chain of the sea.

forced draft. Archaic term indicating that the ship's firerooms were under increased air pressure and thus that the ship was going faster than normal. All modern steam vessels, except for nuclear ships, operate at all times under forced draft, even at anchor.

force majeure. A marine insurance term; an Act of God.

fore-and-aft. Lengthways on a ship, from bow to stern as opposed to athwartships which means from side to side.

fore-and-aft sail. A sail that is rigged in line with the keel, in contrast to a squaresail that is rigged perpendicular to the keel.

fore. Forward; always an adjective denoting the front or forward direction, towards the bow. At the fore describes a flag flown at the foremast.

forebody. The forward part of the hull of a ship.

forecastle. In modern usage, the forward section of the main deck or weather deck. The forecastle head is the extreme forward part, the bow, near the ground tackle; also sometimes the forward living space for the crew. In a yacht, the same area topside is called the foredeck. Forecastle is pronounced fohksul.

forecastle card. A copy of the shipping articles, the sailor's legal contract of employment, posted in the crew's living spaces.

foredeck. The extreme forward part of the weather deck of a sailing yacht where the headsails are handled.

forefoot. The forward, outboard end of a ship's stem where it is made fast to the keel.

foreguy. The line that holds the spinnaker down. In some gaff-rigged ships, it was a line leading forward from the end of the mainsail boom to control the boom when the ship was running free.

forehand. To take a strain by hand on a piece of gear near the moving block so that the line or tackle may be belayed was to forehand it. In more modern usage, an Officer of the Deck is trained to be alert and forehanded.

forehook. Same as breasthook.

foreign trade zone. Part of a port terminal in which cargo can be stored free of duty until removed or processed in a manner which reduces the final duty. Also called a free zone.

Forel scale. A standard scale used to measure the color of seawater.

foremast. The forward mast of a sailing ship. In a two-masted yacht where the forward mast is much larger than the one aft, as in a yawl or ketch, it is called the mainmast and the after mast, the mizzenmast or jigger.

forenoon watch. 0800 to 1200.

forepeak. The tank, compartment, or space in a ship between the collision bulkhead or forward watertight bulkhead and the stem. *See* peak. Also the forward cabin in a small yacht.

forereach. The movement ahead or into the wind that a sailboat makes when tacking or luffing or when hove to.

foresail. A general word for any sail set forward of the most forward mast of a fore-and-aft rigged sailing vessel. It can be a jib, staysail, genoa, or a reaching foresail. Also a sail set abaft the foremast of a schooner. Originally it was the lowest squaresail set on the foremast of a square-rigger and was also called the fore course.

foresheets. The forward part of a boat, in contrast to the stern sheets. In modern usage most commonly referred to as the bow.

foreshore. Part of a beach or shore that lies between high and low water at normal tides. *See* backshore.

forestay. The wire running from near the top of the foremast forward to the stem or bowsprit; often same as headstay.

foretop. A platform erected high on the foremast of a warship, originally for snipers and later for fire control gear in the early steam warships. Modern warships have an integrated superstructure with no foremasts or foretops as such.

foretriangle. The area between the most forward mast of a sailboat and the forestay.

forklift truck. A 3 or 4 wheel powered device for lifting, carrying, and stacking cargo either as bags, boxes, or barrels, or mounted on pallets. Also called a fork truck.

form drag. The resistance or water drag of an object, such as a ship moving in water due to its shape. More precisely, form drag is the difference in water pressure forward and aft.

fother. Old word meaning to stop a leak in a ship's hull by covering the hole with canvas or other handy material. This may be a collision mat or fothering blanket.

forward. Towards the bow-up front.

forward bow, or quarter, spring. A mooring line on a ship's bow, or quarter that leads forward from the ship to the pier. *See* mooring line.

forward perpendicular. The most forward frame station of a ship, usually at the intersection of the waterline and the forward part of the stem.

foul. 1. Jammed, tangled, not clear for running. **2.** Covered with sea growth such as a foul bottom. **3.** Unsafe for mooring or anchoring as a foul berth or foul ground. **4.** To entangle, confuse, or obstruct. **5.** To foul up is to do something badly or to get into trouble.

foul anchor. Anchor that is entangled in something such as its own chain.

foul bill of health. Bill that is not "clean" and thus indicates an infected port of departure or an unhealthy ship.

foul hawse. A twisting of the anchor chains when moored with two anchors.

foul hook. To hook a fish anywhere but in its mouth.

foul lading. A bill of lading listing damaged or badly packed cargo.

foul weather. Bad or stormy weather.

found. Equipped with stores and provisions. All found means having all necessities aboard; well found describes a ship thoroughly and well equipped for a voyage.

foundation plate. A fore-and-aft horizontal steel sheet fitted on top of floors upon which the keelson rests. Also the structure upon which a heavy piece of machinery rests.

founder. To sink.

fourfold purchase. A tackle consisting of two blocks with two sheaves in each block.

fox. Old word for a strand formed by twisting several rope yarns together or two yarns twisted against their lay.

foxtail. A naval word for a short handled brush used for sweeping. Also a short line attached to a jackstay.

FPC. Fish Protein Concentrate; a tasteless white powder derived from any edible marine life. It is a valuable food additive for the under-nourished of the world.

frame. One of the transverse girders of a ship's hull, extending from the keel to the highest continuous deck. Often numbered from the bow aft.

frame stations. In ship construction plans, the transverse vertical plane at equal intervals along the length of the ship from bow to stern.

franchise. In marine insurance, the percentage or amount of the insured value which in case of loss must be borne by the insured.

frap. To wrap with line or small rope which is called frapping gear or frapping.

frapping lines. Lines used to steady a boat when being raised or lowered from a ship. They are passed around the boat falls of the davits and tended on deck.

Franklin buoy. A ring-shaped lifebuoy fitted with a light that is lit when the buoy is thrown overboard to assist someone in the water at night.

frazil ice. Crystals that form in supercooled water too turbulent to permit coagulation into sheet ice. Also called lolly ice, frazil crystals, and needle ice.

free. Loose, adrift, not made fast as in free for running. A ship sails or runs free with the wind near or abaft the beam in contrast to close-hauled.

free alongside. The cargo is delivered within reach of the ship's tackle for loading.

freeboard. Vertical distance from the waterline of a ship to the main or weather deck.

freeboard mark. Lines and letters indicating maximum permissible load a ship can carry in different ocean areas or freeboard zones at different seasons of the year. *See* Plimsoll marks, load waterline.

freebooter. A pirate; a sea-going thief.

free dispatch. *See* dispatch.

Freedom of the Seas. A doctrine agreed upon internationally which states that the open seas, beyond announced territorial limits, are free of any nation's rule or control. Territorial limits are now approaching 200 miles for all countries.

freeing port. An opening in a bulwark that permits the escape of water. Also called a freeing scuttle, a bulwark port, or a wash port.

free of address. *See* address commission.

Free On Board. Same as FOB.

free pratique. A clean bill of health.

free port. Port where buying and even manufacturing can be carried out free of most duties and taxes. Also called a free zone.

freer. *See* lift.

free surface. Liquid in a partially filled ship's tank or compartment that is free to move from side to side as the ship rolls. Large free surface areas are dangerous to the ship's stability since they can involve a large shift of weight. Washplates are built in to reduce free surface.

free wave. Wave that continues to exist after the generating force, the wind, has died down. Same as a swell.

freight. Charges made for carrying cargo in ships. Advance freight is payable before delivery of cargo; lump sum freight is that paid for all or part of the capacity of the ship; dead freight is that claimed for space not provided by the charter despite written agreement. Back freight is that claimed when cargo is refused or cannot be delivered at destination and is returned to shipper; pro-rata freight is that paid for carriage only part of the way to destination; ad valorum freight is that added for unusually valuable cargo.

freighter. A cargo or freight carrying ship.

French bowline. Bowline having two loops, handy for putting a man over the side. Same as a double bowline or a bowline on a bight.

French sennit. A kind of flat plaited cordage made with 5 or 7 rope yarns.

fresh breeze. A wind of 17-21 knots, number 5 on the Beaufort Scale.

freshen. To shift the position of a rope, line, or chain that is exposed to friction and wear at one place.

freshen the nip. To shift the nip or part of a line exposed to wear.

freshet. An area of comparatively fresh water at or near the mouth of a stream flowing into the sea.

fresh gale. A strong wind of 34-40 knots, number 8 on the Beaufort Scale.

freshwater mark. A ship's maximum permissible draft when in fresh water. A ship floats lower in freshwater because it is less dense than saltwater.

Fresnel lens. Lens used to magnify and direct the light of a lighthouse.

friendship sloop. Originally a fishing boat out of Friendship, Maine; its seaworthiness and comfort led to yacht designs for boats to 35 feet.

frigate. In days of sail, it was a medium-sized, heavily armed, fast warship. Today it is a warship of medium size, smaller than a destroyer, used for anti-submarine, general escort, and patrol duties.

frigate bird. Family Fregatidae, the sailor's man-o'-war bird, very fast, aggressive, and predatory with a long forked tail, 4–7 foot wing spread, whitish below, dark above and found in tropical waters.

frogman. General term for any free diver using an aqualung.

frog's leg. The foot of a spinnaker when made up in stops to which the spinnaker sheet is made fast.

front. Meteorological term for when two air masses of different densities and usually temperatures come together.

frostbiters. Persons who race small, frostbite dinghies in the winter; a sport known as frostbiting.

frost smoke. Steam fog over newly formed leads, lanes, or pools in ice; may be called Arctic frost smoke or barber. *See* steam fog.

Froude number. A constant used in calculating the resistance of a ship model towed in a model testing basin. Similar but not equivalent to a Reynolds number.

frustration of the adventure. A clause used in charter parties implying that a delay due to circumstances beyond the control of either party will be grounds for cancellation (thus frustrating the adventure). It also applies to marine insurance.

frustrule. The siliceous shell of a diatom; the principal constituent of diatomaceous ooze at the bottom of the sea.

fry. A general term for the young of fish and other sea life.

full and by. A sailing ship with all sails set and full, sailing close-hauled but not so close to the wind as to slow the vessel.

full and change. In reference to the tides, the times of the full and of the new moon.

full and down. A cargo ship with all spaces filled and at maximum allowed draft.

full outturn. Describes cargo that arrives without a shortage.

full reach and burden. A chartering expression describing the cargo space which is normally available for use including legal deck capacity.

full rigged ship. A fully square-rigged vessel with three or more masts. The sails from bottom up are, on each mast: courses, lower topsails, upper topsails, lower topgallants (t'gallants), upper t'gallants, royals and skysails. Also called a square-rigged ship, a square rigger or just a ship.

full rudder. The maximum amount a rudder may safely be turned.

full scantling vessel. Vessel built in accordance with the most demanding requirements of the classification societies in regard to structural strength. Minimum freeboard is measured up to the main deck, the freeboard deck, which is equipped with permanent means of closing the openings to the weather. *See* shelterdeck.

full speed. In naval usage, a higher speed than standard but less than flank. *See* flank speed.

fully found. Describes a ship that is completely equipped for whatever its purpose or mission may be.

fulmar. An Arctic bird of the petrel family that feeds at sea, similar in appearance to the herring gull. There is also a giant fulmar in the antarctic.

funnel. The smoke stack or chimney of a powered ship. The galley funnel is known as Charlie Noble.

furl. To take in or roll up a sail to its yard or boom and fasten it there with a gasket. Furling in the bunt describes the usual way a squaresail is furled at sea.

furniture. In marine insurance terminology, all the equipment of a ship not fixed in place that is necessary for her efficient operation.

futtocks. In wooden shipbuilding, the curved pieces of wood that make up the ship's frames.

futtock shrouds. Chains or rods that are downward extensions of the topmast shrouds. They stiffen the top as well as take the stress of the topmast rigging.

FWG. Foul Weather Gear.

fyke net. Same as pound net. Sometimes spelled fike.

G

G. International signal code alphabet flag. When hoisted singly means: "I require a pilot." When made by fishing vessels operating on the fishing grounds, it means: "I am hauling nets." Spoken: "golf."

gaff. A spar for supporting the top of a four-sided fore-and-aft gaff sail as in the old-fashioned gaff-rigged sailboat. Also the steel hook attached to a pole or a handle when used to boat a hooked gamefish.

gaff foresail. A sail set abaft the lower foremast of a schooner.

gaff-headed. A four-sided fore-and-aft sail rig with a gaff at the head or top of the sail. Now largely replaced in modern yachts by the jib-headed or Bermuda rig.

gaff jaws. A fitting which attaches a gaff to the mast. *See* throat.

gaff trysail. A storm trysail using a small gaff.

gag. U.S. and West Indian local name for grouper.

gage. *See* gauge.

gale. A strong wind; moderate, fresh, strong, or whole gales range from 28 to 55 knots. *See* Beaufort Scale.

gale warning. Warning predicting winds of 34 knots or higher, issued by the National Weather Service. *See* Small Craft Advisory, storm warning.

gall. To chafe or wear. Also *see* wind dog.

galleass. A fast, heavily armed, combined sailing and rowing Mediterranean warship of the 15-17th centruies. It was a descendant of the ancient galley and now survives after a fashion in the felucca.

galleon. A large merchant and warship of the 15-17th centuries that was developed from the carrack. Most of the boats in the Spanish Armada were galleons.

gallery. The balcony over the stern of a wooden ship with access through the stern windows (now rare). In modern usage, the partial deck below the flight deck which looks down upon the hangar deck of an aircraft carrier.

galley. 1. Nautical word for kitchen. **2.** Classic rowing and sailing ship of the Greek, Roman, and Phoenician Bronze Age and continued in some form by the Europeans until the 18th century. It had one or more banks of oars and a square or lateen sail. **3.** In the British Navy, an old word for an Admiral's barge or Captain's gig.

galley stroke. A rowing technique used in ancient galleys in which men stood up on the backstroke and then fell back on their benches as they pulled on the heavy oars.

gallows. 1. In a fishing trawler, especially a side trawler, the A-frame that supports the warps or towing lines. **2.** The U-shaped frame from which a trawl block is suspended. **3.** Any frame work shaped like goalposts aboard ship designed to support booms, spars, spare oars, cargo derricks or similar gear. Sometimes called a gantry.

Galofaro. A whirlpool in the Strait of Messina between Italy and Sicily; known to the ancients as Charybdis, a hazard to ships under sail or oars.

gam. A herd, pod, or school of whales.

gamming. Term used by sailing whalers for paying a visit or having a meeting.

gamefish. Those aggressive, sight-feeding fish or sharks that will take a bait or an artificial lure and resist capture.

gammon. To make fast the bowsprit in the stem, originally by lashing with rope or chain in a special cross-over fashion known as gammoning; later using metal plates and bands. Associated terms are gammon plate, gammoning hole, gammon knee or timber, gammon iron, and gammoning fish or batten.

gangboard. An old word for brow or gangplank.

ganger. Any short length of chain or rope used to haul a heavy cable into position.

ganging, gangion. Same as snood.

gang of rigging. An old term for the mixture used to slush or tar down the standing rigging.

gangplank. Same as brow in modern usage. Also a plank running from the stem of a boat to the first thwart. Old word was gangboard.

gangway. 1. The opening in a ship's rail or bulwark that is used for the passage of people or cargo by means of a brow, gangplank, or accommodation ladder. **2.** The command or request "gangway" means make way or let me through.

gangwayman. A signalman in a stevedoring crew who directs the winch operators in loading and unloading into and from the ship's hold.

gannet. A large white seabird with black wing tips, much bigger than a gull. It can be identified at a distance by its steep dive into the water from a considerable height with folded wings.

gantline. Line rove through a fixed single block, a whip, to send something aloft such as a man up a stack.

gantline, dummy. A gantline made of a piece of old rope that is kept rove through a block to be used as a messenger to pull through the actual gantline when necessary.

gantry. Any overhanging or spanning structure containing a crane that rolls on railroad tracks; used in shipyards and on piers. Also called a gantry crane. A similar stationary structure, with or without a crane, is found on container ships and on large fishing vessels.

gap. The governing dimension of a fishhook, the shortest distance between its point and its shank. *See* fishhook.

gape net. *See* stow net.

garboard strake. Row of planks or steel plates nearest to the keel extending fore-and-aft. Also called a sand strake.

garibaldi. A small bright orange fish of the giant kelp beds of the Pacific North America.

garland. Old word for a grommet or ring of rope around a spar or mast.

garnet. Old word for a tackle of two blocks, similar to a gun tackle, used in hauling a course up to its yard.

garua. A heavy fog common to the coastal areas of Chile, Peru, and Ecuador; similar to the inversion fogs of coastal California.

gasket. 1. Traditionally a small line or strip of canvas used to fasten a sail when furled to its boom or gaff. Some yachtsmen call them tiers (tie ers). **2.** The seals on machinery and on watertight doors and ports; the British word is seating ring or seating strip.

gastroliths. Stones found in the stomachs of some marine mammals such as walruses.

gas turbine. Turbine driven by the hot, expanding gases of burning fuel oil instead of by steam. Multiple gas turbines are now widely used for small warships, such as destroyers, and in some merchant ships.

gat. A natural or artificial channel or passage through shoals, banks, or extending inland, often marked by current. Sometimes spelled gut.

gate. Door to a drydock or canal lock.

gate valve. A common fluid control device using a wedge-shaped block, the gate, to move across and close off the opening.

gather. To take in, as gather in the jib. A ship gathers way as she gets underway.

gatline. British word for a line specifically rigged to send a man aloft in a boatswains chair.

gauge. 1. A measuring device. 2. A position of a sailing ship relative to another and to the wind. If upwind of another; a ship is said to have the weather gauge, downwind she has the lee gauge. Also spelled gage.

gauge glass. A vertical glass tube that shows the water level in a tank or boiler to which it is attached.

gear. 1. A common collective nautical word for equipment, supplies, baggage, or anything aboard ship that has no more specific designation. 2. A sailor's baggage. 3. A standard device used to change the speed, force, or direction of rotation of a machine.

gelcoat. The finishing coat of polyester resin on a fiberglass boat.

GEM. Ground Effects Machine; an aircushion vehicle or a Hovercraft (trade name). Modern term is Surface Effect Ship (SES).

gencon. A standard charter party form. *See* charter party.

general average. In marine insurance, an expression of joint financial responsibility of the owners of the ship, the owner of the cargo, and of the master and crew. Loss or damage due to an Act of God, such as a severe storm, would be shared by all. If caused by a collision which was the fault of the master alone, it would be a particular average loss. *See* particular average. The word average above is used in a sense unrelated to its meaning ashore.

general inference. A description of the general weather pattern and pressure distribution giving the weather forecast for a certain area.

General Prudential Rule. Same as the Rule of Special Circumstance.

General Quarters. Stations for battle or other emergency aboard a warship. The general alarm is sounded and the word is passed over the general announcing system. The modern British equivalent is action stations which has long replaced the traditional beat to quarters.

general trader. British term for tramp; a cargo ship that has no regular or scheduled route.

gennaker. A sail that is a cross between a genoa and a spinnaker. It is set flying like a spinnaker but is cut more like a ballooner or reaching jib.

genoa jib. A triangular headsail, larger than a normal jib that is used by cruising and racing yachts when reaching. It overlaps the mainsail; also called a jenny. *See* ghoster, yankee.

gentle breeze. Breeze of 7 to 10 knots, number 3 on the Beaufort Scale.

geo-navigation. As distinct from celo or celestial navigation; fixing a ship's position by observing or sensing terrestrial objects, land, the bottom, etc. Known more commonly as piloting.

georef. A geographic reference system used internationally at sea to report one's position or for search and rescue operations.

Germanischer Lloyds (GL). The West German national ship classification society located in Berlin. *See* classification.

ghoster. A very light headsail similar to a genoa jib and a yankee but with its luff extending to the top of the forestay; used only in very light airs. Also sometimes called a drifter and a windfinder.

ghosting. Sailing with little or no apparent wind. Once called fanning.

giant clam. The largest of the bivalve mollusks, up to 5 feet across, that lives fixed in a coral reef. Its normally open, fluted shell closes quickly to trap an intruder, actuated by a shadow sensing organ. There is no recorded evidence of a diver having been trapped. Also called tridacna.

giant squid. A large cephalopod of the genus *Architeuthis*, the major food of the sperm whale. With a body up to four meters long and tentacles to 15 meters, this little known and rarely seen monster of the mid depths may be the original Kraken, a legendary Scandanavian sea monster.

gibe. Same as jibe.

Gibson Girl. A portable radio for liferafts that broadcasts on the distress frequencies. Now largely replaced by the EPIRB.

gig. In the United States, a naval Commanding Officer's personal power boat. Formerly and still used in the United Kingdom, a clinker built, square stern rowing boat sometimes used by senior naval officers. Also a spear used to catch fish, a trident, as well as an arrangement of hooks used to snag fish.

gig stroke. A long, sweeping pull and recovery on the oars of a boat with a two second pause after the blade leaves the water before starting recovery.

gilguy. Any rope temporarily used as a guy or lanyard, such as the light line to hold a halyard away from the mast when the boat is anchored or moored.

gilhickey. Slang for anything whose specific name is not known.

giligan hitch. Any unseamanlike, messy, or inefficient knot, hitch, or bend.

gill. The respiratory organ of a fish through which water passes in order for oxygen to be extracted.

gill net. Net that entangles fish with mesh too small to permit passage but large enough to allow the fish to enter. The fish cannot then retreat because of its gill covers. Now made of nearly transparent mono-filament.

gill netter. A fishing vessel that uses a gill net, either setting it and leaving it for a period or drifting with it attached, using the net as a sea anchor to windward. Latter is called drifter.

gimbals. An arrangement of metal rings and levers permitting a chronometer, galley stove or table to remain level while the ship or boat rolls and pitches.

gimlet. To turn something around such as to gimlet the anchor which means to turn the anchor around at the hawse.

gin block. The iron block with a single sheave used at the end of a boom when handling cargo. Also called a gin or a whip gin.

gin pole. Any improvised hoisting spar set up as a derrick.

gin tackle. A purchase with a double and a triple block and the standing part of the fall being attached to the double block.

gipsy head. An auxilliary drum on a windlass, winch or capstan used for handling lines; gipsy for short and sometimes spelled gypsey. Also called a warping head, whipping drum, or winch head. British word for wildcat.

girder. A heavy, continuous member of a steel ship's structure usually running fore-and-aft and designed to support the deck.

girding. The accidental and dangerous broadside pull by a ship on the line made fast to a tug. If the line leads out abeam of the tug, she may be capsized and is thus said to be girded.

girdling. Increasing the stability of a ship by adding to its beam, once a common practice with wooden ships. The material used to increase its beam (wood or steel) is added at the waterline.

girt. Said of a ship moored with two anchors whose cables are too taut to permit her to swing. Also to distort the shape of a sail by means of a line stretched across it.

girt band. A strip of canvas sewn across the middle part of a sail to strengthen it.

girth. A ship's measurement from gunwale (deck edge) to gunwale around the ship's bottom at any specified frame; used in measuring yachts for comparative ratings for time allowance in racing. The procedure is known as girthing. Also the horizontal dimension of a sail from luff to leech.

girth stick. In ship construction, a stick of wood with rivet hole spacings marked on it that is used to check the proper spacing of the rivets. Now somewhat outmoded.

give way. An order by the coxswain to his men to begin pulling stroke together.

give-way vessel. The vessel that, under 72 Colregs, must give way (change course and/or speed) in deference to the stand-on vessel that has the right of way. Formerly called the burdened vessel. *See* stand-on vessel.

GL. Germanischer Lloyds.

glacon. A fragment of sea ice ranging in size from brash to medium floe.

gland. A seal around a propeller shaft, submarine periscope, or any other revolving mechanism to prevent leakage of water, oil, or steam. Also called a gland seal and for turbine rotors, steam is forced into the seal to prevent the entry of air and the escape of turbine steam.

glass. Shortened word for any shipboard instrument made partly of glass such as a barometer, hand-held telescope or long glass, feed water gauge on a boiler, or magnifying glass to help read a chart. The barometer may be called a storm glass or weather glass. A night glass or glasses is a long glass or a pair of binoculars having high light-gathering properties.

glass sponge. Sponge in which the internal skeleton, spicules, is composed of silica; found at great depths.

glim. A light or candle once used inside a ship as in the crew's quarters. Thus the expression "douse that glim" meaning put out the light. A glimmer of light is a very small amount of light.

glitter. Light reflected from the surface of the sea which, when photographed at a distance, as from a satellite, reveals the sea state.

globe buoy. Buoy mounting a sphere on a staff. Also called a staff and globe buoy.

globigerina. A very small marine animal, a foraminifera. Their chambered shells, when very abundant, form the globigerina ooze or mud of the ocean bottom.

glory hole. The opening into the inside of a firebox under a ship's boiler to permit visual inspection. Also any one of a number of small spaces or compartments on a ship, especially the fireman's or steward's living quarters.

glory hole steward. Steward on a passenger ship who looks after the ship's stewards.

glue, marine. A special waterproof glue used in wooden ship construction. Now many modern glues are waterproof, even some for household use.

glut. A becket, a piece of rope with a thimble, fastened to the center near the head of a squaresail to assist in furling.

glut herring. An American waters, herring-like, small food fish closely related to the alewife.

GM. Metacentric height.

GMT. Greenwich Mean Time.

gnomonic projection. A chart that shows all great circles as straight lines. It is produced by projecting part of the earth, a sphere onto a flat plane, the chart, which touches the sphere at one point. *See* mercator, and projection, chart.

go about. To go about is to tack.

gob. Slang for a Naval enlisted man; not considered good usage in the Navy.

gob line. A rope fitting over the dolphin striker under the bowsprit of a sailing ship.

gob stick. A fisherman's wooden club. Also called a persuader.

goby. A small fish of the large kelp beds or forests of the North Pacific.

godown. A warehouse or waterfront storehouse, especially in the Far East.

gollywobbler. A main topmast balloon staysail that extends from the masthead to the deck and overlaps the mainsail; used on schooner yachts.

gondola. A long, narrow, mostly open, boat used for centuries in the canal of Venice.

gongbuoy. Buoy similar to a bellbuoy but having for identification the distinctive tones of two gongs which sound as the buoy moves in the seaway.

good ship. Used in the preamble of a charter party meaning a fully seaworthy vessel.

goose or gooseneck barnacle. *See* barnacle.

gooseneck. A fitting which secures the hinged end of a gaff boom or derrick to the mast, allowing the spar to move in all directions. Also any pip or vent making an 180° turn as it emerges from the deck, particularly those used as ventilators.

goosewinged. Same as wing and wing.

gore. Any diagonally cut or triangular piece of canvas added to a sail. A sail may be gored or made with a certain goring.

gorge. In its simplest form, a short double pointed piece of wood used as a primitive fishhook hidden in bait and swallowed by the fish.

grab, dredge. *See* dredge.

grabrail. Any small section of wood or metal railing fitted on the side or top of a ship's deckhouse as a handhold for men moving about the deck.

grab rope. A safety line or hand rope made fast above a boom or brow. The knotted lifelines hanging from the span wire of boat davits. Any lifeline attached to a lifeboat, liferaft or life preserver used in an emergency.

graft. To cover a ringbolt, stanchion, block or other fitting with a weaving of small cord.

grain. In the maritime sense, includes all varieties of seed foods: wheat, corn, rye, barley, oats, rice, pulse, seeds, and nuts. Wheat, rye and corn (maize) are considered heavy grains whereas barley and oats are classified as light. Also any small spear or gig having multiple barbed prongs that are used to catch for example eels, frogs, or flounder.

grain cubic. The capacity, in cubic feet, of the cargo hold in a ship measured to the inside of the shell plating. If measured to the inside of the frames or cargo battens, it is bale cubic. *See* bale capacity.

grampus. Same as killer whale.

Grand Banks. A shallow fishing area hundreds of miles long off the coast of Newfoundland, famous for cod and other groundfish. Now overfished, it has historically been a rewarding but dangerous fishing ground for Europeans because of fog and gales.

granny knot. A false, unsymmetrical square knot; one to avoid because it slips. Also called a lubber's knot.

grapnel or grappling iron. A small device with 4 or 5 claws that can be thrown and used at the end of a line to recover objects in the water or on the bottom. A heavier version is a hawk. The British word is creeper.

graticule. The network of latitude and longitude lines on a chart.

grating. Any open framework or latticework in wood or metal used as a removable deck, something to stand on. There are such gratings as engineroom gratings, fireroom gratings, hatch gratings, wooden shower gratings, the fantail gratings of a tug, and skylight gratings. The platforms at the top and bottom of an accommodation ladder are usually gratings and the steersman at the wheel on the bridge traditionally stands on a grating to keep his feet dry in rough weather.

grave. 1. An obsolete term meaning to scrape off the barnacles from a ship's bottom; same as bream. It included treating the scraped bottom with tar or other compounds. 2. To inlay a piece of wood.

graveyard shift. The 0000 to 0800 shift in a shipyard working three 8-hour shifts.

graveyard watch. The middle watch, midwatch, 0000 to 0400.

graving dock. A basin or a structure with a gate that can be pumped out. Originally used only for repair and maintenance, whereas a drydock was used for new construction; now the two terms are used interchangeably.

graving piece. A piece of wood fitted into a plank on a wooden ship to replace a knot or damaged wood.

gravity band. A band with a shackle fitted to the shank of an old-fashioned anchor near its center of gravity.

gravity davit. A mechanical holding and lowering device for ship's boats which depends on the force of gravity to roll the boat to the ship's edge where it can be lowered and raised by boat falls.

gravity waves. Waves actuated by gravity and inertia when the wave length is greater than 1.73 centimeters.

graybeard, grayback. A big, curling storm wave, especially when seen from a small boat.

grease ice. A sludge of ice crystals not yet formed into solid ice that reflects little light, thus having a matt or greasy appearance.

greaser. British term for maintenance mechanic on a merchant ship.

great circle. The circle formed by the intersection of the earth's surface with a plane through the earth's center. A great circle course is the shortest distance between places on the earth. A great circle chart showing these courses is used for great circle sailing. *See* rhumb line.

Greek Fire. A liquid charge made mostly from petroleum and thrown, after being lit, from tubes against ships. Developed in the Byzantine Empire in the 7th century A.D. and used with some success until gunpowder was invented.

Green Flash. A short, half to one second-long glimpse of bright green light seen on the upper edge of the sun as it drops below the horizon or when it rises. It is caused by the refraction of the different colors of light in different degrees. Green is seen last, or first at sunrise. Unusually clear weather is required to see this phenomenon.

greenheart. A strong and durable tropical wood used in shipbuilding. It is resistant to marine borers.

greenhorn. Originally a seaman's term for a landsman; a man new to the sea.

greenhouse effect. On or near the sea where a layer of fresh or low salinity water overlays denser, saltier water, the short wave-length radiation of the sun is absorbed in the lower, denser layer. The consequent radiation given off by this layer is far infra-red and cannot escape through the fresh water above. The result is a temperature rise in the water which under controlled conditions can nearly reach boiling and thus can provide energy for a low temperature turbine.

green turtle. A large, up to 200 pounds, herbiverous, deep sea turtle that was long hunted for its meat. Sailing ships often carried live turtles for fresh meat.

Greenwich hour angle. *See* hour angle.

Greenwich Mean Time (GMT). Mean solar time measured from the meridian, (longitude) of Greenwich, near London. *See* time. GMT is used for celestial navigation and, corrected by the zone description, for ship's time. *See* zone time.

gremlin. Surfer's name for the beach bums who give surfing a bad name and whose antics often lead to restrictive local ordinances against surfing.

greyhounding. The acrobatics preformed by some gamefish above the water when hooked.

gribble. An invertebrate, aquatic animal; any of 4000 species of isopods ranging from a quarter inch to a foot long that feeds on wood, including boats and docks; found in freshwater and saltwater from the shoreline to the sea bottom. Also known as sea roach.

grid navigation. A system of grid coordinates to be used in polar regions instead of latitude and longitude.

grilse. A young salmon as it returns from the sea to the river of its birth.

grinder. A large pedestal hand winch on a sailboat. Also the man who turns it.

gripe. *n* 1. A device for securing a boat in its davit or cradle. 2. In old wooden ships, the area near the junction of stem and keel as well as the curved timber joining keel and cutwater. *vb* 1. To gripe in means to haul in and secure a boat in its cradle or its shocks. 2. A sailboat is said to gripe when she tends to come into the wind, thus carrying weather helm.

grog. The traditional rum and water drink of seamen, still served in the Royal Navy. Slang for any alcoholic drink, particularly one made of rum.

groin. A jetty or pier of stone projecting out into the water to protect the beach or bank from erosion, or to direct the current and maintain a scoured channel. The large stones that face the waves are armor rocks and the core rock is made up of smaller pieces. British spelling is groyne. *See* jetty.

grommet. 1. In modern usage, a reinforced hole or eyelet such as in a sail, awning, or canvas bag to which a line can be made fast or rove through. 2. A word for gasket as well as for a ring of wire or rope made of a single strand laid up around its own part. 3. The wire or plastic ring supporting an officer's cap. *See* cringle.

gross form charter. Charter by which the owner pays all regular expenses for the voyage from the time the ship is first berthed until the cargo is discharged.

gross ton. *See* ton.

ground. 1. The floor of the sea; the bottom. A ship is said to run aground. 2. Good holding ground is a bottom that will hold an anchor. 3. A ship may take the ground when she touches the bottom at low water.

Ground Effects Machine (GEM). A vehicle supported above water by a blast of air forced downward, an air cushion. Also called an air cushion vehicle although the latest term is Surface Effect Ship (SES).

groundfish. Fish that live on the bottom of the ocean such as flounder, cod, and halibut. British word is whitefish. Also called demersal fish.

grounding. Any contact between a ship's hull and the bottom in which the ship comes to rest intentionally, accidentally, or purposefully. *See* stranding.

grounding clause. An exception to a marine insurance policy wherein grounding in certain rivers and canals is not be considered stranding.

grounding keels. False keels added to each side of the centerline (keel) to provide better weight distribution when the ship is resting on blocks in a drydock.

ground rope. A heavy rope, wire, or chain used at the bottom of a trawl or dragnet.

ground speed. Velocity in knots made good over the ground.

ground swell. Same as swell; not to be confused with ground wave.

ground tackle. The equipment used in achoring and mooring, including anchors, anchor chains, connecting shackles and links, swivels and stoppers, cable jacks, and mooring buoys.

ground wave. Part of a radio wave system that moves along the earth's surface instead of being projected upwards as a sky wave. Not a ground swell.

ground ways. In a ship-building slipway, the blocks and timbers on both sides of the keel that hold the ship up during construction and upon which she is launched when completed. Also called launching ways.

grouper. A sedentary and solitary fish of warm water, often very large, edible, curious, and slow, that lives near reefs and in underwater caves.

group flashing light. Navigational aid that shows groups of two or more flashes at regular intervals.

group occulting light. Navigational aid showing two or more eclipses at regular intervals; the dark periods, eclipses, being shorter than the lighted periods.

grow. An anchor cable was said to grow in the direction it was lying. Modern American usage is tend or lead.

growler. A piece of floating ice, smaller than a bergy-bit, that often appears green in color and barely shows above the water. It may originate from sea ice or glacier ice and presents a hazard to ships and especially smaller crafts because it is often difficult to detect by radar.

GRP. *See* fiberglass.

GRT. Gross Registered Tonnage. *See* tonnage.

grunt. A small, colorful, tropical fish found near reefs whose teeth when grinding, amplified by its air bladder, make a loud and distinctive noise.

guano. The excrement of coastal marine, fish-eating sea birds that is harvested as fertilizer, particularly off the coasts of Chile and Peru.

guard rail. A fence aboard ship, lighter than bulwarks, erected along the deck edge as a safety measure. Also a timber bolted fore-and-aft horizontally above the waterline and serving as a fender. In this sense, also called a fender guard, fender rail, belting, bull rail, or sheer rail.

gudgeon. A steel ring on the sternpost or rudderpost of a ship or boat into which the pins or pintles of the rudder fit, thus permitting rotation.

guess-warp. 1. A rope or line passed through a thimble on a boat boom that is made fast at one end on deck and hanging free when not in use. It is used for the convenience of boat crews in hauling out to the boom. **2.** A rope run along a ship's side as a grab line, guy rope, or to assist in towing astern. **3.** A line run out by boat to, for example, a buoy, wharf, dolphin, or bollard to assist in warping (moving) the ship. Also called a gueswarp, guess-rope, or guestwarp. The British spelling is guest-rope.

guest flag. Flag flown from the starboard side of a yacht to indicate that guests are aboard in the owner's absence. It is a rectangular blue flag with a white diagonal bar.

Guiana Current. A northward flowing ocean current off the northeast coast of South America that joins the North Equatorial Current to form the Caribbean Current, the start of the Gulf Stream System.

guillotine. A cable (chain) holding device; a hinged bar that can be made fast across the links.

Guinea Current. A branch of the Canary Current that turns southeast and then east at the Cape Verde Islands. *See* Canary Current.

gulf. A very large indentation of the coast line, larger than a bay, an area of water partly enclosed by land.

Gulf Stream System. In general terms, it is that ocean current system originating in the Caribbean with the Caribbean Current that flows through the Gulf of Mexico as the Yucatan Current and then the Florida Current passing Florida and north to be known as the Gulf Stream off Cape Hatteras. It then flows in a complex pattern generally northeast to become the North Atlantic Current off the Grand Banks. This relatively warm water divides as it approaches Great Britain and Ireland, with some water passing to the north of them and the other going south along the coasts of France and Portugal to form the Canary Current and join the North Equatorial Current and thus complete the cycle.

gulf weed. Any of the pelagic brown weeds, *Sargassum,* that float in and near the Gulf Stream. Common in large drifts in the Sargasso Sea.

gull. A gregarious, long-winged, web-footed sea bird of the family Laridae common to all waters and often found far inland; does not swim underwater and is often seen as a scavenger. Also an old word for wear, as a pin wears in a block causing the sheave to wobble.

gulleting. The part of the leading edge of a boats rudder near the pintles that is cut away to permit them to fit into the gudgeons.

gunboat. A relatively small, armed escort and general patrol warship.

gun captain. In the Navy, a petty officer in charge of a gun or gun mount. If in charge of a missile mount, he is a missile captain.

gundeck. U.S. Navy slang meaning to fake or falsify a report or other document.

gundelo or gundalow. An old rig of a lateen sail on a short mast, seen until recently on Arab dhows.

gunkholing. A yachtsman's word for cruising in sheltered waters, anchoring at night in a quiet cove or other protected anchorage known as a gunkhole.

gunport. The square hole in the side of a wooden sailing ship through which a gun was fired.

gun room. Old name for the junior naval officer's messroom.

gun salute. The blank rounds usually fired by the saluting gun of a warship as part of a ceremonial greeting or farewell to important people or as a mark of celebration such as on a national holiday.

gunstocking. A broad deck plank of teak or other hard wood inlaid at the curved ends of the deck planking.

gun tackle. Tackle with two single blocks.

gunter. The sliding topmast of the gunter rig, also the triangular sail spread in such a rig. Now rarely seen, the gunter rig is extended by a gunter yard secured to a short mast by two iron travellers, gunter irons, which hold the yard upright. A variation of this rig is the gunter lug, similar to a standing lug, very high in the peak with the yard nearly vertical.

guntline. *See* cantline.

gunwale. Upper edge of the side of a boat. Pronounced gunnel.

gurdy. A frictionless bearing or roller fitted into the gunwale of a boat to facilitate hauling in lines. Also called a line or trawl roller. A modern gurdy, common on commercial fishing vessels, is a powered reel used to haul troll lines. Also spelled gurdie.

gurry. The offal or waste after cleaning fish. Sometimes refers to bait stowed in a gurry pen or box.

gusset. A reinforcing or connecting steel plate of different shapes used in shipbuilding as a uniting and stiffening member where a gap in the plating exists.

gust. A sudden, brief increase in wind velocity. A wind may be described as blowing at 20 knots, gusting to 25. Gusts are momentary while squalls may last several minutes or longer. *See* flaw.

gut. Same as gat.

gutterway. Drainage gutter or waterway that runs fore-and-aft on the lowest deck of a trawler.

gybe. British spelling of jibe.

guy. Any line, rope, or wire used to hold, steady or support, for example, a boom, mast spar, or derrick. The particular name depends on its function such as forward guy, after guy, davit guy, boom guy, jib-boom guy, martingale guy, or travelling guy. Sometimes called a vang. *See* vang, lazy guy. The British use guy to describe a breast line which is a mooring line.

guyot. A flat-topped submarine mountain rising at least 1000 meters above the ocean floor. Also called a tablemount, which is now preferred.

gypsy. Same as gipsy.

gyre. A closed circulatory system, larger than a whirlpool or eddy, such as that involving ocean currents in the major oceans. The adjective is gyral.

gyrocompass. A modern ship's compass that uses a gyroscope.

gyroscope. A rapidly spinning device that maintains itself steady and level, and also aligns itself with the axis of the earth, thus pointing to true north. It is the basis for the gyrocompass now found on all modern ships.

gyro pilot. An automatic steering device using a gyrocompass on which a course can be set and automatically maintained. Also called an iron mike or a metal mike (slang).

gyro repeater. A direction indicator, fed from the master gyrocompass, located at the ship's wheel for the helmsman as well as on the wings of the bridge for taking bearings.

gyro stabilizer. Any mechanism using a gyro to establish a level platform or a level plane of reference.

H

H. International signal code alphabet flag. When hoisted singly means: "I have a pilot on board." Spoken: "hotel."

haar. A wet sea fog off the coast of Scotland and England; common in the summer.

hachures. Marks on charts indicating the direction and steepness of the coastal shore line.

hack chronometer or watch. The working timepiece used in taking sights for celestial navigation so as not to disturb and bring topside the major or standard chronometer. Frequent radio time signals now make elaborate combinations of watches and chronometers unnecessary.

hack, under. A naval officer confined to his quarters or room as punishment was said to be under hack or under hatches (slang).

hadal. Pertaining to the greatest depths of the ocean.

haddock. A food fish of the north Atlantic, similar to cod. When dried it is finan haddie, a popular smoked fish in Europe.

Hague Rules. An international agreement defining the minimum responsibilities and liabilities as well as the maximum rights and immunities of ocean shipping, particularly cargo carriers.

hail. 1. A ship was said to hail from a certain port. **2.** In the Navy, boats are hailed when they approach a ship at night in order to identify the passengers. **3.** To hail is to call out as in "boat ahoy."

hailing port. The port from which a ship or boat is registered or documented.

hake. A groundfish related to, but smaller than a cod, family Gadidae; once popular in Europe but now being caught in large numbers worldwide. Through a governmental ruling, hake may be sold as Pacific whitefish.

half model or half block model. A solid wooden ship model showing in outboard profile half of the hull form. Dozens may be seen in the famous model room of the New York Yacht Club.

half-breadth plan. A plan or top view drawing of half a ship divided along the keel line, the other half being identical. Part of the sheer draft.

half hitch. A knot formed by passing the end of a line around the standing part and bringing it up through the bight.

half mast. To fly a flag from the center rather than from the top of a mast is to half mast it. Colors are half masted as a sign of mourning. Also called half staff or at the dip.

half-rater. A class of small, sloop and fore-and-aft rigged open sail boats popular with yachtsmen and used at the U.S. Naval Academy for sail training.

half seas over. Well on the way to being drunk.

half sheave. A curved metal insert at the top of the mast of a small boat to provide a fairlead. Also called a dead sheave.

Halon. The trade name for a new, very fast and effective fire extinguishant used in boats.

halibut. Largest of the flat groundfish who swim on their sides, Genus *Hippoglossus*. A fine food fish of up to 300 pounds, common to northern waters.

halyard. Any line, rope, tackle, or wire used to raise and lower sails and flags. In many modern sailboats, the halyards are run inside the hollow mast and are known as internal halyards.

hambro line. British word for a small three-stranded rope used for lashing and lacing aboard a sailboat.

hamlet. An edible, brightly colored fish of the genus *Hypoplectrus*, common to the Caribbean reefs and south to Brazil.

hammerhead shark. Shark with a unique laterally expanded head, shaped much like a hammer; has been known to attack people, common in north Atlantic waters.

hammerlock moor. A procedure to reduce violent yawing or horsing of a ship at anchor in a strong wind. A second anchor is dropped when the vessel is at one end of a yaw, anchor cable is eased out and the ship or boat rides to two anchors.

hammock. The traditional sailor's bed, now rarely used, that is made of canvas and slung beneath the overhead of a compartment. Hammocks were hung by means of clews and stops, covered by hammock cloths, and stowed in hammock nettings.

hammock ladder. A non-existent item sometimes demanded of new men in the days of sail, just as new men aboard ship today may be asked to get a bucket of steam or a swab comb.

hamper. *See* top hamper.

hand. *n* A sailor or may be anyone aboard ship as in the expression "all hands." *vb* **1.** To take in, furl, or stow, such as a sail. **2.** To bear a hand is to hurry. **3.** To lend a hand means to assist.

hand hole. A small opening in a tank or boiler giving access for inspection and cleaning, and covered with a bolted plate.

hand lead. A sounding weight, 5 to 15 pounds, cast and retrieved by hand and used in comparatively shallow water; now largely replaced by the echo sounder.

hand-lining. Fishing with hand lines.

hand log. Same as chip log.

hand, reef, and steer. The traditional qualifications of an Able Seaman or **AB**.

handsomely. Carefully, deliberately as the helmsman may be told to change course handsomely.

handspike. A bar of wood or metal used as a lever for various shipboard purposes such as moving weights or turning a windlass. Now rare.

handy. Maneuverable, nimble, easy to handle, as a boat is said to be handy.

handy billy. Traditionally a portable, general purpose tackle such as a luff tackle once used aboard a sailing ship. Now refers to a portable, powered pump used to fight fires or to pump out flooded spaces aboard ship.

hanging five (ten). Riding a surfboard with all five (ten) toes curled over the edge of the board.

hanging keel. Same as bar keel.

hank. A metal or plastic ring, shackle or hook, often with a spring-loaded closure (a piston, plunger or snap) for securing the luff of a headsail to its stay. Sometimes called a clip.

happy hour. A convivial late afternoon period of relaxation aboard a yacht, at a bar, or a club when the drinks are reduced in price.

harbor. Any area of water, protected naturally or artificially, that provides shelter for a ship to anchor or moor and handle cargo.

hard. Part of a beach where the sand provides a firm surface. Also an adjective meaning full or extreme, as in hard right rudder or hard alee. To harden a sail is to trim it flat for going to windward.

hard chine. *See* chine.

hard lay. In making cordage, an angle of lay or twist greater than normal. Also called a short lay. A soft lay involves an angle less than average.

hard patch. *See* patch.

hardtack. An unleavened biscuit or bread made of flour and water; a durable ship's biscuit. Also known as sea biscuit or pilot bread. Normal soft bread is sometimes known as softtack.

hardwood. In the nautical sense, any timber from a tree having leaves instead of needles.

hare along. To sail fast down wind.

Harmattan. A dry and dusty, steady wind blowing off the Sahara across the Gulf of Guinea and the Cape Verde Islands.

harmonic analysis, tidal. A mathematical prediction of times and heights of tides from the duration and height of the solar and lunar tide-waves. *See* Indian tide-plane.

harness cask. In old sailing days, a keg of saltwater used to soak and soften the salted and dried beef called the salt horse.

harness, safety. Worn by all prudent sailors when topside at night or in heavy weather in a yacht or small fishing boat. Straps over the shoulder and around the chest are connected to a line with a snap hook to make fast to, for example, a lifeline, shroud, or stay.

harpoon. A spear, sometimes fired from a gun and having an explosive head, that is used in whaling and swordfishing.

Harrison cargo gear. A cargo handling system aboard ship and ship to shore using overhead cranes instead of the usual booms and winches.

hashmark. Slang for the stripe worn on the sleeve of a sailor in the U.S. Navy; shows years of service.

hatch, hatchway. Any opening in a ship's deck, usually rectangular, used for the passage of people and cargo. A cargo hatch is fitted with a hatch cover.

hatch beam. A steel support for hatch covers that fits into sockets on the inside of the coaming.

hatch book. Book prepared by the purser when underway that lists the cargo alphabetically by mark and shows place of stowage.

hatch boss. A supervisor or foreman of a group, a gang of longshoremen. In the United Kingdom, he is called a foreman stevedore.

hatch coaming. The steel rim built around a hatch to keep out water and provide a support for the hatch cover.

hatch cover. Traditionally a series of planks laid over hatch beams and covered by a tarpaulin secured in place by battens and wedges. Modern steel hatch covers fold or slide under power to open and close the hatch.

hatch hood. A removable canvas cover for companion hatchways.

hatch list. A record of the cargo loaded through a particular hatch.

hatchway. *See* hatch.

haul. 1. A proper nautical word for pull or drag as in "haul in the anchor." The hauling part of a tackle is the moving or free end in contrast to the standing part. **2.** When the wind changes direction clockwise, it hauls or veers. *See* back. **3.** A ship hauls up, off, or offshore meaning goes. **4.** A boat hauls out to the boat boom. **5.** To haul down a flag is to pull it down.

haul ashore. A British expression meaning to retire from the sea or to swallow the anchor.

hauling line. Old name for heaving line. Any line used to pass, for example tools aloft or to assist in handling mooring lines.

haul out. To take a boat out of the water, for example, for storage or repairs. *See* haul.

haven. An enclosed and protected harbor.

hawk. A multipronged device, similar to a grapnel, used at the end of a cable to recover a lost anchor or other heavy object on the bottom. Also a wind direction indicator at the top of a mast.

hawksbill turtle. A large sea turtle, weighing up to 150 pounds and long hunted for its shell, the source of commercial tortoise shell.

hawse. Part of the bow where the hawsepipes are located and through which the anchor chains pass. Also the space between the ship and the anchor when it is on the bottom. When a ship was moored to two anchors, she had a clear or open hawse if the two cables did not touch; otherwise she had a foul hawse if the chains crossed.

hawse buckler. The metal cover for the hawsepipe that keeps out the water.

hawsepipe. A metal cylinder leading down from the deck out to the bow plating through which the anchor chain passes. Often called hawse for short. Modern achors are housed and secured at the lower end of the hawsepipe.

hawser. Any large fiber or wire rope over five inches in diameter. In the United Kingdom, the word hawser means mooring line.

hawser-laid rope. Same as plain-laid or right-handed rope.

hawser rudder. A length of hawser streamed astern; used as a jury rudder by hauling on guys at its end run forward on each quarter. Not feasible today with modern, non-buoyant hawsers of wire or synthetic fiber.

hawsing. Driving home the caulking by striking a hawsing iron with a hawsing mallet or beetle; a two-man operation. Rare today.

head. 1. Foremost or projecting part, or the highest part, such as in the ship's head, pier head, rudder head, davit head, or head of a sail. 2. Toilet aboard ship. 3. The expanding seaward part of a rip current. 4. Down by the head describes a ship having more draft forward than aft. 5. Head on means bow to bow.

headboard. The fitting at the head of a triangular sail to which its halyard is made fast.

header. A wind shift in sailing that requires a course change away from the wind; opposite shift is lift.

headers. Reservoirs into which the tubes of a marine boiler or heat exchanger terminate.

headfish. Same as sunfish.

heading. The direction in which a ship is pointed; also known as the ship's head.

headland. A precipitous cape or promontory. Also called head.

headline. The floating line of a fish net. Also any mooring line leading from forward of a ship's pivot point.

headreach. The distance made to windward by a ship when tacking. Headreaching is sailing to windward, especially when leeway is minimum.

headroom. The distance in a ship or boat between the sole or deck and the overhead or deckhead.

headrope. Part of the boltrope sewn to the head of a sail.

headsail. Any sail forward of the most forward mast. Same as kite. *See* foresail.

headsheets. Sheets attached to the headsails.

headstay. In a small craft, the stay from the top of the forward mast to the top of the stem or to the bowsprit. In large sailing ships, it extends to the end of the jibboom. Often same as forestay.

headway. Forward movement of the ship through the water. The opposite is sternway or sternboard.

head wind or sea. Wind directly opposite to the course of the ship.

heart. A circular or heart-shaped wooden block used as a deadeye. Also a slack-twisted strand forming the core of a shroud-laid rope or the fiber rope in the center of a wire rope.

heave. 1. To draw, pull, or haul as on a rope. 2. To move into position as in "the ship hove in sight." 3. To rise and fall, the vertical bodily movement of a ship in a seaway; distinct from pitch. 4. "Heave out and lash up" was an order given to men in their hammocks. 5. To heave the lead is to cast it and take a sounding with a hand lead.

heave down. Same as careen.

heaver. A short tool or bar used for tightening line, as well as when splicing.

heave short. To haul in on the anchor chain until the anchor is at short stay, just short of breaking ground. A preparation for getting underway.

heave to. In very heavy weather, a ship often chooses to reduce speed to that needed to hold her bows up to the sea; for a sailing ship, minimum storm canvas is set and in a steamer, the engines are slowed to maintain bare steerageway. At this point, a ship is hove to or lying to. At normal sea conditions, a ship may heave to for inspection or to lower a boat when she also slows to bare steerageway and may be said to have rounded to.

heaving line. A light line weighed down with a monkey fist and thrown across from the ship to the pier or to another ship when going alongside. A messenger is attached and the mooring line is then pulled across. If weather or timid ship handling require the use of a line-throwing gun or bolo, the messenger is made fast to this light line.

heavy. Describes a rough sea. In a storm, a ship may be said to be making heavy weather of it. A top heavy ship is one unstable because its weight is mostly topside.

heavy cruiser. A large gun and missile carrying warship, smaller than an aircraft carrier but larger than a destroyer; usually equipped with helicopters and capable of speeds of over 30 knots.

heavy lift. Describes a ship especially equipped to handle large and heavy items of cargo.

hectocotylus. The arm of a male cephalopod (octopus, squid, or cuttlefish); used as his sexual organ in penetrating the female.

heel. The temporary inclination or leaning of a ship to port or starboard caused by wind and sea or by the inertia of a ship that heels in a high speed turn. It is a dynamic condition and not static as list; not to be confused with rolling. Also the lower end of a mast or boom. *See* list.

heel and toe. One after the other as in a heel and toe watch which is watch on and watch off. Also called watch and watch.

heel block. Block acting as a fair lead to a winch at the lower end of a cargo boom.

heeling error. Part of the deviation or magnetic compass error due to the motion of a ship in departing from an even keel; corrected by heeling magnets.

heeling magnets. Vertical magnetized iron bars placed in the compass binnacle.

heeling tanks. Tanks built into some ice breakers in order to induce a rolling motion to help break free of ice.

heel piece. A steel angle bar used as a connecting piece for two larger angle bars. Also called a frame butt strap or heel bar.

heel rope or lashing. Any line made fast to the heel or end of a boom, spar, or other object.

heel tackle. Tackle used for holding in position the heels of sheer legs or similar gear.

height of eye. A consideration in measuring the altitude of a celestial body. It is the distance above the water of the observer's eye. A table in the Nautical Almanac is used to correct a sextant altitude for height of eye.

heliocentric. Concentric with the sun, a word used to describe a celestial body's position. Heliocentric latitude is its angular distance north or south of the plane of the ecliptic as seen from the sun's center. The corresponding angle east or west is heliocentric longitude.

helm. Normally means the tiller or wheel but sometimes it includes the whole steering gear with the rudder. In powered vessels, orders to the helm or helmsman are now always given in terms of right or left, not starboard or port and indicate the direction which the ship's head will take. In sailing ships or boats, the helm is still put up to windward or down to leeward. A sailing vessel may carry lee or weather helm while a steamship carries right or left rudder. Shift the helm and ease the helm are the same as shift or ease the rudder.

helmsman. A seaman or petty officer who steers the ship upon orders of the conning officer. Also called a steersman.

hemp. A plant of the genus *Cannabis* that produces natural fiber for rope as well as certain narcotics. Now largely replaced by synthetic fibers.

hennequen. The plant from which a natural rope fiber, sisal is obtained.

herd. Sometimes applies to marine mammals when the group is larger than a pod.

hermaphrodite brig. *See* brigantine.

hero platform. Platform rigged out over the deck edge of a ship, such as on an oceanographic research ship that is used to simplify the lowering of instruments.

Herreshoff anchor. An improved model of the old-fashioned anchor having a movable stock for easier stowage.

herring. A small, prolific, popular food fish, *Clupea harengus,* found in North Atlantic waters. Other similar fish such as alewives, menhaden, sardines, pilchard, and sprat are often called herring.

herring drifter. A small trawler that sets out herring nets and then drifts to leeward of them. Common near the British Isles.

Highfield lever. A handle situated where the running backstay is secured to the deck; used to quickly slack or pull taut the backstay when tacking and thereby change the direction of stress on the mast. Also hyfield lever.

highline. A simple rig for transferring personnel and light freight between ships underway; the procedure is called highlining.

high pressure area. An air mass of high atmospheric pressure that helps govern the weather at sea. In this area, the wind blows clockwise in the northern hemisphere and counter-clockwise in the southern. Also called an anticyclone.

high seas. All of the ocean outside of territorial waters. *See* territorial waters. Also a term describing wind driven storm waves, 15-25 feet high. *See* sea.

high water. The maximum height of a rising tide. High water is a better nautical expression than high tide.

hike, hiking. To lean out on the gunwale of a sailboat, thereby counteracting the excessive heeling. In maximum hiking, a crewman swings out in a strap supported by a wire or trapeze secured at the masthead. British term is sit out and use a toe strap.

hiking seats and straps. Seats and straps often rigged to assist and magnify the effort of hiking.

hiking stick. A stick attached to the tiller to permit the helmsman to hike out.

hipping. Increasing the beam of a wooden hull by adding wood on the outside. Rare today.

hiring hall. A union procedure that provides seamen for merchant ships. The ships state their needs and the men are assigned in the hiring hall.

hitch. A knot whose loops normally jam together under strain yet remain separable when strain is removed. *See* knot.

HMS. His or Her Majesty's Ship; initials used before the name of a Royal Navy ship.

HO. Hydrographic Office of the U.S. Navy, now part of the Defense Mapping Agency Hydrographic Center.

hobbler or hobbling pilot. British term for an unlicensed pilot with sufficient local knowledge to be useful.

hobbyhorsing. Excessive pitching into a head sea, a common problem to small yachts; reduces speed and tortures crew.

hobgob. British word for a confused, choppy sea where reflected or joining waves of different wave trains meet.

hockle. Yachtsmen's slang for a kink in a line or wire.

Hoey. *See* protractor.

hog. *n* An obsolete device made of brushes and timbers that was used to clean the hull of a ship by dragging it along the bottom of the ship. *vb* A ship hogs when the bow and stern droop below the level of amidships; opposite to sag.

hogging line. Line passed under the ship as on a collision mat and secured again at the opposite side.

Hog Islander. A mass-produced cargo ship of World War I.

hog-piece. A fore-and-aft plank or timber bolted to the inside top of the keel of a small boat.

hogshead. A large cask or barrel holding 63 U.S. gallons, 52.5 Imperial gallons, or 238.5 liters.

hoist. *n* 1. The vertical side of a flag nearest the halyard to which it is bent. 2. The quantity of cargo hoisted out in one sling load; more commonly a draft. 3. A tackle used for lifting something. *vb* 1. To raise or lift. 2. To hoist in a boat means to hook on, raise, and stow it. Hoist out is the reverse process.

hoist, flag. A group of signal flags flown together in a single vertical line making up a signal or message.

hoisting eye or ring. Ring secured to a hoisting pad.

hoisting pad. A steel fitting bolted to the boat fore-and-aft; used for hoisting purposes.

hoke valve. Valve in a deep-diving recirculating helmet that permits the gas mixture the diver breathes to go into a canister for purification.

hold. The major subdivision or compartment of a cargo ship in which cargo is stowed and numbered from forward aft. Some related terms include hold crew, hold boss, hold ladder, batten, and beam. The undefined area between holds where cargo can be stowed is called no-man's land.

holdfast. The giant kelp's root-like tentacle by which it anchors to the bottom. A favorite food of the sea urchin whose excessive numbers threaten the kelp beds when their natural enemies and predators, the sea otter in the Pacific and the lobster in the Atlantic, decline in numbers.

holding ground. A classification of the bottom as to its anchor holding properties; termed good, fair, or poor.

holding tank. Any tank aboard ship or boat designed to hold, for example, sewage or contaminated water until discharge ashore.

hold water. A command to oarsmen to immerse oar blades and hold steady in order to stop the boat or just break the headway.

holiday. Nautical term for any accidentally neglected, unpainted, or unscrubbed area on the deck or bulkhead.

hollow sea. An uncommonly used British word for a very steep and dangerous sea, usually caused by tide against wind and producing waves with concave fronts.

holystone. A piece of soft stone with a hole in it for the end of a swab handle; used with sand and water to clean wooden decks. Also called a bible.

home. In the direction of the ship or where it should come to rest, such as the anchor comes home when it is hauled in or when one pulls home a sail by hauling on its halyard.

home port. For a vessel in the U.S. Navy, the port where the ship is based and where the families live. For a private yacht or vessel, the port designated by the owner and approved by the appropriate documentation office. Place where all the ship's papers and documents are recorded; the vessel's port of registry.

homeward bound pennant. A long narrow pennant flown by Naval ships after being abroad more than a year. The British equivalent is paying off pennant.

homeward bound stitches. Extra long stitches made in canvas, to get the job done sooner.

honey barge. Slang for garbage scow.

honor policy. Same as wager policy, a marine insurance term.

hood. Any canvas or metal cover as a hatch hood or a brass binnacle hood.

hood seal. A large North Atlantic seal marked by an inflatable sac for protecting its head.

hook. 1. Any bent piece of steel used for a specific purpose such as a fishhook, chain hook, cargo hook, and swivel hook. **2.** A spit of land or a narrow cape whose ends curve inward as does Sandy Hook, New Jersey.

hook, mud. Slang for anchor.

hook rope. A special line and hook used in clearing a foul hawse (untangling an anchor chain).

hook, snap. A hook that has a spring snap to close it.

hoop. A movable ring of wood or metal to which the luff of the sail is fastened and which slides up and down the mast. Replaced in most sailboats by slides that move in a track.

hope in heaven. A light sail carried aloft in fair weather in a square-rigger. *See* kites.

hopper barge. Barge used to receive mud and sand (spoil) removed from the bottom by a dredge. Also a double-hulled barge used to carry bulk cargo, either open or decked over.

hopper dredge. A dredge that incorporates a compartment to take the spoil.

horizon. The apparent intersection of sea and sky known as the apparent or visible horizon. For celestial navigation, the horizon is a plane passing through the center of the earth and perpendicular to a line connecting the observer's position and the earth's center.

horn. *n* **1.** One of the side pieces that forms the jaw of a gaff. **2.** The outer end of a crosstree or one of the arms of a cleat. **3.** A noise making device. *See* fog signal. **4.** A projecting fitting on the stern of some vessels that holds and supports the rudder. *vb* In shipbuilding, to align the frames and bulkheads square with the keel is to horn them.

horn cleat. Cleat with a single projecting piece or horn about which a line can be made fast. *See* cleat.

hornpipe. Originally a wind instrument of Welsh origin which gave its name to the traditional sailor's dance.

horn timber. A center-line timber that forms the backbone of the stern section of a wooden ship.

horse. 1. In a sailboat, any rope or bar on which something slides as the bar or traveler placed athwartships on which the main sheet slides when coming about. In square-riggers, it was an iron bar between the fife rail stanchions to which the lead blocks were made fast. **2.** The footrope supported by stirrups under the yard of a square-rigger. **3.** A pattern of a curved area as made from a mold-loft drawing in shipbuilding.

horse mackerel. Another name for the large mature bluefin tuna.

horse latitudes. Areas of high atmospheric pressure just north of the northeast Trade Winds in the northern hemisphere and south of the southeast Trade Winds in the southern hemisphere, at about 30° latitude. They are marked by light winds and calms, especially in the summer. *See* doldrums.

horseshoe crab. A fairly large round marine arthropod with a stiff pointed tail found on sandy beaches of eastern North America. Not edible.

horsing. A corruption of hawsing; the sometimes violent swinging of a ship at anchor in a strong wind. Same as sluing or slewing.

hose. Aboard ship fire hoses are coiled against the bulkhead ready for use and wash-deck hoses are broken out topside to wash down the decks. Special heavy hoses are used in fueling ship and are handled on tankers by hose davits.

hose testing. The testing of the water tightness of riveted joints in shipbuilding by spraying water from a hose at a 30 pounds per square inch pressure.

hospital ship. A floating hospital that by international agreement is always free from attack and must treat the wounded of all belligerents. Hospital ships are generally exempt from tolls, taxes, and pilotage.

hotchpot. A word used in admiralty law to describe the collective sum of all damage costs resulting from a collision in which both parties share the guilt.

hot dog. To perform tricks and do trick riding on a surfboard.

hotwell. Part of a marine condenser in which the condensed water is collected.

houndband. The ring around the upper mast used for attaching the shrouds.

hounding. Part of the mast below the hounds.

hounds. 1. Traditionally the projections or wooden blocks at the side of a mast supporting the trestletrees. 2. Hounds of the rigging are the eyes of the shrouds as they pass over the trestletrees. 3. In modern yachts, the point where the shrouds and the spreaders meet the mast. 4. The point on the mast where the jib halyard block is made fast.

hour angle. Arc in degrees on the equinoctial marked by the observer's meridian and the hour circle of the celestial body. The Greenwich hour angle is the angle or arc measured from Greenwich at longitude $0°$ west to the longitude of the celestial body.

hour circle. The projection of a meridian or line of longitude upon the celestial sphere.

hour glass. Same as sand glass.

house. *n* A structure on deck or a compartment topside such as the cook house, chart house, or pilot house. *vb* 1. To house (pronounced houz) something is to bring it down from aloft such as a topmast or to store it or put it away. 2. Housing an awning is to pull its stops down and secure them to the rail or housing line. 3. An anchor is housed when it is secured up into the hawse.

houseboat. Boat designed for living aboard in sheltered waters although modern houseboats are often seaworthy enough to cruise in the summer in waters such as the Caribbean and the Adriatic.

housefall. A cargo handling system in which power is applied only at the ship end. A line is then rove through a block rigged ashore or on another ship.

house flag. The distinguishing flag of a shipping company flown at sea from the mainmast.

houseline. A three-threaded tarred cord spun from left to right and laid from right to left; stronger than marline and smaller than roundline. Now replaced largely by synthetic small stuff, much stronger, more durable, and free of tar.

housing line. The middle of the three lifelines of U.S. warships and some merchant ships. The top line is the lifeline and the bottom, the footline. In old sailing ships, the housing line was used when housing the awning.

housing chain stopper. A length of chain fitted with a turnbuckle, one end secured to the deck and the other fitted with a pelican hook that seizes the chain of the anchor and holds the anchor up snug into the hawse. Sometimes the turnbuckle is made fast directly to the deck.

hove. The past participle of heave, as in the ship hove in sight or the line was hove taut. Hove to is the same as lay to.

Hovercraft. Trade name for the original, successful British air cushion vehicle that moves over land and water on a cushion of air. Also known as a Ground Effect Machine or, more currently, a Surface Effect Ship (SES).

hoy. Once a decked sailing vessel under various rigs used on the north European coast for passengers and cargo. Now a lighter or barge for heavy cargo. A word rarely used in the U.S..

hub. The central part of a ship's propeller to which the blades are attached and which keys onto the propeller shaft.

Huelett unloader. A complex and rapid ore handling system for loading and unloading that involves movable gantries, clamshell buckets, and chutes.

hug. Keep close to, as a ship hugs the shore or, in sailing, she hugs the wind.

hulk. Generally a bare hull, unfit for sea, used as storage in port.

hull. The body of a ship. A ship is said to be hulled when its skin is pierced by a projectile, a rock, etc. *See* displacement hull, vee-bottom hull, planing hull.

hull balance. A characteristic of good sailboat design that ensures no excessive pull to the right or left when the sailboat is heeled over to the wind.

hull down. Said of a ship seen over the horizon with just her top hamper showing. If seen on the horizon with the hull showing, she can be said to be hull up.

hull girder. The collective term for the longitudinal strength members of a ship considered as a single girder in hull strength calculations.

hulling. *See* ahull.

hull speed. Speed for which a ship's or boat's hull is designed as the effective maximum speed.

Humboldt Current. Another and less accurate name for the Peru Current.

hummock. A ridge or mound of sea ice caused by pressure.

hunt. The oscillation around mid-point of an instrument such as a gyrocompass.

hurdy-gurdy. A hand windlass or crank and drum used by fishermen in taking in trawl lines.

hurricane. The Atlantic, Caribbean and eastern Pacific word for a cyclone or typhoon; a very strong and dangerous tropical storm of devastating power. Any storm at sea with a wind velocity of over 65 knots.

hurricane deck. The upper deck in a passenger ship.

hurricane lamp. Lamp designed for use in a storm emergency.

Hurricane Warning. An official notification from the National Weather Service (NWS) that a hurricane is expected in a specified area within 24 hours. *See* storm warning.

Hurricane Watch. A warning by the National Weather Service (NWS) that a hurricane is possible in a specified area at an indicated time.

husband, ship's. An old-fashioned British term for a person responsible for the management of a ship on behalf of the owners. His pay or commission is known as husbandage.

hydraulic current. Current flowing through a narrow passage joining two bodies of water which have different times and ranges of high and low waters.

hydrofoil. A high speed vessel partly lifted over the water surface by submerged foils acting in a similar fashion to airplane wings that provide lift in the air. Modern hydrofoils use movable rather than fixed foils and can thus adjust the lift to permit high speed and comfort in moderately rough waters.

hydrography. In a restrictive sense, the science of determining the condition of navigable waters as an assistance to navigators. In its broad and modern sense, the scientific analysis of the physical characteristics of the world's waters. *See* oceanography.

hydroplane. A fast boat in which the hull has steps to lift most of it above water when it reaches the required speed. At this point the boat is planing or on the step. A boat that does not plane is a displacement hull.

hydroplot. An integrated, very accurate ship's positioning system using all navigational aids, especially electronic ones; specially suitable for cableship operations.

hydrostatic pressure. Pressure at a given depth due to the weight of the water; normally measured in pounds per square inch.

hyfield lever. Same as Highfield lever.

hygrometer. *See* psychrometer.

hypoxia. Diver's word for shortage of oxygen.

hypoplankton. Plankton living below 1 000 fathoms. *See* plankton.

I

I. International signal code alphabet flag. When flown singly means: "I am altering my course to port". Also called the interrogatory flag. Spoken: "india".

IALA. Internatinal Association of Lighthouse Authorities.

ice anchor or hook. A special stockless, single-fluke hook used to hold a ship close to the edge of the ice; often just a piece of timber frozen into the ice to which a ship's line can be made fast. *See* anchor ice.

iceberg. A large floating mass of ice that has broken off or calved from a glacier in the Arctic or from the great ice shelf in the Antarctic. An iceberg or berg is over five meters above sea level; smaller masses are called bergy bits or growlers.

ice blink. The reflection in the sky of the sunlight's glare on the ice. Also known as ice sky. *See* blink.

icebreaker. A powerful ship of solid construction designed to move in sea ice and open the way for other vessels. Its spoon bow allows it to ride up on the ice and break it.

ice field. An area of sea ice more than 10 kilometers across or one whose limits cannot be seen from the crow's nest. *See* floe.

ice floe. *See* floe.

ice fog. A type of fog composed of ice crystals occurring at very low temperatures in clear, calm weather at high latitudes.

ice foot. Sea ice frozen to the shore at the high tide line and unaffected by tides. Known under various local names, it is formed by the freezing of ebb tide waters and spray, and separated from floating sea ice by a tide crack.

ice lead. A passage of open water through the ice.

ice pack. *See* pack ice.

ice rafting. The transportation of rock fragments and sediment by floating ice.

ice rind. A thin elastic shining crust of ice formed by the freezing of slush or sludge on a quiet sea surface.

ice shelf. A thick ice formation with a fairly level surface fastened to the shore and often reaching the bottom. Usually an extension of land ice, it may grow hundreds of miles out to sea where its front floats freely. The calving of an ice shelf forms tabular icebergs and ice islands.

ice yowling. A long, high pitched sound heard during the formation of contraction cracks in the ice.

ichthyology. The study of fish.

idler. A Naval idiom for a man who does not stand night watches because of his demanding duties during the day, such as the ship's cooks or messmen. The British word is dayman.

IHO. International Hydrographic Organization.

IMCO. International Maritime Consultive Organization; part of the United Nations.

immersion. *See* tons per inch immersion.

impeller log. Log that uses a propeller to generate an electric current with a frequency that is a direct measure of the ship's speed.

inboard. Inward, towards the center of the ship, as opposed to outboard which means away from the center or outward.

inboard-outboard. Another name for stern drive; also outboard-inboard.

Inchmaree clause. In marine insurance, the clause stating that damage to the machinery of a ship caused by the negligence of the crew is not a maritime peril and owners are not covered under a standard policy. Also called the negligence clause.

inclining experiment. A shipyard test of a ship's stability that is done by shifting weights to cause a list and thereby obtain an angle of heel. The metacentric height or degree of stability can then be calculated.

inclinometer. An instrument using a bubble or a pendulum to measure the angle of roll or list of a ship. Same as clinometer.

index arm or bar. The movable part of a sextant carrying the index mirror or index glass which indicates degrees of arc or angle. *See* sextant.

index error. A constant error in the angle measured by a sextant due to the horizon and the index glass not being parallel when the pointer on the vernier scale indicates zero. *See* sextant.

indiaman. Sometimes applies to any ship sailing in the western Pacific trade but in a more restricted meaning one of the sailing ships once owned by the East India Company.

Indian Ocean. Now considered to be the waters bounded by Antarctica, Asia, Australia, and Africa.

Indian tide plane. A reference level or datum computed by harmonic analysis and used on British charts in coastal areas where the diurnal inequality is considerable. Also called Indian spring low water and harmonic tide-plane.

inertial navigation. Navigation by using the inert or stable properties of a gyroscope, measuring and converting minute components of acceleration into course and distance from a known point of departure. *See* Ship's Inertial Navigation System.

inference. *See* general inference.

Inglefield anchor. A stockless, double-fluked anchor whose arms can rotate separately up to 45 degrees from the shank.

Inglefield clips. British interlocking C-shaped metal hooks whose tension keeps them closed when used to connect lines or gear such as signal flags to their halyards. The U.S. snap shackle or hook that has a spring-loaded closing piece has a similar use.

inhaul. Any line or rope used to pull something towards the ship in contrast to an outhaul.

inherent vice. An expression used in marine insurance to describe a particular cargo that is difficult or dangerous to handle such as goods that can ignite spontaneously or spoil without cause.

in irons. Said of a sailboat that when tacking cannot get through the wind and thus fill its sails on the new tack. She is said to have missed stays. Also applies to a tug that cannot move freely because of the way it is made fast to another ship.

injector. A device using a jet of steam to force water into a ship's boiler.

Inland Rules of the Road. The International Rules now do not apply to harbors, rivers, lakes and other inland waters of the U.S.. Among the special rules that do apply are the Inland Rules (Title 33 of the U.S. Code), Pilot Rules, Great Lakes Rules, Pilot Rules for the Great Lakes, Western Rivers Rules, the Motorboat Act of 1940, and Army Corps of Engineers Rules. Most foreign countries also have special regulations effective in their inland waters.

Inland Waters. The areas shown on most coastal and harbor charts, in which the Inland Rules of the Road apply. Inland waters are those inland of a line roughly parallel to the coast drawn through the outermost aids to navigation such as buoys. Not to be confused with territorial waters.

inlet. A relatively short narrow waterway connecting one body of water with another or merely extending inland from the sea or other body of water.

inner space. An informal term for the depths of the sea about which we know so little and where current research and exploration goes on.

in ordinary. A ship not in commission and maintained in reserve by a skeleton crew is so classified. Not a U.S. Naval term.

INS. Integrated Navigation System.

inshore. Close to the coast, as opposed to offshore. It describes, for example, fisheries, currents and navigation all near land; same as nearshore. *See* nearshore current system.

in stays. While tacking, a sailing vessel is in stays momentarily when sails are flapping prior to the boat falling off and the sails filling. If she cannot get her bow through the wind and fill out her sails on a new tack, she is said to be in irons.

Integrated Navigation System (INS). A Ships Inertial Navigation System plus an automatic star tracker with associated gear used in space vehicle tracking by NASA range instrumentation ships.

intercardinal points. Northeast, southeast, southwest and northwest, the four points on the compass in between the cardinal points.

intercept. Used in celestial navigation; the difference between the observed and the calculated zenith distances of a celestial body. Its determination leads to plotting a line of position.

intercoastal. In U.S. shipping terms refers to traffic between the Atlantic and the Pacific or between different coastal ports on the same coast. The Intercoastal Waterway is a series of canals, bays, rivers, and inlets that provide an inside sheltered passage from New England to Florida.

intercostal. A general shipbuilding word describing the structural members that fit between other larger ones and are not continuous.

Intergovernmental Maritime Consultive Organization (IMCO). A United Nations agency concerned with maritime matters such as a new tonnage mark system to ensure standard tonnage measurement for the world's merchant ships and ship routing procedures for ships at sea. *See* tonnage mark.

interlock. A safety device that cuts off the electricity when the door or cover of an instrument such as a radar is removed. Particularly important in a ship where the steel deck forms a perfect ground and electric shock hazard is great.

intermediate ship. Any vessel carrying both cargo and passengers (more than 12).

internal waves. Waves formed beneath the surface at the boundaries between waters of different densities. There are short internal waves that produce the dead water effect as well as long ones that occur everywhere to some degree wherever water densities vary. Also known as boundary waves.

International Association of Lighthouse Authorities (IALA). An organization representing the major maritime powers. Now engaged in devising and promoting world-wide uniform systems of buoyage. *See* System A, B.

International Code of Signals. A universal system of communication at sea using flags, light displays, or flashing light transmissions of code. A multilingual signal book, first printed in 1902, explains the 40 flags and pennants.

International date line. *See* date line.

International Hydrographic Organization (IHO). An organization based in Monaco comprising over 40 member states. It is engaged in vital world-wide hydrographic study, research, coordination and services.

International Ice Patrol. Patrol made by the U.S. Coast Guard with its ships and aircraft under international agreement and funding to protect north Atlantic shipping from icebergs.

International Load Line Certificate. Certificate required of all cargo and passenger carrying ships over 150 tons showing permissible loading under various conditions; issued by governments and the classification societies.

International Low Water (ILW). A datum or reference plane below mean sea level calculated by multiplying half the range between mean lower low water and mean higher high water by 1.5.

International Maritime Law. A code or system of rules which civilized maritime states agree upon relating to maritime operations, public and private. It is assisted by an International Maritime Committee in attaining uniformity and effectiveness.

International Offshore Rule (IOR). The regulations issued by the International Yacht Racing Union by which ocean racing sailboats are measured and rated in order to provide equitable handicaps.

international radio silence. Three minute periods of silence on the distress frequency starting 15 minutes and 45 minutes after each hour so that ships in distress may be heard.

International Regulations for Preventing Collisions at Sea. Commonly known as the Rules of the Road; last revised in 1972 and ratified by Congress for U.S. ships in 1977. Short title, 72 Colregs.

International Rules of the Road. *See* International Regulations for Preventing Collisions at Sea.

International waters. Waters outside territorial limits, thus outside the jurisdiction of any country, generally considered to be three miles. Some countries, including the U.S., claim jurisdiction over fishing out to 200 miles.

International Weather Code. A five-figure group of numbers used by ships at sea as well as shore stations in reporting and in receiving weather data.

International Yacht Racing Union (IYRU). The governing body of all international yacht racing that administers racing rules such as the International Offshore Rule.

interrupted quick-flashing light (i. qk. fl.). A navigational light showing a number of quick flashes followed by a period of darkness.

intertidal. Pertains to the zone of the seashore between low and high water. *See* littoral.

inversion. A weather condition common to the west coast of temperate zone land masses; important to seamen as it causes heavy fog. For example, in California, cold air is blown onto the coast by the prevailing westerly winds thus displacing the warm air along the coast and causing the temperature gradient of the air to be inverted.

inwale. A piece of wood fastened inside the frame of an open wooden boat along the top strake of planking. If outside the gunwale, it is an outwale.

inward. Towards the land, as inward bound. Thus inward charges are levied on a ship entering port who must also get an inward clearance and must provide an inward manifest.

I/O. Inboard/outboard. *See* sterndrive.

IOR. International Offshore Rule.

Irish moss. A brown edible seaweed, *Chondrus cispus,* found in Europe and North America and harvested as a source of carrageenin, a colloidal material used as a food and drug emulsifier and thickener.

Irish horse. In the days of sail, described as especially tough salted beef known as salt horse.

Irish hurricane. A jocular term among ancient mariners for a flat calm.

Irish pennant. Any loose, unsightly rope or line aloft or on deck which should be secured, stowed, or made fast. Also called a deadman.

Irish splice. In the days of sail, a quick way to shorten a line by twisting it.

Irminger Current. One of the terminal branches of the Gulf Stream System flowing west off the south coast of Iceland.

ironbound. Describes a coast with no shelters or anchorages.

ironclad. The first armored ships made of wood and covered with iron plates.

iron mike. Slang for the gyro automatic pilot. Also called metal mike.

irons. Sharp steel hand tools used in traditional wooden ship building that include making, spike, crooked, rimming, fleeting, and reef irons. *See* in irons.

iron-sick. An old sailor's description of a wooden ship whose iron fastenings had corroded and loosened. Term rarely used today.

isallobars. Lines of equal change of barometric pressure of a cyclone during a standard interval, often plotted to show the direction of travel and the estimated rate of advance of the disturbance.

Isherwood system. In steel ship construction, a method of longitudinal framing instead of the traditional transverse framing.

island. Any land completely surrounded by water. Also any raised superstructure above the main deck, a castle or a poop, such as on an aircraft carrier.

islet. A small island.

isobar. A line on a weather chart showing equal atmospheric pressures.

isobath. A line on a bathymetric chart showing equal depths.

isogon. A line on a chart connecting points or places of the same magnetic variations.

isohaline. Describes two or more sea areas having equal salinity.

isophase. Describes a flashing aid to navigation with equal periods of light and darkness.

isopleuth. Describes a condition of equal wave height.

isotach. Descirbes a condition of equal current velocity.

isotherm. A line on a chart connecting areas of the same water temperature.

isthmus. A narrow neck of land joining two land masses.

IYRU. International Yacht Racing Union.

J

J. International signal code alphabet flag. When hoisted single means: "I am on fire and have dangerous cargo on board. Keep well clear of me." Spoken: "juliett."

jack. *n* 1. Short for the Union Jack flown at the bow of a warship at anchor. 2. A mast funnel. 3. A local name for the fish pompano. 4. Short for telephone jack or plug, or for cable jack. *vb* To jack over the main engines is to turn them over with jacking gear.

jackass. Any device or cover that keeps water out of the hawseholes and hawsepipes.

jackass rig. Any rig of a sailing ship that differs from the usual, such as a jackass bark or a jackass brig. Now used to describe any unseamen-like, confusing arrangement of gear aboard ship.

jack block. Block kept aloft for hoisting and lowering top gallant yards in a square-rigger.

jackbox. Receptacle into which telephone plugs or jacks are fitted.

jack crosstrees. Single iron crosstrees at the head of the topgallant mast used for spreading the royal shrouds in a square-rigger.

jack-in-a-basket. A cylindrical daymarker made of vertical slats mounted on a pole and used to mark a shoal or the edge of the channel.

jacking gear. A device that rotates the propeller shaft slowly and in turn rotates the turbines to ensure an even heat distribution when starting up the engines or when they are temporarily stopped.

jack lines, rods, ropes, yards. Depending on local usage, the various pieces of used for special purposes aboard ship.

Jack-of-the-Dust. In the U.S. Navy, the man in charge of the food issue room aboard ship. British equivalent is Dusty Jack.

jack pin. A belaying pin.

jack rod. A length of metal rod or small pipe welded to the ship's structure to which, for example, awnings, weather cloths, and canvas covers are made fast. Also called a jackstay.

jackrope. A line used to secure the foot of a sail to its boom.

jackscrew. A device using a large screw to apply force or pressure, such as to lift a weight or to stow baled cargo more compactly.

jackstaff. A short flagpole in the extreme forward part of the bow from which the Jack or Union Jack is flown.

jackstay. Wire or rope used aboard ship for a wide variety of purposes such as supporting a sail, an awning, a number of seabags, the throat of a gaff sail, or passed to a wreck to take off people.

jackup rig. An offshore oil rig or platform held in position by a submerged mat above which the platform is jacked up or raised above the water on supporting legs.

jackyard. Any extension of a yard, gaff, or spar; mainly used to enlarge the size of a sail set as a topsail.

jacobs ladder. A portable rope ladder with wooden rungs slung from a boat boom or over the side for temporary embarkation such as when a pilot is coming aboard. Also called a pilot ladder or jack ladder and, less accurately, a sea ladder. *See* ladder.

jaeger. A swift, gull-like seabird of the genus *Stercorarius* that snatches food from other birds. Often confused with the skua.

jag. *n* A short pull or tug as in the expression "take a jag on that jib sheet." *vb* 1. To lay out a rope or chain in loops and to secure it with stops. 2. To caulk a seam in a steel plate or a leaky rivet.

jam or jamb cleat. Traditionally a steel or wooden block secured to the ship's side and used to hold a supporting shore timber just prior to launching. Jam cleats are now popular on sailing yachts since they are designed to hold a line but will release it quickly when necessary.

Jamie Green or Jimmy Green. A light sail often rigged below the bowsprit of a clipper ship.

jamming fiddle block. Block whose slot design allows self cleating or holding action; usually used with vangs.

jamoke. A U.S. Navy slang word for coffee; now replaced for the most part by Joe.

Japan Current. Same as Kuroshiwo.

jason clause. Part of a voyage charter party that concerns the shipowner's right to recover from the cargo owner his share of the general charges in the event of a casualty or accident.

Jaunty. The British term for the Master-at-Arms.

jaw. 1. Forward end of a gaff or boom which half encircles the mast and whose prongs are called cheeks or horns. Also called a throat. 2. The length of a strand of rope as it makes one full turn. *See* long in the jaw.

jaw rope. Line holding the jaw to the mast and passed through beads to reduce friction as it is raised and lowered.

jeers. Heavy tackles with multiple blocks used to sway up the lower yards for the largest sails or courses in a square-rigger. These yards and sails were too heavy for ordinary halyards.

jellyfish. A marine coelenterate related to coral polyps and sea anemones, sometimes luminescent; umbrella-shaped, free floating and transparent body surrounded by passive tentacles studded with tiny stinging cells. Also known as medusae.

jenny. Same as genoa jib.

jerk or jerque. A colloquial British expression for a final customs inspection of a ship done by a jerker or jerquer. He may issue a jerk note as a result of his inspection.

jerk string. A light line attached to the jib of a sailboat to control the fore-and-aft location of the jib's draft.

jet drive. *See* waterjet.

jetsam. *See* jettison.

jet sled. *See* lay barge.

jettison. To throw overboard, especially to lighten an endangered ship. The material jettisoned is called flotsam if it floats, jetsam if it sinks, and lagan if it is buoyed for future recovery. The British label all goods jettisoned as jetsam and those accidentally lost overboard as flotsam. These two terms are sometimes used together to define anything thrown or lost over the side and thus the distinction between them is often blurred.

jetty. A waterfront structure such as a wharf or pier built to influence current or protect the entrance of a harbor or a river. If its primary use is to protect from erosion, it is called a groin but if it is used mainly to break the force of waves, it is a breakwater. For the British, jetty describes a pier of solid construction intended to berth vessels, not T-shaped. *See* seawall, training wall, bulkhead.

jewel block. A small single block usually made fast to a yard or masthead that is used for reeving flag halyards.

jew fish. Several large fish of the family Serranidae similar in size and in behaviour to the grouper but not as highly esteemed as food.

jews harp. A ring or shackle at the shank head of an anchor to which the anchor cable is made fast. Also any lyre or harp-shaped shackle.

JG. Short of Lieutenant (junior grade); a one and a half striper in the U.S. Navy, rank senior to an Ensign and junior to a Lieutenant.

jib. A triangular sail rigged forward of the most forward mast. Square-riggers and large schooners usually had multiple jibs known from aft forward as inner, middle, outer and flying jib. Balloon and genoa jibs are large headsails carried by yachts in moderate or light winds. Also the end of a crane used for handling cargo.

jibboom. A separate wooden extension of the bowsprit in wooden ships; now part of the bowsprit in modern ships.

jibboom saddle. The block of wood to which the jibboom was fitted; now rarely found.

jibe. A sudden and often unplanned change of tack when sailing before the wind in which it swings the boom quickly across the stern and over to the other side as the stern passes through the wind. If accidental, a jibe can be dangerous but if planned, it is the same as wearing. Also spelled gybe, the British version.

jib head. A piece of wood, plastic, or metal forming the head of a jib that is used instead of canvas.

jib-headed. Describes a sailing vessel with triangular sails, a Bermuda or Marconi rig rather than the older gaff or four-sided sail rig. All of these refer to fore-and-aft rigs.

jib iron. Same as jib traveller.

jib netting. A triangular safety net under the jibboom.

jib-stick. A light pole or spar used to hold ouboard a jib or staysail when the sailboat is running before the wind. In small crafts, a boathook may be used.

jib traveller. An iron ring used to secure the tack of a jib to the bowsprit when not made fast to a stay; rarely used now. Also called a jib iron or tack-ring.

jib tricing line. A small line fastened to the center of the jib, used in taking in the jib or spilling its air.

jiffy reefing. Same as slab reefing.

jig. 1. A small tackle aboard a sailing ship. Also called a jigger. 2. A fishing lure that spins and flashes; used in jigging.

jigboat. A tuna fishing boat that uses hooks and lines instead of nets.

jigger. A small sail set on a jigger mast, the mizzenmast of a yawl or ketch. The aftermost mast on a four-masted ship, sometimes called a spanker. *See* mast. Also a small purchase or tackle aboard ship, a jig.

jigger bumkin or bumpkin. A spar overhanging the stern of a yawl fitted with a block for the jigger sheet. Also called a jigger boom.

jigging. A method of hand fishing, often through ice, in which a lure or jig is pulled up and down with regular motion. British word is pilking.

Jimmy Green. *See* Jamie Green.

Jimmy Legs. The slang nautical term for a Master-At-Arms, police petty officers or any security police.

jingle bell. A special bell used in early steamers before the engine order telegraph. Sounded by a bell pull or wire from the bridge, it indicated full speed. Used with a gong, it meant, for example, ahead, stop, slow, or back, according to the numbers of strokes, as a result "and a jingle" means full speed.

jockey pole. A British term for reaching strut; a short wooden or metal spar used to hold a headsail guy away from the shrouds or stanchions.

joe. A slang term in the U.S. Navy for coffee; once known as jamoke. Every gang, watch, and workshop on a warship has a joe pot if authorized.

jog. The thin end or scarf of timber used in boat building. Also called lip, scarf, or nib.

jogging. In boat building, the notching of a boat's frames. In fishing, the suspension of fishing due to bad weather. Also running at slowest speed in heavy weather that will maintain steerageway.

joggle. A shipbuilding term meaning to bend, crimp, or fit a plate or bar around some other material. This can result in joggled frames or joggled plates and may be done by a joggling machine or a joggler.

john boat. A square-ended and flat bottomed boat. Also called a jonboat. *See* scrow.

John Doree or Dory. A small, golden food fish of the family Zeidae found in European waters.

joiner. A shipbuilding term used to describe work and fittings that involve sheet metal and various synthetics. These have replaced wood working in ship's interiors. Also a craftsman who does joiner work.

joiner door. A normal interior door in contrast to a steel watertight door.

joint. In ship building, when parts come together squarely or end to end, they form a butt joint. An expansion joint permits expansion or contraction. A flange joint involves overlapping flanges or edges while a scarf or lap joint involves scarfs.

jolly or jolly boat. A small rowing or sailing boat carried aboard ship and used mainly today for recreation.

jolly jumpers. Collective term for the sails set above the moonrakers in clipper ships.

Jolly Roger. The traditional but probably fictional pirate flag bearing white skull and cross bones on a black background.

Jonah. The person on board ship traditionally blamed for the ship's bad luck or misfortune.

jonboat. Same as johnboat.

jumbo. On American schooners, a forestay sail or jib.

jumbo boom. In modern usage, an extra heavy cargo or heavy lift boom.

jumboize. To increase the size of a ship by inserting an additional section or piece of hull. Also describes a ship newly fitted with a jumbo boom.

jumper. 1. Any rope, line, or wire, such as a jumper stay or jumper guy, which maintains items in position. 2. A connecting wire, hose, or pipe used to make an emergency connection in damage control aboard ship. 3. The buttonless blouse worn by sailors.

jumper stay. A truss-like stay on the upper forward side of the mast of a sailboat. It supports the top of the mast and is held away from the mast by a jumper strut.

jump ship. Slang for leaving a ship without permission or deserting. A pier head jump is, by British usage, a last minute assignment to a ship. By U.S. usage it means a sudden and precipitous departure or arrival involving, theoretically, a last minute jump across from the pier onto the ship or into the last boat.

junk. Old, condemned rope and cordage used, when untwisted and picked apart, to make such items as small stuff and oakum for caulking; now rare. Also a Chinese craft of distinctive shape and rig, slow and cumbersome although seaworthy.

jury. In its nautical sense, an adjective meaning temporary or improvised such as a jury rig of any kind, a jury anchor, a jury rudder, or a jury mast.

jute. A natural fiber once used widely for making cordage.

K

K. International signal code alphabet flag. When hoisted singly means: "I wish to communicate with you." Spoken: "kilo."

kalema. A heavy surf that breaks on the coast of Guinea usually as a result of distant storms.

kamaaina. Hawaiian word for an old timer or native islander and thus now, a surfer's word for an experienced surfer.

Kamchatka Current. The branch of the Japan or Kuroshiwo current that flows northeast towards the Aleutian Islands.

kapok. The silky fibers that surround the seeds of the tropical ceiba tree; used as buoyant stuffing in lifejackets and lifebuoys.

kaus. A moderate to strong southeasterly wind, usually marked by rain and squalls, that blows in the Persian Gulf. Also spelled quas and called shaski.

kayak. A small wooden-framed, skin-covered canoe used by Eskimos in the Far North, usually paddled by a man.

keckle. Traditionally meant to apply keckling material. Now means to fasten mooring lines together with small stuff as they are doubled up in use; more to improve appearance than to prevent chafing.

keckling. Traditionally, the chafing gear made of old rope.

kedge. To move a ship by laying out an anchor by boat and then heaving in on the line out to the anchor. Usually an old-fashioned anchor called a kedge anchor was used. The procedure was called kedging; now uncommon except for salvage work. Yachtsmen and fishermen often refer to the old-fashioned anchor as a kedge anchor.

keel. A ship's centerline, fore-and-aft structure running along the bottom and from which the frames and side platings arise. A ship is on an even keel when it draws the same amount of water fore and aft. *See* slab keel, bilge keel, fin keel, bar keel, hanging keel, box keel, duct keel, drop keel, center keel, centerplate keel, docking keel, false keel, flat-plate keel, sliding keel.

keelage. In the United Kingdom, a duty or toll charged to a ship for using a port or harbor.

keel block. A strong, solid wooden block or pile of blocks on which the keel of a ship rests while in drydock or during construction in a building way.

keelhaul. Historically, it meant to punish a man by pulling him under the ship from side to side by means of ropes. Now, a slang term for giving a severe reprimand.

keel slab. A narrow stiffening bar or plate on each side of the vertical plate extending below the ship's bottom to form the center-plate.

keelson. Originally a long structure inside the ship over the keel designed to strengthen it. Now any interior strength member, fore-and-aft or athwartships, used to strengthen the hull or support a heavy weight.

keep. To hold or maintain, as in the expression "keep that buoy to port" or "keep off that cape by two miles." Keeping ship in the U.S. Navy means observing the ship's routine without any special drills or exercises.

keeper. Any locking or securing device.

kellet. A weight suspended from an anchor cable or rode in bad weather to reduce the angle that the cable makes with the bottom as it leads to the anchor, thus improving the anchor's holding power. Also called a sentinel.

Kelly's eye. Fisherman's term for the steel ring used at the end of the wire or chain trawl line.

kelp. A very large seaweed or algae that grows on the bottom in moderately deep and cold waters near the coast; habitat for kelp fish and, in some areas, sea otter.

kench. A storage bin or space aboard ship used in kenching.

kenching. A primitive method of salting fish by layering them in salt.

Kenter shackle. The first and best known of a number of detachable links or shackles used to connect the anchor chain. Now largely replaced by more modern designs.

kentledge. Pig iron or metal scraps used as ballast.

ketch. A small, two-masted sailing yacht with a shorter mizzenmast or jigger abaft the mainmast and stepped forward of the waterline aft or the rudder post. *See* yawl.

ketch, bomb. In the old days of sail warfare, a small ship used to carry mortars that fired a primitive projectile called a bomb.

kevel. A heavy piece of wood on or near the bulwarks used for securing the mooring lines and other heavy ropes such as the topsail halyards of an old sailing ship; replaced in modern ships by steel cleats which may still be called kevels. Also called cavil.

Kevlar. A synthetic fiber used in modern rope and sail making.

key. *See* cay.

kick. Swirl in the wake of a turning ship caused by the turning of the rudder. Same as knuckle.

kicker. Same as a kicking strap. Also a slang term for an outboard motor.

kicking strap. Originally, any line used to restrain something such as the short line around the spokes of a steering wheel used in heavy weather. Also called a martingale or kicker for short. In modern usage, a line from the spinnaker pole to a cleat aft that keeps the spinnaker from lifting. Also a line or tackle on a boom used to restrain it when sailing downwind or to flatten the sail of a racing dinghy. The British call a boom vang a kicking strap. *See* vang.

kick plate. A bright metal plate that absorbs scuff marks on the vertical parts or risers of steps and ladders aboard ship. Also the dark stripe along the deck on a light-colored bulkhead.

kid. Aboard ship, a small container once used for various purposes such as a mess kid for food or a spit kid as a spittoon; sometimes spelled kit; now rarely used.

kill devil. A local word for a dip net.

killer boat. Same as catcher boat.

killer whale. The largest member of the dolphin family (genus *Orca*) that grows to 30 feet. A sea-going, predatory mammal that feeds on fish and other sea mammals; highly intelligent and normally no threat to man unless it is injured or threatened. Also known as grampus, orc or orca.

killick. Originally a stone, later any heavy object usually fitted with crude hooks or crooks of wood or iron used as an anchor.

killick hitch. Hitch used to make fast the anchor rope to a killick.

killie. A small bait fish.

king crab. A large, edible and commercially important crab of North Pacific coastal waters. Also another name for horseshoe crab.

kingfish. *See* cobia.

king plank. A centerline hardwood board in a planked deck from which the deck planks are laid.

kingpost. 1. A short heavy mast aboard a cargo ship that supports a boom; often built in pairs with a connecting member at the top (king bridge). Also known as a samson post. 2. The centerline pillar in a ship's hold.

Kingsbury thrust bearing. A device that receives and transmits the force or thrust of the ship's power to turn the propellers against the thrust block. The bearing consists of a collar on a shaft that engages a series of babbit-faced shoes through a film of lubricating oil under pressure.

king spoke. The radial spoke of the steering wheel that is up and vertical when the ship's rudder is amidships; usually marked by a turk's head or a brass cap.

kipper. A salted and smoked herring; a kippered herring. Also a male salmon or sea trout in the spawning season.

Kirsten-Boeing propeller. Propeller in which a number of fixed blades rotate in a horizontal plane about a vertical axis. *See* Voith-Schneider propeller.

kit. A British measure used in fishing equal to 12 stone or 168 pounds. *See* kid.

Kitchen rudder. A steering and reversing mechanism in a small craft consisting of two adjustable blades that forms an aperture just abaft the propeller. This permits the boat to go astern without reversing the propeller.

kite drag. A sea anchor made of two or more spars and some canvas fastened together.

kites. Formerly the highest and lightest sails on a square-rigger set only in very light winds above the royals, such as skysails, moonsails, moonrakers, stargazers, skyscrapers, raffees, hopes-in-heaven, puffballs, savealls, trust-in-God, Christ disturbers, cloud ticklers, and angels. Now a general word for all light sails such as spinnakers and genoas set forward of the mainmast on sailing yachts and included under headsails.

kittiwake. A gull with black, unspotted wing tips; similar to the common gull but less urban in habitat and more sea roving. Often seen following ships.

kiyi. A naval word for a small brush used to scrub canvas or clothing.

knacker's yard. British slang for shipbreaker's yard or scrapheap.

knee. In shipbuilding, a plate, often rectangular, used to connect intersecting structural members such as beams, frames, and deck girders. In wooden ship or boat construction, timber knees are named for their location and use. A knee that lies flat is a lodging knee; upright, a hanging knee; at an angle, a dragger knee. A knee that locks a clamp, stringer, or shelf to the stem is a breasthook. A trail knee supports a trail board.

knife edge. The rim or edge of a watertight door, hatch, or port designed to meet against the gasket set in the frame in order to have a watertight fit.

knight. In old sailing ships, a vertical timber or bit used to make fast the running rigging.

knighthead. In old sailing ships, the most forward timbers that supported the bowsprit. Also called apostles.

knighthead frame. The frame near the stem in old steel sailing ships for the bowsprit to pass through.

knittle. Old version of nettle; small stuff made from rope yarn.

knockabout. Generally, a small single masted sailboat without a bowsprit and rigged only with a mainsail and jib.

knock down. A sailing boat or ship is knocked down by wind or sea when she is forced over on her beam ends with sails in the water. Also when a trolled, baited line clipped to an outrigger is pulled free.

knock off. A slang term in the U.S. Navy for stop, as in the familiar word passed over the general announcing system aboard ship "knock off work."

knoll. An elevation rising less than 500 fathoms from the ocean floor and of limited extent across its summit.

knorr. The Viking merchant ship counterpart of the longship rigged with a single mast supporting a square sail.

knot. Any combination of loops, mostly interlocking, used to fasten ropes together, to anything, or to enlarge the end of a rope. A bend is a special form of knot which can be cast off easily when necessary. A hitch is a knot whose loops normally jam together under pressure but remain separable when strain is released. Also a unit of speed: one knot equals one nautical mile per hour.

knotmeter. A sophisticated recording yacht speed indicator using a paddle wheel, a transducer, and a digital averaging readout or display dial.

knuckle. Same as kick. Also in shipbuilding, any abrupt local change of direction of the hull plating, particularly at the intersection of the counter and the upper part of the stern. The distortion in a welded joint of steel plate is called knuckling.

Kochab. A bright star in the Little Dipper often used in celestial navigation that indicates true north. Also known as lodestar.

kogia. A variety of small sperm whale known as a pigmy sperm.

koku. A Japanese unit of volume equal to 10 cubic feet used in shipping measurements.

Kona wind or weather. A south or southwest storm wind in the Hawaiian Islands that at times interrupts the normal northeast trades with rain.

kook. A derogatory surfer's word for an inexperienced beginner who blocks and endangers other surfers.

Kort nozzle. A cylindrical steel casing fitted around the propellers of certain shallow draft vessels such as tugs that is used to increase efficiency.

Kraken. A large, mythical sea monster said to lurk in waters off Norway and Sweden. Sometimes shown as a giant squid in old drawings, making it possible that the little known giant squid was the basis for the legend.

krill. A small and abundant crustacean, a euphausiid, found in cold waters; the major food of baleen whales, sea birds, seals and penguins. It is now being harvested for human consumption.

Kuroshio or Kuroshiwo System. Similar to the Gulf Stream System, this series of ocean currents in the North Pacific flows first northeast along the coasts of Taiwan and Japan where it is known as the Kuroshio or Japan Current. As the main stream curves eastward it divides into the North Pacific Current moving east, a south curving component, and the Tsushima Current that passes into the Sea of Japan. The system originates with the North Equatorial Current. Sometimes called the Black Current.

kymatology. The science of waves and wave motion.

L

L. International signal code alphabet flag. When flown singly means: "You should stop your vessel instantly." Spoken: "lima."

labor. A ship labors in heavy weather when her rolling and pitching is so violent that it places unusual strain on her hull and top hamper.

Labrador Current. An ocean current in the North Atlantic setting south out of Davis Strait and flowing down the coasts of Labrador and Newfoundland until it meets the Gulf Stream drift with which some of it moves east and north. It is a cold current often bringing down ice that can endanger shipping. Also called the Arctic Current.

ladder. Nautical word for stairs or steps made of wood, metal, or rope. A pilot's ladder or jacob's ladder is made of rope or chain with wooden or metal steps rigged for temporary use. Also called a sea ladder. In the Navy, a sea ladder describes more accurately metal rungs welded to the side of the ship to form a ladder.

ladder screen. Screen made of canvas and lashed alongside or under a ladder.

laden, lading. A heavily loaded ship is said to be heavily laden. A bill of lading is a list of cargo carried in a cargo ship.

lag. To cover with asbestos or other insulating material; steam pipes are always lagged. The covering is known as lagging.

lagan. Under maritime law anything cast overboard in an emergency that is buoyed for eventual recovery. Also spelled ligan or logan. *See* jettison.

lagging, tidal. An increase in the time between successive high tides due to the relative position of the sun and the moon; opposite of priming or acceleration. Little used today as tidal movements are no longer of as great importance as in days of sail.

lagoon. A body of shallow water separated from the ocean by a reef or a spit of land.

lagoon blink. The reflected sunlight from the white sands of a lagoon which is often visible on clouds a long distance away. *See* blink.

laid. A descriptive word for rope or wire as plain laid, back laid, cable laid, etc. Laid rope is wire rope made of 6 strands of 7 wires each.

laid deck. Deck in which the planks are put down parallel to the gunwale.

lampara net. Net shaped like a dustpan with a wing or extension on each side; used to surround a school of fish near the surface.

lamp locker. Traditional small compartment formerly used to store and service the oil-burning lamps and navigational lights; usually forward in the ship.

lamprey. An eel-like fish of the family Petromyzonidae living in the North Atlantic. Grows to a length of two feet and feeds on other fish by attaching itself by the mouth and boring into the victim. Once a serious menace to the fish of the Great Lakes, now brought under control.

LAN. Local Apparent Noon; the optimum time to take a sun line.

LANBY. Large Automatic Navigational BuoY (British).

lancelet. A small, 2 to 3 inch marine organism of the genus *Amphioxus*, resembling a fish but without a true skeleton; lives in tropical waters.

land. Part of the longitudinal plank that overlaps in a clinkerbuilt wooden boat. *See* landing.

land boards. Planks laid down near a cargo hatch to protect the wooden deck when handling cargo. Modern ships have steel decks.

land breeze. At night, the offshore breeze resulting from the land cooling off faster than the sea. It blows in the opposite direction to the sea breeze of the daytime when as the land heats the warm air, it rises and the cooler sea air comes in to replace it. Land and sea breezes are also called solar winds. *See* breeze.

landed terms. In commercial shipping, the freight charges including all costs incurred in landing the goods at the destination port.

landfall. An approach to land at the end of a sea voyage. Also seeing land.

land ho. The traditional report of the lookout in sighting land. Usually he is asked where away and replies with the direction as in "broad on the port bow."

landing. *n* **1.** The amount by which two steel plates overlap each other when fastened together. **2.** The distance between the center of a rivet hole and the edge of a piece of steel. **3.** The place alongside a dock, pier, or wharf where ship's boats may load and unload if the ship is anchored or moored in a stream. **4.** In amphibious warfare, the arrival of forces on a beach either as an assault landing or as an administrative one. *vb* To direct or to steer a ship or boat alongside a pier or of another ship is to make a landing.

landing card. Card provided to disembarking ship passengers to facilitate customs and immigration clearance.

landing craft. Craft designed to land directly on a beach; used in amphibious naval operations or in commercial traffic in remote places lacking proper port facilities.

landing party. Any group of people going ashore for a specific purpose such as armed men from a warship; once called the landing force in the Navy.

landlocked. Surrounded by land such as a bay or protected harbor.

landlubber. Person unfamiliar with the sea or life at sea and thus liable to behave in a clumsy or lubberly fashion aboard ship.

landmark. On shore, any fixed object whose position is marked on a chart.

landsman. In the British Navy, an old rating describing an ordinary seaman seccond class.

lang lay. *See* lay.

langouste. Another word for spiny lobster.

lantern. In times before electricity was available, a designation for all the ship's lights, such as for internal use, signaling, and navigation.

lantern fish. Small, deep-sea fish equipped with luminous spots or glands used to attract its prey.

lanyard. Originally a rope rove through deadeyes or wooden blocks used to set up or tighten the rigging. Now, any small line used to fasten or hold something temporarily such as a pistol or a bucket lanyard.

lanyard stopper. A rope used as a stopper or holding line on a heavy rope or hawser being hauled in and about to be taken off the winch and secured to a cleat or bitts. Also called a rope stopper.

lap. The distance that one piece of material is laid over another in a lapped joint. The process is called lapping.

lapper. A sail very similar to a mule, a headsail. *See* mule.

lapstrake. Describes the clinker or lap construction of a wooden boat in which each plank or strake overlaps the other.

lapstrake boat. Same as a clinker-built boat.

larboard. Old name for port; the left hand side looking forward.

large. A seldom used word today; once used in sailing to describe a favorable wind or course. Survives in the term "by and large" which originally meant a ship's ability to sail well close hauled as well as free.

lark's head. A hitch used for fastening a line to a ring or spar when the same tension is exerted on both standing parts. Same as cow hitch.

Lascar. An Indian seaman employed in British ships in the Far East.

lash. *n* **1.** Sailors were once flogged with a lash. *vb* **1.** To secure, fasten, or repair with rope or wire by wrapping closely and making fast. **2.** Cargo may be lashed down on deck with such items as lashing posts, ring pads, or shackles. **3.** Wind and sea lash the shore and a whale's flukes lash the sea. **4.** A sail adrift may lash about. *See* rose lashing.

LASH. Lighter Aboard SHip; a system of carrying lighters or barges already loaded aboard ship, thus facilitating loading and unloading. The lighters have a capacity of up to 400 tons. *See* **BACAT**, Seabee, **FLASH**.

latchings. Series of loops of small stuff by which the foot of a sail is fastened to a bonnet.

lateen. An ancient sailing rig where a triangular, loose-footed sail on a long yard is slung on a short mast at about a 45 degree angle; still popular where sail is used commercially and it is also used in small pleasure boats such as canoes and catamarans.

lateral system of buoyage. An arrangement of buoys of different shapes, colors, numbers, and lights used to indicate the side of the buoy on which a ship should pass to avoid danger when proceeding in a given direction, as in "Red, right, returning." Used in the U.S. *See* cardinal system. *See* System B.

latitude. The angular distance of a point north or south of the equator measured in degrees, minutes and seconds. Latitude and longitude provide the coordinates with which all ships navigate across the oceans.

Laughlin plow anchor. A patented, plow-like yacht anchor with a long shank.

launch. 1. To release a newly-built ship from its building ways or to float it from its building dock. **2.** A ship's boat, especially in the Navy where it is an open, diesel powered boat for personnel and stores.

launching cradle. A structure built on the ground or on launching ways to hold and launch a finished ship. It consists of sliding ways or timbers, a first layer of packing timbers called a wedge rider, and vertical or nearly vertical timbers attached to the hull known as poppets.

launching ways. *See* ground ways, slipway.

launching wedge. *See* slice.

lay. *n* **1.** The share of the catch due to each member of the crew of a fishing vessel. *vb* **1.** To lay is to go, as in lay aft or lay aloft. **2.** A ship lays alongside the pier or if she is stopped for some reason at sea she lays to. 3. A ship may be laid up for repairs. 4. To lay out an anchor is to carry it out.

lay of wire or rope. The direction of rotation of the wires, fibers, yarns, or strands making up the rope; left for counterclockwise, right for clockwise. The individual wires should be laid in the opposite direction to that of the strands to produce regular lay wire rope that does not tend to unwind when holding up a load. If the wires and strands are laid in the same direction, the result is a lang lay. The strength of rope depends partly on the degree of lay or twist, thus a rope is soft, medium, or hard laid.

lay barge. A large vessel designed to join together and then lower over the side or stern, pipe for gas or oil transfer under water. The pipe is normally fed over the stern by a stinger into a trench dug out of the bottom by a jet sled.

lay days. The time allowed for loading and unloading a cargo ship under the terms of the charter party. If it exceeds the allowed time, the charter pays demurrage; if it is met or bettered, dispatch may be paid by the owner. Non-lay days are clear days. *See* clear days.

layer depth. The distance between the surface of the sea and the thermocline. It is measured as the thickness of the mixed layer of water nearest to the surface at about the same temperature.

lay off or laying off. In ship building, to develop the lines of the ship's hull with full scale drawings on the mold-loft floor and making templates therefrom in order to make steel plates and parts. Also called laying down.

lay on the oars. An order to the crew of a rowing boat or shell to stop rowing and hold the oars straight out and horizontal. To lay in the oars is to unship them and place them in the boat. To lay out on the oars is to pull harder.

lay the keel. To place the first plate or timber of a new ship on the keel blocks as the first step in building. Slang for fathering a child.

lay up. To apply the various layers of fiberglass cloth, mat roving, and gel coat that make up the hull of a fiberglass boat.

lay up refund. The return of premium for marine insurance by reason of a ship being laid up and not underway. British term is lay up return.

lazaret. A space or small compartment aft in a boat or ship. Also an isolation area or hospital for people with contagious diseases from ships in quarantine.

lazy. Describes any one of a variety of light lines used for purposes not involving much strain. *See* lazy guy, jack, line, tack.

lazy guy. 1. A wire or vang connecting two adjacent cargo booms that keeps them from separating when used together. Also called a schooner guy. **2.** A line or light tackle used to steady the boom of a fore-and-aft sail. 3. A line not under strain such as one of the two sheets of a headsail. *See* guy, vang.

lazy jack. A bridle of light line from the topping lift or mast of a sailboat to each side of the boom between which the sail is contained as it is hoisted and lowered. Also called a boom guy.

lazy line. Line used on a fish or shrimp trawl to pull it in close to the ship when hauling the trawl.

lazy tack. A line securing the tack of a course or squaresail until a tack tackle can be rigged in a square-rigger.

LBP. *See* Length Between Perpendiculars.

LCL. Less than a Full Container Load (FCL).

lead. 1. A narrow channel of open water in an ice field. 2. The direction a rope lies which when free for running has a fair lead. 3. A measure of hull comparison in sailing vessels; the distance between the center of effort and the center of lateral resistance expressed as a fraction of waterline length. Pronounced leed.

lead block of leading block. Block rigged to provide a fair lead, usually when the line changes its direction. Lead blocks are used in sailing yachts to handle sheets in connection with a slide or traveler.

lead, depth measuring. Short for a sounding or hand lead. The small, 5 to 15 pound hand lead is the one mostly used today. It can measure depths down to 20 fathoms while the ship is slowly underway. A coasting lead was once used in waters to 60 fathoms; over that, a deep-sea or dipsey lead, or a sounding machine was used. The echo sounder replaces all leads except for the hand lead. The lead itself is a sinker with a concave bottom which was traditionally armed with tallow to reveal the nature of the bottom. Rarely done today. Pronounced led.

leader. 1. A fence built out from the shore to guide fish into a pound net, fyke net, or weir. 2. A wire or other line between the fish hook and the fishing line proper to prevent a hooked fish from cutting it. Also called a snood or a snell. The British word is cast.

leading lights and marks. British terms for range lights and range marks. *See* daybeacon.

lead line. The rope attached to the lead weight. Fathoms, called marks and deeps, are indicated by bits of cloth and leather on a hand lead line. Coasting and deep-sea leads were marked somewhat differently but are no longer used. Also a modern, lead-filled weighted bottom line of a gillnet or seine used instead of lead weights. Pronounced led.

leads. The parts of a fall or tackle between two blocks. The leading part is the hauling part.

leadsman. The seaman who stands in the chains to take soundings with his hand lead. He reports depths in fathoms by marks and deeps as the ship moves forward for example "by the deep six," "and a half five," or "no bottom at 13."

league. Archaic measure of distance; three nautical miles.

leather. Part of the oar that fits against the oarlock or thole pin.

leatherneck. Slang for a U.S. Marine Corps enlisted man, a sea-going soldier.

leave. Authorized absence of naval personnel from their duty station over 24 to 48 hours. *See* liberty. Term shore leave is not applicable to the U.S. Navy.

lebeche. A warm and dry southwesterly wind off the southeast coast of Spain.

ledge. A shelf-like projection or a ridge of rocks under water near the shore. In wooden ships, a piece of the deck frame running athwartships.

lee. The side away from the wind. If the wind blows from the port side then the starboard side is the sheltered or lee side and the port side is the exposed, weather, or windward side. A ship may anchor in the lee of an island. To the old sailing ship crews, everything about the ship was usually referred to as either lee or weather instead of port and starboard. This persists today only in some yachts. Note that the lee shore is one on which the wind blows.

leeboard. A flat wooden or steel device lowered over the side of a sail boat to provide lateral resistance when sailing close-hauled; serves the same purpose as a centerboard and takes effect on the lee side of the boat.

lee-bow. To sail a boat against the current so that the current on the lee bow reduces the leeway or side slipping.

leech. The after edge of a fore-and-aft or triangular sail, opposite the luff. Also one of the vertical, side edges of a squaresail into which is sewn the leech rope.

leecloth. A canvas strip secured to both sides of a bunk in a sail boat to keep the occupant from falling out.

lee shore. Any land or coast towards which the wind is blowing and thus a danger in heavy weather to a ship under sail or a ship anchored. To avoid this danger, a ship anchors in the lee of the land.

leeward. The direction away from the wind as a boat should come alongside a ship to leeward or on the lee side. Pronounced looard. *See* alee.

leeway. The sideways movement of a ship to leeward of her course or heading due to pressure from wind and sea. Sometimes called drift or sag.

leg. 1. A portion of a ship's tack or plotted course along a single heading; same as a board or tack. 2. Part of a rope bridle, boom crutch or sheerlegs. 3. One of the shores used to hold a boat upright if stranded by a receding tide. 4. One flange of a steel shape or angle bar.

legging. The procedure for pushing a canal boat through a narrow tunnel; men lie on deck and push against the walls with their feet.

leg-of-mutton sail. A fore-and-aft triangular sail whose tack extends down below the boom; used in windsurfing.

lemonfish. *See* cobia.

length between perpendiculars (l.b.p.). *See* perpendicular.

length on the load waterline (l.w.l.). Length measured on the waterline with the ship loaded.

length over all (l.o.a.). Linear distance from the most forward part of the stem to the most aftermost part of the stern.

leptocephalus. A small elongated, transparent planktonic larva of the eel or anguilla.

leste. A hot dry easterly wind of the Canary and Madeira Islands originating in the North African desert.

let. In its maritime sense, it combines with various words to initiate action as in "let go the anchor," "let go by the run," or "let run" (meaning to let a line go out under strain) or to "let fly" a sail. To let go by the run is to cast a line off a cleat and let it run free.

Letter of Marque or Mart. Historically, an authorization by a government to capture vessels of a particular country as a matter of retaliation. The ship authorized was a privateer. A limited Letter of Marque was also a Letter of Reprisal, sometimes known as a Letter of Countermart.

levant. The old word for east. Levante is the ancient but still used word for the easterly wind of the mediterranean.

levanter. A ship engaged in trade with the Middle East.

level-luffing crane. A shipboard cargo handling rig which maintains the load at a nearly constant elevation during transfer.

Leviathan. A huge, legendary sea animal described in ancient writ, including the Bible; mostly probably a crocodile, a giant squid, or a whale.

liberty. Authorized absence for Naval personnel from their ship or station; usually from the end of working hours until the next morning of a working day. A longer period is leave which requires written permission. Men leave the ship as the liberty party and are known in the British Navy as libertymen. Not to be confused with shore leave which is not a Naval term.

Liberty Ship. Originally of British design, a simple, mass produced 10,000 ton cargo vessel built in the U.S. by Henry Kaiser during World War II. These ships could reach a speed of 10 knots. Similar ships serving under the British flag were called SAM ships. *See* Victory Ship.

Licensed Officer. A Merchant Marine officer who has been authorized, after examination, to serve as master, mate, engineer, officer, and so on.

lie. A ship or boat lies off when it is stopped nearby and waiting. A ship lies to or heaves to when stopped and waiting. A ship stopped outside a harbor lies off that harbor. Large sailing ships when lying to in heavy weather with some canvas set were said to lie atry.

lie ahull. Describes a ship that merely drifts in very heavy weather without sails or power. Also called hulling.

lieutenant. A junior officer in the Navy, equivalent to an Army or Air Force captain; senior to a lieutenant junior grade and junior to a lieutenant commander.

lieutenant commander. A naval officer junior to a commander; equivalent to a major in the Army.

lifeboat. In merchant ships, a boat required by international agreement and of specified characteristics. In a warship, it is one of the ship's boats, usually a motor whaleboat with an assigned and trained crew. Shore based lifeboats are in the U.S. manned by the Coast Guard and are specially designed to withstand extreme weather. Lifeboats ashore are now often replaced by helicopters.

lifebuoy or ring. A buoyant object that can be thrown from a ship or a pier to assist someone in the water; may be a simple cork ring attached to a line or a metal or plastic ring equipped with a self-starting light.

lifefloat or raft. Any buoyant device, but not a boat, designed to support a number of people in an emergency in the water. Most modern ones inflate automatically and contain water, food, a radio, and provide shelter.

life jacket. Any individual flotation device or life preserver that is worn to sustain a person in the water. Some are equipped with such items as flashlight, whistle, and shark repellent.

lifeline. Any of several lines rigged on deck, fore-and-aft, to keep people from going overboard; either rigged in heavy weather or normal lines on stanchions along the edge of the weather decks. Normal lines are collectively termed lifelines but used more specifically to designate the top line of the three. The middle one is the housing line and the bottom one, the footline. Also any protective line rigged on a boom brow, yard, or a rope thrown to someone in the water, the grab ropes on a lifeboat or liferaft, or those hanging from the span wire of boat davits for the boat crew to grasp as the boat is lowered or hoisted.

lift. *n* **1.** A rope or chain used to raise the end of a boom, spar, or spinnaker pole. Also called a topping lift. **2.** A particular load or piece of cargo that, if heavy, requires a heavy lift boom or jumbo boom. **3.** Broadside movement of a ship turning due to the effect of the rudder. **4.** A shift of wind when sailing that allows a course change into the wind or permits the sail trim (sheet) to be eased without changing course. Also known as a freer. *See* header. *vb* To lift a template means to make one the same size as the structure to be built using mold loft lines or the ship itself.

lifting. Describes the luff of a sail that is shaking so that the sail must be trimmed or the course changed.

lift net. A fishing net rigged to be raised vertically out of the water with the net horizontal; used either from a boat or from shore. Also called a blanket net.

lightening hole. Hole cut in a steel plate or member to save weight yet without sacrificing much strength.

lighter. *n* A broad, usually rectangular, open vessel used for transporting cargo on water but mainly for loading and unloading ships. In sheltered waters, a lighter is normally towed or pushed but it can be self-propelled. The cargo is usually carried in the open whereas in a barge or scow it is at least partly decked over. Lighter, barge, and scow are terms often used interchangeably in accordance to local usage. *See* barge. *vb* To lighter is to move something by lighter and the fees involved are called lighterage.

Lighter Aboard SHip (LASH). A type of cargo vessel in which the cargo is loaded in barges or lighters which are themselves transported. The lighters may have a capacity of up to 400 tons and provide great flexibility in loading and in discharging the freight. *See* BACAT, seabee, FLASH.

lighthouse. A structure on or near the shore showing a strong white or colored light, flashing or occulting over a specified arc or sector. Systems for magnifying and concentrating the light are catoptric (reflecting), dioptric (refracting), or a combination of both (catadioptric).

light line. The line of immersion at which a cargo vessel floats when in ballast or light trim. Also called the light load line or light waterline.

Light Lists. Lists published by the U.S. Coast Guard that describes the characteristics of all lighted aids to navigation in waters of the U.S. and its possessions.

It includes lighthouses, buoys, daybeacons, ranges, fog signals, and radiobeacons. *See* Lists of Lights (another publication for lights abroad).

light money. The tonnage tax imposed on a foreign ship entering the U.S.

light, occulting. A navigational light whose periods of darkness or eclipses are more than its periods of light. Its eclipses or occultations are all of equal duration and are repeated at regular intervals. *See* flashing light.

light off. Literally to start the fires under a ship's boiler; often used in a general sense to mean "start a piece of machinery."

lightship. An anchored vessel showing a light to assist navigators at critical junctions of ocean traffic; almost all have been replaced by large automatic lighted buoys. In the U.S., there is one off Nantucket.

lights, navigational. Lights installed on lighthouses, lightships, buoys, and beacons; may be white or colored and may show all around or in certain sectors; may be fixed, flashing, occulting, or in any combination singly or in groups. Their characteristics are found in the Light Lists or in the Lists of Lights.

lights, ships. Running lights most commonly shown by ships underway, under both Inland and International Rules, are range, masthead and stern lights, and sidelights. There are many other special lights, some not common to both Rules, such as anchor, flare-up, towing, fishing, not-under-command, man overboard, pilot, dredge, and submarine construction lights, as well as lights shown by ships doing surveying or servicing aids to navigation. There are also special lights shown by warships.

lignum vitae. A heavy, durable, resinous wood of an American tropical tree traditionally used for machinery bearings aboard ship such as rudder gudgeon bearings.

lima coast. Coast characterized by many lagoons or limans.

liman. A shallow coastal lagoon with a muddy bottom. Also an area of mud deposited near the mouth of a stream.

limber. A passage on each side of the keelson for bilge water, hence limber holes to permit free movement of the water, limber boards used to free obstructions, and limber chains that were once used to clear the limber holes of trash.

limb. The upper or the lower edge of the sun or moon that is aligned with the horizon when measuring the altitude of that body by sextant is known as the upper or lower limb. Also the graduated arc of a sextant from which the reading of the observation is made.

Limey or Lime-Juicer. Slang for a British sailor.

limpet. A small edible mollusk found in tidal pools and that feeds on algae.

line. 1. Equator. 2. A shipping business; its ships are called liners.

line, as cordage. Often synonymous with rope. *See* rope.

line officer. In the Navy, an officer who is concerned with ship operations and is eligible for command at sea whereas a staff officer is not.

line of position. In celestial navigation, after solving the spherical triangle using the measured altitude at a known time, the result is a line that is part of an arc. Somewhere along this line of position is the ship's position that can be determined by the intersection of other lines of position. Also called a position line.

liner. A merchant (cargo or passenger) ship that travels on scheduled routes as a public carrier at regular intervals; in contrast to a tramp ship. *See* tramp. Also in ship construction a flat or tapered steel strip placed under a plate or other structure to bring it into proper alignment.

lines of a ship. Lines laid out in the plans or sets of drawings from which the ship is built.

lines or lines drawings. Same as sheer draft; a set of ship building drawings showing the form of the hull. *See* sheer draft.

linesider. Same as striped bass. *See* bass.

line squall. A sudden and violent storm marked by a line of black clouds along the horizon.

line-throwing gun. A kind of rifle that fires, at low velocity, a projectile to which a very light line is attached; used in reaching the shore, a pier, or another ship when the distance is too great for a heaving line or a bolo. It can be dangerous to personnel if they are not alerted. *See* heaving line.

ling-cod. Not a true cod, a food fish common to North Pacific waters of the genus *Ophiodon elongatus.* Not the same as the ling of North Atlantic waters which is related to the cod and also a popular food fish.

lining. A method of deep sea fishing using a principal buoyed line to which multiple small baited lines are attached. There is long lining or great lining using very long lines in deep water and there is short lining for restricted shallow water. *See* longline.

lip. Same as jog.

lipper. A slight ruffling or roughness on the surface of calm water. Also a light spray from small waves.

liquid gas ship or tanker. A specially designed ship used to carry the high pressure, low temperature liquid propane, butane, methane, and other petroleum products; a very explosive and dangerous cargo requiring specially qualified crews. LPG is liquid petroleum-derived gas and LNG is liquid natural gas.

list. The static, fixed inclination or leaning of a ship to port or starboard due to an unbalance of weight; does not mean that the ship is unstable. *See* heel, loll.

Lists of Lights. Published by the Defense Mapping Agency Hydrographic Center to characterize the lighted aids to navigation and fog signals (but not lighted buoys within harbors) of foreign waters and limited sections of the U.S. coast. *See* Light Lists.

littoral. Pertaining to the seashore. The littoral or intertidal zone is from the high water line out to 200 meters.

littoral benthic. Describes sea life on the ocean bottom in waters up to 600 feet deep. *See* bathybenthic, bathypelagic.

littoral current. Current in the littoral zone such as a rip current or longshore current.

littoral transport. Deposits of sand, gravel, and so on, moved along the shore.

Liverpool rig. A cargo-handling rig used with a single standing derrick or boom rigged to plumb over the ship's side.

Liverpool splice. A wire eye splice made around a thimble with the end tucked under with the lay and without locking turns.

live well. A tank of sea water aboard a fishing vessel in which fish, especially bait, are kept alive.

lizard. A short length of rope having a thimble spliced into one end. A traveling lizard moves on a fixed wire or rope span.

Llüngstrom rig. An unusual sail boat having a single triangular sail attached to a rotating, unstayed mast.

Lloyd's Agents. Men in all the important ports of the world who represent the Corporation of Lloyd's and keep Lloyd's informed about shipping; not to be confused with Lloyd's Underwriting Agents that are specialized in marine insurance.

Lloyd's of London. A corporation and association of insurance underwriters specializing in maritime matters. The members share capital and risks; not to be confused with Lloyd's Register with whom it has no official connection.

Lloyd's Register of Shipping (LR). An association of ship owners, shipbuilders, and underwriters of marine insurance that exists primarily to establish standards for the construction and maintenance of ships and to provide technical services to owners and builders. It is the British classification society upon which the American Bureau of Shipping (ABS) was modeled and has counterparts in all major maritime counties; not to be confused with Lloyd's of London.

Lloyd's Salvage Agreement. A standard form, widely used in the signed agreement between a salvage tug or company and the master of a vessel in distress. It follows the doctrine of no cure-no pay.

LNG. Liquid Natural Gas. *See* liquid gas ship.

l.o.a. Length over all of a ship expressed in feet or meters.

loading charge. *See* wharfage.

load waterline or loadline. The marks and lines, also known as freeboard marks, that indicate the ship's permissible draft according to international agreement, to which a ship may be loaded in different ocean areas at different seasons. *See* Plimsoll marks. Not to be confused with a ship's draft marks at bow and stern.

lobby. In old sailing ships, the space just forward of the Captain's cabin traditionally occupied by the ship's surgeon.

loblolly. A thick porridge. Also an old word for medicine.

loblolly boy. A surgeon's helper in a sailing warship.

lobscouse. In old sailing ship days, a sailor's stew. Thus a sailor might be called a lobscouser.

lobster. A large, up to 40 pounds, crustacean with two prominent claws; valued for food and found worldwide. *See* spiny lobster.

Local Apparent Noon (LAN). Midday as indicated by the actual position of the sun at its maximum altitude, as on a sundial, in contrast to midday as measured by the mean or average sun. It is the optimum time for the navigator to take a sun line to determine his latitude.

local attraction. Any magnetic disturbance of a compass due to iron in the vicinity but not part of the basic ship's structure.

local time. Determined by the time zone of the observer and as specified by local authority.

loch. A lake as well as a long arm of the sea in the United Kingdom; Scottish for lake. The Irish equivalent is lough.

lock. A structure having movable gates for ships and boats to pass up or down to different water levels in a canal, river, or tidal basin.

Lodestar. The sailor's name for Polaris, the North Star. Also known as Kochab and as the Polestar. *See* Polaris.

loft. *n* A large room or building used in laying out plans and drawings for ship construction as a mold loft, or a sail loft where sails are cut and sewn. *vb* To loft is to lay out the plans and take measurements.

log. A device for measuring ship's speed, distance, or both. *See* speedometer. Modern logs are either pitot-static (which measures differences in pressure generated by the ship's movement), impeller type (that uses a turning propeller to generate an electric current, or electromagnetic (that uses an induction coil to develop a signal voltage that varies with speed). Older logs were the screw log, chip log, and Dutchman's log. Log is short for logbook. *See* logging race.

logbook. Originally a record of a ship's distance sailed each day by log. Now an official record of all significant events and data. It may be a deck log maintained on the bridge underway or on the quarterdeck (Navy) in port or the engineer's log. Most logbooks are first kept in the rough in pencil and should not be erased since they are a legal record. In British and Merchant Marine usage, an offender is logged; in U.S. Naval usage, he is placed on report.

loggerhead. The wooden bit in the bow of a whaling boat around which the harpoon line was passed and controlled.

loggerhead turtle. A large, edible, sea-going turtle of the U.S. Atlantic coast. It lays its eggs on southern beaches and the young, when hatched, hasten out to the Gulf Stream to take refuge in the sargassum weed until they are about 10 inches long. An endangered species.

logging race or log race. More accurately a contest in which the power yachts predict their time of passage over the course and the winner is the boat that has made the most accurate prediction. Also called a predicted log race.

log room. The engineering office aboard ship.

loll. A ship which has a list that makes her unstable is said to loll or to have a loll. A cargo ship just unloaded is said to be lolling before she is ballasted or reloaded enough to correct the list and restore stability. *See* list, heel.

lolly ice. *See* frazil ice.

Lonars. An improved Loran C navigation system being developed by the U.S. Navy.

long blast. Blast of more than six seconds on the ship's whistle.

long boat. Formerly a ship's largest boat carried by merchant sailing vessels.

long glass. A hand-held telescope. Same as spyglass. *See* glass.

long in the jaw. Said of an old rope that has stretched and thus increased its jaw (the length occupied by a strand making one full turn).

longitude. One of the two major navigational coordinates, the other being latitude. It is a measure of angular distance on the earth, east or west of the prime meridian of Greenwich to the point for which the longitude is expressed, measured in degrees, minutes and seconds.

longitudinal. Pertains to the fore-and-aft direction in a ship rather than athwartships; therefore there are longitudinal framing, bulkheads, metacenter, and so on. *See* transverse.

long legged. Describes a ship with high endurance that carries much fuel.

longline. An extensive fishing line with many baited short lines called gangions or snoods attached. The ends are anchored and buoys, sometimes lighted, support the line which is often many miles long. It is called a setline in the Pacific, a trawl line off New England, and a trotline in southern U.S. waters. Longlining boats are known as longliners.

longship. The Norse or Viking galley with which the Vikings raided and explored. It was a rowing ship also provided with a single squaresail.

longshore current. Current produced by waves deflected at an angle by the coast line. Also called a littoral current. *See* nearshore current system.

longshoreman. A man who loads and unloads ship cargo on the U.S. waterfront. Generally synonymous with stevedore, although the latter is also a supervisor and a contractor. In the United Kingdom, he is a dockman, docker, or quayman if he works ashore and a shipman, if he works aboard ship. Stevedore is also sometimes used in the United Kingdom in accordance with local customs.

long splice. Splice that provides a minimum increase in the circumference of the lines spliced together.

long ton. Ton weighing 2240 pounds or 1016 kilos.

loof. Part of a ship where the sides begin to converge towards the stem; the rounded part of the bow.

loofah sponge. The fibrous interior of a tropical gourd, once used as a filter for ship's boiler feed water in reciprocating steam engine plants. Also spelled loofa, luffa.

lookout. As required by law, a sailor stationed on the bridge, in the eyes of the ship or aloft to watch out, for example, for land, ships, and buoys. In whaling ships, he was called a masthead.

loom. 1. The glow of a light from just below the horizon. 2. The shaft or central part of an oar between the blade and the handle. British usage limits the loom to that part of the shaft from the end of the handle to the leather. 3. Sometimes a loom refers to a small trunk or passage for pipes and wiring in a yacht.

looming. A mirage causing the elevation of distant terrestrial objects above the horizon. It is due to the refraction of light waves in atmospheric layers of different characteristics such as temperature.

loop. *See* wave, standing.

loose. To let go, such as a sail.

loose boat. *See* fast boat.

loose-footed sail. A sail without a boom.

lop. A state of the sea marked by short, steep waves.

LORAN. LOng Range Aid to Navigation; a system of radio position finding that uses shore stations that emit simultaneous high frequency radio waves. By measuring the time difference in receiving the signals, a ship can locate herself on a Loran line of position. Loran C is the latest model as Loran A is being phased out.

lorcha. A sailing junk of the Far East that has a European hull and a Chinese lugsail rig.

Lord Nelson. On a square-rigger, a rope ratline rigged above (higher than) the wooden ratlines, usually above the top.

lost or not lost. A term used in marine insurance policies to signify that the contract is retrospective and applies to any loss not already known about.

loud-hailer. A hand-held voice amplifier.

lough. *See* loch.

louver. An opening in a vertical weather bulkhead of a ship used for intake or exhaust of a powered ventilation system. Usually rain proof but not spray proof. *See* air lift, ventilators. The British use punkah-louvre to describe an air distribution device that controls the force and direction of ventilation air in a ship's compartment.

low. A cyclone or area of low atmospheric pressure that brings rain and storms in contrast to a high or anti-cyclone that is associated with good weather.

lower the boom. Slang for severe punishment or reprimand.

low water. The minimum height reached by a falling tide. Term is more seamanlike than low tide.

loxodrome. Same as a rhumb line.

loxodograph. An instrument that records the courses steered by a ship.

LPG. Liquid Petroleum-derived Gas. *See* liquid gas ship.

LR. Lloyd's Register of Shipping.

lubber. Short for landlubber.

lubberly. Unseamanlike and clumsy.

lubber's hole. In the old sailing ships, a hole in the deck of a top through which a man could go further aloft without the risk of going out and up over the rim of the top.

lubber's knot. A granny or false square knot; should never be used on board ship.

lubber's line. Reference mark on a compass or on a radar scope indicating the ship's head.

Lucky Bag. A compartment or locker aboard ship where various articles found adrift are stowed until claimed.

luff. *n* The forward edge of a fore-and-aft sail, next to the mast. *vb* **1.** To luff or flag when sailing is to bring the bow up into the wind until forward motion is slowed and the sails shake. **2.** To hold your luff is a command to the helmsman to keep the boat pointing up close to the wind. **3.** To luff an opponent in a sailing race or to engage in a luffing match is to prevent, if possible, an opponent from passing you to windward. **4.** The end of a cargo handling crane, the jib, is luffed when it is raised or lowered.

luffing davit. *See* davit.

luff puller. A cunningham or line attached to the sail to flatten the luff.

luffrope. The rope or line sewn into the luff or leading edge of a sail, traditionally on the port side of the edge. In some small sailboats, the luffrope of the mainsail fits into a groove or slide on the mainmast.

luff tackle. A general purpose tackle consisting of a double and a single block. The standing part is secured to the single block and the hauling part comes out of the double block. Often used as a handy billy or watch tackle.

luff upon luff. A purchase consisting of two luff tackles together.

lug. 1. A small piece of steel or angle iron used in shipbuilding to make various small fittings or pad-eyes. **2.** Any fitting on a mast or spar that includes an eye. Also called a lug piece. **3.** The yard on which a lugsail is set. Short for lugsail.

lugger. A small, coastal, 2- or 3-masted lug-rigged sailing craft, now uncommon except in the developing countries. The four-masted fishing schooners on the Grand Banks, often Portuguese, were sometimes called luggers.

lugsail. A four-sided, fore-and-aft sail with the head shorter than the foot and the luff shorter than the leech. It is bent to a lug or yard that is raised and lowered with the sail and may be loose-footed. Widely used abroad in small craft. The major types are dipping lug which has no boom (the yard must be dipped around the mast when tacking), the standing lug which has a boom whose forward end pivots at the mast, and the balance lug that has a boom and lug both projecting forward of the mast.

lumper. Old term for an unskilled worker on the waterfront and in a shipyard.

lunar. Pertaining to the moon.

lunar distance. The angle between the moon and another celestial body.

lunar inequality. The negligible fluctuation of a magnetic compass due to the attraction of the moon.

lunar method. An obsolete way of finding longitude by lunar distances.

lunch hook. A yachtsman's light anchor used mostly for short stops such as when cruising and anchoring for lunch.

lunitidal interval. The time between the moon's upper or lower transit and the next high or low water at a given place. The average lunitidal interval is known as the establishment of that port. Also called vulgar establishment on days of full or of new moon; has lost its importance with the advent of tide tables.

lurching. An abnormal, deep, and sometimes sudden roll of a ship in a seaway. *See* roll.

lutchet. Similar to a tabernacle.

Lutine Bell. Bell salvaged from the frigate "Lutine" which went down in 1799. It hangs in the Room at Lloyd's of London and is traditionally rung before making any important announcement such as a disaster at sea.

luting. A mixture of putty, white lead and oil that is used on the contacting surfaces of planks and timbers in wooden boat building.

lwl. *See* length on the load waterline.

lying to. *See* lie.

Lyle gun. Trade name for a line-throwing gun.

M

M. International signal code alphabet flag. When flown singly means: "My vessel is stopped and making no way through the water." Spoken: "mike."

MACH. Modular Automated Container Handling.

MacIntyre tank. An early type of double bottom construction for steel ships.

mackerel. A broad and often confusing name for nearly 60 species of deep sea, wide-ranging popular food and game fish of the family Scombride; included in the group are tuna, albacore, bonito, and wahoo. They live in large schools and are being seriously overfished. Some of these can be as large as the horse mackerel or the blue fin tuna of North Atlantic waters, reaching more than 1 000 pounds; all have deeply forked tails and smooth iridescent skin. The mackerel shark is part of the Lamnidae family, therefore not related.

mackerel sky. One of the cirro-cumulus clouds whose design resembles the bars or ripples on the back of a Spanish mackerel. Off the coast of the British Isles and of the U.S., this sky may indicate good weather to follow, but in southern Europe it may mean just the opposite.

Macnamara Lace. Fancy curtains and trimmings worked with white cord and made by the boat's crew for Naval barges and gigs. Nautical slang for the word macrame.

madrepores. *See* coral.

Maelstrom. Traditionally considered to be a powerful and destructive whirlpool. Originally, a very fast tidal current off the coast of one of the Lofoten Islands on the coast of Norway; combined with and sometimes opposing strong winds, the current can produce eddies that are dangerous to small boats.

Mae West. Slang for an inflatable life vest or jacket. Also slang for a parachute spinnaker.

magazine. A compartment aboard ship especially designed and equipped for storing explosives.

magnetic chart. Chart showing lines of equal magnetic variation.

magnetic compass. A free floating magnet is attracted to the earth and tends to align itself with the earth's magnetic field thereby pointing to magnetic north and forming a magnetic compass.

magnetic storm. A large scale but short disturbance of the earth's magnetic field associated with sun spots and disrupting radio signals.

maiden voyage. The first trip to sea of a newly-built ship exclusive of trials and shakedown.

mailbuoy. Expression used to confuse new men. It was supposed to be a buoy at mid-ocean for exchanging mail.

main. In a poetic sense, part of the ocean, as the Spanish Main. The main battery of a warship is its principal armament.

mainmast. Traditionally, the principal and heaviest mast of a full-rigged ship, the second one from forward. In a yawl or ketch, the most forward mast. In a schooner, the after mast if there are two, the center mast if there are three masts.

mainsail. Traditionally, the principal sail or course on the mainmast. In a square-rigger, the lowest sail on the mainmast. In a modern sailboat, the largest sail set abaft the mainmast.

mainsheet swivel block. Block secured to the bottom of the cockpit of a sailboat that anchors the mainsheet gear. It should swivel 180 degrees.

make. To accomplish, to do. A ship makes leeway; she makes good 10 knots; she is making water; the mate makes sail or makes a line fast to a cleat. In response to a report that it is 12 o'clock, the Commanding Officer of a warship replies "make it so." Tides make or are making when they rise in maximum height constantly between neap and spring tides. If they fall, they are said to be taking off.

make and mend. In the British Navy, an afternoon without ordered work or drills; U.S. equivalent is ropeyarn Sunday. Usually specified after a strenuous night of work or in very heavy weather.

make-up feed. Boiler water taken from the reserve feed tanks, purified or treated and added to the feed water condensed in the main condenser to make up for water lost in the system.

making iron. A caulking iron; a chisel-like tool with a groove used in finishing a seam after the oakum is driven in. Also called a creasing iron and a common iron.

mako. A shark. *See* shark.

malahini. A Hawaiian word for newcomer or stranger and thus a surfer's name for an inexperienced and beginning surfer.

Malibu Board. An Australian term for a modern, light surfboard.

man. To man a ship is to provide and organize a crew. A boat's crew mans its boat. The crew may man the yards or the rails or man the side of a ship on a ceremonial occasion.

manatee. An almost extinct coastal equatic mammal of the order Sirenia which includes dugongs; found along the tropical shores of West African, North and

South American bays and rivers, feeds on grass and sea weed. They grow to about 10 feet and are also called sea cows.

maneuvering board. A compass rose with polar coordinates printed on a sheet of paper and used in solving the geometric problems of relative motion involved in ship maneuvering.

manger. The perforated deck or flooring of the chain locker. Manger boards or plates were once used as the after boundary of a space called a manger near the hawse-pipes to divert water over the side.

mangrove. A shrub or small tree with multiple prop roots that grows in salt water along many tropical coasts.

manhelper. A long wooden pole with a paint brush attached that is used in painting the ship's side. Also called a long arm.

manhole. A round or oval access to, for example, compartments, tanks, and boilers that is fitted with a bolted watertight cover.

manifest. A detailed list of a ship's cargo; may be certified by a consular officer to meet importation requirements. A manifest is made out after loading is completed, usually based on the bills of lading, and contains complete information on the nature of the cargo and to what ports it is destined.

manila hemp. A fibrous material from the abaca plant. Manila is the name of the rope made from this natural fiber; once widely used, it is now being replaced by synthetic fibers such as Dacron or nylon which are smaller, stronger, more elastic and resistant to rot.

man-of-war bird. *See* frigatebird.

manrope. The side or guard rope of a ladder or any rope used as a safety line or lifeline.

manta ray. A huge skate, as much as 20 feet across, that appears to fly under water by flapping its wings. Strong but unaggressive, it is feared by divers into whose hose lines it may blunder. Often seen near the surface, it sometimes leaps clear of the water, presumably to free itself of parasites. Also known as devil fish.

map. *See* bathymetric map.

MARAD. MARitime ADministration.

Marconi rig. A triangular sail, same as Bermuda or jib-headed rig.

Marcq St. Hilaire method. The first modern solution of the astronomical triangle in celestial navigation that produced a line of position. Long since replaced by Ageton, Dreisonstock, H.0.214 and others.

mare's nest. Slang for any mess or disarray aboard ship. Nearest British equivalent seems to be dog's breakfast.

mare's tails. A popular name for tufted cirrus clouds that usually accompany good weather.

margin. In its nautical sense describes a number of angles, plates, brackets and planks in shipbuilding.

margin angle. The connecting piece to the shell of the ship.

margin bracket. The connecting piece to the side framing. Also called bilge bracket.

margin line. An assumed line parallel to and approximately three feet below the bulkhead deck at the side of the ship. If the ship takes on water, it cannot safely sink below the margin line.

margin plate. The outboard steel strake of the inner bottom of a ship which, when turned down at the bilge, forms the outboard boundary of the double bottom.

mariculture. Short for marine agriculture. Same as sea farming.

marigram. A graphic representation of the rise and fall of the tide, obtained by an instrument called a marigraph which records these data at a specific station. Also called a tidal curve or diagram.

marigraph. *See* marigram.

marina. A harbor facility providing, for example, fuel, food, ice, showers, washing machines, and telephones for the convenience of small boat owners having permanent or temporary berths. Also a seaside park or promenade.

marine. Seagoing vessels considered collectively as in Merchant Marine. A member of the Marine Corps is a Marine. As an adjective, it means anything relating to the sea as in marine geology or marine engineering. Sometimes synonymous with maritime.

marine adventure. A term for a commercial voyage.

marine agriculture. *See* sea farming.

marine belt. Same as territorial waters.

marine borer. Any of the wood-piercing mollusks, especially the teredos, who attack wood underwater. Same as shipworm.

Marine Check Radar Detector. A trade name for a portable, battery-powered device that detects and gives the bearing of any radar. Small boats not equipped with radar are thereby able to detect the presence of other ships that might present a danger at night or in low visibility.

marine geochemist. Person who studies the minerals and rocks of the ocean in order to understand the distribution of elements in the earth's crust.

marine geologist. Person who studies the mountain ranges, rocks and sediment of the ocean, especially in relation to their distribution.

marine geophysicist. Person who studies the composition and physical aspects of the undersea world, particularly in relation to its electric, magnetic, and gravitational fields.

marine glue. British term for a modern caulking compound; not an ordinary adhesive.

marine insurance. Insurance that covers cargo, hull, freight or any insurable interest related thereto against perils of the sea or perils incident to a marine adventure. There is ocean marine insurance and inland marine insurance that covers only commerce on inland waterways.

mariner. Person who goes to sea, such as seaman or sailor; one whose vocation is the sea.

marine railway. A device that moves on railroad tracks; used for hauling boats out of the water and onto the shore for repair or painting.

marine salina. A body of salt water separated from the sea by a sand or gravel barrier through which salt water percolates. *See* salina.

mariner's anchor. An old-fashioned anchor.

marine soap. Same as saltwater soap; usable in saltwater.

Marine Weather Services Charts. Charts covering all U.S. waters; issued by the National Weather Service (NWS) and available from the National Ocean Survey. They show NWS broadcast stations and frequencies, storm warning display locations, stations whose observations are included in NWS broadcasts, and Coast Guard and Marine Police stations.

maritime. Pertaining to the sea and anything associated with it; often synonymous with marine.

Maritime Academy. A college for training and educating Merchant Marine officers. Five are state-operated, in Maine, Massachusetts, New York, Texas, and California. There is also a national, federally-operated U.S. Merchant Marine Academy at King's Point, New York.

Maritime Administration. An office in the Department of Commerce responsible for developing, regulating, and subsidizing U.S. shipping; once called the Maritime Commission, it's abbreviation is now **MARAD**.

mark. 1. A line, notch, piece of cloth or leather or a structure indicating a measure, a limit or a danger. A load line mark or Plimsoll Mark indicates maximum allowable draft of a ship. These may be called birth marks in a newly built ship. 2. A mark on a leadline is a measure of depth and is reported by the leadsman as "by the mark .. ". 3. A bench mark is cut in metal or stone and indicates a reference point aboard a warship for calibrating gun and missile control or, if cut in stone, indicates a tidal datum. 4. A daymark indicates a shoal or obstruction. Also called a landmark or shoalmark.

mark, sail racing. A buoy, other floating object or a stake that a sailboat must pass on a designated side when racing. Line marks show the starting and finishing lines, rounding marks determine how far the boats must go, and guide marks outline the allowed racing area.

marl. To fasten or secure with a series of marline hitches, such as a sail to its boltrope or canvas around a large rope (known as parceling).

marlin. One of the large oceanic gamefish of the billfish family distinguished by its protruding beak or bill; has been caught up to 1000 pounds. The black marlin is the largest of the genus *(Makaira* and *Tetrapturus)* that also include the white, blue and striped marlins.

marline. Small stuff or cord used for lashings, mousing, and seizing. Once lightly tarred to stop rot but now usually made of synthetic fibers.

marlinespike. A round and tapered steel tool, similar to a fid, used for example in splicing wire and rope, and screwing shackle pins. *See* fid.

marlinespike seamanship. The art and technique of using rope and wire to make knots, bends, hitches, and splices.

marry. To join two ropes together, either before splicing or side by side before seizing. Two cargo whips attached to a single cargo hook is married gear.

martesia. A clam-like marine borer.

martingale. One of the ropes or chains in a large sailing ship under the bowsprit and jibboom that is used to counteract the stress of the headstay upon the end of the jibboom; extended by the dolphin striker. Also a kicking strap or kicker when used to hold a boom down.

Maru. A word following the name of most Japanese merchant ships meaning good, fulfilling, calm whose exact derivation is lost in the mists of antiquity. Since not required by law, it is now sometimes replaced by the prefix Japan, followed by the ship's name.

mascarat. Same as bore.

mask. A contrivance of heavy timbers braced at the stern of a ship being launched in confined waters; slows the ship as it becomes waterborne.

mass transport. In the nautical sense, the net movement of water by wave action in the direction of wave travel.

mast. The wooden, metal, or composite pole or structure rising vertically from the ship's deck; used to support, for example, sails, signal gear, and cargo handling gear. In two-masted vessels with the higher mast aft, such as in schooners, the masts are called foremast and mainmast; in three-masted ships, add a mizzenmast aft (also the name for the after mast on a ketch or yawl). For square-riggers and schooners of 4 to 7 masts, the names follow local variations but, in general, going from forward to aft, they are called fore, main, mizzen, jigger, spanker, driver, and pusher. In large sailing ships the masts are separated into several sections known as lower mast, topmast, topgallant mast, royal mast, and sometimes includes a skysail pole.

mast bed. In wooden boats, the pieces of wood in the decking around the mast hole.

mastboot. *See* mastcoat.

mast cheek. *See* cheek.

mast cloth. The lining of a squaresail that prevents chafing against the mast.

mastcoat. A heavy canvas fitted around the base of the mast where it meets the deck; keeps out water. Called a petticoat or mastboot in small vessels.

Master. A person or officer in command of a merchant or fishing vessel, qualified by experience, examination and certified by his Master's papers. His courtesy title is Captain. In sailing warship days, Masters did the navigating and shiphandling while under the command of a senior officer who fought the ship.

Master-At-Arms. A shipboard policeman. The Chief MAA in the U.S. Navy is called the Sheriff and in the Royal Navy, he is known as Jaunty.

mast eye. A metal ring made fast to a mast, usually by means of a strap.

mast funnel. A metal band at the head of an upper mast of a sailing ship around which the rigging fitted or was made to rest. Also called a jack.

masthead. *n* The part of a mast from the topmost standing rigging to the cap or truck. *vb* To masthead a yard or other piece of gear is to hoist it as far as it will go; sometimes called full-mast or two-block.

masthead man. A lookout sent aloft to a crow's nest or barrel.

masthead float. Float at the masthead of a multi-hulled ship or a catamaran that is used to right the boat if it is knocked down; may be solid yet buoyant or a bladder that is filled automatically with compressed gas.

masthead fly. A wind direction indicator on top of a mast.

masthead light. A 20 point (255°) white light at the forward masthead of a ship showing an arc from dead ahead to 2 points abaft the beam on both sides; required to be displayed by the Rules of the Road.

masthead rig. A jib-headed rig in which the headstay is made fast to the top of the mast. In a 7/8ths rig, the headstay is made fast 7/8ths of the way up.

mast house. *See* bridge deck.

masting. The optimum location of masts when designing a sailing vessel.

mast partner. The timber or plank on the deck of a boat through which the mast passes.

mast step. The timber at the bottom of a boat on which the mast rests.

mast trunk. Same as tabernacle.

mat. The foundation structure of an offshore oil rig that rests flooded on the bottom when the rig is in position.

match hook. Same as sister hook.

mate. In the Merchant Navy, the title for a ship's officer, such as Chief or First Mate or Second Mate; in the Navy, an assistant to a Warrant Officer such as Boatswain's Mate or Carpenter's Mate. Also a fellow sailor as a shipmate, messmate.

mate's cargo. Slang for valuable cargo requiring security stowage.

mate's receipt. A document signed by the mate or chief officer acknowledging receipt of cargo on board. It forms the basis for the final bill of lading.

Mathew Walker knot. A good stopper knot, formed by passing each strand around the rope in the direction of the lay and then tucking it upward through its own bight or loop.

Mayday. The internationally known and authorized distress signal by voice radio; the equivalent of SOS in code.

meal flag. Any flag that indicates that owner, officers, or crew are dining. Navy ships fly the E flag which is sometimes called the meal break, bean rag, or chow rag.

mean. A middle or average quantity or position between extremes such as mean draft and a mean tide.

mean time. Time based on the mean sun; an imaginary body whose movement in relation to the earth is regular and uniform. *See* time.

measured mile. The distance in deep water offshore, whose limits are clearly marked by ranges on the shore, over which ships test their speed in relation to the revolutions per minute (rpm) of their propellers.

measurement rule. A formula for handicapping sailboats of different design and size for racing.

mediterranean. In general sense, any large inland sea of saltwater surrounded by land but with one or more narrow openings to the sea. Specifically there is the Mediterranean Sea between Africa and Europe.

Mediterranean moor. *See* moor.

medusa. Same as jellyfish.

meet her. A command to the helmsman to shift the rudder or to use more rudder in order to stop the swing of the ship; usually followed by a specific course to steer or an object to steer for.

meeting. Two ships approaching head to head so that at night both sidelights would be visible are considered, under the Rules of the Road, to be meeting.

Meirform bow. A modern streamlined shape for the bow of certain ships that is marked by a bulbous rather than a pointed forefoot.

meltemi. The strong northerly wind that blows across the Greek Islands in the summer. Also called the etesian wind.

mend. In the old days of sail, it meant to refurl a sail that was badly made up and secured to its yard.

menhaden. A small and abundant, oily fish, *Brevoorita tyrannus*, that is used as bait, chum, or for fish oil or fertilizer. Also called pogy, oldwife, mossbunker, mossbanker, or bunker.

Meon anchor. Similar to a Danforth with deep flukes that pivot around the stock at the bottom of the shank, a British anchor designed for big ships.

Mercator charts. Charts done as a result of Mercator projections and used in latitudes under $75°$.

Mercator projections. A method of projecting a sphere, such as the earth, onto a flat surface. The parallels of latitude are shown at proper intervals as straight lines and meridians of longitude at right angles to them.

Mercator sailing. *See* sailing.

merchant. Pertaining to maritime trade and commerce such as the Merchant Navy, Merchant Marine or merchant sailor, or merchant vessel.

mercury or mercurial barometer. Barometer that measures atmospheric pressure by the varying height of a column of mercury. *See* barometer.

meridian. An imaginary great circle passing through the poles and corresponding to a line of longitude.

meridian altitude. The altitude of longitude body when on the observer's meridian.

meridian distance. The difference of longitude in time or arc between two places.

mermaid. A mythical sea creature, half woman and half fish, believed to have been inspired by the sea mammals, dugong and manatee, whose torso can have some resemblance to that of a woman.

mermaid's purse. The egg case of certain rays and skates; often found on the beach.

mesh, meshing. A space in a fish net enclosed by adjacent knots.

mesobenthic. Describes sea life on the ocean bottom at depths of 600 to 2000 feet. *See* bathybenthic.

mesopelagic. Describes life in the sea in depths of water of 600 to 2000 feet. *See* bathypelagic.

mesoplankton. Plankton living in ocean water in depths of 600 to 2000 feet.

mesoscale eddies. *See* eddy.

mess. Food or meals aboard ship as well as the compartment in which they are served. A sailor dines in the general mess in the crew's messhall with his messmates while officers and passengers enjoy their own mess served in a saloon or wardroom. A wine or cigar mess is a special Naval cooperative in the wardroom for the benefit of mess members.

messcook. Person who serves or prepares the food. Also called messman.

message. The proper nautical term for any rapid form of communication (electronic, visual or messenger) to and from ship.

messenger. Any line used to haul in or handle a heavier rope as in putting over mooring lines when a ship goes alongside the pier. A line throwing gun, a bolo or a heaving line is used to establish contact, then a medium-heavy line (the messenger) is used to haul the mooring lines into position.

messroom. A dining room aboard ship.

metacenter. The point of intersection of the verticals through the center of buoyancy of a ship when she is in equilibrium.

metacentric height. The vertical distance between the center of gravity and the metacenter measured in feet. An important measure of stability. *See* inclining experiment.

metal mike. Slang for gyro or automatic pilot. Also called iron mike.

meteorology. The science of weather. A British term for weather bureau is met office.

metric ton. 1000 kilograms or 2205 pounds.

MFV. A British acronym for Motor Fishing Vessel.

mic. Short for microseconds, a common word in electronic navigation. Pronounced mike.

Micro-Omega. A form of differential Omega in which the adjusted sky wave corrections for actual propagation conditions are transmitted continuously and are automatically applied to the standard Omega receiver.

middle body. Part of a ship's hull amidships in which a constant cross-sectional shape exists.

middle ground. A shoal or shallow area with deep water on each side; found in buoyed channels and marked by a middle ground buoy.

middle watch. The watch from midnight to 0400 or 4 am. U.S. term is midwatch.

mid-latitude sailing. One of the sailings that uses in its determination the middle or mean latitude of the area the ship traverses. *See* sailing.

mid-ocean ridge. A 40,000 mile long continuous median mountain range underwater from the Arctic south through the Atlantic around Africa into the Indian Ocean; usually found at 3000 to 8000 feet depth.

mid-ocean rift. A deep and narrow (15-30 miles wide) cleft or valley along the crest of the mid-ocean ridge. The Gulf of Aden, the Red Sea, the Dead Sea, the Jordan Valley and the East African rift system are all considered to be extensions of the mid-ocean rift.

midshipman. A male or female student officer, either at the U.S. Naval Academy at Annapolis, at one of the various Merchant Marine Academies, at the Coast Guard Academy, or at a university under the Naval Reserve Officer's training program. In the British Navy, he serves at sea. A midshipman, while not commissioned, is considered an officer in a limited sense.

midships. Same as amidships; the central or middle part of a ship.

midwatch. *See* middle watch.

mile. A nautical mile by international agreement is 6076 feet or 1852 meters or one minute of arc at the Equator. A statute or land mile is used in navigating lakes and rivers and is 5280 feet. The nautical mile is known as an Admiralty mile in the United Kingdom.

millepora. A variety of coral, usually bright yellow, that is equipped with tiny barbed stings and is thus known as stinging coral.

miller-dog. A shark. *See* tope.

millibar. A thousandth part of a bar that is used as a measure of atmospheric pressure under the metric system. A bar is 29.92 inches of mercury at sea level and at $32°F$.

MINDAC. Miniature Inertial Navigation Digital Automatic Computer; a general purpose computer in the SINS system designed primarily to calculate present ships position.

mind your rudder. A caution to the helmsman to steer more precisely or to be careful in applying rudder under special circumstances.

mine. An underwater bomb detonated by contact with its horns, by sound, by increased water pressure of a passing ship, by magnetic influence of a ship's hull, or from the shore. Usually planted as a minefield by minelayers or aircraft and swept (exploded) by minesweepers often towed by helicopters.

minute. 60 seconds. As an angular measure, it is 1/60th of a degree. There are 360 degrees in a circle or a sphere. Also 15 minutes of arc in longitude is an hour.

mirage. At sea, the presence of dry desert air, and thereby different atmospheric characteristics, causes refraction and distortion of light, radio and radar waves.

miss stays. In tacking a sailboat, to fail to bring the ship's head through the wind so that the ship can fall off on the new tack and fill her sails. The ship is said to be in irons if she should miss stays.

mist. An air mass filled with tiny white droplets; a cloud touching the ground with visibility over 1000 meters. *See* fog.

mistral. A strong, dry northerly wind of the Mediterranean sea particularily felt in the Gulf of Lyons where the funneling effect of the Rhone Valley increases its velocity. Similar to the bora of the Adriatic and the tramontana from Italy.

mitchboard. Boom crutch or rail used to support the boom when the sail is lowered.

miter. The seam in a sail, usually the headsail, that joins the cloths running in two different directions. In a miter cut, the cloths are perpendicular to the leech and to the foot of the sail.

mitten money. An additional pilotage fee charged in cold weather.

mizzen. Pertaining to the mizzenmast, the aftermost mast in a full-rigged ship, bark, barkentine, three-masted schooner, yawl and ketch; the gaff sail on the mizzenmast of a bark or barkentine. In yawls and ketches, it is the smaller after mast, also called a jigger, forward of which can be set a mizzen staysail and a mizzen spinnaker.

Moby Dick. The great white sperm whale pursued by Captain Ahab in Melville's classic novel of the same name.

mock-up. A model or replica of a machine, weapon, control center or device used for training, planning or design.

model basin. A large instrumented tank or pool used for testing such items as models of ships, propellers, and torpedoes.

moderate breeze. *See* Beaufort Scale.

modern log. A speedometer or knotmeter in a boat.

mold. A wooden pattern or frame from which steel beams and plates can be cut and shaped in shipbuilding. The design (lines) of a ship are laid down full size in a mold loft.

molded breadth. The greatest width or beam of a ship's hull measured to the outside of the frame, inside of the plating.

molded depth. The vertical distance in a ship measured from the top of the keel to the top of the upper deck beam amidships.

molded displacement. Displacement computed in measuring capacity to the outside of the frame not including the submerged volume of the planking or plating.

molded draft. The vertical distance from the waterline to the lowest intersection of the outside plating and the keel. Also called fairbody draft.

molded surface. An imaginary surface of a ship having zero thickness. It is equivalent to a thin membrane spread over the shell of a ship.

molding. Any decorative or useful strip of metal or wood such as the half round on the outside of a boat at deck and gunwale. Also called a rubbing piece or nosing ribband.

mold loft. *See* loft.

mole. A strong protective masonry structure forming the wall or breakwater of a harbor and usually fitted on the inside with facilities for loading and unloading boats and ships.

mollusk *or* **mollusc.** Part of the large phylum Mollusca which includes marine invertebrates with shells such as clams, oysters, and limpets.

monitor. An obsolete iron warship having one or more revolving guns and a low profile; designed for harbor and coastal defense. Also a watercannon, a nozzle on a high pressure portable pump for fire fighting aboard ship.

monkey. A vague and usually irrelevant adjective used to describe something unusual or undersize such as the short white messjacket or an officer's evening dress jacket which is called a monkey jacket. A ship is called monkey sparred or rigged when her rig is considered too light or too unorthodox. Used as a noun, it defines the container into which the rum ration is poured for each mess.

monkey block. A loose term for any small block, usually with an attached swivel used in the running rigging of a sailing ship.

monkey fist. A heavy weighted knot at the end of a heaving line.

monkey pipe. Same as chain pipe.

monkey rail. A light, decorative wooden fence above the main deck in the after part of an old sailing ship.

monkey rope. A lifeline made fast to a man going over the side.

monkey spar or gaff. A short spar or gaff.

monkey tail. A short line used to assist a man in hooking on a boat fall when hoisting a boat and then used as mousing for the hook.

monofilament. A strong, nearly transparent line made of a single continuous thread of synthetic fiber usually nylon; widely used for fishing. Often referred to as mono.

monsoon. Specifically a seasonal wind of the Far and Middle East (China Sea, Indian Ocean, Red Sea) which changes direction and intensity in winter and summer as the land masses gain and lose heat. Monsoon is used in a more general sense for a seasonal wind anywhere in the Orient.

Monsoon Current. An Indian Ocean current oriented in a general eastward direction off India and Ceylon.

moon dog. *See* parhelion.

moon pool. The center section or well of a drilling ship over which the derrick or tower is mounted.

moonraker. Same as moonsail.

moonsail. A squaresail once carried in light winds above a skysail in a square-rigger. Also called a moonraker. *See* kites.

moor. 1. To secure a ship alongside another or to a pier, dock, a mooring buoy. 2. To anchor with more than one anchor. A Mediterranean moor involves dropping an anchor or two anchors in succession inside a harbor, then backing down and adjusting the scope so the stern can be made fast to a pier or seawall and a brow rigged. The British term is stern-to moor.

mooring. The location where ships moor with anchors or mooring buoys.

mooring anchor. Any heavy device, mass or clump of cement or anchor used to secure, for example, a mooring buoy, lightship, or buoy firmly to the bottom.

mooring buoy. A large floating, well-anchored, usually flat, round structure with a heavy ring to which a ship's wire or anchor chain is made fast.

mooring chock. A heavy casting with incurving horns located along the edge of the weather deck and designed to provide a fairlead for a ship's mooring lines.

mooring cleat. A large cleat or kevel to which mooring lines can be made fast aboard ship.

mooring line. Wire, manila, or nylon rope used to secure a ship to the pier or to another ship; named from forward aft: #1 bow line, #2 after bow spring, #3 forward bow spring, #4 breast line, #5 after quarter spring, #6 forward quarter spring, #7 stern line. British term is berthing hawser.

mooring ring. An oval or circular opening in a ship's steel bulwark that permits the passage of a mooring line.

mooring shackle. Shackle used to fasten the end of the anchor chain to the ring on the mooring buoy. The screw pin of the shackle has a large eye for easy turning. *See* mooring swivel.

mooring staple. *See* staple.

mooring swivel. A special heavy triple swivel to which both anchor chains are attached outside the hawse as well as a single chain leading up through a hawsepipe on deck of a ship mooring with two anchors. Sometimes inaccurately referred to as a mooring shackle.

mooring whip. A device to hold a boat away from the pier made of several flexible poles on the pier which lead out over the boat. Short lines are attached to both poles and boat. The same device can keep a yacht's towed dinghy away from the stern.

moorish idol. A small disc-shaped tropical reef fish with a very long raked dorsal fin and broad yellow and black stripes.

Moorsom tonnage system. The basis for nearly all methods of tonnage measurement. It provides for computing the volume of the space under the tonnage deck plus the between deck spaces. In general 100 cubic feet of internal cargo capacity is a ton.

moray eel. A snake-like, finless, tropical saltwater fish of the family Murrenidae that swims with a serpentine movement and hides in a hole during the day. Its sharp, back-slanting teeth can be dangerous to an unwary hand groping in a hole for lobsters. Grows to 12 feet and is related to the conger eel with which it is sometimes confused. *See* eel.

morning watch. 0400 (4 am) to 0800 (8 am).

Morse Code. The series of dots and dashes representing letters of the alphabet and used in radio and flashing light communications at sea.

Morse lamp. An electric, directional, hand-held light for sending messages by Morse. Also called a blinker gun or light.

mossbunker. *See* menhaden.

Mother Carey. The traditional, fictitious owner of certain sea birds found in the open sea, especially petrels which are known as Mother Carey's chickens. Mother Carey's goose is the giant fulmar.

motorboat. A craft propelled only by a motor.

motor launch. The traditional 24–50 foot open, diesel-powered U.S. Navy boat used for personnel and stores; carried aboard large warships.

motor, outboard. A portable internal combustion or electric motor fitted with a steering propeller and attached to the stern of a boat.

motor sailor. A cross between a sailing yacht, usually sloop rigged, and a cabin cruiser; sails adequately, has a reasonably powerful motor, and comfortable accommodations.

mouse. To mouse a hook is to fasten small stuff or wire across it to prevent the escape of the line or wire it is holding. Also to seize both shanks of sister hooks or to fasten together similar items.

mousetrap. A quick-release gear used to release the power skiff from the seine boat in setting a purse seine.

mousing. The small stuff used to mouse.

mud drum. The water tank or drum in some marine boilers.

mud hook. Slang for anchor.

mudskipper. An amphibious fish common to Africa, Asia, and Australia that can walk out of the water on its pectoral fins.

mule. An upper staysail such as the one used in a ketch above the mainsail. Also a small genoa.

multihull. A collective term for boats with more than one hull such as catamarans, trimarans or proas.

murderer. An English fish rake, equipped with sharp hooks, used to impale ground fish when dragged over the bottom.

Murman Current. A warm ocean current running southeast off the coast of the Kola peninsula.

mushroom anchor. A special type of anchor shaped like a mushroom and used as buoy anchors and to hold in a muddy bottom.

mussel. Part of the Mytilidae family; elongated, tapered bivalves, usually dark in color and similar to oysters. Considered a delicacy in Europe but not widely consumed in the U.S.

mutiny. Rebellion or serious widespread and organized disobedience aboard ship.

mutton fish. An Atlantic food fish resembling the sea bass that is part of the Gerridae family.

mutton sail. *See* spanker.

muzzler. A strong wind or gale blowing from dead ahead.

Mylar. Trade name for a relatively new sail material that is a plastic film, not woven.

N

N. International signal code alphabet flag. When flown singly means: "No." Also known as the negative flag. Spoken: "november."

nacre. Mother of pearl; the lustrous inner layer of the shells of certain mollusks.

nadir. The point on the celestial sphere directly under the observer and opposite to the zenith.

nail-sick. Describes a wooden hull whose fastenings are too corroded to be reliable.

naked. Said of a wooden ship without copper sheating.

name and hail. Old term for the stem and stern scrolls and carvings that reveal the name and the homeport of the vessel.

Nantucket sleigh ride. A whaleboat towed by a harpooned whale; often fast and dangerous until the whale tires. Method used before the explosive harpoon was developed.

Napier's diagram. A curve of deviation error on various courses for the magnetic compass that are displayed on a board conveniently near the binnacle.

naphtha engine. An obsolete, multi-cylinder boat engine that vaporized naphtha instead of water to drive the pistons and at the same time used naphtha (petroleum spirits) as fuel; replaced by the internal combustion engine.

narrows. A navigable, relatively short passage in, for example, a river, bay, or sound with a limited width. Not as long as a reach.

narwhal. An Arctic sea mammal of the dolphin family, distinguished by a long round ivory tooth or tusk in the front of its head; believed to have been the inspiration for the mythical unicorn.

National Cargo Bureau. A non-profit trade association with offices in all major U.S. ports that assists and advises on proper and safe cargo handling.

National Ocean Survey (NOS). Formerly the Coast and Geodetic Survey, a government office that produces charts of the U.S. as well as tide and current tables, Coast Pilots, and Notices to Mariners. It is part of the National Oceanic and Atmospheric Administration (NOAA).

National Sea Grant Program. Program that provides a means for public and private institutions, organizations and agencies to cooperate and to develop the resources of the sea. It is partially funded by the U.S. government and is run by the National Science Foundation.

nautical. Pertaining to ships, shipping, navigation, and seamen. Not as broad in meaning as maritime since the latter relates to the sea and everything associated with it.

Nautical Almanac. Tables of positions of celestial bodies used in navigation, times of sunrise, moonrise, and other data of interest to navigators. Prepared jointly by the U.S. Naval Observatory and the Royal Greenwich Observatory near London.

nautilus. A small mollusk, an invertebrate sea animal, a cephalopod related to the octopus that lives in a chambered, spiral shell. The last chamber contains the body while the others, filled with liquid and gas, control its vertical movements (175-900 feet) in the tropical waters in which it lives.

nautophone. A sound-making device used as a fog signal by shore stations; similar to a diaphone but using an oscillating metal diaphragm instead of compressed air to make a loud noise.

navaid. An aid to navigation.

naval. A word that, according to U.S. usage pertains to the U.S. Navy and other navies. Older usage has a broader sense, as in naval architect and naval stores. In the United Kingdom, naval is still used in the wider sense.

NAVDAC. NAVigation Data Assimilation Computer; a real-time, general purpose, digital computer originally designed for the Polaris missile submarine program.

navel pipe. British term for chain pipe.

navicert. Short for navigation certificate. Certificate used by a belligerent power testifying that certain cargo being carried in a ship was not subject to seizure.

navigable semicircle. The area near a hurricane or typhoon away from its direction of advance and thus subject to less violent weather. The opposite, the area towards which the storm is advancing, is known as the dangerous semicircle.

navigate. To control the course of a ship or aircraft; to make a passage or voyage.

navigation. The art and science of directing ships' movements over and under the sea. It can be celestial, by the observation of heavenly bodies, bathymetric (by depth of water) or electronic with radar, radio, satellite, and inertial guidance. Piloting and dead reckoning are the earliest forms of navigation and with SINS dead reckoning has been perfected. *See* Navstar, doppler navigation system.

navigation calculator or computor. A small, battery powered, hand-held, solid state device for working out sights, solving the astronomical triangle. The data from the sight reduction tables and the air or Nautical Almanac is programmed, requiring only as input the corrected observed altitude and time. An accurate digital or quartz watch is sometimes included and many other standard calculations can be made.

navigation, electronic and radio. *See* radio navigation.

navigation lights. *See* lights. The term is also a synonym for running lights.

navigator. A person who navigates; specifically responsible for navigation.

NAVSAT. The Navy NAVigation SATellite system that provides accurate all-weather world-wide position finding for ships and aircraft. It is highly accurate, passive and uses Doppler shift to measure the signals emitted by the satellite and calculate the position of the receiver. Also called transit; available to all.

Navstar. An advanced world-wide Global Positioning System (GPS) using satellites broadcasting signals. Highly accurate and partly coded for security, it follows NAVSAT as a second generation system.

NAYRU. North American Yacht Racing Union; once important to yachtsmen because it organized and supervised ocean and coastal racing. Now the USYRU.

Navy anchor. *See* stockless anchor.

Navy top. Same as Bimini top.

neap. *n* The tides which twice in a lunar month rise and fall the least from the mean level; in constrast to spring tides. *vb* A ship that has run aground at high water is said to be neaped or is beneaped.

neap tides and tidal currents. Tides of decreased range or velocity occurring semi-monthly as a result of the moon being in quadrature with the sun. *See* spring tide.

nearshore current system. Current caused by surf. It includes the shoreward mass transport of water by the breaking waves, longshore currents parallel to the beach that include feeder currents, rip currents perpendicular to the beach fed by feeder currents, and the expanding heads of the rip currents. Nearshore currents are also called inshore currents. *See* rip current, longshore current.

neck. In oceanography, the stream of a rip current. *See* rip current. Geographically, a narrow piece of land between two water masses, an isthmus.

nef. A French ship of the 15th and 16th centuries, three-masted and square-rigged. The word is now used for the elaborate, sometimes silver, ship models used as dining table decoration.

negligence clause. *See* Inchmaree clause.

nekton. One of the three components of pelagic sea life marked by the ability to swim effectively against the current at sea and thus migrate. The others are phytoplankton, tiny free drifting plants and zooplankton, the minute sea animals that cannot swim strongly.

nematocyst. A minute capsule containing a stinging, poisonous filament equipped with tiny barbs; used as a defense by some coral and anemones.

Neptune. The Roman god of the sea (the Greek counterpart was Poseidon) who often appears aboard ship during Crossing-the-Line ceremonies.

Neptune's Sheep. A poetic term for whitecaps or white horses, the tops of waves breaking and spilling as driven by the wind.

neritic. Describes the part of the sea that is near the coast, a subdivision of the pelagic or surface layer of the ocean. The other subdivision in the open sea is oceanic.

nest. Ships berthed together to a single mooring buoy or anchor are said to be nested or in a nest. Ship's boats are sometimes stowed one inside another on deck in a nest. *See* raft.

nets. Cargo nets are made of rope, used to load and unload loose freight, and in emergencies or when disembarking troops are rigged over the side as mass ladders. Various fish nets, trawls and seines are now made of synthetic fibers in various shapes and sizes. Steel wire nets are used in wartime to protect harbors from enemy submarines and torpedoes.

nets, fish. Meshed and knotted devices made of synthetic fibers and used to catch, trap and hold fish. Also called seines and trawls. *See* seine, drag net, purse net, basnig, gill net, lampara net, fyke net, dip net, lift net, trawl net, blanket net, cast net, trammel net, butterfly net, channel net.

netsonde. A device on the headline of a mid-water fishing trawl that records and transmits to the towing vessel the depth of water at which the trawl is being towed. Thus a trawl can be towed where the fishfinder indicates the fish are.

nettle. Small line once made of twisted yarns in handy lengths and used for odd jobs such as hammock clews and clothes stops.

nib. Same as jog.

niggerhead. A gipsey or warping head; the drum end of a winch around which turns of line are made when hauling. Also the heavy bitts for making fast a towrope to a tug as well as those bollards which line a pier or wharf for ship's mooring lines.

night glasses. Binoculars with large fields and good light-gathering qualities for use at sea at night.

nilas. A thin elastic film of ice that forms in sheets on a calm sea; may be dark or light in color.

nimbus. *See* cloud.

nip. *n* Sharp turn or bend in a rope or wire. *See* freshen the nip. *vb* To stop or seize a taut rope against another as in a tackle, to jam a rope in a block.

nipper. A short length of rope or a metal clamp used to bind the messenger to the manila anchor hawser in the days of sail when fiber anchor cables were too large to go aground the capstan and a messenger was used.

Nippon Kaiji Kyokai. The Japanese classification society; also called the Japanese Marine Corporation. *See* classification society.

NMFS. National Marine Fisheries Service.

NOAA. National Oceanic and Atmospheric Administration.

nock. The upper forward corner of a quadrilateral fore-and-aft sail where the head and luff join. Also called throat.

nocturnal. A medieval handheld device for telling time at night by lining up the pointer stars of the Big Dipper or Ursa Major. The stars of this constellation appear to rotate during the night.

nodal point. In tidal phenomena, the place where the rise and fall of the tide is a minimum despite maximum current.

noddy. A large tern, dark brown with some white on the head, common to the tropics.

nodes. *See* wave, standing.

nodules, ocean bottom. Potato-size lumps of nearly pure manganese, cobalt, iron, and nickel found on the ocean floor in deep water. Efforts are being made to recover these minerals while at the same time the problems of ownership and jurisdiction are being discussed.

nog. An old word for treenail.

nogging. A tub made from half a keg.

NOMAD. Naval Oceanographic Meteorological Device; an automatic weather reporting station anchored at sea.

no man's land. *See* hold.

nondisplacement craft. A ground effect machine such as a Hovercraft.

nonmagnetic ship. Ship made of non-magnetic materials such as wood, copper, or plastic that would not disturb the earth's magnetic field. Used for some minesweepers as well as for special research ships.

non-return valve. Merchant Marine term for the one way valve the U.S. Navy calls a flapper valve.

noon. The time of the sun's passage across the upper branch of the meridian. At LAN or local apparant noon, a ship's latitude is most easily determined by sextant. A noon position is traditionally found and reported daily by the navigator to the captain.

norman. Any pin or bolt of wood or metal used to hold or contain rope or cable such as the horizontal pin through the top of a bitt.

Norske Veritas. Norway's official ship classification society.

North American Yacht Register. A listing of U.S. and Canadian yachts; replaces Lloyd's Register of American Yachts.

North Atlantic Current. The most northerly part of the Gulf Stream System originating off the Grand Banks as the end of the Gulf Stream. It flows in a complicated and varying pattern north, northeast and east towards Europe as well as south. The easterly and southerly drifts eventually join the North Equatorial Current.

Northill folding anchor. Trade name for a popular, collapsible boat anchor.

North Cape Current. *See* Norway Current.

North Equatorial Current. The major east to west flow of water in the North Atlantic in the Trade Wind belt north of the Equator. It is fed by southeasterly currents off the coast of Africa and, powered by the Trades, it piles up water in the Caribbean Sea where, as the Yucatan Current, it provides the major source of the Gulf Stream System. A similar current with the same name flows westward in the Pacific and is the source of the Japan Current. Another flows in the Indian Ocean from October to July. *See* South Equatorial Current.

Norway Current. A continuation of the North Atlantic Current, by now slowed and widened to a drift, which moves north along the coast of Norway. This warm drift becomes the North Cape Current as it flows northeast and then east into the Barents Sea.

NOS. National Ocean Survey.

nose. The stem or most forward part of a ship or boat. Also the metal fitting protecting the stem of a small boat.

nose port. A small rectangular glass or plastic window set into a yacht's hull above the waterline that cannot be opened.

nosing. Same as molding.

notch block. Same as snatch block. *See* block.

Notice to Mariners. Contains chart and Light List corrections, warnings of wrecks and obstructions and other matters of importance to mariners. Published weekly by the Hydrographic Center of the Defense Mapping Agency and prepared jointly by the National Ocean Survey and the Coast Guard. Local notices are published by each Coast Guard headquarters. *See* Daily Memorandum.

not-under-command. Describes a ship which through some exceptional circumstance is unable to maneuver as required by the Rules of the Road. During the day such a ship must show two shapes in a vertical line, at night two red, 32-point lights in a vertical line. The lights are also called breakdown lights and in warships are flashed if a man should fall overboard.

NRT. Net Registered Tonnage. *See* tonnage.

nudibranch. A sea slug, a mollusk without a shell that lives in the kelp forest and other dense underwater vegetation feeding on anemones, sponges, etc.

nuggar, nugger. The traditional trading sailboat of the lower Nile, two-masted, lateen rigged.

number. A ship's four letter identification assigned when registered or commissioned and hoisted as a flag signal; also used as a radio call sign. Also known as her call sign, signal letters or call letters. Not to be confused with a warship's class number that is usually painted on her hull. The expression to make one's number means to call upon someone usually a superior or senior.

Number One. British naval slang for the First Lieutenant, especially when he is also the Executive Officer.

number tax. A license fee or royalty paid to the class association by the builder of a class yacht. After the boat is inspected and accepted by the class association, it is given a number which is displayed on its mainsail and under which it may race.

nun buoy. Buoy-shaped like a truncated cone and even-numbered in U.S. waters. It is anchored to the right of the channel when entering from the sea and painted red; thus the rule "Red, right, returning." *See* can buoy.

nut. The iron ball on the end of the stock of an old-fashioned anchor.

NWS. National Weather Service.

nylon. A very strong, rot resistant and elastic synthetic fiber used widely aboard ships and boats for ropes, cordage and sail cloth. Nylon hawsers, under stress, have considerable stretch and if parted can backlash with dangerous force.

O

O. International signal code alphabet flag. When flown singly means: "Man overboard." Spoken: "oscar."

oakum. Caulking material traditionally made from rope fibers picked from old rope. It was driven down between the planks of wooden ships with caulking tools and then the seams were payed or sealed with tar.

oar. A bladed, wooden pole used to propel a boat by rowing. The different parts are handle, loom or shaft (*See* loom), neck, blade or peel. If the blade is rounded, that part is called the feather. The leather is that part of the shaft that engages the oarlock.

oarlock. Any device holding an oar while it is pulled; a grommet or a swiveling crutch, fork, or ring. British word is crutch or rowlock.

OBO. Oil-Bulk-Ore carrier; a ship designed for all three types of cargo.

occlusion or occluded front. A weather phenomenon in which the leading edge of a cold air mass overtakes a warm air mass. The latter is thus occluded, closed out or dispensed with as the cold air comes in beneath it and displaces it on the surface.

occulting. *See* light, occulting.

ocean. The intercommunicating body of salt water occupying the depressions in the earth's surface and divided into various parts by the continents and the Equator. The five oceans are the Atlantic, Pacific, Indian, Arctic, Antarctic. They cover 70% of the earth's surface.

ocean current. A large mass of water moved by wind, temperature and density differences and subject to Coriolis force. Some are narrow and fast stream currents; others are wide and slow drifts. Together, they form great circulatory systems in each major ocean area.

ocean engineering. Engineering concerned with the development of new equipment and systems and the improvement of techniques to enable man to operate beneath the surface of the sea to exploit its resources. Short term is sometimes oceaneering.

Oceania. The South Seas; specifically the area bound by Hawaii, Easter Island, New Zealand and New Guinea. The eastern part is Polynesia, with Micronesia in the northwest and Melanesia in the southwest.

Oceanlab. An advanced and mobile undersea research laboratory.

oceanography. The study of all aspects of the sea, including its physical boundaries, the chemistry of sea water, marine biology, and submarine geology. In a strict sense, oceanography is the description of the marine environment whereas oceanology is the study of the ocean and related sciences.

oceanology. *See* oceanography.

ocean station. *See* weather ship.

ocean sunfish. *See* sunfish.

octant. An instrument similar to a sextant but using an arc of 1/8 of a circle (45°) instead of an arc of 1/6.

octopod. *See* octopus.

octopus. An invertebrate sea animal that is part of the cephalopod mollusk group, more precisely an octopod because it has eight arms equipped with suction disks. An octopus has a strong, parrot-like beak, moves by jet propulsion and ejects ink in self-defense. Although it can reach a weight of 150 pounds and a width of 25 feet that includes the tentacles, it is a shy and friendly creature with no record of unprovoked attack on man. Plural is octopuses or octopi.

oculus. The symbolic eye painted or carved on the bow of ships and crafts worldwide.

officer. One of the licensed members of the ship's crew who assist the master in running the ship; often known as a mate in the Merchant Marine. In the Navy, there is always an Officer of the Deck or of the Watch who is responsible under the Captain for all the ship's activities.

offing. A ship gains her offing from the shore when she is a safe distance from the coast and no longer needs a pilot.

offset. In shipbuilding or repair, a measurement taken off the plans of a ship.

offshore. At sea; away from the coast. Ships cruise offshore if not along the coast. Also a direction meaning towards the sea, as an offshore wind which blows away from land. Compare onshore. In technical terms, offshore is the zone between the surf line seaward to the outer edge of the continental shelf.

offshore oil rig. A large structure designed to drill, pump and store oil at sea in moderate depths of water.

off soundings. Outside the 100 fathom curve. *See* on sounding.

off the wind. A sailboat not close hauled, on a reach. If close hauled, she would be on the wind. *See* close hauled, on the wind, reach.

oil bag. A canvas bag, traditionally filled with animal or vegetable oil and pierced with holes by a sail needle. It is slung over the side of a ship to release small amounts of oil that will form a film and reduce the severity of the sea. Not commonly used today.

oil canning. The snapping in and out of the hull plating of some ships in heavy weather.

oiler. A tanker; a ship that carries petroleum.

Oil King. A Naval petty officer who maintains fuel oil records, transfers oil between tanks, and inspects oil received aboard.

oil rig. *See* offshore oil rig.

oil skimmer. A ship specially designed to clear up an oil slick spilled on the water.

oilskins. Traditionally, the heavy yellow, waterproof jacket and trousers worn at sea in wet weather. Modern raingear is light and made in many styles and colors including an orange that is the most visible color for rescue from the water.

oil stop. The caulking used to make a riveted joint water tight.

old-fashioned anchor. The common and traditional anchor of the past with a central shaft or shank, a ring or shackle at one end (often called the Jew's harp) to which the anchor cable is attached, a cross piece, the stock, and a crown or lower extremity from which branch two arms perpendicular to the stock, each curving up to a broad palm or fluke ending in a bill or pea. It is called a stock anchor in the U.S. Navy and a fisherman's anchor in the United Kingdom, also often referred to as a kedge, mariners, yachtsman's or Herreshoff anchor by yachtsmen and fishermen. *See* anchor.

old man. The master of a merchant ship or the commanding officer of a warship. An admiral is the old gentleman. In shipbuilding, a Z-shaped steel holder for a portable drill.

oldwife. Same as menhaden.

Oleron, Laws of. A code of maritime law enacted by Eleanor of Aquitaine and brought to England when she married Henry II in 1152; probably derived from the older doctrines of the Mediterranean, especially those of Rhodes. They were codified in the Black Book of the Admiralty in 1336.

Omega. A long-range and worldwide, very low frequency, hyperbolic radio navigation system developed by the U.S. Navy to provide a global all-weather positioning system for ships, aircraft, and submarines (surfaced and submerged).

omnirange. A radio aid to navigation providing direct indication of magnetic bearing (omnibearing) of a station from any direction. Also called omnidirectional range or beacon.

one design. Describes an organized class of identical racing boats.

onshore. Direction towards the coast from the sea. Compare off shore.

on soundings. Within the 100 fathom curve.

on the bow or quarter. Towards the bow or quarter; within that direction. *See* broad on the bow.

on the wind. Same as close hauled. If not close hauled, a ship is sailing off the wind or reaching.

ooching. An illegal procedure in a sailboat race whereby a crew member lunges forward and then stops abruptly in order to propel the boat.

ooker. Slang for a cunningham.

open. Range lights or marks, when not in line, are said to be open. A bay or other body of water may open in a certain direction which indicates accessibility.

open cover. In marine insurance, an agreement that the insured is automatically covered for all shipments for a specified time, at specified premiums, or at rates to be arranged.

open hawse. *See* hawse.

open harbor. An unsheltered harbor.

open port. A port that is free of ice.

orca. The genus of sea mammals that includes killer whales; the name for such whales, sometimes shortened to orc.

ordinary seaman. In merchant ships, an untrained, generally new man who may be promoted to able seaman after experience at sea and an examination.

ore carrier. A ship specially designed to withstand the concentrated weight and special handling problems of carrying ore.

Orlon. Trade name for a modern synthetic fiber sometimes used at sea for lines and cloth.

orlop. Now the fourth or lowest deck in a merchant ship having four or more full or partial decks. Orlop is no longer used in warships where once it was the lowest deck.

ormer. An abalone peculiar to the Channel Islands. *See* abalone.

oropesa sweep. A towed wire used over an area when surveying shoals or wreck-strewn waters.

orthodrome. Any line on a chart representing a great circle track between two points.

orthophoto chart. Chart produced by a combination of aerial photographs and conventional chart symbols.

osprey. A fish-eating hawk, dark on the back and white below. Also known as a fish hawk or sea eagle.

otary. Members of the family of eared seals and walruses.

otolith. A small diamond-shaped bone in a fish's skull that reveals its age. Also called an ear stone.

OTSR. Optimum Track Ship Routing; a U.S. Navy procedure for routing its ships to avoid bad weather.

otter. An amphibious, fish-eating mammal, approximately the size of a small dog that lives along the coast in most northern waters. Not to be confused with the sea otter which lives in the kelp beds of the North Pacific. *See* sea otter.

otter board. A towed wood or steel board, rigged with a bridle and used to stretch a line out at an angle from straight ahead. Used mostly in fishing to keep the net or trawl open; also used in minesweeping. Sometimes called a door.

otter trawl. *See* trawl net.

outboard. Away from the centerline; towards the side of the ship. The opposite direction is inboard.

outboard-inboard. *See* sterndrive.

outboard motor. *See* motor, outboard.

outdrive. Another word for sterndrive.

outfall. The location, any structure involved, and the liquid itself related to the discharge into the sea of sewerage and waste.

outfit. *n* All equipment and necessities on board ship ready for a voyage. In shipbuilding, there is a fitting out period during which the ship undergoes outfitting with, for example, rigging, deck machinery, furniture (in the maritime sense), and boat davits. *vb* To outfit a ship is to provide this type of material.

outfoot. To sail faster close hauled is to outfoot a rival sailboat.

outhaul. A line used to pull something outboard or away from the ship such as in swinging out a boom. Compare with inhaul.

out oars. A command to the crew of a rowing boat to let the oars fall into the oarlocks with the blades held horizontally.

outpoint. A sailboat is said to outpoint another when it can sail closer to the wind.

outreach. The effective working distance of a cargo handling rig beyond the ship's side or edge of hatch. Also the length of a cargo boom is its outreach.

outrigger. A balancing float, usually a shaped log, attached to a boat or canoe to keep it upright against the pressure of a sail. Any gear that supports something beyond the vessel's side such as the outrigger on a racing shell supporting the oarlocks. Spreaders are sometimes known as outriggers.

outrigger canoe. A classic, long distance sailing canoe with a single auxilliary float used by the Polynesians to travel over the wide Pacific.

out shipment. Passengers and/or cargo refused as shipment because the ship was already loaded.

outturn. The final tally of cargo landed. In marine insurance, the word may also refer to the condition of the cargo on discharge.

outwale. *See* inwale.

outward bound. Said of a ship departing on a voyage. Now also used to describe a youth program, often involving sailing, in which young men and women develop self confidence, good sportmanship, and sound human relationships under conditions of stress and mild physical hardship.

over. The width of a fishing net.

overboard. Over the side; into the water.

overcarriage. The act of transporting certain cargo past its destination.

overfalls. Short breaking waves marking the meeting of contrary currents, the passing of a strong current over a shallow irregular bottom, or the meeting of a current and an opposing wind. Also called rips or rip tides.

overhang. The projection of a ship's bow or stern beyond the stem or sternpost.

overhaul. 1. A nautical term for spreading a tackle, thus moving the blocks further apart. The opposite is round in. 2. To overhaul a rope is to move it back towards the nearest block to ease the strain. 3. A ship passing another overhauls it. 4. A ship is periodically overhauled when it is, for example, painted or repaired. A U.S. ship goes into overhaul while a British ship has a refit.

overhead. The interior, horizontal surface of a compartment or space aboard ship that is above the floor or deck. Also called the deckhead. *See* ceiling, deckhead.

overlap. The extension of the foot of a genoa abaft the luff of the mainsail in a sailboat.

overrake. Said of heavy seas that come aboard over a wreck, over the bow of an anchored ship, or over the ship in a storm.

overtaking vessel. According to the Rules of the Road, ship that is coming up from astern and passing another ship from a direction more than two points abaft the beam of the overtaken vessel.

owl eye. A portable, battery-powered electronic device that greatly assists vision in the dark. It can magnify light by a factor of at least 100,000. A special model may be used underwater.

oxball. Small ornamental sphere at the top of a flagstaff or mast. On a mast, it forms the truck.

oxter plate. A steel shell plate fastened to the stern frame of a ship near the rudderpost. Also called a tuck plate.

Oyashio. An ocean current flowing southwest from the Bering Sea along the southeast coast of Siberia and the Kuril Islands, then curving south and eastward to join the North Pacific Current.

oyster. A small marine bivalve mollusk grouped in three genera and some 100 species. Highly valued as food, it is found in a broad band between the latitudes 64°N and 44°S.

P

P. International signal code alphabet flag. When hoisted singly, in port, means: "All persons return to the ship which is ready to depart." Spoken: "papa." Also known, particularily among the British, as the Blue Peter.

Pacific iron. The iron cappings at the ends of the yardarms of a square-rigger. Also the gooseneck at the deck end of a cargo derrick.

Pacific Ocean. The largest of the world's oceans; named by Magellan who encountered a very rare calm day as he passed around South America from the Atlantic.

pacifier. A short and heavy club used to subdue a boated fish that is thrashing about. Also called a priest.

package freight. Cargo in boxes, barrels, and other containers as opposed to bulk freight or cargo.

packer. A boat that buys fish from the fishermen at sea on the fishing grounds.

packet. Old fashion word for a regularly scheduled mail and passenger boat.

pack ice. An area of sea ice of variable shape and form and different from fast ice; may be open pack (1/10 ice) to close pack (9/10 ice). Also called drift ice, ice pack.

packing gland. *See* stuffing box.

pad. A small piece of plate welded to the deck or bulkhead, for example; used to attach a removable bolt, hook, or other fitting.

pad, lifting. A piece of plate fitted with an eye and fixed where needed for lifting something heavy such as on a ship's counter to lift the propeller.

paddle. A short oar used to propel a small boat or canoe by being swung freely with both hands; may be single or double bladed.

paddleboard. A light and hollow surfboard made of plywood or fiberglass used more for rescue work by lifeguards than for surfing.

paddle wheel. A nearly obsolete, early form of steam propulsion in which a large circle or wheel of paddles was rotated in a vertical plane either from the stern or on each side of the ship. Although not as efficient as propellers, paddlewheelers are still used in some shallow waters, lakes and rivers as harbor tugs. Also called a sidewheel.

paddy. A trade or shipping word for rice with the husks attached in contrast to clean rice. Cargo rice is a mixture of about 75% clean and 25% paddy.

Paddy's Hurricane. A flat calm.

pad eye. A metal ring welded to deck or bulkhead.

paint. At sea, anti-corrosive paint is an important base coat for all painted iron and steel. Anti-fouling paint is required for all ship's hulls below the waterline to inhibit the growth of barnacles and other sea life. Fire resistant paint is used on all modern ship interiors.

painter. Small rope or line used on boats; usually attached to the bow where it is used for towing or making fast.

paint locker. The small compartment aboard ship where paint is stowed.

pair trawl. A large net towed by two ships that are known as pair trawlers. Also called a bull trawl.

pale. A temporary shore or brace used to hold beams or timbers during wooden ship building.

palinurus. An outmoded gimbaled instrument with time and latitude scales once used to estimate a true steering course by sighting a celestial body.

pallet. A wooden, portable platform used for moving cargo on forklift trucks and slings. Also called a tray or a skip.

pallet ship. A ship carrying most of its cargo fitted on pallets and that is loaded and unloaded through side doors instead of using the hatches.

palm. 1. The flattened end of an old-fashioned anchor arm. Also called a wrist or fluke. **2.** A sailmaker's leather semi-glove worn over the palm of the hand and used to drive a needle through the canvas. **3.** Any flattened piece of steel used in shipbuilding such as the top of the rudder post.

palolo worm. A type of edible saltwater worm that spawns in vast free-swimming swarms over the reefs of Samoa and Fiji during the lowest tides of October and November.

pampero. A violent westerly storm blowing mostly from July to November offshore on the coast of Argentina.

Panama Canal. A major man-made shipping waterway connecting the Atlantic and Pacific oceans across the Isthmus of Panama that links North and South America. Toll charges are based on a Panama Canal tonnage.

Panama plate. A metal piece bolted over a chock or fairlead resulting in a Panama chock that does not permit a line therein to jump out.

pan fishing. Fishing for small to moderate food fish such as sole, bass and snapper in contrast to game fishing for sport alone.

pan ice. A piece of ice from several to hundreds of yards in diameter formed by the effect of wind and sea on field ice.

pancake ice. The circular pieces of ice measuring up to six feet in diameter which appear before the solid floe is formed. This occurs during the formation of new sea ice. *See* spicule.

pan pan pan. Indicates an urgent radio telephone message and thus requests priority on the circuit. Less urgent than mayday but more urgent than a safety message.

panting. The alternate bulging in and out of the plating of a ship, caused by water pressure, as the ship pitches into a wave. Also a similar phenomenon in a marine boiler caused generally by a shortage of air. Panting beams, frames, and stringers are used in the construction of a ship's bow to prevent or minimize panting; also called tin-canning.

papagayo. A strong, dry winter northeasterly wind blowing off the west coast of Central America.

parachute flare. Flare fired from a pyrotechnic pistol such as a Very's pistol, that is used as a warning or distress signal. A small parachute delays the descent of the colored flare.

parachute spinnaker. A large light, triangular racing sail used in light winds, sometimes fitted with circular holes to achieve balance. Also called a Mae West and a balloon spinnaker.

paraffin. British word for the diesel oil used in boat engines and stoves.

parallax. In navigation, the error in altitude of a celestial body caused by the observer being on the surface and not at the center of the earth. Correction for it is found in a table and must be applied to the sextant altitude to get the true observed altitude.

parallel. The imaginary lines around the earth parallel to the equator are known as parallels of latitude or parallels for short. *See* latitude. In the celestial sphere there are parallels of declination and altitude. Parallel sailing means sailing east or west along the known parallel of latitude of the objective.

paraselene. *See* parhelion.

paravane. A torpedo-shaped device towed on either side of the ship's bow to deflect and cut adrift moored mines.

parbuckle. A primitive system for raising or lowering heavy weights, especially loaded casks, by passing a rope or two around the object, making one end fast and hauling or easing on the other end, thus rolling the object up or down.

parcel. An old and largely out-moded method of protecting a rope by winding strips of tarred canvas around it with the lay, known as parcelling, after worming and before serving. The whole procedure was known as worm, parcel and serve. *See* worm, serve.

parhelion. An optical illusion, a bright light or mock sun appearing near the sun, also called a sun dog. A similar phenomenon at night is a paraselene or moon dog.

parrel. Rope, chain or metal collar by which a yard or gaff is kept close to the mast yet free to move up and down. Common in the past in square-riggers and included parrel cleats, lashings, ribs and trucks. A parrel moved freely on parrel beads or balls, also known as trucks. Also spelled parral.

parrot fish. A small colorful tropical reef fish, any of several species who feed on coral and thus have a strong, parrot-like mouth or beak.

part. *n* The different sections in a tackle such as the standing part which is fixed and the hauling part which is movable. *vb* To part means to break in a proper nautical sense as in the expression: "a line parts under strain."

particular average. A loss of ship and/or cargo caused by an act of God and relates to damage caused by stranding, fire and collision. *See* general average.

partners. Pieces of timber inserted between beams in wooden ship construction to form a frame to support whatever passes down from the deck, such as a mast.

party. A Naval word meaning a group of men or women organized for a special task or purpose such as a repair party, rescue and assistance party, or liberty party.

party boat. A public fishing boat that takes out parties or groups of anglers for a day's offshore fishing on an individual basis.

pass. To pass a line or pass a stopper is to place it and make it fast.

passage. A one-way trip or crossing, part of a voyage. Also a narrow navigable channel through reefs or islands or between two bodies of water. In this sense, may be called a pass for short and in New England waters, a hole.

passageway. Nautical word for corridor or hallway aboard ship.

passarado. An old name for the rope used to haul down the sheet blocks of the courses of a square-rigger.

passaree. A rope used in square-riggers when running before the wind to haul out the clews of the foresail to the ends of the studding-sail booms.

Pass Down the Line (PDL) Book. Book used in the Navy as a guide for oncoming watch officers. It contains permanent directives and orders.

passenger. Any person aboard other than the master, officers, crew, owner and family (and sometimes the master's wife) who pays a fare.

pass the word. Means to broadcast or disseminate the information.

patch. Used for damage control aboard ship; a piece of steel plate (hard patch) riveted or welded or top-bolted (soft patch) over a hole or crack that must be sealed. Piping is sometimes repaired by a soft patch of gasket material or lead sheet held in place by wrapping with wire or cord.

patent anchor. A general term for a stockless anchor. Patented anchors are sold under various trade names.

patent block. A modern block in which the traditional simple pin holding the sheaves has been replaced by plastic or steel bearings.

patent log. Same as screw log or taffrail log.

patent sheave. Same as roller sheave.

paternoster. A British, multi-hooked, hand-fishing line.

patrimonial sea. A British term for territorial waters.

paunch. A thick anti-chafing mat made by interweaving strands of old rope.

pay. 1. In the nautical sense, to pay out a line is to allow it to be pulled away but under control. 2. A ship or boat under sail is said to pay off when she turns away from the wind to fill her sails after coming about on a new tack. 3. To fill or coat a seam after caulking.

P.D. On most charts, it indicates a reported reef or other hazard to navigation as "position doubtful".

pea. The point or extreme end of a fluke of an anchor. Also called a bill, peak, or pee.

peacoat. A heavy woolen short jacket worn by sailors. Called a peajacket in the Merchant Service and a reefer in the Old Navy.

peak. *n* 1. The upper, after end or corner of a fore-and-aft four-sided sail. 2. The outboard end of the gaff from which the colors are flown underway. 3. The extreme internal ends of a ship, called the forepeak and afterpeak are located forward and abaft of the first and last collision bulkheads and contain the peak tanks. 4. The pea or bill of an anchor fluke. 5. A seamount rising more than 500 fathoms above the sea floor and having a pointed or rounded top. *vb* To peak or peak up is to adjust, as a radio, for optimum performance.

peak cleat. A piece of wood fitted in a boat and used for resting the inboard end of an oar when blades were elevated at a common angle.

peak oars. A command to oarsmen in a pulling boat to raise their oars to the same elevation and resting the handle ends on peak cleats.

peapod. A colloquial word for a very small light boat towed astern or secured on the deck of a yacht or fishing boat.

pearl. 1. The familiar gem found within mussels, clams, conchs, and particularily oysters. 2. In surfer's slang, it means to lose control of your board and dive towards the bottom when trying to catch a breaking wave. The board, when released, comes up fast and jumps clear of the water.

pea soup fog. A very thick fog.

pectoral fin. *See* fin.

pegging. Hand line fishing in which the bait is pulled up and allowed to sink down in a certain tempo similar to jigging.

peel. Broadest part or blade of an oar or paddle.

pelagic. 1. Pertains to the open sea such as in pelagic fish or birds. 2. One of two primary divisions of the marine environment; the other being benthic. *See* abyss, bathal zone.

pelagic fish. Fish who roam the ocean such as tuna rather than cling to the coast as grouper.

pelican. Any of the large, pouched, coastal birds of the genus *Pelicanus* who dive into the water to catch fish. Now struggling to survive against pollution of the ocean.

pelican hook. A quick release device consisting of a hook closed by a ring or bail shackle. When the bail is knocked away, the hook opens and releases quickly the anchor chain it is holding. A pelican hook is part of a chain or cable stopper and is also called a slip hook. *See* cable stopper.

pelorus. 1. In all modern ships, it is a compass repeater set in gimbals on the wings of the bridge or anywhere with a wide arc of vision on which a bearing circle, azimuth circle or alidade can be positioned. 2. The whole assembly used for taking true bearings, including the stand.

Pelorus Jack. The historic guide for ships passing through Pelorus Sound, New Zealand. It was believed to have been a Risso's dolphin.

pelt. A circular, inflated fabric buoy used by British fishermen in the North Sea to mark their nets. Also called a pellet.

pelvic fin. *See* fin.

pen. The backbone of a squid or octopus. Also a British word for a slip or berth formed in a marina between two docks or pontoons.

pendant. Any single rope or chain secured at one end to, for example, a mast, spar, or sail and having at its other end a block or a thimble. A whip or tackle is usually made fast to the block or thimble. There are many special purpose pendants such as brace pendant, burton pendant, clearhawse pendant, and fish pendant whose name explains their use. Pendant is the British spelling for pennant meaning a flag. *See* pennant.

pendant tackle. A two-fold purchase hooked to a pendant and used for various tasks on deck such as moving weights.

penguin. A flightless, fast-swimming, fish-eating bird of the Antarctic found as far north as the Galapagos Islands off Ecuador. The four most common penguins are the gentoo, chinstrap, emperor, and adelie and their major enemy is the leopard seal.

peninsula. An elongated portion of land nearly surrounded by water and connected to a larger body of land.

pennant. A special flag, usually longer than wide (having a greater fly than a hoist) such as a commission pennant or a broad command pennant. The ten pennants of the International Signal Code indicate numerals. A mess pennant indicates that the crew is at a meal. The Irish pennant refers to a loose, untidy object about a ship. *See* Irish pennant. Sometimes spelled pendant by the British but pronounced pennant on both sides of the Atlantic. *See* pendant.

penny-dog. A shark. *See* tope.

perch. 1. An aid to navigation mounted on a buoy or ashore and consisting of a pole or staff on which is often attached such items as a ball, cage, or cross to mark a shoal, rock, or reef or turning point in the channel. 2. A sea perch is a popular food fish of European and American waters.

perigee. The orbital position of an earth satellite, such as the moon, when it is closest to the earth. Compare apogee.

perils of the sea. As used in marine insurance, it relates only to collision, stranding, fire, heavy weather and other abnormal accidents. Ordinary action of the waves and the sea, human errors and mistakes, damage from rats, poor packaging are not considered perils of the sea.

period. The span of time a lighted aid to navigation takes to complete one cycle of its characteristic impulses; one of the principal means of light identification at sea.

period of roll. The time a ship takes to make one roll from one side to the other and return when rolling freely in calm water. From this time, in seconds, a ship's stability can be estimated; a short roll indicates a high metacentric height.

periplus. The ancient word for sailing directions, the first known having been written about 500 B.C. as a sailing guide for the Mediterranean.

periscope. An optical instrument composed of a pipe with mirrors that is used to view the surface while submerged as in a submarine.

periscope feather. The wake made by a periscope of a moving submerged submarine.

periwinkle. A marine snail, smaller than a conch. Also called a winkle. *See* conch.

permeability. A measure of a ship's space that, if flooded, can be occupied by water. It depends on the nature of the cargo carried and thus different cargoes are assigned different permeability factors, in percent, by international agreement.

perpendicular. In ship measurements, a line drawn at right angles to the keel. The after perpendicular is the one that coincides with the stern post and the one forward intersects with the stem. Between them we have the length of a ship between perpendiculars.

Personal Flotation Device (PFD). A general term for all types of lifejackets, belts, vests and other devices to prevent drowning.

Peru Current. A cold ocean current flowing north along the coast of South America. Near the equator it curves westward to join the South Equatorial Current. Also, but inaccurately, called the Humboldt Current.

petal. A metal clip on a stanchion used for securing a wire or a lifeline.

Peter's fish. The haddock, so called from the dark spots behind its gills which are supposed to be St. Peter's finger prints.

petrel. A small, white-rumped black tube-nosed bird of the open sea that often follows ships, flying close to the surface. Petrels are known as Mother Carey's chickens and as stormy petrels because they seem to delight in high winds and big seas.

petticoat. *See* mastcoat.

petty officer. A non-commissioned, experienced and trained supervisor in the Navy.

PFD. *See* Personal Flotation Device.

photophores. The special organs on certain sea animals that produce luminescence.

phytoplankton. The minute pelagic ocean plants (diatoms, dinoflagellates, and nannoplankton) that form the basic unit in the food chain of the sea. Zooplankton feed on these plants.

picket boat. Boat used for guard or sentry purposes in harbor.

pier. 1. A structure built at an angle to the shore and used for mooring boats or ships or used for sightseeing and pleasure. It may be T-shaped. *See* dock, wharf. **2.** A support for the span of a bridge. The British use pier as a synonym for jetty.

pierhead. The seaward end of a pier.

pierhead jump. A last-minute arrival aboard a ship or a departure.

pigboard. A surfboard with a pointed bow and a broad flat stern.

pigeon hole. *See* capstan bar.

pigstick. Small spar at top of mainmast from which the commission pennant flies.

pigtail. The end of a rope or line, the end of a lashing, or the untidy end of a line that is also called a cowstail.

pilchard. European name for sardine.

pile. A wooden, steel or concrete pole or stake used in pier, wharf, or cofferdam construction. Mooring piles or pile moorings are arranged so ships can be made fast to them. Wooden pilings are grouped together at a ferry slip to cushion and guide the landing of the ferry in the slip. A piling, another name for pile, is sometimes called a dolphin or a rack.

pilking. *See* jigging.

pillage. Describes an ancient and legal practice wherein the captors of a ship taken as a prize of war were entitled to take anything found above the main deck except the ship's furniture and guns.

pillar. Any vertical support member below deck, usually supporting a deck. Also known as a stanchion.

Pillars of Hercules. The ancient name for the Straits of Gibralter long considered the end of the known world. It is marked by two highly prominent rocky mounts-Gibralter and its African counterpart, Jebel Musa.

pillow. Any block of wood or metal used as a support or rest. A pillow-block supports a propeller shaft bearing; a bowsprit pillow held in place the bowsprit of an old wooden ship.

pilot. A qualified, licensed man with local knowledge who directs a ship in a harbor, channel or narrow passage. He does not relieve a master or commanding officer of any of the final responsibility for the ship. A volume of sailing directions is known as a pilot.

pilotage. The act or business of piloting. Also the fee paid for a pilot's services.

pilot bread. Same as hard-tack or ship's biscuit.

pilot chart. Chart that contains important information to assist in safe navigation such as ocean currents, ice at sea, force and direction of seasonal winds, storm tracks, isotherms, and magnetic variation; issued monthly by the Defense Mapping Agency Hydrographic Center.

pilotfish. A small brightly banded fish that accompanies sharks, living off their scraps and giving the appearance of guiding the sharks by often swimming in front of them.

pilothouse. The space in the ship's bridge superstructure that encloses the steering wheel or helm, the engine controls, and so on, from which the ship is piloted or conned. Also called the wheel house.

piloting. The part of navigating a ship that involves such items as radar, radio and visual bearings, ranges, soundings, and navigation aids and is associated with relative nearness to land.

pilot jack. In the United Kingdom, a union jack with a white border once flown to indicate that a pilot was needed.

pilot ladder. A handy, light, flexible, and portable ladder slung over the side of a ship to assist the pilot in climbing the ship's side. *See* ladder.

Pilot Rules. Rules of the Road issued by the U.S. Coast Guard that supplement the Inland Rules for U.S. Waters.

pilot whale. A toothed cetacean 12-15 feet long, found on the Atlantic coast of North America. Also called a blackfish.

pin. *See* belaying pin, clevis. Slang for mark among sail racing yachtsmen.

pinch. To sail a boat so close to the wind that her sails shiver and headway is reduced.

pinky. A New England fishing schooner first built in 1820 and now being revived by hobbyists. Also called pinkey or pink.

pinnace. In the days of sail, a small two-masted sailing vessel as well as a ship's boat rowed with 8-16 oars. Not a common word today.

pinniped. Collective word for seals, sea lions, and walruses; members of the order Pinnipedia.

pinrail. *See* fife rail.

pintail. A surfboard with a long pointed tapering stern.

pintles. The heavy pins or bolts on the forward edge of the rudder that fit and rotate in the gudgeons secured to the ship's sternpost or rudderpost.

pipe. 1. A cask for carrying wine and spirits with a capacity of about 100 gallons depending on contents. 2. Short for boatswain's pipe. In the Navy when the word is passed, it is also piped and an important person may be piped over the side. When side honors are given the boatswain's mate pipes the side.

pipe berth. A bed or bunk aboard ship made of canvas stretched over a frame of metal tubing and hinged so as to fold up. British word is cot.

pipe down. A nautical expression meaning to be quiet, make less noise.

pipefish. A close relative of the seahorse, living in shallow grass and seaweed beds along the coast.

pipe up. Sailor's term meaning to speak louder or to start a song. The wind pipes up as it increases in strength.

piping the side. The act of giving side honors to an important person arriving on or departing from a Naval ship. Side boys stand at salute in two ranks through which the person passes as the boatswain's mate sounds his pipe. Also the name of the call that is piped during the ceremony.

piracy. Robbery and murder on the high seas, not considered acts of war. *See* privateer, corsair. Still a danger to yachtsmen in remote parts of the world as well as in local waters by drug smugglers. A pirate is one who commits piracy.

pirogue. A small double-ended, flat-bottomed, open boat used for fishing and hunting along the Gulf Coast, particularly Louisiana.

piston hank. British term for snap hook.

pitch. 1. A natural vegetable or petroleum based tar or glue used to seal the caulking between the wooden planks. The pitch is usually heated for this treatment called paying. **2.** The vertical movement of a ship or boat on its transverse axis; an up and down movement in a seaway distinct from roll, surge or heave. *See* heave. **3.** In riveting, the space between the centers of adjacent rivet holes usually expressed in number of rivet diameters.

pitchpole. A vessel is said to pitchpole or be pitchpoled when it is thrown end over end in very large sea or in surf; usually happens when the vessel is struck from aft by a rogue wave with a vertical face.

pitch, propeller. The angle a propeller blade makes with a plane perpendicular to the axis of the propeller. This angle varies along the length of the blade. With a controllable pitch propeller, the blades can be rotated about their axes. If the blades can be rotated to produce reverse thrust, it is a controllable reversible propeller or a CRP. Propeller pitch is also expressed as the distance the propeller would move forward in one revolution if it were screwing through a soft solid.

pitch ratio. The pitch divided by the diameter of the propeller.

Pitometer Log. *See* pitot-static log.

pitot-static log. A speed measuring device having a rodmeter assembly that detects both dynamic and static pressure, the former due to boat speed, the latter only to depth of water in which the device is rigged. Thus both boat speed and distance traveled can be recorded. Two examples are the Pitometer Log and the Bendix Underwater Log.

pivot or pivoting point. The point about which a ship pivots when making a turn, usually located about one third of the way abaft the bow.

plain-laid rope. A three-strand, right-hand laid fiber rope. If laid left-handed, it is backhanded or back-laid rope. Also called right-handed or hawser-laid rope.

plain sail. The sails normally carried in average weather. In light winds, additional and lighter weight sails would be set while in rough or heavy weather, the heavy canvas or storm sails would be used.

plain sailing. Originally a maritime term, plane sailing, which meant to sail in a rhumb line instead of great circle sailing.

plan. A diagram or drawing to scale from which a ship is built; may be a sheer plan (in the longitudinal plane), body plan (in the transverse plane), or half-breadth plan in the horizontal plane. *See* lines of a ship.

plane. A boat planes when its hull rises and friction is reduced. *See* hydroplane.

planets. Heavenly bodies most useful for celestial navigation, such as Venus, Jupiter, Mars that revolve around the sun as the earth does and thus, unlike stars, change their position daily. Planets do not twinkle, as stars do, and are brighter.

planimeter. An instrument used by naval architects to measure areas on a drawing.

planing hull. A hull that can partly rise above the water and plane. *See* displacement hull.

plank. Any of the special purposes planks used in wooden ship building such as carvel, clinker, spline, strip, diagonal, cross, garboard, and others whose names usually identify their use.

plankowner. In the U.S. Navy, a man who has served in the ship since she was commissioned.

plank-sheer. In wooden shipbuilding, a horizontal fore-and-aft timber that forms the outer limit of the upper deck at the sides.

plankton. The minute plant (phytoplankton) and animal (zooplankton) life floating or drifting submerged in the sea; divided into epiplankton down to 100 fathoms, mesoplankton from 100 to 1 000, and hypoplankton below 1 000 fathoms. The adjective is planktonic.

Planning Guide. *See* Sailing Directions.

Plan Position Indicator (PPI). A radar screen that shows an actual true outline picture of surrounding land and anything floating that returns a radar beam.

plat. To braid small lines.

plate. A flat piece of steel used in shipbuilding that is thicker than a sheet. There are many special purpose plates whose names reveal their use such as bow-chock plate and doubling plate. Also an old word for treasure. *See* plating.

plate clamps. Clamps used to lift and stow plates.

plate door. Door made of a steel plate bolted over an opening in a tank or compartment aboard ship.

plate wedges. Wedges used when fitting plates in place before welding.

plateau. A comparatively flat-topped elevation of the sea floor that is greater than 60 miles across and rises more than 100 fathoms.

platform. Removable flooring aboard ship made of steel plating and used in engineering spaces. Also any wood or metal stand, for example, at the top or bottom of an accommodation ladder or around a magnetic compass, that is not a grating. *See* grating.

platform deck. A partial deck below the lowest complete deck.

platform, ocean. A fixed or leg-supported structure used to drill and produce oil and gas, to store oil, or for undersea mining or underwater research. *See* drilling rig.

platform tide. *See* stand.

platier. A level reef.

plating. An arrangement of steel plates such as deck plating, shell plating or skin plating, or tank top plating; may be clinker (forming lap joints), flush (forming butt joints), in and out (both edges of a strake either inside or outside of adjacent strakes), or joggled (fitted around a projecting part). Special plating may be aluminum, alloy, or copper and brass for non-magnetic purposes.

pledget. A roll of oakum used for caulking the seams of planks.

Plimsoll marks or lines. Load waterline or loadline marks painted on the side of a ship indicating the maximum draft to which it may be loaded under different conditions. By international agreement, each country's classification society establishes the levels. Starting with the lowest line, Winter North Atlantic (WNA), there are six ending with Tropical Fresh water (TF). A circle bisected with a straight horizontal line identifies the marks and letters indicate the relevant classification society (LR means Lloyds Register for the United Kingdom). Also called load waterlines, loadlines, or freeboard marks.

plot. *n* A diagram of ship position and movement. *vb* To plot a position is to find or locate it and thereby indicate and label it.

plotter. Basically a combined protractor and straight edge made in various designs and available under various trade names that is used in piloting and plotting lines and measuring courses and bearings on a chart.

plotting sheet. Special blank sections of chart, large scale, showing only latitude and longitude lines, for plotting the lines of position and the resultant ship's position in celestial navigation.

plow anchor. A stockless anchor whose flukes are plow-shaped. Efficient for small vessels but not easy to stow in a hawsepipe. In large sizes it is used to anchor mooring buoys, platforms, etc. Called a ploughshare or CQR anchor in the United Kingdom.

plow-steel rope. A particularly strong wire rope made of open hearth or high carbon steel.

plug. 1. Any removable piece of wood, metal, or plastic designed to fill a hole. A boat plug is removed for drainage when the boat is hoisted clear of the water. A deck plug is a wooden cylinder fitted over a deck bolt and cut flush with the wood deck, also called a bung. Fusible safety plugs melt when the water level in a boiler drops dangerously low. There are also numerous drain or bleeder plugs in a ship. 2. The frame around which the mold for a fiberglass boat is built. 3. An artificial lure used in sport fishing.

plumb. To plumb a line from a derrick or boom over the side or over a hatch is to direct or guide it there.

plumb bow. *See* bow shapes.

plumber block. Same as plummer block.

plummer block. One of the pillow blocks supporting the tunnel shafting or propeller shaft bearing. Also called the pillow block or line shaft bearing since it often designates combined pillow block and bearing.

plummet. A piece of lead or other weight used in sounding tanks and compartments for level of liquid.

plush. An old British naval term meaning the amount of rum left over after a daily issue.

ply. *n* The thickness and strength of small line as indicated by combined threads and yarns as in 8-ply twine. *vb* 1. To make regular voyages between ports. 2. To beat to windward or to tack (obsolete).

pneumercator. An instrument for measuring the level of liquid in a tank using air pressure.

pneumofathometer. A device for measuring a diver's depth. Air is released from a hose attached to the diver and air pressure, indicating depth, is read at the surface in the support boat.

pod. A small group of whales, porpoise or seals. A large group is a school or gam. Also short for peapod or a small double-ended boat.

pogy. Another word for menhaden.

point. *n* 1. One of the 32 divisions of the magnetic compass circle, each equal to 11 1/4 degrees of arc. Before the introduction of the gyro compass and its 360 degree scale, points were in wide usage but now they are seldom used in steering. They are still used in reporting or indicating relative bearing as in "ship 2 points on the port bow". 2. A projection of land on the coast. 3. A sailing ship points high if she sails close to the wind. 4. Dew point is the temperature at which the moisture in the atmosphere condenses. 5. Flash point is the temperature at which a combustible mixture burns. *vb* To point a line or rope is to taper the end.

pointer. A timber or steel girder fitted diagonally into the fore and after ends of a ship, extending from the deck to the keelson or deadwood.

point-line. In a square-rigger, the light line or cord, often a 21 thread manila used in making reef-points.

point oars. A command to a pulling boat's crew given when the boat is aground. Oars are lowered into the water, downward and forward, and the boat is freed at the command "shove off".

polacca. A two- or three-masted Mediterranean vessel of the days of sail rigged differently in different countries. Sometimes called a polacre but rarely seen today.

polar. Pertaining to the Arctic or Antarctic, north and south of latitude 66° 33′ N or S.

polar chart. A great circle projection whose point of tangency is one of the geographical poles.

polar whale. The bowhead whale or Greenland right whale.

Polaris. The North Star or polar star, an historic guide to navigation whose direction is always within a degree or two of true north and whose altitude is nearly exactly equal to the latitude of the observer. Also called Lodestar Stella Maris and the sailor's star by sailors.

pole. The part of the ship's mast above the shrouds; also a flag-staff. Loosely used as a synonym for mast as in "She ran before the gale under bare poles."

Polestar. Another name for Polaris or the North Star.

pollack. A food fish of the cod family found in the North Atlantic.

Pollywogs. Persons aboard ship who have never crossed the Equator and who are initiated at the Crossing the Line ceremony, becoming shellbacks under the kindly supervision of Father Neptune.

polyethylene. A modern synthetic fiber used for cordage.

Polymode Project. *See* eddy.

polynia. An area of water in sea ice, other than a lead, lane, crack, or flaw, that is surrounded by ice but is not large enough to be called open water. Also spelled polynya.

polyp. *See* coral.

polypropylene. A synthetic fiber used for cordage. It is strong and light enough to float.

pompano. Related to the tuna and mackerel group, part of the Carangidae family which also includes the jack, crevalle, and yellowtail. All are medium size tropical and temperate zone popular food and game fish with blue or green backs and gold or silver sides and deeply forked tails.

ponente. The ancient but still used name for the westerly winds of the Mediterranean.

pontoon. Any flat, rectangular, barge-like floating structure used for loading and unloading ships and supporting derricks, cranes, portable bridges, and so on.

pontoon hatch. A metal hatch cover fitted with rings for lifting.

pontoon lifeboat. A wide and shallow boat built of steel or wood and having several watertight compartments.

pontoon pier. A pier made of hollow steel sections, usually carried to the site by ship; temporary ones are often used in amphibious landings.

pony board. A small auxilliary otter board used on a fishing trawl.

poop. A superstructure above the after part of the main deck, extending from side to side. Its original purpose, in early ships, was to provide additional buoyancy aft as well as quarters for the master and officers. The old word for poop was aftercastle.

poop deck. Deck that extends over the poop and may include a poop rail and a poop staff.

pooped, to be. For a ship to be pooped means that a large sea or wave has broken over the stern or poop when the ship was running before a storm.

poppet. One of the various timbers and blocks of wood used in the construction of wooden launching cradles and craft.

poppet board. The sill or sole on which the poppets of a launching cradle rest.

poppet hole. A hole in an old-fashioned capstan head that is used to receive the capstan bars. Sometimes called a pigeon hole.

poptop. A collapsible cabin top that can be raised to provide more headroom in a small boat.

porbeagle. A small game shark of the North Atlantic and North Pacific. *See* shark.

porcupine fish. A small to medium globe fish of the Diodonidae family which, like its cousins the puffers or blowfish, inflates its body when threatened. In addition its many spines protrude at the same time.

porgy. A small bottom food fish of the U.S. East Coast, resembling a fresh water sunfish, of the family Sparidae. Also called a scups and a fairmaid.

pororoca. Same as bore.

porpoise. 1. A relatively small (up to 12 feet) toothed whale that feeds on fish and squid. Technically only the family Phocaenidae include porpoises while members of the Delphinidae are ocean dolphins but there is some controversy among naturalists and thus confusion among laymen. One may use the words interchangeably unless the specific animal can be identified such as the bottle-nosed dolphin, the common dolphin, or the harbor porpoise of Europe. Porpoise live at sea and are often enmeshed and drowned by tuna seiners. *See* dolphin. 2. A torpedo is said to porpoise when it periodically breaks the surface while running.

port. 1. A harbor or shelter for ships where loading and unloading facilities are provided as well as other logistic conveniences. 2. An opening in a ship's side in form of an airport, cargo port, or side port. A freeing port permits the escape of water.

portage. The transportation of cargo overland from one waterway to another.

portage bill. A statement made out at the end of a voyage by the master showing the earnings of each member of the crew, including overtime and shares, if any.

portainer. A special container-handling crane for fast loading and unloading, consisting of a gantry supporting a horizontal boom which is stored in a vertical position when not used.

port capacity. The estimated ability of the facilities of a port or of an anchorage to clear cargo, expressed in tons per 24 hours.

portfolio, chart. A collection of charts, assigned a number and covering a specific area.

porthole. An opening in a ship's side fitted with hinged glass and metal covers; same as airport. British word is scuttle or sidescuttle.

portlast. An old word for the upper edge of a boat's gunwale or for the bulwark rail. Also called portoise.

portlight. The fitting inside a porthole or airport holding the hinged glass cover that can be dogged down Sometimes used synonymously with airport but an airport or porthole is more accurately the opening itself, not the fitting.

port marks. Insignia of distinctive but simple shapes and colors on all items of a ship's cargo to indicate the port where that item will be off-loaded.

portolano. A form of sailing directions; a book used in the 12-15th centuries which included charts. Also called a portulan.

port side. The left side of a ship looking forward (the fact that both port and left have four letters helps an easier recall), opposite to starboard, the right side. A sailing ship is on the port tack when the wind comes over the port side; not to be used in steering in which right and left rudder is used.

port speed. The rate at which cargo is handled at a particular port. For bulk cargo, it may be called the custom of the port.

Portuguese Current. Part of the huge North Atlantic gyre (including the Gulf Stream System) that circulates clockwise. The Portuguese Current passes south along the coast of Europe to join the Canary Current. A side branch passes into the Mediterranean through the Straits of Gibraltar.

Portuguese man-of-war. A hydroid or jellyfish with long stinging tentacles found floating on the sea worldwide.

portulan. *See* portolano.

Poseidon. The Greek god of the sea, corresponding to the Roman Neptune. Also the name of a nuclear submarine-launched missile system that is being superseded by Triton.

posh. Supposedly derived from Port side Out, Starboard side Home, which meant the shady side at all times for the English who went back and forth to the Far East by steamer. Now generally used to mean superior and luxurious.

position buoy. An anchored marker showing the location of a submerged object such as a wreck, anchor, or cable. Also a towed spar once used by warships steaming in column in low visibility to assist in station-keeping. This was also called a towing spar or fog spar.

position line. Same as a line of position.

post captain. An obsolete naval rank for an officer posted to command with the actual rank of captain; now an officer of lesser rank given the courtesy title of captain because he was in command.

pot. A baited trap that crabs, lobsters, and other crustaceans enter and then are unable to leave; used in large numbers by crab fishermen.

potrero. An accretionary ridge offshore separated from the coast by a lagoon and barrier island, as along the Texas coast.

pound. *See* weir.

pounding. The motion of a ship or boat in a head sea when there is heavy contact with the oncoming waves. If so violent that damage may result, it is called slamming.

pound net. A fixed fishing enclosure of vertical netting supported by stakes and used close to shore in shallow water. Fish wander into the interior pound or pocket where they are trapped. Also called a fyke or fike net.

power block. *See* block, power.

power boat. A boat propelled by mechanical means; a motorboat.

power curve. A curve showing horsepower needed to drive a certain hull at various speeds.

power skiff. A powerful, small open boat, usually steel, that is used to assist the seine boat in making a set of a purse seine.

power tonnage. *See* tonnage.

PPI. Plan Position Indicator.

pram. A light dinghy or small boat with a square, cut off bow and stern used primarily by yachts as a tender. *See* scow.

prao. *See* proa.

pratique. Technically, a ship's certificate of health but commonly used to mean permission granted by port authorities to a ship arriving from a foreign port to communicate with the shore after a quarantine inspection or certification. Now usually granted by radio after assurances that the arriving ship has no communicable disease aboard.

prau. *See* proa.

prawn. *See* shrimp.

predicted log race. *See* logging race.

press gang. In the days of sail, sailors used to abduct men ashore for service in the Royal Navy.

pressure pattern routing. *See* routing, ship weather.

preventer. Any rope or wire used for additional security to keep something in place such as a preventer backstay or preventer shroud. Other gear could be used in a similar manner such as a preventer fid (a bar of iron put through the mast above the fid hole) or a preventer plate (a steel piece made fast to the lower end of a chain plate).

pricker. A small marlinespike.

pride of the morning. A light mist or fog hanging over the sea at sunrise soon dispelled by the sun of a fair, bright day.

priest. *See* pacifier.

primage. Once paid as a lump sum or a percentage of freight charge to a ship's master for the care and protection of his cargo. Now applies to any special, extra charge for the use of ship's gear or any unusual expense due to special transportation problems.

prime meridian. On the earth's surface, the imaginary great circles passing through the poles from which longitude and time are measured. The prime meridian at the Royal Observatory at Greenwich, England is zero longitude and zero time zone.

prime vertical. A great circle passing through the observer's zenith, as well as through the true east and west points of the observer's celestial horizon.

priming. 1. The undesirable carry-over of fine water particles from a ship's boiler to the machinery such as into the turbines. 2. Steel is primed with an anti-corrosive mixture before the final painting. 3. A shortening of the interval between the times of successive high tides. Also called acceleration; the opposite is lagging.

prism, tidal. The total amount of water, excluding fresh water, that flows into the harbor (or out) with tidal movement.

privateer. Once a privately owned war vessel authorized by Letters of Marque to attack and plunder ships of a specific country. It was abolished by international agreement in 1856. To be in a privateer as a privateersman was to be engaged in privateering.

privileged vessel. Now called the stand-on vessel. *See* stand-on vessel.

prize. A ship captured in wartime, usually sent back with a prize crew to a prize court that awarded prize money. A feature of warfare at sea in the days of sail. Prize money is no longer paid.

proa. A general word for the native craft of Indonesia, Malaysia and the Philippines. Spelled prao in Portuguese and prau in Malay.

profile plan. Same as sheer plan.

projection, chart. A representation of a spherical earth on a flat sheet of paper. The Mercator projection is the one most commonly used although gnomic and polar projections are often seen. *See* Mercator, gnomic, polar chart.

prolonged blast. A signal of 4-6 seconds on the ship's whistle as specified by the International Rules of the Road.

promenade deck. An upper superstructure deck on passenger ships.

propeller. A rotating device used to propel a ship. Two to four blades are spaced evenly around a hub or boss into which a power-driven shaft is fitted. The blades are shaped to propel the water and thus cause the ship to move. Adjustable or variable pitch propellers permit rotation of the blades to change the amount of thrust or reverse the movement. A ducted or shrouded propeller has a surrounding shield to increase its efficiency. A propeller is right-handed when it turns clockwise viewed from aft when the ship is moving ahead. Also called a wheel.

propeller diameter. The diameter described by the tips of the blades when turning.

propeller disc area. The area enclosed by the revolving tips.

propeller guard. A framework of steel overhanging the propellers when they project beyond the ship's hull.

propeller pitch. *See* pitch.

propeller shaft. *See* shaft.

propeller slip. *See* slip, propeller.

propeller, vertical axis. Propeller in which a number of blades rotate in a horizontal plane about a vertical axis. It is efficient for tugs and other ships requiring high maneuverability. *See* Voith, Kirsten.

protest. An affidavit known as a writ of protest made before proper authority by the master of a ship immediately upon entering port when he fears litigation on loss of or damage to cargo or when a charter party has been seriously violated. Also the sworn statement made by the survivor of a shipwreck. *See* protest flag.

protest flag. International alphabet flag B flown by a yacht during or just after a race if a violation of rules by a competitor is claimed. Flag is noted by the race committee who must rule on the matter before a winner is declared.

protractor. A transparent plastic semi-circle whose curved edge is marked in degrees. A Hoey or single arm protractor has an attached swinging rule, used in plotting bearing lines and courses on a chart. A three-arm protractor has three rules that can each be lined up on a bearing to a landmark or aid to navigation. The pivot point is then the ship's position and can be obtained without the use of a compass by using relative bearings. The British term for a three arm protractor is station pointer.

prow. The extreme forward part of a vessel or the bow; word rarely used by seamen, mostly a poetic word or one used by landsmen. Also a variant of prao.

psc. per standard compass.

psychrometer. An instrument for measuring the relative humidity of the air by comparing the readings of a wet and a dry bulb thermometer. Also called a hygrometer.

PTC. Personal Transfer Capsule; used in deep diving operations.

pudding. Chafing gear usually made of yarns or matting that is used to protect, for example, a boat, spar, towline from rubbing. British spelling is puddening.

pudding chain. Before flexible wire was available, the short link chain used in running rigging of sailing ships.

pudding fender. A small fender or bumper made of old rope and covered with matting or canvas; now usually replaced by a hollow and durable plastic cylinder or ball. Sometimes called a dolphin.

puff ball. In a square-rigger, a light sail set aloft in fair weather.

puffer. A globe fish, swell fish, or balloon fish that inflates itself as protection when threatened. *See* blowfish.

pull. To pull a boat is better nautical usage than to row a boat. A rowboat is used on a lake but a pulling boat is used at sea by a sailor who pulls an oar. However, he does not pull on a rope, he hauls on it.

pulpit. A platform on a bow extension or bowsprit for a harpooner, particularly for one who harpoons swordfish. *See* stern pulpit.

pump. An important device aboard ship. *See* bilge pump, submersible pump. The barometer is said to pump when it oscillates due to passing squalls or heavy pitching.

pumping. Frequent rapid trimming and releasing of sails with no particular reference to a change in wind direction. This practice, also known as fanning, is not always legal in sailboat racing.

puncheon. A large wooden cask containing 84 U.S. gallons or 70 imperial gallons; larger than a hogshead.

punkah-louvre. *See* louver.

punt. Any small, flat-bottom, usually square-ended, boat used for odd jobs such as painting the ship's side. Perhaps the best known punts are those used socially in punting on the Thames at Oxford.

purchase. 1. A general word for any arrangment of blocks and ropes (tackle) that produce a mechanical advantage. 2. The mechanical advantage; the number of moving parts (ropes or lines) at the moving block, disregarding friction.

purchase block. Block having two or more sheaves and used in a multiple tackle for moving heavy weights.

purser. Aboard a passenger vessel, the administrative officer in charge of passenger lists, accomodations, and so on.

purse seine. A fishing net built like a long shallow curtain without a bag in the middle. The top is buoyed with floats and the lower end is weighed down. A purse rope pulls the bottom together when the fish have been enclosed. Also called a tuck seine or surrounding net. *See* seine, drag seine.

purse boat. Boat designed for purse seining.

pushboat. *See* tug, pusher.

pusher mast. The seventh mast on a seven-masted schooner. On other schooners, it was the 5th or 6th mast from forward.

pushing lights. In accordance with the Rules of the Road, two amber, 12 point (135°) lights displayed in a vertical line at the stern of a vessel pushing a tow.

pushpit. *See* stern pulpit.

put. To move, bring about, or take a certain action. A sailing ship puts about when tacking. A ship puts out to sea and may put into port. A ship is put into commission.

pyx. A very old and obsolete word for the box or the binnacle in which the magnetic compass was kept.

Q

Q. International signal code alphabet flag. When flown singly the quarantine flag means: "My vessel is healthy and I request free pratique". Spoken "quebec."

Q-ship. A disguised warship used to decoy enemy submarines or merchant raiders into close range where they can be sunk.

quadrant. A portable device having an arc length of 90 degrees and used to measure angles; similar to a sextant but smaller.

quadrantal deviation. A deflection of the magnetic compass caused by the induced magnetism of the ship's horizontal iron. It is corrected by the quadrantal spheres or correctors.

quadrantal spheres. Round iron balls mounted on each side of the compass on the binnacle. Sometimes referred to as the navigator's balls.

quadrant (or quadrantal) davit. Davit in which the lower end of the arm is a quadrant of steel fitted with gear teeth that enable the arm to be cranked out away from the ship's side in order to lower the boat.

quadrant, rudder or tiller. A fitting shaped like the quadrant of a circle, that is used to attach chains or cables to the rudder.

quadrature. The relationship between two celestial bodies, the moon and the sun, when they are 90 degrees apart in reference to the earth. When the moon is in quadrature, or 90 degrees from the sun, their effect on the tides is less (neap tides) than when the moon and sun lie in a line to produce their maximum or spring tides.

quahog. A large, hard-shelled clam of the genus *Mercenaria* that usually lives in deeper water than the soft-shelled and surf clams. *See* clam. Spoken: "co-hog."

quarantine. The detention period for a ship entering port, unless she has been granted pratique, to ensure that she is free of disease. Also the medical regulations governing this procedure as well as the area where the ship is detained. This may be a quarantine anchorage marked by a quarantine buoy. *See* pratique.

quarter. 1. The part of the stern 45 degrees or 4 points on each side of the center-line. **2.** A direction; an object is described as being sighted broad on the port quarter or 225 degrees relative. **3.** To quarter the wind and sea is to bring them astern on the quarter. **4.** In square-riggers, the quarter was the part of a yard outboard of the slings. **5.** A man-of-warsman might be granted quarter in battle, meaning that he could submit to capture instead of being killed.

quarter bitts. Bitts located topside on each quarter and used for securing mooring lines.

quarter block. Any of various lead blocks on a square-rigger for sheets and clew lines. Also a metal sheave which acts as a fairlead for the wheel chain or cable to the rudder quadrant.

quarter boards. Light boarding which extended around the stern above the quarter rail of old ships.

quarter boat. Any boat hung on davits near the ship's quarter.

quarterdeck. Traditionally, the part of a ship aft and topside from which the master or captain conned or directed the ship. It was the domain of officers, the scene of ceremony, and the rituals of punishment. In modern warships, it is the designated deck area near the brow or accommodation ladder from which the Officer of the Deck, for example, manages the ship and carries out the routine, meets visitors, organizes honors and ceremonies and dispatches ship's boats and vehicles.

quartermaster. A petty officer or senior able seaman who traditionally steers the ship and assists in navigation, piloting, taking soundings, and signaling.

quarter rail. On large schooners, a light open fence fitted above the bulwarks around the stern and quarters, serving as a guard rail for the quarterdeck. Also called a quarterdeck rail or monkey rail.

quarter rope. A mooring line leading to the ship's quarter, usually called the quarter breast or a quarter spring line. In a trawl net, one of the lines fastened to the foot of the bosom.

quarters. 1. The accommodations on a ship, such as the crew's quarters. 2. A formation or group of men on a warship as quarters for inspection. 3. U.S. Navy sailors fall in at quarters for muster daily and in times of emergency they go to general quarters or their battle stations.

quarter sling. One of the supports of a yard on either side of its center.

quasi-derelict. A judicial term that describes a ship that while abandoned temporarily is not "forever abandoned to the mercy of wind and sea."

quay. Usually a solid masonry structure, a landing place along the shore for ships and boats. Often called a wharf if made of wood and sometimes called loosely a pier, dock, or mole. Pronounced kee . . . . .

quayage. The payment made for the use of a berth at a quay.

quayman. *See* longshoreman.

queen staysail. A triangular sail set on the main topmast stay of a two-masted schooner.

quick-flashing light. A navigational light that flashes continuously and quickly; not more than 60 flashes per minute. *See* flashing light.

quicksand. Loose, water-saturated sand into which any heavy object will sink.

quinquereme. An ancient galley having five banks of oars.

quintant. A rare old instrument similar to a sextant but with an arc of only 72 degrees, one fifth of a circle.

quoin. A wedge used to elevate a smoothbore gun in the days of sail. Still used as dunnage to secure casks and barrels when stowed on their sides.

R

R. International Signal Code alphabet flag. Spoken: "romeo."

rabbet. A shoulder or recess; a channel made to receive the edge of a board or steel plate in order to make a smooth fit.

rabbet line. The line formed by the intersection of outside plating or planking with the stem, sternpost, and the side of the keel.

rabbet plank. Also called hog-piece.

race. 1. Any fast, visibly turbulent water such as a tide race or a screw or propeller race. 2. A propeller is said to race when it is lifted partly out of the water in a heavily pitching ship and it speeds up. 3. Boat racing involves race boats, racing flags, racing numbers, racing rules, etc..

rack. 1. Any device designed to stop items from going adrift such as a pot rack on a galley range, or fiddle or table rack, or a belaying pin rack. Ships are made fast to the piling called a mooring rack and the piles that shoulder a ferry into her slip are called a ferry rack. 2. To seize two ropes together, side by side, to prevent their relative movement is to rack them. 3. A thin mass of wind-driven clouds is a wrack or rack.

racking. Spun yarn or small stuff (seizing) used to rack two lines together. Also the lateral stress or deformation of a ship's hull due to violent rolling.

racking stopper. *See* stopper.

racon. A RAdar beaCON that returns a coded signal providing identification of the beacon as well as range and bearing when triggered by the ship's radar. *See* ramark.

radar. RAdio Detection And Ranging; an electronic device used to obtain a visual presentation of ships, aircraft, landmarks, etc. by means of the reflection of radio waves. Of great value to ships in low visibility.

radar beacon. *See* racon.

radar reflector. Any metallic device that ensures a strong reflected radar signal as used on buoys, small boats, etc..

raddle. To interlace lengths of rope as in making boat gripes.

radio. Used as an aid to navigation in the form of radio direction finders (RDF), radio beacons, radio fog signals, etc. The advent of small and cheap radars has made such systems less important, however the wide use of voice radio in controlling ship traffic in restricted waters has become of major significance.

radio beacon. An aid to navigation that broadcasts an identifiable signal whose direction from the ship can be determined.

radio direction finder (RDF). A radio receiver using a directional antenna that determines the bearing of a radio signal such as a radio beacon or a radio broadcasting station. Late models automatically scan and show the direction of radio stations by indicating lights that glow on a 360° scale.

radiolarian. A single-celled planktonic protozoa with a siliceous skeleton; mostly pelagic and many luminescent.

radio navigation. A system of navigation by which radio waves are received and evaluated to determine the ship's position; it includes radar and satellite navigation. Electronic navigation, a broader term, includes depthfinders, inertial systems, Doppler equipment, etc..

radiosonde. A device carried by balloon that is used to record weather information at various altitudes and transmit this information by radio to ships and shore stations in the RAOB system.

radio time signal. A broadcast of Greenwich mean time useful to navigators who can thus get a time tick accurate to 1/10 of a second. All information is in the publication H.O. 205, Radio Aids To Navigation, issued by the U.S. government.

raffe or raffee. A triangular sail once set above the upper yard in a schooner carrying a square topsail. It was also sometimes a word for moonsail or moonraker. *See* kites.

raffle. In the nautical sense, a tangle of cordage, blocks, spars and other debris associated with a wreck or with a ship's topside rigging carrying away.

raft. Any floating device used to transport people or goods on water; usually made of logs and having no hull as such or interior; may be propelled by oars, sail or poling. Logs are often fastened together into a large raft for moving to a mill. Ice is said to raft when sheets pile upon sheets of field ice. Boats that moor side by side are said to be rafted or nested or may be said to raft-up.

rail. 1. The nautical word for an open fence aboard ship, usually along the edge of a weather deck. **2.** A plank, timber, or piece of metal forming the top of a ship's bulwark. Also called a railcap. **3.** A hand rail, ladder rail, or safety rail is there to assist those using the ship's ladder. **4.** Surfer's slang for the edge of a surfboard. *See* fender rail, sheer rail, guard rail.

rail cap. *See* rail.

rail screens. Screens made of canvas that are sometimes used along a ship's rail.

railway. An old word for the track or metal strip on a mast on which the clips of a sail are fastened and on which they travel. *See* marine railway.

rainmaker. Navy slang for the meteorologist or weather man. Also slang for any device that converts shore-supplied steam into freshwater for use to a ship alongside a pier.

raise. 1. In the nautical sense, it means to bring into view as in the expression "We shall soon raise Fire Island". 2. The wind raises a choppy sea. 3. One attempts to raise another station by radio.

rake. The inclination forward or aft of a mast, funnel, or other piece of tophamper or hull above the waterline.

rake of a propeller. The difference between the angle of slope of its blades and the perpendicular.

rakish. Having a smart appearance suggestive of speed.

rally. Progressive and even blows on the wedges along a ship's side that transfer the weight from the keel blocks and shores to the cradle and sliding ways just prior to launching a ship from the building ways.

ram. Once an underwater extension of the stem of a warship which itself was called a ram.

ram bow. The bow of a boat that recedes aft above the waterline.

ramark. A RAdar MARKer beacon that transmits continuously a signal indicating the direction of the beacon.

RAMOS. Remote Automatic Meteorological Observing System; installed by the National Weather Service. It is solar powered with each station reporting temperature, dewpoint, wind speed and direction, pressure, and rainfall each hour.

ramp. To sail a boat rather full when on the wind is to ramp her.

randan. An English three-man pulling boat with two men pulling single oars and one between pulling two oars or sculls.

range. 1. Distance to the target. 2. The effective range of visibility of a navigational light. 3. The direction indicated by two marks when in line to show a channel. 4. The markers that show a channel.

range light. In accordance with the Rules of the Road, a white light abaft and above the masthead light. The two form a range that reveals the course of a ship at night to other ships. For sea-going steam vessels, it is a $225°$ light.

range of tide. The difference in feet between high and low water.

range. 1. To range an anchor chain is to lay it out on deck or on the pier alongside. 2. A ship coming alongside another or a pier is said to range alongside.

ranging. Said of a ship at anchor that is moving or horsing around its anchor in a blow as she changes course.

RAOB. A RAdar OBservation system of land stations and ships that receive weather data sent by radiosonde.

rap full. With all sails filled and the sailboat not quite close-hauled; same as clean full.

rapture of the deep. A form of narcosis induced by nitrogen in the blood system. A great hazard to scuba divers since it impairs their judgement. It occurs at depths of about 135 feet and below.

RATAN. Radio And Television Aid to Navigation; a system in which a central station transmits a radar picture of a harbor or congested waterway to ships by television to ensure them a safe course.

ratchet block. Block whose sheave is controlled by a ratchet, often used in a mainsheet system since the sheave can move only in the trim direction.

rate. 1. A level of proficiency within a Naval classification or rating, thus the rate of a second class radioman is second class and his rating is radioman. A ship is rated for insurance purposes by a classification society. **2.** The daily change of a chronometer is its error. **3.** Slang for deserve as in the expression "the senior seaman rates the lower bunk".

rat guard. A conical metal shield fixed around a mooring line to prevent rats from coming aboard.

rathole. A sailor's private storage or hiding place for personal valuables.

rating. 1. A general Naval grouping or classification such as quartermaster. *See* rate. All Naval petty officers wear a rating badge. **2.** A number assigned to a racing yacht by the IOR that is derived from her measurements and which is her racing handicap. **3.** The British word for enlisted man.

ratline. A short length of rope crossing the shrouds at regular intervals and used by men going aloft as a kind of ladder. Traditionally made of ratline stuff, somewhat larger than seizing stuff. Pronounced ratlin.

RATT. Radio Teletype.

rattail. The tapered end of a rope.

rattan. The fiber or stem of a climbing palm of the genus Calamus and native to the Far East that is widely used in making light and strong furniture. Once used in the Orient to make large cables such as anchor cables; it is now used to make large fenders.

rattle down. To secure the ratlines to the shrouds by means of eye splices and clove hitches.

rave hook. A caulking tool used to remove old oakum from a seam before recaulking.

rawin. The radar observation of a released balloon and then tracked to learn the direction and force of winds up to 100,000 feet. When combined with radiosonde, it is a rawinsonde.

ray. Members of the suborder Rajoidei who are characterized by a dorso-ventral flattened body, great spreading pectoral fins, and a whip tail. The devilfish and manta ray can grow to a width of 20 feet but are never aggressive; the sting ray is much smaller but has a barb in its tail which can inflict a most painful wound if accidentally stepped on in shallow waters. Skates are smaller-sized and are edible.

Raydist. A small portable electronic navigation system used in survey work. It has a range of up to 350 miles.

Raymond releasing hook. A type of hook used on boat falls in which a weighted lever strikes the boat as it becomes waterborne upon lowering and thus releases the hook from the ring permitting the falls to be freed.

Rays of Maui. Polynesian (Maori) term for the rays of sun which appear to reach down to the water from behind a cloud. Sailors refer to this as the sun's backstays.

razee. To modify a wooden ship by reducing the number of decks. It was once done to convert wooden warships from one class to another.

razing. Cutting in the ship's lines on wood with a razing knife. Also called scribing and no longer done.

razing iron. A caulker's tool; same as a ripping iron.

razor clam. A long, narrow, razor-edged bivalve which is highly prized for food. Common in the Pacific northwest where its harvesting is now limited by law.

RDF. Radio Direction Finder.

reach. 1. The straight portion of a river or canal between bends, rapids, or locks. 2. An arm of the sea extending into the land. 3. Sailing with the wind on the beam, or nearly so, between close-hauled and free is sailing on a reach or reaching. 4. To close reach is to sail nearly close-hauled; to be on a broad or beam reach is to have the wind abeam; to head reach is to forge ahead while lying to under canvas; to forereach is to forge to windward while tacking. 5. A leg or a distance sailed on a certain course is known as a reach.

reacher. A lightweight, high-clewed jib or spinnaker used when reaching; normally smaller than a spinnaker. Also called a jibtop.

reacher block. Block used for changing the lead or direction of spinnaker and jib sheets in a sailboat. Similar to a turning block except that the reacher block has a swivel.

reaching canvas. Sails designed for maximum efficiency when reaching; full cut and relatively light.

reaching foresail. *See* foresail.

reaching jib. Same as balloon jib.

reaching strut. A short spar used on a sailboat to hold a headsail guy away from the shrouds. British term is jockey pole.

reach rod. A long handle by which valves below decks, usually in the engineering spaces, can be opened or closed from topside.

reaction turbine. The standard ship's turbine which depends on the reactive force of steam expanding against the blades of a rotor that is free to rotate on a shaft.

ready about. The command given to the crew of a sailboat before tacking or coming about. Also a warning to all hands, particularly in regard to the boom which is about to sweep across the boat.

ream. To enlarge a hole, particularly a grommet or cringle in a sail by means of a fid. Sailmakers also use a reaming stool with holes of different sizes bored in the top. Also spelled rime.

Rear Admiral. A Naval officer, a flag officer, senior to a Commodore and junior to a Vice Admiral, comparable to a Major General in the Army. He flies a two-starred flag and is also known as a two-star officer.

recall flag. A signal to racing yachts that they have crossed the starting line too soon. A Naval signal to ship's boats to return to their ship. A general recall applies to all Naval personnel, may be promulgated by any means, and is used in time of emergency.

Receiver of Wrecks. A British official who has cognizance over, for example, all wrecks, stranded cargo ships, cargo washed ashore and to whom all arriving ship's Masters must report any derelict, wreck, or iceberg sighted or any collisions that have happened.

recta. A bill of lading that specifies the name of the consignee.

Red Duster. Sailor's name for the British Red Ensign that merchant ships fly.

Red Ensign. The national flag of the United Kingdom that is flown by merchant ships.

redfish. A small pinkish groundfish of North Atlantic waters of the genus *Sebastes* that is also a popular food fish.

red lead. An anti-corrosive primer paint, traditionally red in color. Sailor's slang for catsup.

red, right, returning. An expression remembered by navigators, pilots, and ship handlers meaning that red channel buoys are always on the right or starboard hand in U.S. waters when entering the channel from seaward.

red tide. A bloom or very rapid growth of a red, toxic dinoflagellate, a common animal plankton. The surface water of the sea turns red and luminescent at night, fish die from lack of surface oxygen, and mollusks in the area become too toxic to eat. A local and temporary phenomenon.

reduction gear. Gear that reduces the necessarily high speed of a turbine to the slower required speed of the propeller in a steam vessel.

reduction to the meridian. The correction of the observed altitude of a heavenly body near the meridian used to obtain its meridian altitude and thus the latitude of the observer.

reef. A reduction in sail area by any means. To reef is to reduce the sail area. *See* reef, sail.

reef band. A strip of canvas sewed horizontally across a sail as strengthening for the line of reef points.

reef cringle. A rope grommet worked around a thimble in the leech of a sail at the end of the reef band through which the reef earing passes.

reef earing. A short rope used to secure the corner of the reefed sail to yard or boom by passing through the reef cringle.

reefer. A short blue or black woolen coat worn by seamen, same as a peacoat or peajacket. Also a refrigerated cargo ship as well as the refrigerated compartment on any ship.

reef, geographic. Any long rock or coral formation near enough (10 fathoms or less) to the surface of the sea to be a danger to navigation. Coral reefs are made of dead and living coral either fringing the shore and separated by a narrow stretch of shallow water (a fringing reef), or a barrier reef off shore separated by deep water from the land, or random reefs known as platform, patch, or table reefs. *See* coral, atoll, shoal.

reefing cleats. Cleats fitted on the boom of a sailing vessel near the clew and used to take the hauling out turns of the reef earing.

reefing iron. A caulker's tool, same as ripping iron.

reef knot. A square knot, a simple over and under twice with the ends coming out on the same side of the loop. In reefing, one end was often tucked back and under as a bow that could release the knot and thus expedite shaking out a reef.

reef points. The short lengths of rope made fast to a sail at the reef band which, tied with a reef knot, results in a reef being taken in that sail. Also called pointline. *See* slab reefing.

reef, sail. To reef a sail is to reduce its area, usually by tying part of it off by reef points or by rolling some of it up with roller reefing gear. A sailor puts in or tucks in a reef and then may shake out a reef. The word reef was also once used in reefing or shortening a spar.

reef tackle. A small purchase used in reefing a squaresail.

reeming iron. An iron wedge used for opening the seams of a wooden ship or boat to permit caulking.

reeve. To pass through or lead a line, rope, or wire through any opening such as a block, grommet, etc.. Past tense is rove.

reeving line. One of the ropes sometimes fixed to squaresails in heavy weather for reefing or furling more easily. Also any small line fastened to a heavier one to assist in putting the line through a block.

reeving line bend. A way of fastening two lines together to facilitate their passing through an opening. It consists of two half hitches with the ends seized to the standing parts.

refit. British word for overhaul in regard to ship maintenance.

refraction. In a maritime sense, the change of direction of radio and light waves when passing through the atmosphere or passing through air masses of different characteristics. The first appears to elevate a celestial body above its true altitude, the second produces mirages, commonly seen when passing along a coast where dry and warm desert air meets colder and moist ocean air.

refraction of water waves. The change in direction of waves as they pass over shallow water; part of the wave in shallow water is slowed by the friction of the bottom. Well known to Polynesia where the proximity of land can be detected by a slight change in the direction of the swell.

regatta. A boat race or series of races organized for sailing, power, or pulling boats.

register breadth. In measuring the register tonnage of a ship it is the distance between opposite outside hull platings at the widest part of the hull at or below the uppermost full deck.

register depth. In measuring register tonnage of a ship, the distance from the middle of the tonnage deck to the top of the inner bottom.

register length. The length of a ship used in calculating register tonnage, measured on the tonnage deck from the outside forward extremity of the bow or stem plating to the after side of the sternpost plating.

Register of Shipping of the USSR (RS). The Soviet national ship classification society located in Moscow. *See* classification.

register tonnage. *See* tonnage.

Registro Italiano Navale (RI). The Italian national ship classification society located in Genoa. *See* classification.

registry. *See* certificate of registry.

relative. In the maritime sense, the bearing's direction relative to the fore-and-aft axis of the ship instead of using north and south; used in shiphandling.

relative wind. The geometric sum of true wind and the course and speed of the ship. This is important in handling aircraft, including helicopters, from ships.

relief, relieve. In its nautical sense, the act of replacing a man on watch or on duty as in the expression "relieve the wheel and lookout." The man taking over is the relief.

relieving tackle. Any purchase rigged to take the strain off a piece of gear as, for example, the steering gear.

remora. A small fish equipped with a suction disk on top of its head by which it can attach itself to sharks, debris, and ships. It was once thought to be a serious hinderance to a ship's movement thus the name stayship.

rend. Old word for an open split or crack in ship's timber or planking, probably due to the use of green wood instead of seasoned.

render. An old word for easing a line through a block. The line itself renders when it runs free.

Rennell's Current. A seasonal ocean current, usual in the winter, that sets northward across the western approaches to the English Channel.

repeater. A signal flag used to repeat another flag directly above it in a flag hoist. Now called a substitute in the NATO Navies.

reserve buoyancy. The watertight, non-submerged volume of a ship; a critical factor in a ship surviving damage that involves flooding.

resin. Same as rosin.

resistance of a ship's hull. The sum of the friction between water and a ship's wetted surface, the resistance due to the formation of eddies and dead water, and that due to the formation of waves set up by a moving hull.

respondentia. A loan or contract, similar to bottomry, in which a Master pledges his cargo as security for a loan to complete the voyage. Now rare.

Restraint of Princes. A phrase used in bills of lading to show a limitation upon the liability of a shipowner when the ship is detained by government authority against the will of the owners.

restricted visibility. According to the Rules of the Road it means any "condition in which visibility is restricted by fog, mist, falling snow, heavy rainstorms, sandstorms, or any other similar causes."

retained magnetism. Transient or temporary magnetism induced in a ship's iron when the ship remains on the same heading for a length of time.

return block. *See* snatch block.

revenue cutter. Old term for Coast Guard cutter from the days when the Revenue Service was independent.

revenue ton. An arbitrary U.S. commercial unit particular to a specific cargo, port, or carrier. *See* ton.

revolution indicator. An electrical instrument by which the direction and rate of revolution of the propeller shaft can be read in the pilot house.

Reynold's number. *See* Froude number.

rhabdolith. A minute calcareous body contained in deep ocean bottom ooze, classed by some as a protozoan and by others as an algae.

rhumb line. The curve on the earth's surface that cuts all the meridians at the same angle and appears on a Mercator chart as a straight line. Also called a loxodrome. Rhumb is an archaic word for one of the 32 points of the compass but is no longer used.

RI. Registro Italiano Navale.

ria. A long narrow inlet, shoaling as it leads into the shore. Also a creek or broad river opening to the sea.

ria coast. A coast having a series of drowned river valleys, as does, for example the coast of northwestern Spain.

rib. A transverse frame in a boat or ship to which the outside planking or plating is fastened.

riband guide. A strip of wood on the ground or launching ways used to hold and protect the launching lubricant after the launching cradle timbers are laid down.

ribband. A long narrow strip of wood or steel plate especially used in shipbuilding to hold the frames together in the early part of construction. Also called ribbon. In some cases, same as molding.

rice, cargo. *See* paddy.

ride. To lie at anchor riding easy or hard depending on wind and tide. To float on the surface, as "the boat rides out the storm." To overlap or press upon; a mooring line rides over its own part when it is jammed around a bitt. *See* riding turn.

rider. A timber or steel plate that adds strength and stiffness as a rider frame or keelson.

rider plate. A continuous flat steel plate attached to the top or bottom of a ship's girder.

ridge rope. The backbone wire or rope of an awning. In the days of sail, it was one of the two ropes running out to the bowsprit to which men could hold on.

riding bitts. Heavy bitts in the days of sail to which anchor cables were made fast.

riding boom. Same as boat boom or guesswarp boom; a hinged spar rigged out from the ship's side in port to which boats are made fast.

ridge. *See* mid-ocean ridge.

riding chock. Same as controller.

riding lights. Lights displayed by a ship at anchor as required by law. Same as anchor lights.

riding sail. Any small sail used to steady a power boat underway, as in fishing, or at anchor.

riding turn. A turn of the parts of a rope under strain around a cleat, bitts, etc. It lies over the other turns and jams them. Also riding turns are a second layer put over the first in a seizing or whipping.

Ridley turtle. A small sea turtle, rarely over 2 feet, found in both the Atlantic and Pacific and now protected as an endangered species.

rift. *See* mid-ocean rift.

rig. *n* **1.** A distinctive arrangement of sails and masts as on a schooner rig, bark rig, fore-and-aft rig, square rig, etc.. **2.** Any arrangement of gear or machinery. *vb* **1.** To rig something is to set it up and arrange it, such as the forecastle in a ship may be rigged for divine services. **2.** Booms are rigged in or may be rigged out. **3.** A sailor may go ashore rigged out in his best civilian clothes.

rigger. A shipyard worker who sets pieces of structure or equipment in place and thus does the hoisting, lowering and securing in place of all the parts of a ship during building. Traditionally, he carried on his belt a rigger's horn, a length of animal horn filled with tallow to lubricate his gear.

rigger's screw. A portable vise used in splicing rope and wire. Also called a rigger's vise or a splicing vise and sometimes a rigging screw. The latter is also a term for turnbuckle or bottlescrew.

rigging. Everything non-structural above decks in a ship such as masts, shrouds, sails (if any), spars, stays and cordage. Standing rigging is fixed in place while running rigging is free to move.

rigging screw. *See* turnbuckle The old version of this term was rigger's screw.

right ascension. *See* ascension.

righting moment. The force that tends to restore a ship to its normal upright position after it has been inclined. Expressed in foot-pounds, it is the resultant of the forces of buoyancy and of gravity acting as a righting couple.

Right of Angary. The right of a state, under International Law, to requisition ships and goods in time of emergency, subject to adequate compensation.

Right of Approach. The right of a warship under International Law to approach and inspect closely a suspect merchant ship.

Rights of Visit, Search and Seizure. Under International Law on the high seas a neutral merchant ship may be visited, searched, and, if found non-neutral, seized by a belligerent warship.

right whale. Any of several baleen or whalebone whales having a large head and no dorsal fin. So called because the early whalers found that it was a profitable and thus the right whale to kill.

rigol. Same as eyebrow; now often spelled wriggle.

rime. *See* ream.

ringbar. A steel bar used to collect and stack the purse rings when hauling a seine.

ringbolt. A bolt or screw with a ring at the end, common in ship's rigging.

ring, mariners. A later form of astrolabe in the form of a brass ring marked on half its inner surface with degrees. Also called a sea ring.

ring net. A fishing net resembling a purse seine, popular in California because of its speed of employment.

ring rope. In the days of sail, a rope by which the anchor is hoisted to the cathead by its ring.

ringsail or ringtail. An archaic, narrow, auxilliary sail once used with a gaff sail. Part of the associated gear was a ringtail boom. There was also a ringtail topsail set above and abaft a leg-of-mutton spanker.

rip. Disturbed water caused by a meeting of currents or by a current flowing over a shoal or an irregular bottom. If tidal current is involved, it is a tide rip or rip tide but should not be confused with a rip current.

rip current. A strong, relatively narrow stream setting directly away from the shore upon which heavy surf is breaking. It is the result of water piled up inshore by the surf and needing an escape. At times, it is improperly called a rip tide or tide rip and should not be confused with undertow. A rip current consists of a feeder current running along the beach (itself a warning to swimmers), a neck which is the narrow current setting away from the beach, and the head where the neck broadens and dissipates. To escape a rip current, a swimmer should swim parallel to the beach.

rip line. *See* ripper hooks.

ripper hooks. Bare hooks used to snag fish by being cast into fish-filled water. The hooks are attached to rip lines.

ripping iron. A caulkers tool used for clearing a wooden seam of pitch and old oakum. Also called a razing iron, reefing iron, or clearing iron.

riprap. Rocks, concrete blocks, or stones dumped together to form a breakwater or groin. Also the resultant structure itself.

rip tide. *See* rip.

riser. 1. One of the heavy planks or strakes of the bottom planking of a ship adjacent to the garboard strake. 2. A fore-and-aft plank in a wooden boat that supports the thwarts. 3. In a modern ship, the vertical pipe leading to a major line that carries fluids such as a firemain riser.

rising line. A curved line drawn on the sheer plan by which a ship's designer determines the height of the ends of the floor timbers throughout the ship's length.

rising tank. A double bottom space in a ship in which the inner bottom is higher at the center line than at the sides.

rive. To string herring on thin wooden sticks before curing is to rive them.

rivet. A slightly tapered iron or mild steel pin which is heated and hammered on one end as it joins two steel plates together. The shape of the unhammered end may be button, pan, steeple, countersunk, or cone. Riveting is done by riveters with a variety of special tools but has been largely replaced by welding in ship-building.

riveting. The act of joining steel plates with rivets either by hand or by power tools is bull riveting. If the rivets in one row are abreast of those in adjacent rows, it is chain riveting; if the rivets are offset from each other, it is zigzag riveting.

roach. Originally the upward, concave curve or cut away part of the foot of a squaresail. Also a word loosely applied to the convex curve of a squaresail, round is more precise in this case. Now used by yachtsmen to describe the outward curve, aft, of the leech of a fore-and-aft mainsail as well as, more loosely, any curved part of a sail. *vb* To roach a sail is to induce more curve in the leech or a sail.

roadstead. An offshore anchorage with good holding ground and usually some protection from wind and sea. Often roads for short.

Roaring Forties. The area of the ocean between 40° and 50° south latitude famous for almost continuous strong winds, gales, and very high waves because of the long fetch of the prevailing westerlies. *See* brave west winds.

roband. Small stuff once used for fastening the luff of a fore-and-aft sail to the mast hoops or clips, the head of a squaresail to the jackstay, or the head of a gaff sail to its gaff. Sometimes it was called robbin or roving.

robbin. Same as roband.

rocker. A boat having a rockered keel. Looking at the keel from the outside, bow to stern, it has a slight convex curve.

rocket. A device for passing a line to a wreck or stranded ship that cannot be reached otherwise. Also a distress signal fired in an emergency and containing colored lights.

rocket launcher. A special type of multiple rod holder often used in game fishing competition.

rock fish. Any one of a number of edible and usually game fish such as red rock, black rock, rock cod, rock bass, or striped bass. A west coast name for sea bass and scorpion fish as well as a generic name for many species of small food fish caught near rocks or in kelp beds.

rocketsonde. A weather recording and radio transmitting device similar to a radiosonde but using a rocket to reach high altitudes. Sometimes combined with rawin.

rocking. Persistently rolling a sailboat from side to side with manpower. Not permitted when racing.

roddle. The part of a wire rope clip against which the U-bolt is secured.

rode. The line or rope to which a small boat rides when anchored. Also called an anchor line. An anchored vessel is said to be tide-rode when she lies to the tidal current primarily and wind-rode when her position is determined by the wind.

rodmeter. A retractable device that is lowered through the hull as part of a log, containing either a pitot tube, a propeller, or an induction coil depending on the type of log.

rogue's yarn. A different colored identification thread run through the center of one strand of a rope.

rogue wave. The rare but statistically predictable, unusually high wave occurring in the open sea that can and does poop and pitchpole ships and yachts, sweep people off rocks, jetties, and decks of ships, smash in the pilot house windows of ocean liners, and, in general, intimidates all prudent mariners. Also called the ultimate wave.

roll. The rythmic motion of a ship from side to side around its fore-and-aft or longitudinal axis. Period of roll is the time, in seconds, for a ship to roll from one side to the other and is a measure of a ship's stability. The shorter the period, the greater the stability. Surge is a sideways, bodily movement of a ship while lurching is an abnormal, deep and sometimes sudden roll. Rolling should not be confused with heeling or listing.

roller. A long, generally non-breaking swell, usually generated by storms often thousands of miles away. Rollers are the source of big surf, often a menace to small boats but a delight to surfers.

roller chock. Chock having one or more fixed rollers designed to reduce friction on a line lying in the chock.

roller furler. A mechanical device for rolling a jib around its own luff wire. The procedure is called roller furling.

roller handspike. *See* handspike.

roller reef. A reef taken in a sailboat's fore-and-aft sail by rotating the boom, thus winding the foot of the sail around the boom.

roller reefing gear. The mechanism that rotates the boom of a sail to achieve reefing.

roller rule or ruler. Ruler fitted with rollers that permit it to move accurately across a chart without changing direction; used instead of parallel rulers in laying down bearings and courses.

roller sheave. Sheave fitted with roller bearings to facilitate turning. Also called a patent sheave.

rolling chock. *See* bilge keel.

rolling hitch. A knot used where strain is roughly parallel to a spar or rope. It consists of two round turns and a half hitch.

roll line. A north European set line, wound lightly on a wooden prong or fork. It unrolls easily to follow the pull of the fish. Now largely replaced by fishing reels.

Roll On/Roll Off. A cargo ship designed to receive and discharge cargo carried in vehicles that drive on and off through a large door in the stern. She carries wheeled or tracked machinery, large structural pieces and containers. British term is end-door ship. Also called RO/RO.

rombowline. An old sailing ship term for used canvas and cordage that can only be employed as chafing gear. Also rumbowline.

room. A shiphandling word for space, such as swinging room needed when anchoring or sea room required when maneuvering.

room to swing a cat. Describes a space aboard ship large enough to permit a man to be flogged.

root valve. Valve located where a branch line or riser comes off the main line that carries water, steam, oil, etc. aboard ship.

rooting. A sailing ship running before big seas may bury her bow from time to time and is then said to be rooting.

ropack. A pinnacle or slab of heavy sea ice forced by pressure to stand upright on edge for as much as 25 feet.

rope. In general a word for cordage, either fiber or wire, over 1 1/2 inches in circumference and 21 threads. Line is smaller (small stuff, marline, etc.) although in the U.S. Navy all cordage is called line except for specific ropes such as wheel rope, or bell rope. Yachtsmen tend to refer to rope as line only when it is being used afloat for standing and running rigging, anchor and mooring lines, and use rope when it is coiled in a storeroom or when it is used to secure something. Rope may be braided to improve its ease in handling. *See* fiber rope, wire rope, braid.

ropehouse. Same as ropewalk.

ropetack. In wind surfing, to come about or tack using the uphaul is to ropetack.

ropewalk. The traditional name for the facility or factory that makes rope. Also called a ropehouse.

Rope Yarn Sunday. A U.S. Naval term for any day or part of a day when work and drills are suspended, traditionally Wednesday afternoon or during very heavy weather. British term is Make and Mend.

roping. Same as bolt rope. Also a collective term for rope.

RO/RO. *See* roll on/roll off.

rorqual. Any of the members of the Balaenopteridae, large baleen or whalebone whales as different from the toothed whales. They are marked by a dorsal fin, a recessive upper jaw and numerous grooves on the underbody. The common rorqual grows to 80 feet and, like its giant cousin the blue whale, is close to extinction because of hunting.

rose. A circular diagram on a chart. *See* compass rose, wind rose.

rose box. A perforated plate or box used as a strainer over a water inlet, as in a bilge pump, to keep foreign matter out. Also called a strum or strum box.

rose lashing. A special seizing used to make fast a rope to the side of a spar, rail, or harpoon.

rosin. The substance remaining after the distillation of turpentine and widely used in the days of sail for paying seams after caulking and as a general waterproofing and preserving agent. A more common name is tar. Also called resin.

Rossel Current. A seasonal ocean current flowing westward and north westward along the coast of New Guinea from May to September.

rotary current. The circular movement of the tidal flow offshore or in a bay caused principally by the rotation of the earth and thus clockwise in the northern hemisphere.

rotten clause. A marine insurance clause that relieves the underwriter of responsibility if the hull of the ship which he has insured is found to be unsound.

rotten ice. Melting sea ice or brash ice.

rotten stops. Light pieces of basting thread or weak string made fast around a sail to hold it together in bundles or stops when it is sent aloft in stops. A sharp pull on the sheet breaks the stops and thus unfurls the sail, usually a headsail.

Rottmer gear. A patented quick release device that operates under tension for launching lifeboats from a ship.

rough sea. A turbulent sea state in which waves with combing crests, 5-8 feet high are produced by winds of 5-7 on the Beaufort Scale. Rough seas are lower than high seas.

round. Used in a nautical sense and in conjunction with down, in, or up, the term means to haul on a specific slack rope or tackle. To round to or up is to turn a ship into the wind or to heave to. Round in means to bring the blocks of a tackle closer together whereas round down or overhaul means to separate them. The round of a sail is its convex curvature as well as the extra cloth added to a sail along its borders.

round charter. Charter involving a round trip-outward and homeward.

roundhaul. A circular set of a purse seine, used in open water when there is no point of land to partly contain the fish.

roundhouse. In old sailing ships, a cabin in the poop or a deckhouse used as a galley or as a space for petty officers.

rounding. Old rope or strands fastened around a rope to prevent chafing.

roundline. Traditionally, small stuff of tarred hemp used for heavy service aboard ship. It was three strands of two yarns each laid righthanded.

round nets. *See* seine.

round of bearings. A series of bearings (landmarks or other aids to navigation) taken close together in time that provide a reliable fix or geographical position for the ship.

round turn. A complete turn of a line around a bitt, spar, or cleat rather than just a partial turn, thus there is enough friction to permit the line to be checked or held. The expression "brought up with a round turn" means a sudden reprimand to a sailor.

rouse. To haul heavily and with great force on a rope or wire. To rouse out is to wake up or alert as in "rouse out the anchor watch."

rouse-about block. A large, all-around heavy duty snatch block.

routing, ship weather. *See* ship weather routing.

rove. Past tense of reeve. Also the long end or bight of a cargo sling that is hooked to the fall.

rover. A word still used in marine insurance to mean pirate.

roving. Fibers woven into a sort of mat, now made of fiberglass and used to waterproof the wooden deck of a small boat.

row. To propel a boat with oars. The preferred nautical word is pull. A sailor pulls on an oar but hauls on a line or rope. A rowboat is properly called a pulling boat by mariners.

rowlock. Strictly speaking, a piece cut out of a boat's gunwale to take an oar, but now used by the British as a synonym for crutch. Rowlock and crutch are the words the British use when we use oarlock. *See* oarlock.

royal. A squaresail traditionally set in line above the topgallantsail and used only in light winds in a square-rigger.

RS. Register of Shipping of the USSR. *See* classification.

rubbing strip. Any external, longitudinal timber or metal strip extending along most of the side of a ship above the waterline as protection against the sides of piers, docks, or other ships. Often called a molding and also known as a rubbing fender, piece, strake, or rubrail.

rudder. The vertical, flat wood or metal slab that pivots at the stern of a ship or boat and by which the ship can be steered. Most large, modern ships have balanced rudders whose turning axis passes through the approximate center of stream pressure, thus reducing the force needed to turn the rudder. A bow rudder is one fitted on the bow and a drop rudder is a portable rudder for sailboats that extends far enough down into the water to act as a keel or centerboard. A jury rudder is a temporary, improvised one. An underhung rudder is one entirely supported from within the hull and not by the sternpost; also called a spade rudder. An active rudder is one incorporating a motor-driven propeller and is thus effective when the ship has no way on. *See* Kitchen rudder.

rudder angle indicator. A visible pointer forward of the helmsman that tells him the angle to which the rudder has been moved by the steering engine. Also called a rudder telltale.

rudder blade. The main, flat surface of the rudder, fastened to the rudderstock and strengthened, in a steel rudder, by forgings projecting out from the stock or rudder arms. The lowest part of the rudder blade is the rudder heel.

rudder braces. A collective term for rudder pintles and gudgeons, also called rudder hangings and rudder irons.

rudder brake. A compressor or locking device once used on the rudder of large ships to keep it from swinging when shifting from power to hand steering and vice versa.

rudder carrier. A fitting placed inboard under the tiller to take the weight and thrust of the rudderstock and tiller and rests on a rudder bearing.

rudderhead. The upper part or continuation of the rudderstock, above the blade on which the quadrant or tiller is fitted.

rudder quadrant. A casting or forging that is part of the rudder structure and with which the turning force is exerted by chains or wire ropes that fit into the two grooves on the quadrant. Rigged on opposite sides, as the port chain pulls, the starboard chain yields.

rudderstock. The part of a rudder that acts as a vertical shaft through which the turning force of the steering engine is exerted. Also called the main rudder piece.

rudder stops. Small projections on the rudderstock and on the stern post which make contact when the rudder has reached the maximum allowable angle. Also called rudderpost stoppers.

Rule of Special Circumstance. *See* Special Circumstance, Rule of.

Rules of the Road. Short term for the International Regulations for Preventing Collision at Sea. Also known as Colregs. There are also Inland Rules and Pilot Rules. The British say Rule of the Road.

rumbowline. Same as rombowline.

rummage. A thorough search for contraband aboard ship. To move the cargo about during a search for smuggled goods is to rummage it.

run. *n* 1. The aftermost, narrowing part of a ship's hull. 2. A trough used to lead water off a deck to the scuppers. 3. A day's run is the distance sailed in 24 hours, usually from noon to noon. 4. A brook or small creek. *vb* 1. To go, to move as in running gear aboard a ship or to run before a gale. 2. To pass through as in running a line through a chock. 3. To hoist as in running up the colors. 4. A ship may run aground, run down a small boat, or run her easting down which means to sail east on the latitude of her destination.

runaway ship. A somewhat derisive term for those U.S. owned and operated ships that take refuge under a foreign flag to escape expensive labor, safety laws, and regulations. *See* flag of convenience.

runnel. A trough or corrugation formed by waves or by tidal currents in the foreshore or on the bottom just offshore.

runner. 1. A line fastened at one end to a fixed object, such as an eyebolt, and rove through a single block. 2. Any whip or fall used as a working hoist. 3. A ship that does a smuggling trade. 4. A man who solicits business for a hotel, bar, or club from sailors ashore. 5. The running or shifting backstays in a sailboat.

running. Usually describes something that moves such as a running bowline that forms a free sliding noose or a running bowsprit. A heavy sea or surf may be said to be running and the movable part of a rope is the running part in contrast to the standing part. A ship is running free when sailing before the wind.

running block. Block that moves, as opposed to a standing block, in a tackle or that moves with the object to which it is attached while hoisting or shifting.

running lights. Lights required to be shown at night by a ship or boat in accordance with the Rules of the Road.

running fix. A fix advanced by dead reckoning (estimated course and speed made good) to a new position.

running rigging. Ropes, lines, and tackle that move in contrast to the fixed or standing rigging.

rutter. An early fifteenth century English word that describes a book of sailing directions, similar to a portolano, and usually illustrated with sketches of coasts and harbors as seen from the sea. It was often the English mariner's highly personal, secret and valued notebook.

S

S. International signal code alphabet flag. When flown singly means: "My engines are going astern." Spoken: "sierra."

sac. An underwater indentation, a submarine gulf, shown on the contour lines of equal depth on a chart.

saddle. A piece of timber having a rounded notch in which a boom or spar is stowed. *See* boom crutch. Any wood or metal fitting acting as a support such as the device that moves on the span wire of a ship-to-ship refueling rig and supports the hose.

saddle plate. A plate or block on a mast that may support the jaws of a gaff.

safe berth. In maritime shipping usage, a berth in which a vessel will remain afloat and not rest on the bottom at low water. Other safety factors such as political, civil, or weather considerations are not included in this expression.

safety capsule, floatable. Survival gear for men working on ocean platforms in cold and stormy waters. A capsule may hold six men with the necessary food, water, warm clothing, signaling gear, and so on.

Safety Certificate. Certificate issued to a ship by a government attesting to compliance with the latest regulations of the International Convention for Safety of Life at Sea.

safety factor. A multiple unit of measure that represents the relationship between the breaking strength of a rope, wire, or tackle and the maximum load it can carry.

safety hook. *See* cargo hook, hook.

safety message. A voice radio transmission, less urgent than pan, but asking for circuit priority to pass a message concerning the general safety of navigation. *See* security, security, security.

sag, sagging. The droop or bending in the center of a spar or of a ship supported at both ends. The opposite is hog. A ship is said to sag to leeward when she moves sideways due to wind, sea, or current.

sail. Any piece of fabric made of natural or synthetic fibers that is used to propel something in the water by means of the wind. Old-fashioned square or rectangular sails are set perpendicular to the mast as in square-riggers. Fore-and-aft sails are usually triangular and have at least one side made fast to a spar or boom;

these are used on modern sailing ships and boats. The bottom of a sail is the foot and the top is the head. On a squaresail, the two sides are called the leech yet on a fore-and-aft sail, the after edge is the leech and the leading edge, usually made fast to the mast, is the luff. In this one, the corners are the head, on top, the tack at the bottom forward, and the clew at the bottom aft.

sail, to. To go on the water, even under power is to sail, as in the expression "the ship sails at dawn." To travel in a ship or to direct a sailboat is to sail. For recreation, people often go for a sail.

sail area. The vertical hull and superstructure flat surfaces upon which the wind can exert force. An important factor in shiphandling.

sailboard. Same as boardboat.

sailcloth. Once cotton canvas, now it is cloth made from Dacron, nylon, Kevlar, or other synthetic fibers, with Dacron the most common.

sail cover. A cloth covering for a furled sail. British term is sail cloth.

sailfish. A warm water game fish with a bill similar to that of a swordfish and distinguished by a prominent dorsal fin known as its sail. *See* bill, billfish.

sail ho. The traditional cry of the lookout at first sighting a ship at sea. The response is "where away?" to which the lookout may report "broad on the port bow, sir."

sail hook. A sailmaker's tool used to hold the canvas taut while it is being worked on. Also called a bench hook.

sailing. A navigational computation, a course to steer in order to reach a destination across the sea. It may be Mercator, rhumb line, middle latitude, great circle, which are all known as sailings. With the perfection of accurate and world-wide charts, the computation has largely been replaced by merely laying down a course on a chart.

Sailing Directions. Publications of the Defense Mapping Agency Hydrographic Center providing detailed information about the coasts of the world and adjacent waters. They now include Planning Guides and Enroute Directions.

sailing master. Anyone in charge of the shiphandling and navigation of a sailing vessel and not in command. Owners of yachts who are not experienced mariners often have sailing masters aboard.

sailing on a bowline. Said of a square-rigged ship when sailing on the wind or close hauled when the bowlines would be hauled taut. Sailing on an easy bowline describes a ship with sails well filled but not jammed into the wind.

sailing on her own bottom. Said of a boat that is fully paid for.

sailing on the bottom. Describes a sailboat that is stiff and does not heel over so far that she appears to be sailing on her side.

sailing thwart. In a sailboat, it is the fore-and-aft plank on top of the thwarts through which the mast is stepped. It may also be called a gangplank, a gangboard, or a mast carling.

sailkite. A lifting device for the headline of a trawl that holds it more open, a rectangle of canvas sewn to the bosom section of the headline. Developed by the United Nations Food and Agriculture Organization for more efficient fishing to improve world food production.

sail loft. An area or building where sails are made.

sailmaker. Traditionally a man who makes and repairs sails, cutting and sewing by hand with palm and needle. Now he makes such items as awnings, ladder screens, and deck machinery covers all sewn by machine. Known as Sails aboard ship.

sail needle. A heavy needle, triangular in cross section used to sew canvas. It is pushed through the heavy cloth by means of a leather palm.

sailor. In general terms, anyone who goes to sea as a profession or as a hobby. Specifically, it is a man who works aboard ship under officers or mates and petty officers.

sailor's knot. A square or reef knot.

sailor's purse. The egg capsule of skates and of certain sharks that is often found on beaches. *See* skate.

sail plan. A side view, drawn to scale, of a sailing ship with her sails set. A rigging plan is sometimes shown with the sail plan, particularilly for a small, simple sailboat but usually it is a separate drawing.

Saint Elmo's Fire. *See* corposant.

salina. A salt marsh or pond separated from the sea but flooded at high water. Area used sometimes to evaporate sea water for the production of salt and is then called salt garden or saltern. *See* marine salina.

sally. To sally ship is to rock or roll it by having the crew move from side to side in unison. This may be done to measure the period of roll and thus to compute the stability or to help free a ship from a mudbank or shoal by breaking the grip of the bottom.

sally port. In the days of sail, an opening aft in a fireship used for the escape of the crew.

Sally Lightfoot crabs. Very agile, bright orange crabs of the Galapagos Islands.

salmon. A valuable food and game fish of the family Salmonidae that also includes trout and char. They maintain a pelagic existance but return to their river of origin to spawn. Parr, smolt, and grilse are different stages in their development. The Pacific salmon dies after spawning whereas the Atlantic salmon will return to sea.

salmon board. A platform, usually made of wood, that forms the bottom of a cargo sling.

salmon tail. An extension plate added to a rudder to give an increased turning power in narrow and restricted waters. Also called a Danube rudder or a Suez rudder.

saloon. The dining compartment, lounge, or other room for officers and passengers aboard a merchant ship.

salp. A barrel-shaped, transparent variety of zooplankton found drifting in the open sea.

salt, salty. A sailor is a salt, especially an old salt. Salty means sea-going, nautical, professional, raffish, cocky or sometimes earthy. *See* tar.

saltern. *See* salina.

salt garden. *See* salina.

salt horse. Sailor's term for salted beef, once his standard fare. Also called salt junk.

salting. The old custom of filling the open spaces in a wooden ship with salt to inhibit rot, particularly between frame timbers. The boards used to contain the salt were called salt stops.

salt water soap. Soap that lathers in salt water and thus widely used where freshwater is scarce.

salvage. Normally a service voluntarily rendered to save lives and ships at sea, or performed under contract on a no cure–no pay basis by professionals using special ships and equipment. Anyone putting a line aboard a stranded vessel may claim salvage (but not ownership) unless an agreement is made beforehand.

SAM ships. *See* Liberty Ship.

samiel. Same as simoom.

sampan. A general word in the Far East for a small boat used to carry people and cargo. Also spelled sanpan.

sampson post. Traditionally a short vertical timber or metal bar forward of the mast on a sailing vessel to which the anchor rode or warp is made fast. Also called a kingpost.

samson line. A three-strand, nine-thread rope for heavy service aboard ship, somewhat larger than round line.

samum. Same as simoom.

sandbagger. A 19th century racing sailboat in which the crew shifted bags of sand as they tacked. Popular on the east coast of the U.S. from 1850 to 1880 and survived in Australia until 1960.

sand dollar. An oval or heart-shaped sea urchin with short spines and about the size of a fist or smaller. Properly called a spatangus, its skeleton is commonly found on sandy beaches.

sand lance. A small silver baitfish that burrows into the sand when approached by larger fish or when stranded by the tide.

sandspit. A long narrow projecting piece of sandy shoreline.

sand strake. An older term for garboard strake.

Santa Ana. A strong, easterly desert wind that is sandy, dry, and warm. It periodically blows off the coast of southern California and is often responsible for extensive mirages.

SAR. Search And Rescue.

sardine. A small food fish of the genus *Sardinella* related to the herring family. Also the young of the European pilchard when it reaches a suitable size for canning.

Sargasso Sea. A relatively calm area of the North Atlantic, south of Bermuda to latitude 25° N, between longitudes 40° and 65°W, the vortex of the general clockwise circulation of water, part of which is the Gulf Stream System. It is marked by masses of sargassum or gulfweed.

sargassum. The yellow floating seaweed of the genus *Sargassum* of the Sargasso Sea and the Gulf Stream System. It is the home for much sea life including the young of the loggerhead turtle. Also called gulfweed.

sastrugi. Wave-like ridges of hard snow formed on sea ice by wind action.

saury. An edible, long-billed thin fish, up to 20 inches long, that is found in the temperate waters of the North Atlantic.

save-all. 1. A rope net or canvas spread under a brow or under a cargo handling rig and used to catch material that might fall overboard. **2.** Any receptacle rigged to catch dripping liquids. **3.** In the days of sail, it was a small additional sail or bonnet set in fine weather under a studdingsail.

sawfish. A flat fish, of the genus *Pristis,* that is related to the ray. It has a long snout or bill fitted with teeth on each edge.

scale. A large-scale chart that shows a small part of the coast in large dimensions thereby making piloting easier. A small-scale chart is normally used for passages at sea and shows a large area on a relatively small piece of chart. Also a deposit composed mainly of calcium that accumulates on the inside of watertube marine boilers.

scallop. A bivalve mollusk of the genus *Pecten* that is highly esteemed as food and found world-wide. The shell is radially ridged and shallow.

scandalize. To spill wind or reduce sail area by any unusual method such as dropping the peak of a fore-and-aft sail. It was also sometimes used as a sign of mourning.

scantling(s). The dimensions of all structural parts of a ship such as frames, girders, plating that are published for various types of ships by the classification authorities. Full scantling means ship construction of maximum strength.

scaphander. A simple diving gear, once used in shallow water, consisting of a suit, and helmet, with a hand pump kept in the boat.

scarf. The joining or scarfing of two pieces of wood or metal end to end or side by side produces a scarf or jog.

scend. The amplitude of the upward vertical motion of a ship when heaving or pitching. Sometimes spelled send. *vb.* To rise or heave upward.

schooner. A fore-and-aft rigged sailing ship, normally with two masts, the foremast shorter than the mainmast. Late in the 19th century in the U.S., the schooners were built with as many as seven masts.

schooner guy. *See* lazy guy.

scope. The length of the anchor cable from hawsepipe out to the anchor or to a mooring buoy. Greater riding scope is used in strong winds to reduce the angle between the anchor cable and the horizontal at the anchor to ensure greater holding power. Also short for oscilloscope.

score. A groove made in the cheeks of a wooden block to hold the strap. Any groove, notch or cut away section in a spar, rudder, or deadeye.

scorpion fish. An ugly, squat, small fish of the family Scorpaenidae, also known as a rockfish since it lies disguised on the bottom. The venomous spines on its head and back can inflict a very painful death. It is found in both warm and cold waters.

Scotch boiler. A firetube boiler.

Scotchman. A batten or a board made fast in the rigging to prevent chafing. It is also the word used in the United Kingdom for flashplate.

scouring basin. In a tidal lock system, it is a bay or lock in which water is retained until needed at low water to scour or flush out the dock or channel.

scouse. An old sailing ship dish of stewed, preserved vegetables, biscuit, and sometimes meat.

scow. A flat bottom vessel with square, sloping ends and no power. As a general service boat it is stable, easy to build and to beach. Variations are known as John boat, bateau, punt, pram, flatboat, and square ender. In U.S. inland waters sailing scows are fast, shallow draft sail boats with twin rudders and twin bilge-boards. Large scows are used as barges, lighters, houseboats and often carry pile-driving and dredging machinery. Scow, lighter, and barge are often used interchangeably in accordance with local usage.

scowing. Same as becuing.

screw. A synonym for propeller.

screw anchor. Anchor that holds in place a screw mooring or buoy in a soft mud bottom.

screw current. Current generated by the propeller of a turning ship.

screw log. A device streamed astern of a ship that is used to measure speed and distance. A rotor or screw turns the towing line that registers on a counter. Also called a taffrail log, a patent log, a towing log, and a mechanical log.

screw slip. *See* cable stopper.

screw stopper. Same as devil's claw.

scrimshaw. Pictures and designs carved on whale bone or on teeth of whales or sharks; figurines or objects carved from this sea ivory. Once done only by whalers and Indians, hobbyists now do scrimshaw.

SCUBA. Self Contained Underwater Breathing Apparatus; an open circuit diving system by which a diver breaths in fresh air through a mouthpiece that is linked up to a tank of compressed air that he carries on his back. Also called by the trade name Aqua-lung.

scud. *n* Loose, vapory fragments of low clouds moving rapidly, often beneath rain clouds or fracto-nimbus clouds. *vb* To scud before a storm is to head downwind with enough sail set to avoid being pooped.

scull. *n* A light, spoon-bladed oar used to propel a very light racing shell, also sometimes called a scull. *vb* To scull with an oar is to use it over the stern of a boat, perhaps resting in a sculling notch or hole, and pushing it from side to side.

scullery. A compartment in a ship, near the galley, where the washing up is done.

sculpin. A member of the Cottidae family; marine fish with large flat head and many spines. Also called bullhead or sea robin.

scum cock. A valve on a boiler that is used to blow off surface impurities. Also called a brine cock or surface blow valve.

scupper. A deck drain used to carry off rain or sea water either, directly as on a weather deck, or through scupper pipes or hoses that discharge through the ship's side. In the latter case, a scupper or storm valve might be installed. A weather deck scupper usually discharges over a scupper lip to keep the water away from the ship's side. Also known as a freeing port.

scups. Same as porgy, a fish.

scurvy. A disease caused by the lack of vitamin C, a scourge for centuries of sailors who had no fresh food. First prevented by the British with lime juice.

scuttle. *n* **1.** A small opening in a bulkhead or in a deck of a ship usually fitted with a quick-closing cover. **2.** The cover that fits over the opening. **3.** A ventilating air scoop rigged in a deck opening. **4.** The British word for porthole or airport, also side scuttle. *vb* To scuttle a ship is to sink it deliberately.

scuttlebutt. An electric shipboard drinking fountain that provides chilled potable water. Slang for gossip or rumor, especially in the U.S. Navy.

sea. In its broadest sense, a synonym for ocean. Also a subdivision of the ocean such as the Black Sea. Short for sea state as in a rough sea.

sea anchor. 1. Any designed or improvised floating or partly submerged device that is used to hold a ship's bow up to the wind and sea in heavy weather. **2.** A drag sail or drift sail. **3.** When referred to as a drogue, it performs a different function. *See* drogue.

sea arrow. Any of the squid of the genus *Ommastrephes* that resemble feathered arrows in shape and who move so rapidly that at times they jump clear of the water.

sea bag. The traditional cylindrical canvas bag in which sailors carry their clothes and other personal gear.

seabather's itch. *Schistosome dermatitis* caused by the larvae of certain sea worms that penetrate the skin.

seabed. The bottom of the ocean. *See* bed.

Seabee. A merchant ship, barge-carrying cargo transportation system in which especially designed ships carry loaded barges or lighters, usually with a capacity of 850 tons. *See* LASH, BACAT. Also a member of the U.S. Navy's Construction Battalion.

sea belly. A round, branched, six inches high brown and green seaweed that grows on rocks at tide level.

sea biscuit. Same as hard tack, pilot bread, ship's biscuit. *See* hard tack.

seaborne. Transported by ship on the sea.

sea breeze. A breeze blowing from the sea to the shore during the day. *See* land breeze.

sea buoy. The buoy that is the furthest out at sea to indicate a channel or an entrance. Sometimes called the farewell, departure, or landfall buoy.

sea chest. Traditionally a box in which a sailor stows his gear aboard ship. Also the intake in the ship's side between the hull and the first inboard sea valve in the salt water supply system.

seacoast. Land bordering the sea.

seacock. Any opening to the sea, through the hull of the ship, that can be opened or closed. Also a valve fitted to the salt water intake line inboard of the sea chest; a sea valve.

sea connections. The valves that control the passage of water into the ship. These must be watched and checked if a ship is in a drydock that is being flooded.

sea cow. A manatee or dugong, an aquatic, weed-eating mammal of the order Sirenia. The Stellar sea cow is probably extinct. *See* mermaid.

sea cradle. Same as chiton.

sea cucumber. An echinoderm, classs Holothuroidea, a roughly cylindrical, primitive bottom creature known as trepang by the Orientals who value it as a reputed aphrodisiac. Also called a sea slug or beche de mer.

sea dog. An older, experienced sailor. In the Navy, an older man who takes an interest in and advises young sailors is a sea daddy.

sea eagle. A fish-eating bird of prey such as a bald eagle or osprey.

sea elephant. The largest of the seals, up to 20 feet in length, with a long snout. Also called an elephant seal.

sea fan. *See* fan, sea.

seafarer. A person who goes to sea as his profession or hobby; a seafaring or seagoing man.

sea farming. The cultivation, under controlled conditions, of fish, shellfish, and algae for commercial use. Also called mariculture and aquaculture.

sea feather. Any of several flowerlike marine organisms of the family Pennatulidae having a featherlike shape.

seafood. General grouping of edible fish or shellfish from the sea.

sea fire. A brilliant display of bioluminescence near the surface of the sea that is usually seen on a dark night.

seafront. Land on the edge of the sea suitable for housing.

seagirt. Surrounded by the sea.

seagoing. Describes a person, ship or any object that goes to sea or is fit and able to do so. Also nautical, salty.

sea grant college. College that receives money from the National Science Foundation to support research and programs that increase the use of marine resources.

sea grape. A small ascidian or sea squirt; an animal that grows in clusters on rocks, piles and other underwater objects. Also a tropical American shrub of sandy beaches that has broad, rounded leaves and hard purple fruit growing in clusters.

sea gull. Sailor's slang for chicken served at meals as well as for girls who are met in waterfront bars.

sea haze. A phenomenon encountered in some parts of the ocean caused by wind-carried aeolian dust. *See* aeolian dust.

sea horse. A small fish of the genus *Hippocampus* that has a head and upper body suggestive of a horse, a prehensile tail and that swims upright in warm waters.

Sea Islands. Islands in a chain that lie just off the coasts of South Carolina, Georgia, and northern Florida.

sea kindly. Describes a vessel that endures heavy weather without excessive discomfort for her crew.

sea king. A Viking pirate chief of the early Middle Ages.

seal. A sea-going mammal of the families Phocidae and Otariidae; a graceful swimmer who feeds mostly on fish. The fur seal is killed for its coat while the larger seals are hunted for their oil and leather. The grouping includes hair seals, crabeater seals, ringed seals, harp seals, and the voracious leopard seal that feeds largely on penguins.

sealer. A ship used to hunt seals.

sea ladder. *See* ladder.

sea lawyer. Anyone aboard ship who is abnormally argumentative and critical concerning regulations and procedures.

sea legs. The ability to accomodate to a ship's motion in a seaway.

sea lettuce. Any of several green seaweeds of the genus *Ulva* having thin, leaflike irregular fronds, sometimes used as food.

sea level. The mean or average position of the ocean's surface, between mean high water and mean low water, from which elevations ashore and depths of the sea are measured.

sea lily. Any of various marine invertebrate, plantlike organisms usually anchored to the bottom in deep water that have a long stalk and a flower-like body.

sea lion. A seal of the Otariidae family having small external ears. The Stella sea lion of the North Pacific grows to 12 feet and 1400 pounds and was once hunted for its blubber.

seaman. In its broad sense, any person who works aboard a ship. In the Merchant Marine, there are apprentice, ordinary, and able-bodied seamen; in the U.S. Navy, there are seamen recruits, seamen apprentice, and seamen. Under U.S. law a seaman is any person, other than an apprentice, who is employed or engaged in any capacity aboard a vessel owned by a U.S. citizen.

seaman's eye. A mariner's ability to judge speed, distance, wind, and sea in ship and boat handling, and functions such as line throwing.

seamanship. The art and science of managing, operating, and maintaining ships and associated gear. Deck seamanship is concerned with all activities and gear above deck whereas marlinespike seamanship relates to splicing, seizing, and serving rope line and wire as well as all manner of rigging.

seamark. In the broadest sense, any object ashore, a landmark as seen from the sea or a floating object such as a buoy used to assist in navigation and piloting.

sea mew. Any of the gulls that live along the coast of Europe.

seaming twine. Cord or light line used to sew canvas. Also called sail twine.

sea mosquitoes. Tiny, tropical, ferocious isopods, sort of planktonic crabs, whose claws tear off minute bits of flesh when they attack a diver underwater in great numbers. Very painful and dangerous to divers with any exposed skin.

seamount. An elevation of the ocean floor rising more than 1000 meters and having a top that is roughly symmetrical and less than 60 miles across. Sometimes called a seapeak.

sea mouse. A segmented marine worm of the genus *Aphrodite*.

sea otter. A saltwater marine mammal of the family Mustelidae that lives in the giant kelp forests of the Pacific Northwest. About the size of a dog, it eats daily 20 percent of its weight in mollusks, especially sea urchins. Once hunted to near extinction for its magnificent fur coat. It is the only one of the sea mammals that doesn't have blubber for warmth and therefore must depend on its fur coat.

sea painter. A long line leading from the bow of a lifeboat well forward that is used in the procedure of lowering and hoisting the boat.

seapeak. *See* seamount.

seaplane. According to the International Rules of the Road, a flying boat or any other aircraft designed to maneuver on the water.

sea power. The vital and total maritime strength of a nation that includes its Navy, Merchant Marine, and port and harbor facilities.

sea purse. Same as sailor's purse.

sea puss. A dangerous longshore, or a strong rip current, or the channel through a bar scoured by such a current.

seaquake. An earthquake under the ocean bottom.

sea raven. A large sculpin of the western Atlantic.

sea return. Interference on a radar screen caused by radar reflections from waves. Also called clutter.

sea roach. *See* gribble.

sea robin. Any of the various bottom fish of the family Triglidae having a long head and very long pectoral fins on which it appears to walk.

sea room. Space to maneuver a ship at sea, especially in the days of sail when it was of critical importance to avoid, for example, being driven onto a lee shore in heavy weather.

Seasat. A U.S. ocean-watching satellite that scans 90 percent of the world's sea surface and broadcasts data on sea state, wind, currents, schools of fish, and so on.

seascape. A view or picture of the sea.

Sea Scout. The nautical branch of the Boy Scouts who learn seamanship and related skills.

sea serpent. A legendary large, snakelike marine animal often reported by mariners but never identified.

seashell. The calcareous shell of a marine mollusk or similar organism.

seashore. Land lying along the edge of the sea; the seaside.

seasickness. Nausea, often violent, caused by the disturbance of the body's balancing mechanism found in the ear's semi-circular canals. There is no real cure for those strongly afflicted except, in most cases, long periods at sea or being taken ashore at once. *See* Stugeron.

seaside. Same as seashore.

sea slick. An area of the surface of the sea that has an oily appearance or a different color. If not man-made pollution, it is usually caused by blooming plankton. The sliding stern of a ship in a sharp turn will produce a slick as will a drop or change of the wind.

sea slug. *See* nudibranch.

sea smoke. *See* steam fog.

sea snake. Any reptile of the family Hydrophiidae, related to cobras, and venomous. Most live in tropical waters of the Indian Ocean and the western Pacific, some range the ocean, others live near the shore where, as in Malaysia, they are dangerous to swimmers.

sea squirt. A small brightly colored animal that ingests large quantities of food-laden water, squirting out the waste water at the same time. Free floating as larva, they later fix themselves to the bottom. Properly known as an ascidian.

sea star. *See* starfish.

sea state. The wave condition on the surface of the sea. The World Meteorological Organization has a widely accepted table which states: "Read code number for sea state, description, and mean maximum wave height. 0 glassy calm 0; 1 calm (ripples) 0-1; 2 smooth (wavelets) 1-2; 3 slight 2-4; 4 moderate 4-8; 5 rough 8-13; 6 very rough 13-20; 7 high 20-30; 8 very high 30-45; 9 phenomenal over 45. Figures for wave height are in feet." *See* wave, wave height.

sea stores. Tax-free goods such as tobacco and spirits for sale only when the ship is at sea. Same as ship stores.

sea swallows. Same as terns.

sea tangle. Any of the various brown seaweeds, especially those of the genus *Laminaria.*

Seattle head. A galley smoke pipe, "Charlie Noble", that is seen on fishing vessels and yachts. It is a metal pipe in the shape of a T with the two ends of the cross piece slanted down at a 45° angle to avoid taking in water.

sea trials. A short voyage to test a ship's machinery upon her completion or after a major overhaul; occurs after finishing dock trials and before she is ready for service. Sea trials may include builder's trials, standardization trials, endurance, fuel economy and full power trials, maneuvering trials or equipment testing trials.

sea trout. A popular saltwater food and game fish of coastal North America. Also known as weakfish, *Cynoscion regalis,* and as squeteague.

sea turtles. Any of the large marine reptiles of the order Testudinata whose feet have become flippers for more swimming ability. This order includes loggerhead, leatherback, hawksbill, green or Ridley turtles. Sea turtles are most vulnerable on shore while laying eggs and as a consequence they are nearing extinction. In the days of sail they were kept alive on board as a source of fresh meat.

sea urchin. An echinoderm with a hard shell and spines that lives on the sea floor where it feeds on the holdfasts of kelp thereby destroying them. Europeans and Orientals consider the eggs a delicacy but so do sea otters and lobsters.

sea valve. Any valve or cock close to a ship's plating that controls the passage of a liquid, usually sea water. Also called an outboard valve or skin valve.

seawall. A stone structure, usually solid, built along the waterfront to prevent encroachment of the sea. It often acts as a road and as a pier for boats. *See* jetty.

seaward. Towards the sea.

seaware. Sea wrack used as fertilizer.

seaway. At sea; afloat in the ocean. A sea-kindly boat may be described as comfortable and dry in a seaway.

seaweed. A general word for macroscopic marine algae and grass growing in the sea, either attached to the bottom, as kelp is, or free floating like sargassum. Some produce useful products for industry.

seaworthiness certificate. Certificate issued by a classification organization or by a qualified person that permits a ship to go at sea and also to satisfy the requirements of the marine insurance companies.

seaworthy. Capable of safe operation or usage at sea in any weather.

sea wrack. Any material cast up on a beach or shore, especially seaweed.

Secchi disk. A flat white disk, about 30 centimeters in diameter that is used to measure the transparency and clarity of seawater.

secret block. Block which is closed at the top or swallow; the rope or wire entering through holes in the shell of the block prevents the fouling of adjacent gear.

secure. *vb* To make fast, lash tight, lock up, stop or cease. A boat hoisted aboard a ship is normally secured for sea. The Boatswain, after anchoring, reports the forecastle secure. The word may be passed aboard ship "secure from boat drill." *adj* Safe, as in a secure berth.

security, security, security. Preface to a voice radio safety message requesting priority to broadcast a message concerning the general safety of navigation. Less urgent than pan,pan,pan. Spoken: "securi-tay."

seiche. A standing wave oscillation in an enclosed body of water, as in a harbor, that often moves a ship about so violently that she parts her mooring lines as the water level rises and falls rapidly. It is a harmonic vibration in response to waves, storms, or underwater seismic disturbances outside the harbor.

seine. A portable fish net that is used to encircle and haul in fish. It is supported by a floatline or corkline and held vertical by a weighted footrope or leadline. Seines are divided into two groups. *See* drag seines, purse seines.

seiner. A boat used for seining. Modern seiners are built to also trawl, use gill nets and long lines as well as troll.

seismic sea wave. Wave of large amplitude, long period, and often very destructive; caused by seaquakes, volcanic explosions, or large earth slides underwater. Popularly but inaccurately termed tidal waves or tsunami although there is nothing tidal involved.

seize. To bind, lash, or make fast a rope to another or to a spar by using small stuff or seizing.

selatan. A strong south wind of the northern Celebes during the monsoon season.

self-bailing cockpit. Cockpit designed to drain itself if flooded. Also called a self-draining or self-emptying cockpit.

self-righting boat. A specially designed rescue boat with buoyancy tanks and a heavy keel that is used by the Coast Guard. If capsized by breaking waves, no matter how large, the boat can right itself.

selvage. The edges of a net or of a piece of canvas are woven to prevent unraveling. Also selvedge.

selvedge line. A line used in a fishing trawl.

semaphore. A system of communicating within visual range with movable arms whose position indicates a letter. It is still used to control ship traffic in canals. Signalmen in the Navy use handheld flags to send messages between ships, usually when at anchor during the day.

semi-circular deviation. *See* deviation.

semi-containership. *See* containership.

semidiameter correction. A correction of sextant altitude needed to determine the altitude of a celestial body when observing this body (such as moon or sun) that has a sensible diameter and where the upper and lower limb is seen on the horizon instead of the center.

semidiurnal. Having a period or cycle of half a lunar day. Tides and tidal currents are normally semidiurnal having two floods and two ebbs each day.

Senhouse slip. *See* cable stopper.

sentinel. A weight used to increase the holding power of an anchor of a small boat. *See* kellet.

separator, steam. A device used to remove water and impurities from steam before it leaves the boiler steam drum.

sergeant fish. *See* cobia.

sergeant major. A small, yellow tropical reef fish with black stripes. Also called a butterfly fish or a damselfish.

serve, serving. To wrap around with tight turns, as in serving a hawser with marline. A wire rope may be wormed, parceled and finally wrapped in line or served. *See* worm, parcel, and serve.

service. The small stuff used in serving. Also, as in Naval Service or Merchant Service, where it means an occupation or profession.

service tanks. Fuel oil tanks near the ship's fireroom. This oil is used to fuel the fires and is periodically pumped from storage tanks.

serving mallet. A wooden hammerlike instrument used to pass a serving around a rope on top of the parceling.

SES. Surface Effect Ship.

sessile. Describes a sea animal attached directly and permanently to something underwater.

set. 1. The direction towards which a current is flowing. **2.** A ship deflected from its steered course by wind, sea, or current is said to be set and the amount of this deflection may be called set or drift. **3.** A sail is hoisted and set. **4.** A ship sets sail after setting the first watch. **5.** A draft, hoist, or sling of cargo is a set or sett.

setee. *See* settee.

set, wave. Usually set for short, a surfer's word for a group or series of successive waves, perhaps 7 or 8, that are higher than average, the last being usually the highest, for which the surfer has been waiting sitting on his board just outside the normal break line. Between sets there is a smooth.

set flying. To rig a sail loose-footed without its luff being made fast either.

setline. A fishing line that is unattended but visited when it appears that the bait has been taken. Setline is a word in the Pacific for longline or trawl. *See* longline.

set net. An entangling fish net attached to a fixed object on shore, the bottom, or an anchored boat.

set sail. Said of any ship when she starts a voyage. A sailboat sets a sail when it is raised and trimmed.

sett. *See* set.

set taut, set up. To take in the slack; to tighten as in the expression "set up on the jib halyard."

settee. A long, lateen-rigged, decked sailboat of the Mediterranean; now rare. Also written setee.

settee rig. A four-sided lateen sail with a very short luff.

settling tank. Tank in which the engineers separate fuel or lubricating oil from contaminating water.

sett piles. Piles driven into the ground as the foundation for a building ways.

seven-eighths rig. *See* masthead rig.

Seven Seas, the. The North and South Atlantic, North and South Pacific, Indian Ocean, and the Arctic and Antarctic Oceans, while the Atlantic, Pacific, Indian, Arctic, and Antarctic are the world's oceans.

sextant. A portable, reflecting, hand-held instrument used to measure angles, particularly, in celestial navigation, the altitudes of heavenly bodies. By measuring the horizontal angles between seamarks, the ship's position can be fixed. Also used in surveying. A sextant has a length of arc of 60° or 1/6th of a circle although with its reflecting mirror it can measure angles up to 120°. It is the successor of the octant and the quadrant.

shackle. Any metal fitting or link, roughly U- or D-shaped, used to connect or attach wire, rope or chain; has a removable pin across its mouth that fits into lugs or eyes. Sometimes called a clevis. Modern shackles used in yachts have a great variety of shapes, sizes and closing mechanisms and consequently a great variety of trade and regional names. *See* anchor shackle, bending shackle, connecting shackle, mooring shackle, Kenter shackle. A shackle is a traditional measure for a length of anchor chain, now universally accepted as 15 fathoms.

shad. An important food fish found in north American rivers; a member of the herring family but much larger and noted for its roe.

shaft. Short for propeller shaft, the long round steel rod that extends aft from a ship's power plant to the propeller. It passes along the shaft alley or shaft tunnel. The after section carrying the propeller is the propeller shaft or tail shaft; the section fitted into the thrust bearing is the thrust shaft. The stern tube shaft passes through the stern tube. There are shaft bearings, struts, couplings, and brackets.

shaft bossing. *See* boss.

shaft log. In a wooden ship, the heavy piece of wood attached to the keel and the after deadwood through which the propeller shaft passes.

shaft pipe. Same as stern tube.

shaft tunnel. A watertight compartment built around the propeller shaft from the engine room to the stern stuffing box in order to ensure control of flooding if there was a shaft casualty.

shagreen. The rough, dried skin of a shark or ray, once used to smooth and polish wood before the days of sandpaper.

shake. *n* Cracks and flaws in timber caused by defects in growth or by too rapid drying. *vb* **1.** To shake a sailboat is to bring it up so far into the wind that the sails shiver. **2.** To shake out a reef is to release the reef points and set taut the halyard.

shakedown. A new or recently overhauled ship has a shakedown and often, in the U.S. Navy, a shakedown cruise during which the men and officers are retrained.

shallop. Old word for a lug-rigged, two-masted fishing boat as well as for an open boat used for fishing in shallow water.

shallow water effect. The difficulty in steering and the increased resistance to the ship's progress felt in shallow water.

shamal. The dry northwesterly wind of the Persian Gulf that blows for long periods year-round.

shanghai. In the days of sail, to kidnap and deliver aboard ship men to fill out the crew, done in most major ports of the world by crimps who made a business of it. The practice disappeared in the early twentieth century when sailors became organized in unions and the public was aroused in their behalf.

shank. The main or center shaft of an old-fashioned anchor. Also the straight shaft of a fishhook.

shantey. British spelling of chantey.

shape. A ball, cone, drum, basket, or similar object made of light metal or canvas as required by the Rules of the Road to be hoisted in the rigging of ships, for example, at anchor, fishing, or dredging. In modern shipbuilding it is any rolled steel bar of constant cross section such as an angle, bulb angle, and channel.

shape-up. The normal method of hiring men for longshore gangs. The men who want to work report daily to a hiring hall where the supervisors choose the men they want.

shark. A variety of fish with multiple gill openings and a cartilaginous skeleton instead of bone. They have a worldwide distribution of some 250 species of whom only a dozen are known to attack humans. Of these, the great white shark is the most feared, followed by the hammerhead. The largest, the whale or basking shark is a placid giant who feeds on small fish, squid, and plankton. Most sharks are scavengers but a few will take bait. Those grouped as game fish include the blue, mako, white, porbeagle, thresher, and tiger sharks.

shark billy. A short stick fitted with nails at one end that is used by divers to fend off small aggressive sharks. The nails keep the billy from slipping on the shark's snout but do not pierce his skin.

sharpie. A distinctive long, flat-bottomed, centerboard fishing and pleasure sailing boat found along the east coast of the U.S.

shaski. *See* kaus.

shearwater. A pelagic seabird, larger than a petrel but with the same low-flying, wave-cruising habits. It has white underparts and is dark on top.

sheathing. A covering of copper, zinc, or galvanized iron once widely used over wooden hulls to protect them from marine worms and sea growth. Now poisonous paints have replaced sheathing.

sheave. A grooved wheel in a block over which a rope or wire passes. Some sheaves are a solid disc, others have spokes and are called spoke sheaves. Sheaves traditionally moved around a pin but modern blocks are fitted with plastic or steel bearings. Pronounced shiv.

sheepshank. A hitch made in a rope to shorten it; formed by making a long bight or loop and passing a half hitch over each end of the bight.

sheer 1. The upward curvature of a ship's main deck from amidships to each end. 2. A sudden heading change of a ship due to shallow water or to bank effect in a narrow channel. 3. To sheer off is to steer away from.

sheer batten. *See* sheer pole.

sheer cleat. Same as whaleboat chock.

sheer draft. A series of drawings which show the ship's lines in actual size and which can be laid out on the floor of the mold loft; consists of the sheer plan, the half-breadth plan, and the body plan. Also called sheer drawings, lines, body lines, and lines drawing.

sheer drawings. Same as sheer draft.

sheer molding. Molding on the outside of the hull of a ship that follows the upper deck line. Also called the sheer rail.

sheer plan. Plan showing the longitudinal, vertical section passing through the median line of a ship. Part of the sheer draft. Also called a profile plan.

sheer pole. An iron bar or wooden batten seized across the shrouds of a large sailing ship above the upper deadeyes or turnbuckle that served as the first ratline. It was often provided with belaying pins and is also called a sheer batten.

sheer rail. The guard rail or fender rail on a small craft; a timber sometimes fastened horizontally along the side above the waterline to act as a fender. Also used as a synonym for sheer molding.

sheer ratline. A name given to every fifth ratline that extended to the after shroud of a large sailing ship.

sheers, sheer legs. A tripod arrangement, usually temporary, of spars rigged to lift a weight with the tackle being rigged from the top.

sheer strake. The line of steel plates or planks in a wooden ship next to the main deck whose upper edge follows the sheer of the ship.

sheet. A rope, tackle, or chain with which a sail is held, hauled flat, sheeted home, or eased. Head sheets are those used with headsails. A sailor's axiom—never belay a sheet—means not to make a sheet fast because a sudden puff of wind could cause trouble if the sail could not be eased instantly. Also a sheet is a large flat piece of metal used in shipbuilding, usually less than 1/8 inches thick. If thicker, it is called a plate.

sheet anchor. A spare anchor, the largest one aboard, once carried in the waist of a ship for use in an emergency. No longer used.

sheet ice. Ice formed in a smooth thin layer by the coagulation of frazil or sludge.

shelf. Timbers that follow the sheer of a ship and are fastened to the underside of the deck beams of a wooden ship to strengthen and support the deck. Also short for continental shelf.

shelf ice. *See* ice shelf.

shell 1. The wooden, plastic, or metal casing of a block in which the sheaves revolve. **2.** The outer hull of a ship. Short for shell plating. **3.** A light, narrow, pulling boat fitted with oarlocks on outriggers and sliding seats used in competitive rowing. **4.** A hard and rigid covering of an animal such as a clam, oyster, or crab.

shellback. Anyone who has crossed the Equator in a ship; thus an experienced mariner. *See* pollywogs.

shell bossing. *See* boss.

shell expansion. A plan showing all the construction details in shipbuilding such as seams, butts, thickness of plates, welding and riveting details.

shell landings. The location of the edges of the shell plating on the ship's frames.

shelter deck. Cargo ships, of lighter construction than full scantling, may have an open deck above the main or freeboard deck. If all openings have permanent closures, it is a closed sheltered deck ship; if one compartment or hatchway has a temporary means of closure, it is an open shelter deck ship or shelter decker.

Sheriff. Navy slang for the Chief Master-at-Arms.

shift. *n* The cost of a tug to move a ship from one berth to another. *vb* **1.** To change or to move such as the wind shifts or the ship shifts berths in the harbor. **2.** "Shift the rudder" is a command to the helmsman to apply the same amount of rudder to the opposite side.

shifting backstay. *See* backstay.

shifting boards. A fore-and-aft bulkhead of loose planking temporarily made fast to the middle line pillars in a ship's hold to prevent bulk cargo such as grain from shifting as the ship rolls.

shifting chock. *See* chock.

shiner. A minnow.

shingle. Stones larger than gravel that form a beach. Also that beach.

ship. *n* Any decked vessel used in the open sea. Traditionally a ship was square-rigged and had three or more masts while other rigs with various numbers of masts and combinations of sail were called, for example, barks, brigantines, schooners, and brigs. Modern ships, for the most part, are either Navy or merchant and the latter may be, for example, cargo ships, passenger ships, reefers, container ships, and tankers. *vb* To ship water is to take it aboard accidentally; to ship a rudder or an oar is to put it into place.

shipentine. Old word for bark.

shipbreaking. The business of cutting up old ships to sell as scrap. The men who do this are called shipbreakers.

ship broker. Person who arranges charters, handles freight for clients, sells ships and marine insurance, and in general handles the paper work involved in merchant shipping.

ship fever. Historically is was typhus, not then known to be carried by lice or fleas.

shipfitter. A technician aboard ship and in a shipyard who is skilled in working with sheet metal, pipes and valves, or steel.

shiphandling. The art and skill of directing the movements of a ship, especially under difficult conditions due to congested and narrow waters, wind, tide, current, and low visibility.

ship keeper. A guard or custodian for a cold ship or group of ships that are anchored, moored, or berthed without crews.

shipman. British word for a longshoreman who handles cargo aboard ship when loading and unloading. *See* longshoreman.

shipmaster. The person or master in charge of and responsible for a ship other than a warship.

shipmaster's lien. Under maritime law, the right of a shipmaster to claim part of the freight charges, but not the ship, as reimbursement for his own wages or for any money he has advanced in the interests of the ship.

shipmate. A fellow sailor in the same ship.

ship motion. Heave (up and down), sway (sideways), and surge (fore-and-aft) are translational movements in which the ship moves bodily. *See* scend. Roll, pitch, and yaw are rotational motions about different axes in which the ship's center of gravity is not displaced. Lurching, listing, heeling, and lolling are associated with rolling and are also rotational.

ship of the line. The battleship of the days of sail with guns mounted on three or more decks. Heavy and powerful enough to fight in the line of battle and was thus a line of battle ship.

ship on a lay, to. To sign aboard a fishing or sealing vessel for a share of the profits or lay instead of wages.

ship over, to. A U.S. Navy term for reenlisting.

shipping-over chow. An exceptionally good meal aboard a Naval ship, supposedly provided in the hopes of encouraging reenlistment.

shipper. The person for whom the owners of a ship or the charterers agree to carry cargo or freight to a specified port at an agreed price as written in the bill of lading. Also known as a consignor since he consigns goods to a ship, the consignee.

shipper's export declaration. A custom's form filled by the shippers of goods to a foreign country that provides data for foreign trade statistics. Also called a shipper's manifest.

shipper's manifest. *See* shipper's export declaration.

shipper's protest. Protest drawn up before a notary against the master and owners of a ship because the master refused to sign bills of lading in their usual form, that is, without qualifications concerning the condition of the goods to be shipped.

shipper's guarantee. An indemnity given to a shipowner in exchange for clean bills of lading for goods to which a clean mate's receipt has not been issued.

shipping. The collective word for all ships belonging to a particular country or sailing in particular waters.

shipping articles. The contract or agreement of employment between the merchant seaman and the owner or master of a ship.

shipping board clamps. Threaded U-shaped fittings with an end piece that is fastened with two bolts; used to join wire or to make an eye. Also called clips.

shipping commissioner. A government official who administers the hiring and discharge of seamen and the arbitration of any personnel disputes; under the supervision of the Coast Guard, there is a commissioner in each major U.S, port. In the United Kingdom, the shipping office is under the Ministry of Shipping which performs the same function. It is also known as the marine office.

shipping documents. The papers and forms that involve the carrier or ship and the skipper, consignee, underwriter, and customs in the shipment of cargo.

shipping permit. A written document from the owner giving a shipper the authority to deliver his goods to the pier for loading. British term is shipping note.

ship-rigged. A ship that has all of the masts fitted with yards and squaresails.

ship's bell. *See* ship's time.

ship's boy. Traditionally a young man employed aboard ship to assist in the galley and the food storerooms. Now rare.

ship's company. All hands; everyone on board except the passengers.

shipshape. Neat, orderly, well-stowed, free of Irish pennants and stray gear. Sometimes expressed as "shipshape and Bristol fashion."

Ship's Inertial Navigation System (SINS). Developed by the U.S. Navy as a very accurate, all weather, dead reckoning system of navigation. It uses gyroscopes, accelerometers, and associated electronics to sense and record every change of course and speed of a ship. A similar system is used to guide aircraft, missiles, and space vehicles and is then known as INS, Inertial Navigation System.

ship's name. Every vessel, including yachts, must have an assigned registered name and number. Merchant ships must have the name in letters at least four inches high on both bows and the stern. Yachts must have their name on the stern and both must record their home port on the stern.

ship's number. *See* number.

ship's papers. The documents required by law that include the ship's certificate of registry, clearance certificate, manifest, bills of lading, charter party, and official logbook.

ship's tackle delivery. A specification on a bill of lading or cargo manifest that the consignee will take delivery alongside from the ship's booms or cranes.

ship's time. At sea, a ship keeps time according to its time zone or longitude position. *See* zone time. The ship's bell is struck every half hour in groups of two followed, if appropriate, by one bell according to this cycle: one bell represents 12:30, 4:30, and 8:30 (both A.M. and P.M.); two bells for 1:00, 5:00, and 9:00; three bells for 1:30, 5:30, and 9:30; continuing till eight bells. Therefore a complete cycle is struck every four hours.

ship stores. Items such as alcohol and tobacco that are sold at sea free of tax. Same as sea stores.

ship trials. Same as sea trials.

ship weather routing. The selection of an optimum track for an ocean passage, based on long range weather forecasts. In the U.S. Navy it is known as Optimum Track Ship Routing (OTSR) and done by the Fleet Weather Centrals. Commercial companies do it for private vessels.

shipworm. A marine mollusk that, when young and small, bores a tiny hole into a wooden ship below the waterline and then eats its way, with the grain of the wood, into an adult size of eight inches or so. Metal sheathing was once used but now toxic paint is used as protection against this teredo, also known as a marine borer.

shipwright. A technician in a shipyard skilled in the building and repairing of wooden vessels, as well as other carpentry work necessary on board.

shipyard. A coastal facility used to repair and build ships; historically located well inland on a waterway as a protection in time of war. Short word is yard.

shoal 1. A submerged ridge, bank, or bar of mud, sand, or gravel that is near enough to the surface (less than 10 fathoms) to be a hazard to navigation. If composed of rock or coral, it is called a reef. 2. As water becomes shallower, it is said to shoal or become shoal water. 3. A school or concentration of fish.

shock cord. An elastic line that stretches easily and is sometimes fitted with a hook at one end. It has various uses on deck such as securing canvas and gear. Also called a snubber. The British call it bungee.

shoe. *n* 1. The horizontal connection between the heel of the rudderpost and that of the sternpost in a single screw ship; called a skeg in a small boat. It is generally a protective piece of wood or metal under the keel. 2. The fitting on the cutwater in warships to which a paravane is attached. *vb* To shoe an anchor was an old practice, now rarely done, of bolting timbers to the flukes of the anchor in order to improve its holding power in a muddy bottom.

shole. A flat piece of wood or steel placed under the keel or bottom of a shore. Also called a sole block. *See* sole block.

shooks. Bundles of cask or barrel staves, heads, and hoops as well as sides of boxes and crates shipped ready to assemble.

shoot 1. To shoot the sun or a star is to measure its altitude with a sextant. 2. A fisherman shoots his trawl when he launches and spreads it to start fishing. When finished he hauls his trawl. 3. In sailing, to turn into the wind and maintain headway by momentum.

shooting. Same as trolling.

shoot the breeze. Sailor's slang meaning to have a talk or a discussion on casual and usually unimportant matters.

Shoran. SHOrt RAnge Navigation; a precise electronic navigation system of limited range that uses the time divergence of pulse-type transmissions from two or more fixed stations; used for surveying and for oceanographic research.

shore 1. The land along the edge of a body of water. 2. A prop or timber fixed under a ship's bottom or along her side that keeps her upright while in drydock or in a marine railway; identified according to their specific support: breast shores, side shores, or wale shores. In ship damage control, it is used to prop up a damaged or weakened bulkhead or other structure inside the ship. The collective word for the gear used is shoring. *See* trip shore.

shore boat. A commercial harbor passenger boat that serves merchant and naval ships at anchor. Also called a water taxi.

shore leave. Permission to be ashore given to merchant ship crews. In regard to the U.S. Navy the correct word is either liberty or leave.

shore line. The line where the shore and the water meet.

Shore Patrol (SP). Naval men and officers assigned police duty in any port where Navy men go ashore.

shore seine. Same as drag seine.

short blast. A ship's whistle or horn or a siren's blast that, according to the International Rules of the Road, has a duration of about one second. There are also long and prolonged blasts. *See* blast.

short-handed. Being without enough men or hands to do the job.

short legged. Describes a ship or boat that carries less than a normal amount of fuel and thus has reduced endurance.

short sheet. A length of line, normally with an open hook at one end, that can be used to hold a sheet or lead temporarily to free a winch for another task or to do any other odd job about a sailboat, especially when racing.

short stay. Said of an anchor being hauled in when it is just short of breaking ground. After breaking out, the anchor is hauled in until it is reported by the forecastle to the bridge as being up and down. It is then soon reported "Anchor in sight, sir, clear (or foul) anchor."

short splice. Splice joining two ends of rope by untwisting only a short section of each, resulting in a strong but thick splice that may not always pass through a block.

shot. A length of anchor chain 15 fathoms long. Also called a shackle.

shot line. The light line attached to the projectile of a line-throwing gun. After reaching its target, the line is made fast to a messenger with which the heavy line or wire is passed.

shoulder 1. Any abrupt projection on a structure, timber, or steel member. **2.** The rounded protruding sections just abaft the stem of a ship or boat.

shoulder block. Block with a projection near the upper end so that it can rest against a spar, for example, without jamming the rope.

shove off. Nautical expression for depart or go. *See* point oars.

"show a leg". In olden warship days, women were allowed on board ship while in port and this expression was used by the petty officers to rouse men out of bed in the morning and let women sleep. *See* son of a gun.

shrimp. A small marine decapod crustacean of the suborder Natantia and of several different families living on the bottom, highly regarded for food, and fished for with bottom trawls. Also called prawns which, outside the U.S. usually describe large shrimp. The usage of shrimp or prawn usually depends on local custom.

shrimper. A boat used in trawling for shrimp.

shroud. Rope, wire or metal rods providing lateral support for the mast of a ship. It was usually fitted with ratlines so that men could climb aloft. Also the close-fitting casing around propeller or turbine blades.

shroud band or hoop. A steel collar fitted around the mast with eyes to which the upper ends of the shrouds are attached.

shroud cap. A thimble shaped covering made of brass, lead, canvas, or leather fitted to the upturned end of a shroud to keep out water. Now rare.

shroud laid rope. Right hand laid cordage with or without a hemp core, surrounded by four strands.

shroud rollers. Split tubes of wood or plastic fastened to the shrouds to reduce chafing of sails and lines.

shuga. Spongy white ice lumps a few centimeters in diameter, formed of sludge ice and sometimes anchor ice rising to the surface.

shut out. Cargo refused shipment because it arrived too late.

shutter. The detachable portion of the gunwale of a wooden pulling boat in the way of the oarlocks.

Sick Bay. Naval term for the hospital or dispensary aboard ship.

side. General word for the outside surface of the ship's hull. Looking forward in a ship one has the port side on the left and the starboard side on the right. On and above the maindeck is topside. The lee side is the one away from the wind; the weather side is the windy side. Anything that goes overboard goes over the side.

side-bar keel. Same as center-plate keel.

side boys. Enlisted men stationed in two ranks at the gangway (quarterdeck) of a Naval ship to greet an important person to whom side honors are being given. The number of men lined up depends on the rank of the dignitary.

side coaming. One of the fore-and-aft coamings or protective low metal edges around a hatch.

side honors. The ceremonious reception aboard a Naval ship for important officers and officials. It includes piping the side, side boys, and sometimes the ship's band, honor guard and gun salutes. The same ceremony takes place on departure.

sidelights. The red (port) and green (starboard) 10 point, $112.5°$ lights required by the Rules of the Road to be shown by all ships underway at night; part of the running lights. *See* sidelight screen.

sidelight screen. A wood or metal shield for each sidelight to ensure that the light shines from dead ahead to $22.5°$ abaft the beam.

side plating. The steel plates of a ship that extend upward from the turn of the bilge. The remainder of the plates on each side down to the keel is the bottom plating.

sideport. *See* port.

sideporter. *See* sideport gantry.

sideport gantry. A traveling gantry crane with a retractable boom that is used on ships where cargo is handled through sideport doors. Also called a sideporter.

sidereal. Of or pertaining to the stars.

sidereal time. Used by navigators to locate stars. A measurement in relation to a fixed star instead of the sun and therefore nearly four minutes shorter than the solar day.

sidescuttle. Same as scuttle, the British word for airport. *See* airport.

side shore. *See* shore.

sidewall craft. An air cushion vehicle for over-water use only. The skirts on the side are rigid and project just below the surface.

side wheeler. A paddle wheel boat, ship, tug, or ferry having a paddle wheel on each side. There are still a few side wheeler tugs.

siding. The act of trimming or smoothing the side of a timber to the required size in wooden ship construction.

sight. *n* An accurately timed sextant altitude of a heavenly body that is used to determine the observer's position. *vb.* To sight the anchor is to heave it short and close enough to see whether it is clear or foul. If clear, it may be dropped again.

sight reduction table. A compilation of the data needed by a navigator to solve the astronomical triangle after he takes a sight and thus gets a line of position. Published by the Defense Mapping Agency Hydrographic Office; these tables are numbered without the old prefix HO.

sight vane. Either of the two vertical pieces of an azimuth or bearing circle used by the observer to line up the object whose bearing is being measured. One of the vanes has a peep hole; the other a vertical wire which is placed upon the object sighted.

signal flags. Flags used in visual communications at sea, especially the alphabet and numeral flags of the International Signal Code. Four alphabet flags are assigned to each registered ship as her visual and radio call sign.

signal of doubt. *See* danger signal.

signal stay. Same as triatic stay.

sill. 1. A submerged elevation that separates two oceanic basins such as the one just west of Gibraltar that separates the Atlantic from the Mediterranean. 2. A timber or concrete beam at the bottom of the entrance gate to a drydock. 3. A lip or projecting piece of metal or plastic that acts as a spout to keep the discharge from the scupper pipe from running down the ship's side.

silt. The topsoil washed into the sea from the eroding land, silting up river mouths, channels, and harbor; technically a clastic deposit or inorganic granular material larger than clay and smaller than sand.

silverside. A small fish.

simoom. A very short and violent sandy wind found off the coast of the Arabian peninsula and off the Syrian and Sahara deserts. Also written simoon, samiel, or samum.

singing propeller. Propeller in which the shape of the blades produces a vibration that can be heard within the ship.

single-banked. A pulling boat in which one oarsman sits on each thwart. With two men on a thwart, the boat is double banked.

single up. An order given to the line handlers upon getting underway from a pier or another ship. It means taking in the mooring lines except for a single length at each station, preparatory to taking in the lines. *See* double up.

SINS. Ships Inertial Navigation System.

siphonophore. An open sea, drifting variety of zooplankton that rises from the depths to feed at night, then empties its gas bags and sinks during the day. It dangles long, stinging tentacles.

siren. A noise-making device powered by steam or compressed air, sometimes used aboard ship instead of the ship's whistle. On Naval ships, its major use is as an alarm signal before a possible collision.

sirocco. The ancient but still used name for a southerly, dry, warm wind that blows off the north African desert to the Mediterranean. The word is also used more generally to describe any hot dry wind.

sisal. A variety of natural rope fiber derived from a plant found in Mexico. It is next in strength to manila, but decreasingly used now with the superiority of synthetic fibers.

sister block. Block having two sheaves, both in the same plane; either side by side as in a sheet block or one above the other as in a long-tailed block or tandem block. *See* block, fiddle block.

sister hooks. Two partial circles of metal, suspended from the same link or eye. When in use, the parts close and hold as long as there is tension; used about the deck for securing various lines and small tackles. Also called clip hook, clasp hook, clove hook, sister clip, and match hook.

sit out. British term for hike.

skag. A heavy chain used when necessary in confined waters to prevent a towed barge from taking too violent a sheer.

skate 1. Used in commercial fishing, a long line with many hooks, usually 1800 feet long with about 90 gangions, such as the line used in ground fishing off the coast of Alaska. **2.** The tub in which the line is coiled before setting. **3.** A bottom-feeder, one of the many rays that is caught for food. The egg capsules are oblong, black, and leathery with a curled horn on each corner and are often found on beaches. These are called mermaid's purse, sailor's purse, or sea purse.

skeet. A long handled dipper used to wet down the sides and deck of a wooden ship in very hot weather. It was also used to wet the sails to improve their efficiency in light winds.

skeg 1. Aftermost and deepest part of the deadwood of after structure of a ship or boat; the projection of the keel on which the rudder may sometimes be stepped and which protects the propeller. **2.** The fin aft or fixed rudder of a surfboard that provides some directional stability. **3.** The additional timbers fastened to the keel aft to improve steering. **4.** A knee timber that connects and braces the stern post and the keel.

skeleton crew. A temporary crew used for moving the ship only a short distance.

skew. Propeller blades that are tilted aft instead of being perpendicular to the shaft are said to be skewed or skew-back.

skids. Planks or timbers used to support something heavy on deck or to ease heavy cargo along on the deck of a ship. Boat skids are a framework on deck that hold the cradle or saddle in which a boat is held down by gripes.

skiff. Any small open boat of simple construction, usually lapstrake, with a sharp bow and a square stern used for pleasure and fishing.

skimmer. A tern-like, long-winged sea bird that flies low over the water, often with its lower beak immersed to catch food. Also a beach or surf calm used as fishing bait.

skimmings. A marine insurance word that refers to the removal of damaged or spoiled goods leaving the remainder suitable for sale.

skin. *n* **1.** The plating or hull covering of a ship; sometimes the inner skin is called ceiling. **2.** The last bit of sail that is left exposed when furling the sail. *vb* To skin or skin up a sail is to furl it neatly.

skin boat. A boat made with animal skins covering a wooden frame. It is still commonly used in the Arctic and was once used in Ireland and Scotland.

skin drag. The resistance or water drag of something such as a ship moving in the water, due to the boundary layer of water dragged along by skin friction. Also called skin resistance.

skip. *See* pallet.

skipjack. 1. The traditional broad-beamed, V-bottomed, clipper-bowed, centerboard sailing craft used on the Atlantic coast particularly in Chesapeake Bay. It has a raked mast and was once widely used for fishing and oystering; smaller than a buckeye, it is now often used as a yacht. 2. A variety of tuna. Also known as ocean bonito. *See* tuna.

skipjack boat. A Japanese tuna clipper.

skipper. A word applied officially in Great Britain to a duly certificated master of a fishing vessel. Generally and colloquially used to refer to and address any master, captain, or commanding officer. If a yacht has a paid captain, he is known as the captain while the owner or amateur in charge is known as the skipper.

skau. A predatory, gull-like bird of northern regions; a sea bird of the genus *Cathasacta*. Sometimes confused with a jaeger.

skylark. Sailor's slang meaning to engage in horseplay, friendly banter, and scuffling.

skylight. The wood, metal, or plastic fitting in a deck or on the top of a deckhouse that admits light and perhaps, fresh air below.

sky pilot. Naval slang for the chaplain. Also called the padre.

skysail. A triangular racing sail used between masts on a schooner. Also a small squaresail set above the royal on a square-rigger. *See* kites.

skyscraper. In a square-rigger, a small triangular sail set above the skysail in very light winds. *See* kites.

slab. The slack part of a squaresail that hangs down after the leech lines are hauled up. A bending slab in a shipyard is a solid metal floor used in bending frames and other members.

slab keel. An additional steel plate fastened outside of a plate keel.

slab reefing. Now popular in racing sailboats, this fast system uses reef holes in the sail instead of reef points. Lines are run from clew and tack cringles through cheek blocks to a winch and cam cleats on the boom and then the lines are passed through the reef holes and around the boom. Also called jiffy reefing.

slack. *n* To take in the slack is to haul in until taut. *adj* Loose as in a slack rope; opposite of taut. *vb* 1. To slack a line is to let it out, ease the strain but not let it run or cast it off. 2. A sailboat is said to be slack when she has a tendency to fall away from the wind; the opposite of ardent.

slack water. The interval during which the tidal current is very weak or zero, usually during the reversal of the tides but it can occur at any time. Sometimes called slack tide.

slamming. The pounding of a ship's hull against the water when she is pitching so heavily that bent stanchions and cracked plating may result. It is more violent than pounding.

slant. A course taken by a sailboat under a favorable wind.

slant of wind. A duration of fair wind.

slat. To flap such as a loose sail, awning, or rope shakes and slaps. This occurs mainly when a sailboat is becalmed. Also a thin piece of wood or metal.

slave jib. A jib set more or less permanently in a yacht.

slaver. A ship that used to carry slaves during the slave trade.

slave station. One of the subordinate transmitting stations in Loran.

sleeper 1. One of the heavy timbers forming the foundation of a building way or slipway. **2.** One of the curved or angled timbers or knees used to strengthen the stern framing of a wooden ship. **3.** A deadhead or nearly submerged floating log.

slice. A long hardwood wedge; a launching wedge used to raise a small ship off the ways before launching. Also a chisel-edged bar with a long handle used in a shipyard.

slice (or slicing) bar. A bar used to stoke a coal fire under a ship's boilers.

slick. *See* sea slick.

slicker. A shiny yellow or dull black oilskin raincoat, usually with a matching southwester rain hat.

slide. A small metal fitting that attaches the luff of a sail to a boom or mast track on which it moves as the sail is set or lowered. Also called a clip.

sliding keel. Same as centerboard.

sliding way. *See* launching cradle.

sling. *n* Any arrangement of rope, chain, or canvas used at the end of a crane or boom to lift cargo. The load or draft of cargo is sometimes also called a sling as well as a hoist or set. *vb* To sling a hammock or a yard is to raise and suspend it.

sling-ding. A small metal rod with an eye at each end used by fishermen to keep the leaders or snoods of adjacent hooks from fouling.

slip. *n* **1.** The open water between two piers or between two structures as in a ferry slip. **2.** Short for slipway. **3.** British word for binder as used in marine insurance. *vb* To release; to let run. To slip a cable was to release it aboard ship, buoying the anchor for later recovery, all in the interest of a quick departure.

slip, propeller. The difference between the distance actually made good by a ship and that theoretically possible due to the pitch of the propeller. It is called the apparent slip ratio because a propeller works in a forward moving stream of water, the wake current. *See* wake.

slip hook. Same as cable stopper, pelican hook, or senhouse slip. *See* cable stopper.

slip knot. A simple knot that can be made and released easily such as a reef knot made with a bow. Also a knot in which a loop slides along the standing part as a running bowline.

slip hitch. A hitch made on a cleat so that a sudden pull will release it.

slip rope. Rope that can be released quickly, such as the one that is passed from deck through the ring on the mooring buoy and back on deck after releasing the anchor chain or wire as a preparation for getting underway. When ready to go, the end on deck is released and the rope slips through the ring.

slip stopper. Same as chain stopper.

slipway. The inclined surface in a shipyard that holds the cradle in which the ship is built and on which it is launched by sliding down into the water. The fixed structure is the groundway and the moving part, the sliding or launching way.

slob ice. An accumulation of sludge so dense that it prevents the passage of small boats.

sloop. In modern U.S. usage, a single-masted sailing vessel; usually a yacht. Similar to a cutter but usually with fewer headsails because a sloop's mast is set farther forward. *See* cutter. The British define it as a single-masted sailboat with only one headsail.

slops. A supply of clothing, tobacco, blankets, and other small stores that are sold to crew members from a slop chest and entered in the slop book against their pay. Much abused in the past, the sale of slops is now required by law and the items are sold at a fair price.

slot. The area between the after part of the headsail and the leeward side of the mainsail.

slot effect. Guiding the wind abaft the headsails and around to the lee side of the mainsail thereby increasing the efficiency and the pulling power of the sails.

slough. Same as bayou or marsh.

sludge ice. A mixture of small spongy ice lumps, snow, and seawater having a greasy sppearance; the initial stage in the freezing of seawater. Also called slush ice.

sludge vessel. A vessel that dumps out at sea the residue of sewerage disposal plants ashore. A practice that is largely forbidden in the U.S.

slue, slew. 1. To twist or turn something especially a boom or mast. 2. To sheer or yaw from side to side as a ship at anchor does in strong wind; same as horsing. 3. A towed barge may slue as it takes a sheer in a channel. 4. A backwater or side channel.

sluice. An opening at the lower part of a bulkhead to permit passage of liquid. Controlled by a sluice valve or sluice cock actuated by a reach rod.

slumgullion. An old whaling word for the mixture of blood, oil, and water that flows from the blubber as it is being handled.

slush. Any greasy mixture used aboard ship as a lubricant or as a preservative. The standing rigging was often slushed down.

slush fund. Originally an unofficial welfare fund raised aboard a warship by the sale of surplus grease from the galley.

slush ice. *See* sludge, spicule.

smack. A large fishing vessel, especially one having a well to keep the catch alive. Not common today.

Small Craft Advisory. A warning of winds 18 knots or higher issued by the National Weather Service. *See* gale warning, storm warning.

small. To steer small is to use minimum rudder to keep the course; an important skill in the days of sail.

small stores. Items of personal convenience such as toiletries and tobacco that are sold on board. In Naval ships, small stores are government issue articles of uniform and bedding.

small stuff. The general term for line or cordage up to 15 thread ratline stuff, includes marline, and spunyarn; used for light lashing and seizings.

smelling the bottom or ground. Describes the erratic course and reduced speed of a ship moving in water so shallow that the normal flow of water around her hull is impeded. *See* shallow water effect.

smelt. A small, popular food fish of the Osmeridae family that is related to salmon and trout and that lives along the coast going up rivers to spawn.

smiting line. An old term for a light line used for breaking out a light sail that has been sent aloft in stops.

smoking lamp. In olden days, a source of flame for men that smoke. Now used figuratively in the U.S. Navy to mean smoking is not permitted as in the expression "the smoking lamp is out," may be changed later to "the smoking lamp is lighted" when smoking is permitted.

smoking room. A lounge area aboard ship for officers of British merchant ships that is required by law to be separate from their messroom.

smoke pipe or stack. *See* stack.

smooth. *See* set, wave.

snaking. The line or cord passed in a zigzag fashion as netting between the housing line and the footline of a three-strand lifeline.

SNAME. Society of Naval Architects and Marine Engineers.

snap block. Same as snatch block.

snaphook. A metal hank or hook closed by a spring snap that is generally used for bending headsails such as jibs to their stays. Also called a springhook, a piston hank or snapshackle.

snapper. A valued food fish of the family Lutjanidae that is found in all warm oceans. The red snapper grows to three feet and is found along the north Atlantic coast whereas the yellowtail and gray snappers are common in the Caribbean.

snapshackle. *See* snaphook.

snatch block. Block whose shell opens to take the loop or bight of a line making it unnecessary to find the end of the line and feed it through; used, for example, in sheets, foreguys, cunninghams, preventers, and vangs. Also called a notch block or return block.

snatch cleat. Cleat with a single horn instead of two, often used as a fairlead. Same as a thumb cleat.

sneak boat. A very shallow draft, scow-like sailboat developed along the coast of New Jersey and adjacent states; used also without sails to hunt wildfowl. Also called sneak box or box.

snell. *See* snood.

snib. A handle used to fasten down a watertight door or hatch. Also called dog.

snipe. U.S. Navy slang for a member of the ship's engineering force, also known as the black gang.

snood. A length of fishing line with hooks attached; part of a longline. Also called a dropper, branch line, or gangion. Although sometimes called a snell, the latter is more accurately the gut or wire leader that fastens the hook to the fishing line.

snorkel. 1. A tube that provides air to a submerged submarine. 2. A tube attached to a face mask allowing the diver to breathe while face down near the water surface.

snorter. A strong gale at sea, particularly in winter in the North Atlantic.

snotter. A short length of wire or rope, often with an eye at each end, that is used for a variety of purposes aboard square-riggers. Today it is most commonly used as a strap or sling to handle heavy items of cargo. In modern yachts, it refers to the spinnaker pole bell; a fitting that holds one end of a spinnaker pole on deck.

snow. A sailing vessel, a brig, having her spanker hooped to a trysail mast close abaft the mainmast. Now rare.

snow blink. A bright white glare on the underside of clouds as produced by the reflection of sunlight from snow; lighter than ice blink and much lighter than land or water sky.

snow crab. A large deep water ocean crab of the North Pacific, similar to the king crab and widely harvested for food. Also called a tanner crab.

snub. The act of stopping a line from running. *See* check. To snub a ship is to let go the anchor and then hold or check the anchor cable in order to stop the ship; useful in an emergency if a ship has a steering casualty in a narrow channel.

snug. Safe, secure as in a snug harbor. To snug down was an old phrase in sailing ship days meaning to prepare the ship for heavy weather aloft and alow.

sny. The upward curve of a ship's planking or plating at bow and stern. Also called spile.

snying. The act of laying out the curvature. Also called spiling.

SOFAR. SOund Fixing And Ranging.

soft patch. *See* patch.

softtack. Ordinary ship's bread; in contrast to hardtack.

softwood. In the maritime sense and as defined by law in the United Kingdom, all timber from trees having needles instead of leaves.

solano. A warm and sometimes dusty southeasterly wind blowing from Africa in the summer towards the coast of Spain.

solar time. A solar day is the period of one rotation of the earth in relation to the sun. Also called mean solar time in contrast to sidereal time.

solar wind. *See* breeze.

SOLAS. Safety Of Life At Sea conference.

sole. 1. An old name for the deck or floor (landsman's sense of floor) of a cabin on a ship. Now used by yachtsmen in referring to the deck or floor of a cabin or cockpit of a boat. Removable sections of the sole are known as floorboards. *See* floor. **2.** The sill on which the upright timbers or poppets of a launching cradle rest; sometimes called a poppet board. **3.** Any of several small flat fish of the Soleidae family; a local name for small flounder.

sole block. A heavy, flat piece of wood placed under the heel or lower end of a spar such as a sheer-leg. Also called a shole or shoe.

sole piece. A skeg or heel piece that projects from the after end of a keel for supporting the rudder. Also a timber or plate used on a launching way to keep the ship from starting. When all is ready the sole piece is cut through and the ship is free to move. Also called a tie plank or a sole plate.

sole plate. The bed plate on which a piece of machinery is secured in a ship. Also another name for sole piece.

SONAR. SOund Navigation And Ranging.

Sonar, active. A device or system in which sound waves are generated and projected so that their echoes may reveal objects underwater such as fish (fishfinder) or the bottom (depthfinder).

Sonar, passive. A device or system that detects underwater objects such as submarines by listening for their noises.

sonobuoy. A small sonar receiver-transmitter dropped from aircraft or ships that is used to detect submarines and transmit target data by radio. Battery powered and normally expendable.

son of a gun. A mildly derogatory epithet that questions a man's origin. In olden sailing warship days, while in port women lived on board and on occasion a child was born. If the delivery was difficult, the loud sound of a firing gun allegedly helped hasten the delivery.

soogee – moogee. Traditionally a mixture of strong soap, lye, and water that was used to wash paint work topside. Rarely used today; spelling varies widely.

soot blowers. Perforated stationary and rotating pipes that use steam to remove soot that accumulates on boiler tubes.

SOS. An international radio signal using Morse Code designating distress (. . . – – – . . .). It was selected for its simplicity and it does not stand for save our souls. Mayday is the voice radio equivalent.

soul and body lashing. Lashing that holds or secures something against the ship's motion. A piece of line tied around the outside of a person's rain clothing to keep the rain out and to attach to a lifeline in heavy weather.

sound. *n* **1.** A long and wide body of water, larger than a strait or channel, that connects larger bodies of water. **2.** A long, wide ocean inlet. **3.** The air bladder of a fish with which it can control its buoyancy. *vb* A fish or whale sounds when it dives quickly and heads downward to measure the depth of water.

sound channel. A horizontal layer in the ocean that has uniform physical characteristics and that traps sound waves to permit their travel for thousands of miles.

sounder. Fishermen's name for echosounder.

sounding. To take a sounding in a ship's tank is to measure the amount of liquid. There are sounding rods, lines, chains, tubes, and tables. *See* ullage.

Sounding, Fixing and Ranging (Sofar). An underwater distress signaling system in which a signal such as a small explosive is located by measuring the different times of reception of sound waves at different stations.

sounding lead. A leadline or any heavy weight used with a leadline.

sounding machine. An archaic device that measures the depth of water by using a weight, a wire, and a drum with a hand crank. Now replaced by the echo sounder.

soundings. Depth of water on a chart given in fathoms (traditional), feet (for harbors and restricted waters), or meters (in Europe and becoming universal with the acceptance of the metric system). To be on or off soundings is to be, respectively, inside or outside the 100 fathom curve. British term is "in soundings."

sounding sextant. A special sextant used in survey work.

sounding tube or pipe. A tube or pipe that leads to the bottom of a tank or compartment in a ship and is used to guide the sounding tape or jointed rod that measures the depth of liquid.

Sound Navigation and Ranging (Sonar). A system for measuring distance underwater by means of sound impulses whose reflection from a target provides distance and bearing. The original British name was Asdic from a joint British – French project in 1918. Also called echo ranging, the basis for echo sounding and for fishfinders.

sound-powered telephones. Shipboard phones, especially in the Navy, that are energized by current generated from the voice vibrations of an iron diaphragm placed in a permanent magnetic field in each receiver transmitter.

soup. Surfer's term for the white, frothy, turbulent water where a wave has broken.

soup fin shark. *See* tope.

southerly buster. A sudden, strong, wind of the southern coast of Australia. Also called a brickfielder.

Southern Cross. The five bright stars of the constellation Crux that form a cross, visible only south of the Tropic of Cancer.

South Equatorial Current. A strong westerly flow in the Atlantic, Indian, and Pacific oceans just south of the Equator. Its counterpart is the North Equatorial Current.

South Pacific Current. An eastward flowing ocean current in the South Pacific that passes along the northern edge of the west-flowing Antarctic Circumpolar Current.

South Seas. Another term for the South Pacific.

southwester. Traditional fisherman's yellow or black waterproof hat with a long brim in back. Also called a slicker hat or squam.

sow. A fish wheel rigged on a barge. *See* barge.

spade anchor. Same as plow anchor.

spall, spale. In ship construction, one of the cross members on which planks rest. Also called a stage bearer or thwart. A cross spall is a temporary timber used to brace frames until the deck beams are in place.

span. *n* Any rope or wire running between two points such as on masts and davits that are used to suspend lines or tackles. Spans usually support blocks, bulls-eyes, and fairleads. *vb* A whale is said to span when it swims in a certain direction, blowing at more or less regular intervals.

Spanish burton. A tackle composed of two single blocks with both standing parts fastened to the load to be moved. The strap of one block is tailed and rove through the sheave of the other.

Spanish bowline. Bowline having two loops, neither of which will slip.

Spanish fox. A single yarn twisted up left-handed or contrary to its lay; used for small seizings.

Spanish mackerel. A large species of the Scombridae family, allied to the common mackerel; a popular, somewhat oily food fish.

Spanish Main. Historically, the northern coast of South America.

Spanish trawl. A trawl net without boards, worked by two boats. Also called a pareja.

Spanish windlass. A simple, improvised device for bringing the parts of a rope together by twisting.

spanker. One of the masts on square-riggers and schooners. *See* mast. Also an additional, fore-and-aft sail hoisted on the mizzenmast of a square-rigger and at times known as a trysail. If jib-headed instead of gaff rigged it was called a storm, mutton or trisail. In modern sailboats a jib-like reaching spinnaker with narrow shoulders.

spanking breeze. A fresh strong wind, particularly a quartering wind that keeps the spanker full.

spanner. A tool having a hole, projection or pin for engaging a matching pin or hole on the device to be turned. Found aboard ship near fire hoses in order to connect them. British word for wrench.

span shackle. Any shackle secured to an eyebolt or other deck fitting used to lash down cargo, vehicles, and other material.

spar. General word for a long, round piece of wood or steel used, for example, as a boom, mast, gaff, fender, or buoy. A sailing ship was said to be over or under sparred, meaning she had too much or too little sail carrying capability. A towing spar was one towed astern of a ship in formation to assist others in keeping station in low visibility. It was also called a fog or position buoy or spar.

spar buoy. An anchored spar floating upright marking an obstruction, shoal, or channel.

spar ceiling. Wooden battens or boards fitted along the inside of a ship to keep cargo from having contact with the steel plating. Also called sparring, hold sparring, open ceiling, or open sparring.

spar deck. A weather or open deck above the main deck.

Sparks. Traditionally familiar name for the ship's radio operator in a merchant ship, analogous to Chips, the carpenter and Boats, the boatswain.

spar ladder. A fixed and vertical metal ladder built inside large diameter steel masts and kingposts for access and inspection.

sparring. Protecting with strips of wood all vertical steel bulkheads in the way of shell frames in cargo holds, all sides of storerooms used for bulk storage, and tanks against which cargo is stored. *See* cargo batten, spar ceiling.

spar varnish. A durable varnish designed for marine use and thus resistant to sun and salt; also often used on houses, doors, and outdoor furniture.

spatangus. *See* sand dollar.

spawn. *n* The eggs of, for example, fish, mollusks, and crustaceans as well as their young. *vb* To spawn is to reproduce, as a salmon goes upstream to spawn.

SPCC. Strength Power Communication Cable.

speak. Means to encounter and communicate with a ship at sea. Such encounters were important before the days of radio and were always reported when a ship made port.

spear-fish. One of the genus *Tetrapturus,* closely related to another billfish, the sailfish. It has a long beak and grows to 7 feet.

Special Circumstance, Rule of. An important provision of the Rules of the Road which every mariner should know by heart: "In construing and complying with these rules due regard shall be had to all dangers of navigation and collision and to any special circumstance, including the limitations of the vessels involved, which may make a departure from these rules necessary in order to avoid immediate danger." Also known as the General Prudential Rule.

spectacle. *adj* Describes a fitting, frame, or other piece of gear aboard ship that resembles a pair of eye glasses. In sailing ships, there are spectacle clews and spectacle eyes in rope. In a modern twin-screw ship, the spectacle frame is a large casting at the stern that supports the ends of the propeller shafts and is used instead of shaft struts.

speed. At sea, speed is measured in knots or nautical miles per hour.

speedboat. A powerboat designed primarily for speed rather than cruising comfort such as roominess and stability in a seaway.

speed length ratio. The ratio of speed, in knots, to the square root of the waterline length of the ship in feet.

speed lights. Steady or pulsating white or red lights once displayed by warships steaming in formation. Obsolete today.

speed made good. Speed measured in reference to distance traveled over the ground along the course in contrast to speed through water.

speed, moderate. *See* moderate speed.

speed of advance. The anticipated speed made good or needed to reach a destination at a desired time.

speedometer. A device for measuring speed only in small craft. *See* log.

spencer. A trapezoidal gaff sail, generally without a boom, once set on the fore and main lower masts of square-riggers. Replaced in mid-19th century by staysails. Also called a gaff trysail or trysail.

sperm whale. A large toothed whale, up to 60 feet, that is valued especially for its oil and spermaceti. Feeds on giant squid in deep waters, this animal is endangered yet unfortunately still hunted extensively. Also called cachalot. Its smaller cousin is the pigmy sperm growing only to 13 feet.

spermaceti. A white, waxy derivative of the oil of the head cavity of the sperm whale. It is used for ointments and cosmetics.

spet. A small barracuda found on the southern coast of Europe.

spicule. A minute, needle-like calcareous or siliceous projection that is part of an invertebrate sea animal such as a sponge. The word also applies to ice crystals or Frazil ice.

spider. A triangular metal outrigger used to keep a block clear of a mast or of a ship's side. Also the portable magnifying glass on the face of a magnetic compass.

spider band. An iron band around a lower mast near the deck that has sockets for belaying pins. Also called a spider iron or spider hoop.

spike. *n* **1.** A large nail, over 3 1/2 inches long, 7 to 17 to the pound, that is used to fasten large planks to a ship's framing or to a pier. **2.** Short for malinspike. *vb* To spike an enemy's smoothbore guns was to drive a large nail into the vent through which the powder was ignited.

spile. A wooden plug for a vent in a cask or to serve as a spigot. A small wooden peg used to fill the hole in planking left by a withdrawn spike. Also the same as sny.

spiling. A method used in boat construction by which the desired shape or curvature of a part is inscribed on a template or spiling batten and transferred to the material to be cut out. The dimensions taken from a straight edge or template to different points on a curve are called spilings.

spill pipe. Same as chain pipe.

spiller. A compartment made of netting next to the pot of a pound net. A seine used inside a larger one to remove fish. Small fish multi-hook lines are sometimes known as spillers.

spilling line. Any line attached to a sail that is used to spill the wind and gather in the sail prior to reefing or furling.

spindle. The center of a composite or built-up mast, the main piece, also called the heart.

spindrift. Foam and spray blown by the wind off the tops of waves and the resultant streaks on the water. *See* Beaufort Scale. The latter are also called wind streaks. Another word for spindrift that is somewhat rare is spoondrift.

spin-fishing. Fishing that involves the use of a moving artificial bait such as a spoon, spinner, or plug.

spinnaker. A large light sail boomed out forward of the mainsail with a pole and on the opposite side when sailing before the wind or when reaching.

spinnaker bag. The container in which the sail is stowed and from which it may be quickly hoisted. When used this way or when a special bag is used, the container is a turtle or, in the United Kingdom, a spinnaker chute.

spinnaker, double or parachute. A larger spinnaker that is boomed out on both sides. Also called a Mae West.

spinnaker pole. A light spar or boom used to hold the spinnaker in place. It is governed by an after guy, a pole downhaul, and by a topping lift.

spinnaker staysail. A staysail often set below a lifted and filled spinnaker. Also called a cheater.

spinner. A bright, rotating, artificial metal lure often used in trolling or casting for game fish. Also another word for spinning jenny.

spinner dolphin, shark. Dolphin or shark that often jumps clear of the water and revolves its body before reentry.

spinning jenney. A hand powered device once used in sailing ships for making small stuff by twisting the strands together.

spiny lobster. A saltwater crustacean of the family Palinuridae that is valued as food. Not a true lobster since it has no claws but the tail meat is delicious. Now the approved name instead of crayfish, crawfish, rock lobster, and languoste.

spirketing. The thick strake or strakes of wood ceiling fastened inside the hull on the beam ends. In steel ships, a spirketing plate is a vertical side stringer inside the frames or tapered downward from the stemhead.

spit. A small, narrow, projecting piece of coast line. Often called a sandspit.

spitfire. A small heavy storm jib usually set in a sailboat at the same time as the storm trysail.

spitkid or spitkit. A spittoon or ashtray aboard ship.

splashboard. Board that fits vertically into grooves on each side of a companion way in a sailboat to keep water from spilling below. British word is fashionboard.

splice. The joining of two pieces of rope or wire by interweaving the strands. There are long splices, short splices, cut splices, and eye splices that form a loop or an eye. There are back splices that keep the ends of rope from unraveling. The almost infinite number of splices has produced the expression "different ships – different long splices." Also a slang word for marriage, to be married is to be spliced.

splice the main brace. To have or to serve alcohol aboard ship, usually in celebration of something, after an emergency, or an arduous experience.

spline. A long flexible strip of plastic, steel, or wood for fairing curved lines in shipbuilding drawings. Also a thin strip of wood fitted into a planking seam and smoothed down to make a well-finished deck on a yacht. The process is called splining and results in spline planking.

split fall. One of two separate falls in hoisting cargo as different from the usual double whip or two falls connecting to a common hook.

spoil. Sand, mud, and other materials removed by a dredge.

spoil barge. Barge that carries the spoil to the area in which it will be dumped.

spoil ground. Dumping ground for spoil.

sponge. A simple and passive multicellular invertebrate that is found on the floor of nearly all waters. They may be as small as an inch to a length of six feet. There are over 500 distinct species among which one has a tough and flexible skeleton that when dried is used as a bath sponge.

sponson. A small structure or platform projecting from a ship's side to provide protection or to increase the ship's stability.

sponsor. The person, usually the wife of some dignitary, who christens a new ship as it is launched by traditionally breaking a bottle of champagne on its bow.

spoon. A trolling bait for gamefish that is shaped like a spoon with hooks attached.

spoon bow. An overhanging ship's bow with full round sections shaped somewhat like the bowl of a spoon.

spoondrift. Same as spindrift.

spot. A small food fish of the north Atlantic coast that has a prominent dark spot above each pectoral fin.

spot ship or cargo. A ship or cargo that is on hand and ready for loading or selling.

sprat. The young of oysters. Also a small, herring-like fish.

spratfall. The amount of oyster sprat that is deposited in a particular area.

spray. Water driven by the wind.

sprayrail. On a power boat, an indentation or shelf in the hull near the bow that helps keep spray off the topside.

spray strips. Long narrow pieces of wood fitted along both sides of a boat's hull to deflect spray.

spreacher block. A two-way lead block that combines the spinnaker and reacher blocks to allow two lines through. It resembles a big fiddle block with a swivel.

spreader 1. Any wooden or steel fitting used to push out or extend stays or shrouds. Commonly seen on both sides of the mast of a yacht to spread the shrouds or mast supports. Also called a crosstree although technically a crosstree is continuous while spreaders can be used on one side only. **2.** A hand tool used in fishing to separate the snoods on a fishing line and keep them from fouling.

spreader boot. A rubber or plastic protective cover over the ends of the spreader to prevent sails from chafing.

spring. *n* **1.** A mooring line rigged at an angle with the ship, either a forward or an after spring. British say fore or back spring. **2.** A line used to change the heading of an anchored ship. *vb* **1.** A mast or spar may crack or be bent out of shape and is then said to be sprung. **2.** A ship may spring a leak if she takes in water.

spring bearing. An old name for propeller shaft bearing.

spring hook. Same as snaphook.

spring lay rope. A six-strand composite rope made with alternate fiber and wire strands around a fiber core. Often used for mooring lines because of its strength and flexibility.

spring stay. Stay rigged horizontally between masts of a ship for handling cargo, moving weights, and other activities.

spring tide. Tide with the maximum range resulting from the combined attraction of the moon and the sun. A spring tide occurs twice in a lunar month, at new and full moon. *See* neap.

spring tidal currents. Stronger than normal currents that come at new and full moons.

sprit. A small spar or pole used to extend something. Short for bowsprit. Specifically the spar that extends and holds the peak of a spritsail.

spritsail. A quadrilateral, fore-and-aft sail having a sprit from its lower forward corner to its peak or after top corner. The foot of the sail is loose and the lower end of the heel of the sprit is secured to the mast with a sort of becket called a snotter. A craft with one or more spritsails is said to be spritrigged. Also a triangular sail set between the gaff and the mast of a gaff-rigged sailboat.

spud. 1. A heavy, pointed metal-shod wood or steel post that is used to anchor a dredge in position, usually one at each corner. 2. The legs of an offshore drilling platform and setting them down in place is spudding.

spud cans. The containers for the legs of a jack-up rig into which they are retracted when the legs are up.

spume. Froth or very fine spray or foam, especially caused by breaking seas.

spun yarn. Small, light line made of 2-4 yarns.

spur. 1. Any shore or piece of timber used in a drydock to support a ship. 2. A half beam in a wooden ship. 3. One of the projections of the arms or crowns of a stockless anchor for engaging the bottom.

spur gear. A gear wheel with radial teeth parallel to the axis.

spurling. An old word for running or moving such as a rope in a block.

spurling line. A line used to rig a fairlead.

spurling pipe. A chain pipe.

spurnwater. A V-shaped breakwater abaft the hawse. *See* breakwater.

spur shore. A boom or pole for breasting off a ship from a pier or seawall, especially when room is needed for lighters.

spyglass. Another name for long glass; a hand held telescope used aboard ship.

spy-hopping. The antics of some whales in periodically jumping clear of the water, either in play or, it is thought, to rid themselves of parasites.

squadron. A group of warships composed of several divisions. Two or more squadrons make up a flotilla.

Squali. The race of fish that sharks belong to and thus a collective word for sharks.

squall. A sudden strong wind, usually accompanied by rain or snow, not of long duration. Often accompanied by a single black cloud, a black squall, or a long line of black clouds just above the horizon, a line squall, or no clouds, a white squall. Sometimes very violent, squalls can occur repeatedly over a period of days and thus mark squally weather. A squall is longer than a gust.

squall line. The air ahead of a cold front, marked by heavy showers, strong, shifting winds and sometimes thunder and lightning. Very dangerous to small boats; also called an instability line.

squam. New England word for a southwester; a rain hat.

square. Originally described the yards of a square-rigger when at right angles to the masts and the ship was squared away on her course. Now squared away means well ordered, clean, disciplined. A sailor may be squared away by someone over him who corrects his behaviour.

square-ender. A scow.

square of the hatch. The size of a cargo hatch which determines the size of cargo that can be handled there. Also the space just below.

square-rigger. Same as a full-rigged ship or a square-rigged ship that has all its sails rectangular in shape and set on yards perpendicular to the masts.

squaresail. A quadrilateral, usually rectangular sail having a foot, a head and two vertical edges called leeches. The lower corners are clews and the upper corners are earings.

squat. The lowering of the stern in the water while at high speed, such as that of a destroyer.

squeegee or squilgee. A sort of rubber-shod wooden hoe used to remove water from a wooden deck. Now used mainly as a hand-held device for cleaning windows.

squid. A fast moving, propelled by jet, pelagic cephalopod that has a long body, ten arms, an internal chitinous support, and a pair of fins. Squids are found worldwide and have an increasing importance as food as the amount of fish decreases. *See* giant squid.

squidder. A squid fisherman.

squid hook. 1. A pointed lead weight wrapped in colored cloth and fitted at one end with a number of barbless hooks. **2.** A tin lure with a single hook.

squidhound. Striped bass. *See* bass.

SS. Initials placed before the name of a merchant ship, originally meaning screw steamer as opposed to paddle streamer. At present means steam ship although diesel and turbine power are increasingly popular. USS denotes a U.S. warship and HMS, His or Her Majesty's Ship.

SSB. Single Side Band. *See* radio telephone.

stabber. A small sailmaker's pricker or marline spike, often with three sharp edges.

stability. The vital characteristic that ensures that a ship, when heeled over for any reason or to any extreme, will right itself. A function of design and of loading measured by metacentric height. A rough indication of a ship's stability is its period of roll. A rapid, jerky roll indicates high stability and a long, slow roll, particularly one with some hesitation at extreme angles, indicates marginal stability.

stack. A metal trunk through which the combustion gases are led from the engineering spaces of a ship to the open air. Also called funnel, smoke pipe, or smoke stack.

stadimeter. A hand-held rangefinder used to measure distance, usually to the warship ahead in formation. The height of something on the ship ahead, such as the truck, must be known and is set on the rangefinder which then solves the problem mechanically. Little used today.

staff. 1. Short for flagstaff. **2.** A Naval staff officer is one responsible for administrative and technical matters.

stage bearer. *See* spall.

stage, landing. A floating platform where boats can go alongside.

stage, staging. A platform or scaffold on which men can work on the ship's side or aloft, particularly when the ship is under construction or repair.

staghorn. British word for a heavy cross-shaped bollard that is fitted in big ships to handle large hawsers.

stair. Not a nautical word although sometimes used by naval architects. Ladder is the proper word.

staith. A structure at the end of a pier from which bulk cargo can be loaded by gravity. A word that is more common in the United Kingdom than in the U.S.

stall zone. A sailor's term for the area of haphazard wind eddies that develop near the luff of a fore-and-aft sail when it is pointed too close to the wind.

stanchion. Any wood or metal vertical support member, either above or below deck; pillar, except when it refers to supporting lifelines and awnings topside.

stand. 1. A ship is said to stand off a harbor while waiting to enter or stands out of the harbor when she departs. **2.** To continue on the same course is to stand on. **3.** A man should stand clear of a tackle under strain and may stand easy or stand down if he stops what he is doing. **4.** A sailor stands his watch or he may stand by to man the lifeboats. 5. Stand by is preparatory to many commands, as in "Stand by to let go the anchor."

standard. A capacity measurement used in the lumber shipping trade with different values in different parts of the world.

standard compass. *See* compass.

standard knee. In a wooden ship, an inverted knee timber that is secured to the deck as well as to the ship's side.

standard rudder. In the Navy, the amount of rudder in degrees required to turn a ship with standard tactical diameter. Full rudder is usually maximum that can be used without jamming the rudder.

stand, compass. A binnacle.

stand from under. Literally a warning to those below of something that could fall on them but now used, in a general sense, among those who fear the action of higher authority if they do not take precautions, or in effect, stand from under.

standing. Fixed; not movable. There are standing blocks and running blocks, the standing part of a tackle and the hauling part. Standing orders are those of a permanent nature, usually in writing for the guidance of subordinates.

standing lights. Lights kept lit within a ship during the night. In Naval vessels, they are usually red in order to preserve the night vision of men going on watch.

standing lug. *See* lugsail.

standing wave. *See* wave, standing.

stand of the tide. The interval at high and low water when there is no appreciable rise and fall. It may last for several hours and is sometimes called a platform tide.

stand-on vessel. The vessel which is required by Colregs to maintain course and speed when it has the right of way. Formerly called the privileged vessel. *See* give-way vessel.

staple. 1. Any U-shaped piece of metal that is used for various purposes aboard ship such as the mooring staple (a U-shaped forging) that was once welded to the side of a large warship to hold the mooring chain. 2. Sometimes the word for dog. 3. Sometimes refers to bitts.

staple angle. A short length of metal closely fitted around a steel beam where it passes through a bulkhead.

star. Luminous bodies in the sky that include planets in celestial navigation. Morning and evening stars are visible at morning and evening twilight.

starboard. The right side of a ship when looking forward. By remembering that port and left both have four letters, it is easier to remember which is port and starboard. Right and left are required usage when giving orders to the helm but otherwise port and starboard are used.

star boat. A small, 22 foot popular class racing sailboat.

star chart. A chart that shows the location of stars and planets.

star drag. The brake on a gamefishing reel, actuated by a large wheel with spokes.

star finder. A device used to locate certain stars.

starfish. An echinoderm of the class Asteroidea with multiple arms (star-shaped) and tubelike feet with suction disks. They live on the bottom and feed on mollusks, coral, and crustaceans.

starshell. A projectile containing a bright flare that illuminates the scene as it drops slowly by parachute. Widely used in Naval warfare before the days of radar.

start. 1. To loosen or ease a rope as one starts a sheet. 2. To open and begin drawing upon the contents of a cask or keg. 3. A plank or seam is said to be started when it springs a leak.

starting signal. At the start of a yacht race, simultaneously a gun is fired and a flag is hoisted as a visual signal. Usually five minutes prior to this, the preparatory signal is given in the same manner, by gun and flag.

stateroom. The private room for passengers and for ship's officers aboard merchant ships and for officers in Naval ships. The crew in some merchant ships, especially U.S., also live in staterooms.

station. 1. The place to which a Navy man is assigned aboard ship for duty or for an emergency and listed on a station bill. 2. The position of a ship in formation; maintaining it is station keeping. 3. A government facility on the coast, such as a Coast Guard Station. 4. In ship design, a station is one of a number of verticial transverse planes, perpendicular to the keel, laid off at regular intervals between stem and stern for reference and measurement purposes. Also called transverse sections and ordinates.

station pointer. Another name for a three-arm protractor, especially in the United Kingdom.

stave. 1. To stave in a ship's planking means to crush and damage it. Also stove in. 2. To stave off means to fend off.

stay. *n* 1. Any wire or rope supporting a mast fore-and-aft. 2. A ship is said to be anchored at short stay when the anchor is out to the minimum cable needed to hold the ship, usually before getting underway. If she has a normal amount of anchor cable out, she is at long stay. 3. A ship when tacking slowly with headsails shaking was said to be in stays or slack in stays. *vb* 1. To stay a topmast is to support and steady it. 2. To stay was an old word for tack. *See* triatic stay, baby stay.

stay hole. A hole in the luff of a staysail or jib for the lacing or hanks attaching it to its stays.

staysail. Traditionally any fore-and-aft sail, except a jib, that is set on a stay but now, in relation to yachts it is any additional sail set between masts.

staysail schooner. A schooner in which the usual foresail is replaced by several staysails. *See* fisherman's staysail.

stayship. An old and uncommon word for the fish remora.

stay tackle. Tackle used for setting up a stay or rigged on a stay for handling weights.

steady. A command to a helmsman to steer the course indicated at that moment on his compass, usually spoken as "steady so" or "steady as you (she) go (goes)." Also means unchanging as in a steady bearing as well as stable in a steadying sail often used by power boats to reduce rolling, especially when out fishing.

stealer. A trapezoidal steel plate of about double width at one end used as a single continuation of two tapering strakes as they come together at the stem or at the stern of a ship being built.

steam. To go by any power-driven ship as in "we steamed south all day." Steam turbine propulsion is most common today and many terms exist prefixed by steam that are self-explanatory such as steam chest, steam valve, steam trap, and steam capstan. To steam out a tank is to clean it out with steam.

steamer. A common word for a steamship or any vessel propelled by machinery. *See* SS, tramp.

steamer chair. A folding canvas and wood chair with a footrest that is provided for passengers on deck.

steam fog. Fog formed when very cold air drifts across relatively warm water. Not to be confused with advection fog that results from warm air over cold water. Also known as sea smoke, Arctic frost smoke, and sea mist.

steam lance. A tool used to blow steam through boiler tubes to remove soot or to melt ice topside.

steam separator. *See* separator, steam.

steamship. Same as steam vessel.

steam smothering system. Valves and piping installed to extinguish fire in or remove gas from spaces aboard ship, activated by remote control.

steam vessel. Under the International Rules of the Road, any vessel propelled by machinery.

steep to. Said of a coast or shoreline where the land rises abruptly close to the water and where anchoring is usually difficult because of the great depth of water close to the shore.

steer. To cause a ship to turn or maintain a course; done by a steersman or helmsman at the wheel or helm. To steer small is to use minimum rudder.

steerage. The part or space in a passenger ship assigned to those who travel at minimum cost. Also the effect of the rudder on a ship in motion.

steerageway. The minimum speed of a ship through the water at which she will respond to the rudder.

steering. The act of making a ship turn or of maintaining course.

steering compass. The compass the steersman follows in order to maintain a course.

steering gear. Gear that moves the ship's rudder.

steering light. During night steaming in column, the light on the stern of the ship ahead that the steersman follows.

steersman. The person that steers the ship; traditionally done with a spoked wheel but it may also be a solid wheel or even a lever. Also called a helmsman.

steeve. 1. The angle the bowsprit makes with the horizontal. Also called steeving. 2. A spar used as a derrick. 3. A jackscrew used to stow baled cargo, or to stow cargo by such means.

St. Elmo's fire. Same as corposant. Also St. Elmo's light.

stem. *n* The upright post or bar at the bow of a ship where the side planking or plating ends, extending down to the keel. The upper part of the stem is the stemhead, the lower part is the stemfoot where the stem knee may be fitted in a wooden boat. *See* cutwater. *vb* 1. To stem is to make some headway against the wind or current as in the expression "The ship stemmed the tide." 2. In the United Kingdom, to stem a vessel is to load it within a certain period of time.

stem anchor. Anchor stowed in a stem hawsepipe; not a common arrangement.

stem band. An iron band that protects a wooden boat's stem.

stemhead. The upper part of the stem.

stemming date. A certain date at which a ship is stemmed to load.

stem net. In drift-net fishing, the net nearest the ship in a line of nets.

stemson. *See* apron.

stemwinder. A blue water or deep water sailor's name for a ship used on the Great Lakes that has its pilot house all the way forward, near the stem.

step. In a masted ship or boat the socket, block, or framing into which the mast fits when erect or when it has been stepped. To step off a distance on a chart is to measure it with a pair of dividers.

stepping point. *See* bearding.

stern. 1. The extreme afterpart of a ship or boat. 2. A ship drawing more water aft than forward is said to be down by the stern. 3. "Stern all" is a command to oarsmen to backwater on both sides and to achieve sternway.

sternboard. Same as sternway.

stern chase. One ship pursuing another.

stern chaser. A gun mounted aft.

sterndrive. A modern propulsion system for boats in which the engine is inside the hull, close to the stern, while the rudder and propeller are just outside or abaft the transom. Also called inboard/outboard, 1/0, outdrive, or outboard/inboard, transom drive, or Z drive.

stern fast. An after mooring line for a boat.

stern frame. A heavy strength member combining the rudder post on which the rudder is hung and the propeller post through which the propeller shaft passes; also connects the ends of the shell plating. Sometimes called the sternpost.

stern gland. A short and hollow short casting with a flange at one end to compress the packing in the stern tube stuffing box.

sternhook. A member of a Naval boat's crew who is stationed aft and who handles matters from there when his boat is going alongside or departing. His counterpart forward is the bowhook.

sternlight. A 135° white light showing 67.5° on each side of directly aft. Required by the Rules of the Road in international waters but in inland waters only required if no other light shows from astern.

stern pointer. In a wooden ship one of the timbers fastened diagonally upon the ceiling of the stern.

sternpost. Another word for stern frame, in a wooden ship the major vertical timber.

stern pulpit. Similar to the pulpit forward but often larger, located over the transom to assist in tending an after sail, as the mizzen sail of a yawl. British word is pushpit.

stern shapes. A cruiser stern has no overhang and often has tumblehome. An elliptical stern has a projecting counter that terminates at the deck in a rounded shape. A transom stern has a square or flat counter, usually sloping aft. If it has an open-work extension aft it is a lute stern. A canoe stern is one in which the side plating comes together, producing a double ender. A tunnel stern has a tunnel in which the propeller turns, designed for shallow water. A counter stern is one with a flat overhang; a ducktail stern slants forward.

sternsheets. Space in an open boat, just forward of the stern thwart and abaft the first regular thwart.

sternson. The curved timber uniting the upper deadwood to the sternpost in wooden ships.

stern thruster. *See* thruster.

stern trawler. *See* trawler.

stern tube. The cylindrical casting through which the propeller shaft emerges from the hull. The forward end is fitted with a stuffing box. Also called a shaft pipe and shaft tube.

sternway. The movement of a ship when backing, same as sternboard.

sternwheeler. A river vessel driven by a single paddlewheel aft.

Steulchen rig. A cargo handling rig aboard ship consisting of two supporting masts with a heavy lift boom between them. Four winches are provided, two for hoisting and one for each of the topping tackles.

stevedore. A person who loads and unloads ship cargo or who contracts as a contract stevedore to do so. Roughly the same as longshoreman although stevedore implies a supervisory position. *See* longshoreman.

steward. A member of a ship's company responsible for domestic matters aboard ship such as feeding and cleaning.

stick. A pole, spar or mast, usually the latter.

stiff. A ship not easily inclined, having a quick, snappy roll, is said to be stiff. It is the opposite of crank or tender that describes a ship having a long, slow, easy motion when rolling. A stiff ship is normally a safe ship. Also a strong breeze or current is said to be stiff.

stiffening. Any ballast or cargo taken on board to improve a ship's stability, therefore to make her stiff. Permanent ballast or kentledge is sometimes called stiffening.

stiffening booms or spars. Booms or spars that were once hung alongside in the water to keep a ship upright.

stinger. *See* lay barge.

stinging coral. *See* millepora.

stingray. One of the flat rays or flat fish that can inflict a very painful wound when stepped on in shallow water due to its whiplike tail containing a poisoned barb. Thus on California beaches, one is wise to shuffle in the water rather than step high.

stinkpot. Originally a primitive fire bomb used in Naval warfare. Now a slang word for a power-driven boat in contrast to a sailboat.

stirrup. A short rope suspended from the yard of a square-rigger that supports the footrope or horse on which men stood when handling sail.

stock. The movable cross piece with a ball at each end of a stock or old-fashioned anchor that lies perpendicular to the shank when the anchor is rigged for use. The stock lies parallel to the shank when the anchor is stowed. Also the main inboard vertical member of a rudder. *See* rudder stock. Stocks are the shores, blocks, and timbers on which a ship rests in a building ways.

stockless anchor. The modern, patent anchor made with a number of minor variations or patents, that is housed and secured in the hawsepipe since it has no stock or cross piece such as the Baldt, Dunn and Norfolk and the British A.C. 14. Called by yachtsmen, a Navy anchor.

stokehold, stokehole. Old word for the fireroom of a steamship derived from the days when stokers stoked coal.

stoker. Old word for the fireman who lights off and tends the fires under a ship's boiler. A stoker shoveled coal, spread the burning coal, and removed the ashes.

stolon. An extension of the body of some sea animals, such as sea squirts, that provides a support base for the animal or colony of animals from which new individuals may grow by budding.

stomach-piece. *See* apron.

stone. A British measure of weight equal to 14 pounds.

stonefish. *See* scorpion fish.

stool. Any chock or support for a shaft or piping. *See* backstay stool.

stop. Any projection on a mast or spar used to support something or as a preventer for a fitting or piece of gear. Small stuff is used to fasten something such as clothes stops. Stops are used to secure a furled sail to a boom and may stop up a furled headsail to a forestay. In this case they may be rotten stops since a sharp pull on the sheet will part the weak strands and the sail will be set flying.

stopper. *n* A short length of rope, chain, or any contrivance used temporarily to check the running of a rope, wire, or cable or for holding it while it is belayed. A chain stopper is a short length of chain used to hold the anchor chain. *See* chain

stopper. Also called a housing stopper or slip stopper. Other stoppers are bitt stopper, block stopper, and cathead stopper. *vb* To stopper is to check or hold something.

stopper knot. Knot in the end of a rope to keep it from passing through a block or fairlead. *See* ball stopper.

stop seine. Also called a stop net. *See* drag seine.

stopwater. Any device for stopping a leak; specifically, in wooden ship construction, a dowel driven along a seam that was not easily caulked. In steel construction it is the material, such as canvas, placed between faying surfaces not accessible for usual caulking. Oil stop is the material used to make a steel joint oil tight.

stores. Supplies aboard ship that are kept in storerooms and sold as small stores or slops to the crew. Sea stores are items such as tobacco and spirits that may be sold at sea tax free.

storm. Winds of force 10 (a storm), or force 11 (a violent storm), on the Beaufort Scale, 43–65 knots that are often accompanied by rain, hail, or snow. Higher winds mark a cyclone, hurricane, or typhoon; slightly lesser winds are gales. It is important to note that mariners consider a storm worse than a gale.

storm glass. The barometer. *See* glass.

storm, magnetic. A disturbance of the earth's magnetic field that affects radio communications.

storm oil. Oil, traditionally dispersed in small quantities to calm breaking seas during very bad weather. Animal or vegetable oil was preferred.

storm sails. Heavy small sails that are set in rough weather.

storm signals. Flags, shapes, and lights displayed ashore at Coast Guard Stations and other locations forecasting various degrees of bad weather.

storm surge. A sudden increase in the level of the sea along the coast due to strong storm winds blowing on shore, often reinforced by very low barometric pressure and a high tide. These three factors together can produce devastating flooding and loss of life. Also called storm waves and, inaccurately, a tidal wave.

storm trysail. *See* trysail.

storm valve. A flapper or check valve in the overboard discharge lines of a ship that prevent the entrance of water during bad weather.

storm warning. A NWS advisory of winds over 48 knots. If associated with a hurricane, it is a hurricane warning, *See* gale warning, Small Craft Advisory.

storm waves. *See* storm surge.

stove. *See* stave.

stow. To put away, lash in place, roll up or furl anything aboard ship.

stowage. The act or procedure of packing away or stowing cargo, ammunition, etc. The place where things are kept is stowage. The word may refer to the goods stowed as well as the money paid for this service. Not to be confused with storage. Candy stowage describes cargo that is affected by heat and must be kept cool.

stowage certificate. Certificate provided to the master by an authorized official testifying to the proper and safe stowage of all cargo, required at times for insurance purposes.

stowaway. A person hiding on a ship to make a passage without paying.

stow net. A fishing net used to catch shrimp and small fish with its mouth held open, usually set in a fixed position in a river or tidal stream but sometimes rigged out on both sides of a ship underway. Also called a gape net.

straddle carrier. A vehicle used on piers and in warehouses that lifts and carries containers between its large wheels.

straggler. 1. A crew member in a warship who has overstayed his liberty or leave but not long enough to be considered a deserter. 2. A ship in a convoy that lags behind.

strain. To pull on a line is to take a strain; the tension itself is the strain. When a sailor rests he may be said to be taking an even strain on all parts.

straits. A relatively narrow waterway between two large bodies of water, as the Straits of Gibralter.

strake. A range or line of planks or plating adjacent to each other and extending fore-and-aft the length of the ship. Bilge strakes are those along the turn of the bilge. The garboard or sand strake is next to the keel; next are the broad strakes. The sheer strake follows the sheer line of the ship and is just above the topside strake. The wash strake, in an open boat, is the thin plank fitted above the gunwale to increase freeboard.

strake book. A record kept in a shipyard of the ordered dimensions and marks of each plate used in building a ship.

strand. A poetic word for shore or beach. To run aground or to be driven ashore is to be stranded. In cordage, a strand is one of several twisted yarns or threads that are laid up or twisted together to form rope. A rope is said to be stranded when one of its strands has parted.

stranded wire. Wire rope.

stranding. Legally, in reference to marine insurance, it is the grounding of a ship attended by unusual and accidental features. The ship must be fast aground for an appreciable time. *See* grounding.

strap. A narrow band of flexible material used to secure, suspend, or fasten something. A wire or rope loop with ends spliced together used to sling a weight for lifting. Strop is the British spelling.

strath. A long depression with steep walls found underwater on the continental shelf.

stratosphere. The atmospheric layer above the troposphere.

stratus. Usually a bank of shapeless low clouds; may produce fog or a light drizzle. *See* cloud.

stray line. An additional, sometimes smaller line attached to the major rope to assist in handling. Same as messenger.

stream. *n* 1. Any flow of water such as a river or an ocean current. 2. A ship is said to be in the stream when she is anchored instead of being alongside a pier. *vb* To stream something is to put it into use outside the ship as a log line may be streamed.

stream anchor. A lighter anchor sometimes carried for use as a stern anchor or for warping. Also called a stern anchor.

stream current. A relatively narrow, deep and fast ocean current quite different from a drift current. *See* ocean current.

streamers. Short and narrow pieces of cloth that are attached to the sail of a racing sailboat to reveal the direction of airflow near the sail. *See* tell tail.

streaming. Pilot's language for moving a ship out into the stream from alongside the pier. Also the pilot's fee.

Strength–Power–Communication–Cable (SPCC). Cable used from the surface to a deep diving capsule. Also called the umbilical cord.

stretch. A reach or straight portion of a river, canal, or bay. In older usage, it was the distance sailed on any one tack; the ship was said to stretch or reach. Modern synthetic cordage is often stretched at the factory before use and is sold as prestretched line.

stretcher. In a boat, an athwartship strip of wood against which an oarsman braces his feet. A bar of metal or wood to spread the parts of a sling, or a spreader.

strike. In its nautical sense, means to haul down or pass below, as sails or colors are struck or stores arriving aboard are struck below or struck down. To strike out is to bring cargo topside and remove it from the ship. A harpooner strikes a swordfish; a messenger strikes the ship's bell, and the ship may strike a reef. Merchant sailing ships once struck (furled) their topsails when meeting a man-of-war as a gesture of submission.

strike over. To move a ship laterally off the cradle on which she has been hauled out.

striker. 1. In the Navy, a man who learns a specialty, for example, a quartermaster striker is a seaman who plans on being a quartermaster. 2. An extension handle on a paint brush.

string. 1. The highest strake of ceiling planking in the hold of a wooden ship. 2. In fishing, a group of snoods or skates of line.

stringer. Any longitudinal beam or girder inside the structure of a ship that strengthens the beams or frames. Depending on location, it may be a bilge stringer, a side stringer, or a deck stringer.

stringer plate. A plate attached to the top flanges of any tier of beams at the side of the ship.

stringout. A series of connected vessels or barges, either underway or at anchor.

string piece. A long horizontal timber used to strengthen a wharf.

strip. A long narrow area of pack ice, about one kilometer or less in width, that is detached from the main mass and whose small fragments have run together under pressure of wind, sea, or current.

strobe. A highly visible, quick-flashing, white light that is commonly used by fishermen and yachtsmen as a fog light, anchor warning light, and as a distress signal on personal flotation devices and life rings. Strobes are sometimes used incorrectly as flare-up or flashing lights under the Rules of the Road which does not recognize them or authorize them. There is some confusion as to the usage of strobe lights as they are used as both emergency and routine lights.

stroke. The complete movement of an oarsman in pulling a boat; the pulling stroke as well as the recovery one. A good oarsman keeps a smooth, perhaps fast stroke as he follows the stroke oarsman or stroke.

strongback. 1. A spar against which a boat is secured in the davits. 2. The wooden beam in a stowed boat over which the boat cover is stretched. 3. A wooden beam supporting an awning. 4. A portable timber supporting an old-fashioned hatch cover. 5. The bar that holds closed a cargo port or manhole. 6. A timber or girder used in damage control to shore up a bulkhead.

strop. British spelling for strap.

strum or **strum box.** British term for rose box.

strut. Any bracket or supporting member, specifically the one holding the outboard end of a propeller shaft.

stud. The cross bar of a link of anchor chain that forms a stud link stronger than an open link and less likely to kink.

stud bolt. A bolt that is threaded at both ends.

studding. The vertical timbers in the construction of a wooden deckhouse.

studding-sail. Known also as a stunsail, it was a light sail set outboard of the squaresail of a square-rigger. *See* studsail

studsail. An additional strip of canvas made fast to the bottom of a fore-and-aft sail. Also called a bonnet.

stuff. *n* **1.** A mixture of tallow and pine tar that was used at one time in treating masts, spars, and rigging before the days of synthetic fiber, stainless steel, resistant varnish, and paint. **2.** Another name for light cordage. *vb* To fill a shipping container at a terminal is to stuff it and to unload it is to unstuff it.

stuffing box. A device used to prevent leakage around a moving or fixed part projecting through a watertight bulkhead. A propeller shaft passes through a stuffing while a cable through a bulkhead would pass through a stuffing tube. Also called a packing gland.

stunsail. Same as studding-sail.

Stugeron. A British non-prescription drug found helpful against seasickness.

sturgeon. A large river food fish with a thick skin and bony plates. Its roe is caviar and isinglass is produced from the bladder. One variety of sturgeon, found in the Black and Caspian Seas, provides the famous beluga caviar; not to be confused with the beluga whale. *See* beluga.

stylaster. A bright yellow form of coral that branches into a thicket. It is armed with tiny stinging barbs.

subcavitating. Describes a marine propeller or foil designed to operate always at a speed too low for cavitation to occur.

submarine. **1.** Below the ocean's surface such as a submarine cable. **2.** Any vessel designed to operate submerged such as a warship, research or salvage vessel.

submariner. A person who serves in submarines.

substitute flag. In the International code of signal flags, a flag used to repeat another in the same hoist.

suction, bank. In shiphandling in narrow channels or canals, a force attracting the stern of a ship towards the bank when the ship's propeller is turning over.

suction dredge. *See* dredge.

Sudbury vent. Trade name of an opaque, plastic combination ventilator and skylight (including a water trap) used in yachts.

Suez Canal. A major ocean shipping canal between the eastern Mediterranean and the Red Sea that leads into the Indian Ocean. Toll charges are based on Suez Canal tonnage. *See* tonnage, Suez and Panama Canal.

Suez rudder. Same as salmontail.

sufferance. A British word meaning permission given by Customs to ship certain goods. A sufferance wharf was used for this traffic.

sugar iceberg. Iceberg formed of porous glacier ice that normally falls apart easily.

sugg. To move with the action of the sea when stranded. Rarely used word now.

suit. A sailing vessel has at least one set of sails, one of each of the required sails. This set is known as a suit of sails and more than one suit makes up her wardrobe.

sulphur bottom whale. Another name for the great blue whale.

sumatra. A squall with violent thunder, lightning and rain that blows at night in Malacca Straits, especially during the southwest monsoon.

summer load line. The deepest waterline to which a merchant ship may be legally loaded in summer. Marked by the letter S. *See* load waterline.

summer tanks. Tanks built in an oil tanker for the additional load permitted during the summer months.

Sumner line. A position line used in celestial navigation, perpendicular to the bearing of the body observed. Somewhere on this line is the position of the ship.

sump. A small well or depression in a ship's compartment to facilitate drainage.

sun dog. Same as parhelion.

sundowner. In the U.S. Navy, a very strict and sometimes harsh commanding officer. In the British Navy, a drink at sundown.

sunfish. A large round ocean fish of the order Plectognothic that appears to be all head and little body, often seen on the surface. Also called a headfish.

sun over the yardarm. The traditional sailor's criterion for opening the bar or having the first drink of the day. The sun should normally be above the yardarm about 11 A.M.

sun's backstays. A sailor's term for the apparent rays of sun reaching down to the water when the sun is behind a cloud. Also called the rays of Maui.

supercargo. A person aboard a merchant ship, a freight clerk, who handles the administrative details of handling cargo. Now rare. A friend of the owner or master might make a passage or voyage and be listed as supercargo.

supercavitating. Describes a marine foil or propeller designed to operate at a velocity too great to permit cavitation.

superheater. An arrangement of piping in a marine boiler that raises the temperature of the steam, producing superheated steam, and thus increasing the efficiency of the plant.

superstructure. Any structure extending above the main deck.

support ship. *See* warship.

surf. The waves breaking on the shore as breakers produce surf. Depending on the slope of the beach underwater, the waves either break heavily and suddenly as on a steep slope or rise slowly to a curl and break at the top before gradually tumbling over as on a gradually shelving beach.

surface blow valve or cock. Same as scum cock.

Surface Effect Ship (SES). Any of the new craft, such as Hovercraft, that move over land and sea supported by a downward thrust of air. An old term was ground effect machine.

surfboard. A buoyant, smooth plank used by surfers to catch and slide across a breaking wave front. The original Hawaiian board was thin, solid, long and heavy. Lighter laminated boards were made as were hollow plywood boards before World War II. Modern boards, known as chips or Malibu boards, are made of balsa wood and plastic foam covered with fiberglass, resulting in a very light and buoyant board.

surf boats. Boats designed to be launched in surf.

surf currents. *See* nearshore current system.

surfing. The sport of riding down and across the face of a breaking wave near shore. A surfboard, bellyboard, mat, small boat, canoe, kayak, or sailing catamaran may be used or nothing at all except one's body. The last is known as body surfing.

surf port. Port whose configuration requires unloading and loading of cargo by lighter or surfboat instead of normal entrance into protected waters.

surfsailing. Same as windsurfing.

surge. 1. To slack or ease a line slowly around a winch, bollard, or cleat, as in lowering a weight. 2. The fore-and-aft translational bodily movement of a ship in a seiche or seaway. 3. The horizontal oscillation of water that accompanies a seiche. *See* ship motion, storm surge.

surgeon fish. A small colorful tropical reef fish of the family Acanthuridae that lives in schools. It has a long pointed spine on its side just forward of the tail. Also called a doctor fish.

surrounding net. A general term for purse net. *See* purse seine.

survey. To explore and chart an area. Also, in U.S. Naval usage, to dispose of worn out or damaged material is to survey it if the matter is recorded with reasons given.

survival suit. Plastic, waterproof, buoyant, heat-containing clothing designed to permit survival in cold water. Worn by those who might be accidentally immersed. Also called an exposure suit.

Susu. A blind river dolphin of India.

swab. Nautical term for mop.

swabbing. Cleaning a deck with a wet swab, periodically rinsed and wrung out. *See* clamp down.

swage. 1. A small, hollow tube of metal, cold-rolled around the end of a wire as terminal. 2. The tool used to compress and form the terminal. Also used as a verb. Pronounced swedge.

swallow. The opening in a block through which the rope passes.

swallow tail. A flag or pennant with a forked fly.

swallow the anchor. To leave the sea as a profession; to go ashore and stay there.

swamp. 1. To fill with water, as a boat may do in breaking seas. 2. To swamp a mooring buoy is to remove it, sink the attached gear and mark the location with a small buoy for later recovery. Done where the mooring area is too exposed to permit the mooring buoy to survive prolonged bad weather.

swash. 1. The rush of water as in the movement up onto the beach from a breaking wave. Also called wash. 2. Term used by the British for a shoal not exposed at low tide and swashway for a channel across or between shoals or spits of land.

swash plates. Plates installed in tanks to inhibit the free movement of water or free surface in a tank as the ship rolls. Also called wash plates.

sway. *n* The athwartship motion of a ship in a seiche or seaway; a sideways, bodily, translational movement. *See* ship motion, surge. *vb* 1. To hoist or raise as in swaying up the foremast. 2. To throw one's weight on a line as one sways up the mainsail to get it all the way up.

sweat up. To hoist something, such as a sail to the very top, all the way up, or to two-block it.

Swedish mainsail. A tall, narrow, relatively small sail used for going to windward in heavy weather.

sweep. *n* 1. A long oar used for steering and sculling. Most sailing vessels had sweeps aboard for emergency use. 2. The track on which a tiller quadrant travels. 3. Any long arc of curvature on a ship's structure. 4. The curved piece of wood or plastic used by draftsmen to draw lines. *vb* To sweep an area or channel is to pull a wire drag over it at a certain depth; the channel is then said to be swept to that depth. Moored or bottom mines are swept.

sweep seine. Same as drag seine.

swell. The undulation of the sea caused by wind blowing from some distance away or a wind that has stopped blowing. Also called a free wave. Swell is sometimes called ground swell or ground sea, especially when it breaks over a bar.

sweller. *See* blowfish.

swifter. 1. A piece of line used to bouse or pull together a shroud or lashing. **2.** A single shroud. **3.** A rope fender encircling a boat below the gunwale to protect its sides.

swig. *n* **1.** To tighten a line by pulling at right angles to it. **2.** A sailor might be ordered to take a swig on the main halyard. **3.** A thirsty sailor might take a swig of water or of something stronger. *vb* To swig in or up a jib sheet or halyard is to haul in on it.

swim fins or flippers. Flexible appendages worn on the feet to increase the speed of swiming for divers and surfers.

swimmer's itch. *See* seabather's itch.

swing. 1. A ship swings at anchor because of wind or current. **2.** To swing ship is to take different headings while underway in order to compensate the magnetic compass. **3.** A boat in a davit is swung out before being lowered.

swinging basin. Same as turning basin.

swivel. A hoop or link that turns freely and axially on a bolt or pin.

swivel block. Block suspended by a swivel and therefore free to turn.

swivel, mooring. A heavy steel link used in mooring with two anchors.

sword arm. A device containing a pitot tube or other sensing instrument that is projected from a ship's bottom.

swordfish. A large, worldwide pelagic food and game fish having a long, sword-like beak. Also called a broadbill or billfish, the latter being the collective word for all billed fish including sailfish and marlin. Sometimes harpooned while basking on the surface, they are fished commercially by longline.

synoptic chart. A weather map showing isobars or lines of equal pressure, thus revealing the high and low pressure weather systems from which forecasts can be made.

System A. A new uniform buoyage system now being gradually implemented in Europe, Africa, Australia and parts of Asia. Full name: "System A-The combined Cardinal and Lateral System (red to port)."

System B. A proposed uniform buoyage system; "System B-Lateral System (red to starboard)", designed for North and South America and parts of Asia.

syzygy. The point in the orbit of a celestial body when it is nearest to a straight line between the earth and the sun, i.e., when in conjunction or opposition. Thus a syzygy or spring tide occurs at full or at new moon.

T

T. International signal code alphabet flag. When hoisted singly means: "Keep clear of me, I am engaged in pair trawling." As a freeboard mark, it indicates the load line in the tropics. Spoken: "tango."

tabernacle. A vertical trunk built to take the heel of a mast that does not pass through the deck; used as a pivoted mast step for folddown masts on boats that travel on canals and must pass under bridges. Also called a mast trunk. Sometimes referred to as a lutchet which is a slightly different fitting that serves the same purpose.

table. *n* The outer part of a keel, stem, or sternpost projecting beyond the planking. *vb* To table is to fold over a broad hem on the edge of a sail before attaching the boltrope.

tablemount. A seamount having a smooth and flat top. Also once called a guyot, a term now considered obsolete.

tabling. The hem around a sail.

tack. *n* **1.** The lower forward corner of a fore-and-aft sail. **2.** The weather clew of a course or the rope or tackle holding such clew. **3.** In sailing, the direction or heading of a ship in relation to the wind, such as a ship is on the port tack if the wind comes from the port side. **4.** The distance or duration while on the same tack, also called a leg or board. **5.** The main tack is the weather clew of a square mainsail and there are tack blocks, bumkins, earings, lashings, and cringles, all associated with the tack of a sail. **6.** Short for tackline. *vb* To tack is to direct the ship's head through the wind, changing the side on which the wind strikes the ship's sails. This procedure is also known as coming or going about. *See* wear.

tackle. An arrangement of rope, wire, or chain and blocks rigged to increase the holding power and gain a mechanical advantage, such as relieving tackle that is applied to relieve the strain on a steering gear in heavy weather or watch tackle that is used for odd jobs on deck by the watch on duty. Also, in a general sense it means the same as purchase though this word specifies the mechanical advantage of a particular tackle. Pronounced taykle.

tackle block. Block used to make up a tackle or purchase.

tackline. A six foot length of halyard used as a spacer between groups of signal flags.

tack ring. *See* jib traveller.

tack shackle. A full swiveling snap shackle fitted at the stemhead to permit instant attachment or release of the tack of a jib.

tactical diameter. In the turning circle of a ship, the perpendicular distance between the original course and the new course after a 180° turn with constant rudder.

taffrail. The railing around the fantail or ship's stern.

taffrail log. A towed, spinning ship's speed measuring device with the recording dial attached to the taffrail. Same as a screwlog.

tail. *n* A short piece of rope attached to a block, a larger rope, or a chain. *vb* 1. A ship at anchor may tail into the shore. 2. Men needed to haul on a line may be asked to tail on. 3. To haul on a line around a winch is to tail the line.

tail shaft. Same as propeller shaft. Also known as tail-end shaft. *See* shaft.

taino. Haitian word for hurricane.

take. 1. To measure, such as to take soundings. 2. To lay hold of, such as to take a turn with a rope, to take the helm, or to take in the slack of a tackle. 3. To take in the slack now means to rest. 4. A ship leaving port takes her departure. 5. A ship in heavy weather may take water aboard.

take charge. Go out of control, such as a heavy piece of gear may come adrift in heavy weather and bang about; it is said to have taken charge. A line can take charge when it carries away or parts under strain.

taken aback. *See* aback.

tallboy. An extremely narrow, tall and flat staysail that is used when sailing downwind in some racing sailboats.

take off. Tides on successive days take off when their heights decrease between spring and neap tides. When the heights increase, the tide is said to make.

tall ships. A modern collective term for the world's remaining large sailing vessels.

tally. A record of the number of items of cargo handled. To keep such a count is to tally a shipment.

tally board. A board attached to rescue gear that is passed to a ship in distress, carries instructions in several languages on how to use the gear.

tallyman. A person recording or tallying the cargo. Also known as a checker or tally clerk.

talurit splice. A modern, quick and easy eye splice in a wire rope using a thimble and a collar or ferrule compressed around both parts after the thimble is inserted.

tampion. *See* tompion.

tan. To treat canvas or fishnets with a preservative; not often done today with synthetic fibers.

tang. A fitting, such as a metal strap, secured to a spar or mast to which a stay or halyard block, for example, may be made fast.

tank. A compartment in a ship that is used to carry various liquids such as fuel, oil, and water. Many special purpose tanks exist aboard ship, for example, settling tanks and feed tanks.

tankage. The capacity of a tank or a number of tanks.

tank barge. A barge with double bottoms designed to transport liquids.

tanker. A specially built, large cargo ship that is used to carry petroleum products as well as other cargo to be shipped in bulk such as grain. Also called an oiler. In the Navy, this specifies the ship that refuels the Fleet.

tankerman. A duly certified and qualified hand who can perform his duties aboard a tanker with skill and safety.

tanks, anti-rolling. *See* anti-rolling tanks.

tanks, deep. *See* deeptanks.

tanner crab. Same as snow crab.

tar. 1. A substance, once made from pine tree sap and now replaced by synthetic compounds, that was used by sailors to waterproof and preserve wood, cordage, and canvas. **2.** Another name for a mariner. **3.** "To tar down the rigging" is an expression still used by yachtsmen meaning to spread a preservative over the standing rigging such as the shrouds.

tariff. In shipping, a list of the charges made by general cargo carriers for services rendered in transporting goods. Also the rules and regulations governing the application of such charges.

tarpaulin. Any piece of canvas used to cover and protect something aboard ship. Tarp for short.

tarpaulin muster. Before the days of seamen's welfare organizations, a collection of cash contributions for a needy man or his family.

tarpon. A popular game fish but a poor food fish of the Caribbean. It grows to 6 feet in length and is not an easy catch.

tartan or tartane. A small, sailing coasting ship of the Mediterranean with a lateen rig and a single mast.

taut. Nautical term for tight as in "a line is hauled taut." In a general sense, it means well-disciplined, orderly, efficient such as a taut ship, or as the British say, a ship run on a taut string.

tautog. A bottom game fish of North Atlantic waters, genus *Tautoga onitis*, that grows to over 20 pounds and is known locally as a blackfish.

tease. To open out and separate yarns and strands of rope.

Tehuantepecer. A violent north wind that blows in the winter around the Gulf of Tehuantepec, Mexico.

telegraph. *See* engine-order telegraph.

telegraph block. Block through which several signal halyards are rove, with a long narrow shell having the sheaves one above the other in the same plane. Similar to a fiddle block.

telemotor. A remote control system, hydraulic or electric, by which controls in one place can actuate machinery in another, such as the steering engine aft controlled from the bridge of a ship.

telescope. A magnifying, single tube, hand-held instrument; also known as a long glass, glass, or spyglass. In the past, it had an important usage on the bridge for piloting and spotting signals as well as distant ships. Today's usage is much diminished with the advent of efficient binoculars and radar.

telltale. 1. An inverted compass or compass repeater placed over the master's, owner's, or captain's bunk indicates the ship's course. 2. Any indicator or pointer that shows the rudder angle to the helmsman. 3. A bit of yarn or cloth made fast in the rigging of a sailboat to reveal airflow direction.

tempest. A poetic and literary word for storm or gale; not usually heard at sea.

tend. To watch or to take care of, as when the watertender monitors the water level in the gauge glass of a marine boiler or an officer on duty in a warship may tend the side if he greets someone coming aboard.

tender. 1. A warship, but not a combatant ship, that is specially manned and equipped to service other ships such as a submarine tender. 2. Any small harbor craft that services other and larger ships. 3. A small boat carried aboard a yacht. 4. A ship is said to be tender if she has poor stability; same as crank.

tengusa. Japanese word for the five species of red seaweed that are harvested to produce agar. *See* agar.

tenon. The heel of a mast shaped to fit into the step.

Teredo navalis. The most common of the shipworms that bores into the underwater portion of wooden ships. Commonly known as toredo. *See* shipworm.

Terkoku Kaya Kyokai (TKK). The Japanese national ship classification society located in Tokyo. *See* classification.

terminal, port. A facility on the waterfront designed to berth ships, handle cargo, and provide services such as transshipment inland, storage, or delivery of goods ashore.

tern. A seabird similar to a gull but smaller and less stout. It has a forked tail from which it gets the name sea swallow. *See* gull. Also a three-masted schooner.

terrapin. *See* turtle.

territorial waters. Waters adjacent to the coast of a country and over which it claims jurisdiction. Historically three miles (the range of a smoothbore cannon), now often claimed to 200 miles. Also called a marine belt or patrimonial sea. Not to be confused with inland waters.

test. A hard covering, shell or supporting structure, of many invertebrate sea animals.

TEU. Twenty foot Equivalent Units; a measure of container capacity.

textile cone. A cone-shaped mollusk or seashell that attains a length of four inches and found in shallow tropical waters. With its tiny teeth, it injects venom into its prey, mainly other shellfish; can be dangerous to handle.

Texas tower. A fixed structure erected offshore to provide oceanographic and weather data and to act as an aid to navigation.

thalweg. The line joining the lowest points of a submarine valley. Also the center line of the principal navigational channel of a waterway that is the boundary between two countries.

Thames barge. *See* barge.

Thames measurement. Introduced in 1855 by the Royal Thames Yacht Club, a formula used in the United Kingdom to determine the tonnage of a yacht from its length and beam. The formula is: $(L-B) \times B \times \frac{1}{2}B / 94$ where L is length roughly on the waterline and B, the beam.

thermocline. A layer of seawater marked by different temperatures.

thick. A sailor's adjective for dense, such as thick fog or thick weather meaning very low visibility.

thick and thin block. Block having several sheaves of different thickness to hold different sizes of rope or wire.

thief. A dipper or can used to extract a sample of liquid from its container. The sample is known as a thief sample.

thimble. An oval metal fitting secured in the eye of a rope or wire for protection against wear as well as a convenience in forming the eye.

tholepin. A primitive oarlock for a pulling boat consisting of one (or a pair of) wooden or metal pin secured upright in a hole in the gunwale. The oar is either held between the pair or by a loop of line made fast to one pin.

thorn-of-stars. A tropical starfish that feeds on coral and often does great damage to coral reefs.

thoroughfoot. To coil down a twisted rope against the lay (counterclockwise for right hand laid cordage), bringing the lower end up through the coil and then coiling the line with the lay. This will take out the twist, particularly with new rope.

thrash. A beat to windward in a sailboat.

three arm protractor. *See* protractor.

three-fold or treble block. Block having three adjacent sheaves.

three sheets to the wind. Sailors slang for drunk.

thresher. A game shark. *See* shark.

throat. 1. The forward end of the gaff of a gaff sail where it embraces the mast (with a saddle, saddle plate and parrel). Also called jaws. 2. The upper forward corner of a four-sided fore-and-aft sail where head and luff join. Also called nock. 3. On an old fashioned anchor, the curved part of either arm where it joins the shank. 4. The part of the shell of a block nearest the hook. 5. The midship part of a floor timber over the keel where its depth is greatest. 6. The center part of a knee or breasthook. 7. The insides of knee timbers at the turn of the arms.

thrum. Short bits of rope yarns used to make mats. The yarns are sewed to canvas in the process of thrumming. These shag or pile mats have uses such as chafing gear and collision mats.

thrust bearing. Bearing that receives the thrust or horizontal push of the propeller shaft through a thrust collar fitted on the shaft.

thrust block. The part of the ship that receives the thrust of the propeller shaft through the thrust bearing which it incorporates. Access to the thrust block is through the thrust recess.

thruster. An auxiliary powered propeller or jet, either at the bow or the stern, that improves the maneuverability of the ship by turning the bow or stern; known as bow or stern thrusters, a component of many large new ships.

thrust surface. The after driving surface of a propeller blade that thrusts the water back. Also called face, driving face, or driving surface.

thumb cleat. A piece of wood or plastic, usually triangular, secured to a spar or spreader to keep part of the rigging in place. Also called a snatch cleat.

thundercloud or thunderhead. A cloud likely to contain thunder and lightning; a cumulonimbus.

thurm. A ragged and rocky headland projecting out into the sea.

thwart. A plank or bench at right angles to the keel of a boat on which rowers and passengers sit; naturally runs athwartships. Also a board between two staging uprights on which the stage planks rest; sometimes called a stage bearer or a spall.

tickle. Any narrow passage connecting two bodies of water; a small strait.

tickler. Same as telltale.

tidal basin. The part of a port or harbor where the tidal range is greatest, enclosed and protected by floodgates to keep the water level constant.

tidal bore. *See* bore.

tidal constant. The minutes and feet that are added or subtracted from the data at the reference stations found in the Tide Tables in order to obtain the time and height of the tide at another location.

tidal current. Current resulting from the rise and fall of the tide and which reverses direction in confined waters. It can be evaluated from the Current Tables, Current Diagrams, and Current Charts. In the open sea, they assume a circular movement due to Coriolis force. British term: tidal stream. *See* current, hydraulic current, Current Charts, Current Tables.

tidal interval. Same as lunitidal interval.

tidal range. The average difference, over a month or more, between high and low water.

tidal river. River under the influence of the tide for a considerable distance upstream.

tidal stream. *See* tidal current.

tidal water. Water in a tidal river.

tidal wave. A slow moving bulge of water on the earth's surface caused by gravitational attraction of the moon and the sun. Also called tide wave. As this bulge or wave advances on, and then retracts, from the shore, high and low tides result. Unusually high tides, when driven ashore by very strong winds, can produce destructive coastal flooding, known as storm surges. *See* storm surge. Also an inaccurate term, along with its Japanese equivalent tsunami, for seismic sea wave. *See* seismic sea wave.

tide. The rise and fall of the level of the ocean caused by the gravitational attraction of the moon and to a lesser extent, the sun. A rising tide is a flood tide; a falling tide is an ebb. The time between successive high tides is normally 24 hours and 51 minutes but is about 13 minutes less when the earth, moon, and sun are in a straight line (first and third quarters of the moon). This is called acceleration or priming of the tide. The opposite phenomenon called lag, lagging, or retardation of the tide, occurs when the moon and sun are in quadrature (second and fourth quarters).

tide gage. An instrument for measuring the rise and fall of the tide.

tide race. *See* race.

tide rip. *See* rip.

tide-rode. Said of a ship at anchor when she lies bow to the tide instead of bow to the wind or wind-rode.

Tide Tables. The list of predicted times of high and low water, and their heights, for some 200 reference posts and 6000 secondary stations. It is published by the National Ocean Survey and in the United Kingdom by the Hydrographic Department of the Royal Navy.

tide wave. *See* tidal wave.

tideway. The channel in which a tidal current flows or the current itself.

tie. *n* 1. A small band of canvas that is used to secure a sail or awning. 2. Part of the tackle used in square-riggers to hoist a yard. Also spelled tye. 3. In ship construction, there are many elements used to join things together such as tie rods, tie planks, and tie plates. *vb* To make fast; to secure; to join together. A boat may be tied up astern, although preferred usage among mariners would be hauled out and made fast astern. In most cases, make fast is a more nautical word than tie.

tie plate. A fore-and-aft course of steel plating on the deck beams under a wooden deck.

tier. 1. A row or layer, such as a series of fakes in a hawser or chain ranged on deck clear for running. 2. A row of cargo in a hold or a row of small boat mooring buoys. 3. For the British yachtsman, a sail gasket that is sometimes spelled tie-er or tyer.

tie-tie. A pair of cloth ribbons used to fasten a kapok life jacket or lash up a hammock.

tiger shark. *See* shark.

tiller. Arm or level fitted onto the rudder that is used to turn it when steering a boat. In large boats and ships, the tiller is replaced by the wheel.

timber load line. A special load line for ships carrying deck loads of logs or boards.

timber head. The upper end of a wooden frame timber rising above the deck and supporting the bulwark and/or serving as a bitt. Also called a kevel head.

time. Since the earth rotates at a slightly irregular rate, it is convenient to assume an average or mean rate, thus mean time. Greenwich Mean Time is the time measured at Greenwich, near London, and used as the point of reference in nautical almanacs and by navigators; when corrected by the zone description, it becomes local ship's time. *See* equation of time, zone time, universal time.

timenoguy. A rope or line stretched from one part of a sailing ship to another in order to prevent running gear from fouling or touching the rigging.

time, ship's. *See* ship's time.

time signal. A signal sent by radio worldwide to ships at sea on various frequencies at various hours of the day to provide the exact universal time to navigators. Also called a time tick.

time tick. Same as time signal.

time zone. One of the 24 divisions, $15°$ wide, into which the world is arbitrarily divided. *See* zone time.

tin canning. *See* panting.

tingle. A copper patch used to repair a hole in the hull of a wooden boat.

TKK. Terkoku Kaya Kyohai, the Japanese ship classification society. *See* classification.

tobin bolt. A composition bronze bolt used in wooden ship construction, particularly to fasten lead ballasts.

toe. 1. The edge of the flange of a structural shape or angle. 2. The point of the palm or fluke of an anchor.

toe cleat. A piece of wood that holds the lower end of an oarlock in place in a wooden pulling boat.

toe strap. Same as hiking strap, its British equivalent.

toggle. 1. A piece of wood or metal fitted crosswise in a loop or an eye of a line. 2. A movable barb in a harpoon. 3. The U-shaped metal fitting at the end of a turnbuckle that prevents bending forces on turnbuckle threads.

toll. Same as chum.

tom. *n* In shipbuilding, a short shore or timber such as the one used to hold frames apart before planking. *vb* To tom down is to hold down something such as cargo using timbers extending to the overhead. *See* tomming.

tomahawk. A special hammer used in smoothing or finishing a rivet head.

tombolo. An area of sand or gravel deposited by waves or current that connects a rock or island to another rock, island, or the mainland.

tomcod. A small edible cod-like fish found in north Atlantic and Pacific waters.

tomming. Shoring cargo on deck by rigging the shores to hold the containers down.

tompion. A plug or cover for a ship's gun barrel. Pronounced tomkin and also spelled tampion.

ton. A unit of weight, both ashore and afloat, or of capacity at sea. A short ton is 2000 pounds (907 kilograms), a long ton is 2240 pounds (1016 kilograms), and a metric ton is 2205 pounds (1000 kilograms). For units of capacity a ton is 100 cubic feet which is gross registered tonnage, or 40 cubic feet which is the net registered tonnage, shipping measurement, or freight ton. *See* tonnage.

tongue. 1. A hinged piece of wood placed vertically in the throat of a gaff to bear the thrust of the latter against the mast. **2.** The upper part of a built-up wooden mast. **3.** A spit of land or ice, or an inlet, a narrow rapid current, or a protrusion of water of different characteristics into a larger body of water.

tonkang. A small craft used for lighterage in the Orient.

tonnage. 1. A collective word for all the shipping of a country, port, or waterway. **2.** Describes a ship, either in terms of weight or capacity. **3.** The charge per ton on cargo, in form of a tax or duty at a port or canal.

tonnage, deadweight. The difference between a ship's loaded and her light displacement, therefore a measurement of the cargo she can carry including fuel, water, and stores.

tonnage deck. The second complete deck of a ship up from the keel; used in tonnage measurements.

tonnage, displacement. The actual weight of a ship measured by the volume of water displaced, expressed in long tons.

tonnage, light displacement. A computation using the light or empty water line.

tonnage, load displacement. A computation using the maximum permissible (summer) draft.

tonnage, equipment. Gross tonnage plus the computed weight for any normally exempted spaces; used by the American Bureau of Shipping in specifying the size and strength of the ship's ground tackle.

tonnage, gross. The calculated weight of the total internal cubic measurement (100 cubic feet is 1 ton), less such spaces in which no fuel, cargo, or stores are carried.

tonnage mark. As proposed by IMCO, a 15 inch horizontal line under an inverted triangle that is painted on the side of a ship to indicate maximum draft if the exemption of certain spaces inside the ship is to be maintained in tonnage measurement.

tonnage, power. Gross tonnage plus the ship's indicated horsepower; sometimes used in calculating the wage scale of ship's officers.

tonnage, register or registered. By law, the number of tons represented by the closed spaces within the ship at 100 cubic feet per ton. Gross register tonnage includes nearly all enclosed spaces; net register tonnage excludes, for example, machinery spaces, living, and storeroom spaces, fuel space, galley and perhaps navigating or radar gear spaces below deck, in order to measure the actual cargo carrying capacity. It is net registered tonnage that determines berthing and other port fees. *See* register length, register breadth, register depth.

tonnage, Suez and Panama Canal. Specially computed tonnage that is slightly different than gross register because of different exempted spaces; the basis for canal tolls.

tonnage, Thames measurement. *See* Thames measurement.

tonnage, yacht. Tonnage of a boat using the Thames measurement.

tonne. British word for a metric ton or 1 000 kilograms or 2 205 pounds. The long ton is 2 240 pounds.

tons per inch immersion. The number of tons weight that when taken aboard will increase the ship's mean draft one inch.

top. *n* **1.** A platform aloft on a mast. In square-riggers, this was at the junction of the lower and topmast; used to spread the shrouds and provided a place for men to work aloft. **2.** In sailing warships, the fighting tops were used by sharpshooters and grenade throwers. **3.** The top of a mast is the cap except for the highest mast on which it is the truck. *vb* **1.** To top up a yard or boom is to raise one end. **2.** To top up or top off a tank or hold is to fill it.

tope. A small dogfish or shark common to Europe; sometimes called a soup-fin shark from which the Chinese make soup. British terms: miller-dog and penny-dog.

topgallant. The masts, sails, rigging, and yards above the topmast in a square-rigger.

topgallant bulwarks. Bulwarks that extend above the main rail.

topgallant forecastle. A superstructure just abaft the stem.

topgallant rail. The rail that extends above the topgallant bulwarks.

top hamper. Collective term for all gear, spars, masts, and other items above the main deck of a ship.

topman. A sailor or marine stationed in one of the tops of a sailing warship. Also called topsman.

topmark. The distinctive shape carried by some foreign buoys as an aid in identifying the function of the buoy.

topmast. The mast rigged above a lower or principal mast. In square-riggers, it was just below the topgallant mast.

topping lift. A wire, rope, or chain used to take the weight off, for example, a yard, boom, sail, or derrick enabling it to be topped or raised to the desired level. Also called a lift or topping line. There are many associated pieces of gear such as topping lift chain, bail, block, fall, purchase, and span.

topsail. In a square-rigger, the lowest sail on any mast that could be spread between an upper and a lower mast. A topsail schooner is fore-and-aft rigged on all masts with additional square sails on the foremast. *See* jib topsail.

topside. Describes anything on the main deck of a ship or above the main deck, such as a sailor goes topside or he remains below. Not to be confused with overhead.

topside strake. *See* strake.

torpedo. A self-propelled underwater missile carrying an explosive charge that is fired by submarines, some aircraft, and warships.

tortoise. *See* hawksbill turtle.

toss. To toss oars is to lift them up together vertically at the end of a stroke as a salute or in preparation to shipping the oars.

touch. 1. To touch the wind is to steer a sailboat very close to the wind, causing the luff to shiver a bit. 2. To stop briefly at a port is to touch there.

tow. A ship, lighter, dredge, or other vessel or craft that is pulled or pushed through the water. If no power is used by the ship being towed, it is a dead or flat tow. If power is used, it is a live tow.

towboat. *See* tugboat.

towing lights. Under the International Rules of the Road a tug when towing or pushing displays various combinations of masthead range, sidelight, and stern lights as well as a towing light defined as a yellow light showing astern, 67.5° on each side. Under Inland Rules similar but different combinations of white and red range and masthead lights as well as standard sidelights and stern lights are displayed by the tug but not the yellow towing light mentioned above. In addition, under Inland Rules, a tug when pushing ahead shows two amber 135° lights arranged vertically on her stern.

towing machine. A large powered drum upon which the towline of a tug is wound and held at the pivot point of the tug. The towline can thus be eased under strain or hauled taut. Also called a towing winch.

towing spar. A towed device, usually of wood, pulled astern by warships in column as an aid to maintaining position in low visibility. Also called a fog buoy or fog spar and little used now.

towing winch. *See* towing machine.

track. The path or course of a ship or a storm marked on a chart with the intended direction of movement; a track chart. Also a metal strip on a mast in which the luff of a sail can move up and down.

tractor tug. Tug in which the propulsion gear, propellers with variable pitch blades, is omni-directional and located under the pilot house. The result is a highly maneuverable tug that moves ships in confined waters.

trade winds. Constant and steady winds that naturally flow towards the equator as the sun-heated air there rises and cold air flows in from the polar regions. Their easterly component is a result of Coriolis force and produces northeast trades in the northern hemisphere and southeast trades in the southern.

trailboard. A carved plank on each side of the stem near the deck edge in a sailboat where the bowsprit starts. Originally a brace for the figurehead in a ship, it is now a decoration for yachts.

training wall. A jetty or similar structure, often submerged, built to confine the flow of a river or tidal current.

trammel. A fixed and loosely mounted fishnet consisting of three parallel panels of netting in which the fish entangle themselves.

tramontana. The cold north wind off the west coast of Italy, similar to the mistral off the south coast of France.

tramp. A cargo ship that does not have a fixed and scheduled route but carries freight where she can find business. British term: general trader or cargo boat.

trampoline. The net of webbing or piece of fabric between the hulls of a small catamaran.

transfer. The distance gained by a ship when turning that is perpendicular to the original course. *See* advance.

transire. A customs document furnished to a coasting ship in place of the normal clearance provided to a ship going abroad.

transit. *n* 1. The passage of a celestial body over a specified meridian of the earth. 2. Two objects, such as range lights or beacons, seen in line with each other, are said to be in transit or in range. Transit is the more commonly used British term. 3. Cargo is in transit before final delivery. *vb* A ship transits a canal. Transit is the same as Navsat.

transom. 1. The framework of the stern of a ship at the sternpost, includes the transom floor, frames, and beams. 2. A built-in sofa in a ship's cabin.

transom board. In a small boat, the aftermost athwartships piece in the stern sheets.

transom drive. Same as stern drive.

transom flap. An opening in the stern of a boat that permits the escape of water.

transom stern. Stern with a square or flat counter, usually sloping outward from the sternpost, as different from a sharp or from a rounded stern. *See* stern shapes.

transport. A ship used by the government to carry troops and military supplies.

transtainer. An advanced container handling method on the dockside using an overhead traveling crane and gantry.

transverse. In reference to shipbuilding it indicates a system of framing in which closely spaced frames are used to provide the main supports for the shell, keel, and decks. This is different from longitudinal framing in which many fore-and-aft strength members are used and the frames are more widely spaced.

trapeze. The wire from aloft that supports a crew member who is hiked out in a small sailboat.

trap net. An inshore fixed fishing system in which a number of net funnels, supported by stakes, lead the fish into a final enclosure from which they cannot find their way back.

traveler. 1. Any ring, thimble, or strap that moves on a spar, bar, or rope, such as the sheet or traveler block that moves athwartship on a traveling iron or horse. 2. In modern sailing yachts, the track on which a traveler slide or becket block moves.

traverse. To cross, to sail a compound course, or to pass back and forth. Also an old word that describes the horizontal movement of a gun; the modern word is train.

traverse board. A board used in olden times along with a compass rose to get the resultant of a series of tacks on different headings. The headings were recorded by placing pegs in the right holes every half hour.

traverse table. Table that gives the distance gained both in latitude and in longitude for any course sailed at a certain speed; used in traverse sailing. *See* sailing.

trawl cab. A small sheltered control station facing aft from which large trawls can be governed.

trawler. Any ship that sets or shoots, tows, and hauls a trawl net either from the side as a side trawler, or from the stern as a stern or factory trawler. Stern or factory trawlers are the most modern and have a stern chute or ramp for hauling in the catch. Also called a dragger. A trawler that has a beam to hold the net open is a beam trawler. *See* seiner.

trawling. Fishing with a trawl.

trawl net. A large, conical net bag towed on or above the bottom to catch fish, shrimp, or sponges. Older models used a wooden beam to spread the mouth of the net; modern ones use otter boards. Also a long buoyed fishing line having multiple lines or snoods attached.

tray. Another word for pallet. *See* pallet.

tread. One of the steps on a ship's ladder. Also the entire length of a ship's keel.

treenail. A hard wood peg used at one time to fasten planks and timbers in wooden ship and boat construction. Now largely replaced by such items as nails, driftbolts, lags, bolts, and screws. Also spelled trenail and pronounced trunel.

trebling. Extra planking on the bow of a wooden vessel to resist ice.

trepang. Another name for sea cucumber.

trestletrees. A fore-and-aft framing that rests on the cheeks of a lower mast or topmast of a sailing ship and supports the weight of the crosstrees and of the top. Also called trestles.

tret. The allowance for depreciation and ordinary wear and tear on a ship during a voyage.

trials. *See* sea trials.

triatic stay. A fore-and-aft wire between masts or from a mast to the top of the stack. Often used to support signal halyards and then called a signal stay or a cap stay.

trice. To lift a sail, awning, or spar by means of a tricing stay, line or pendant, or to temporarily hold or support something.

trick. A spell of duty or a turn, as a helmsman does his trick at the wheel.

trick wheel. Wheel at an emergency steering station such as the steering engine room.

tridacna. *See* giant clam.

trident. A three pronged spear, traditionally carried by Neptune. The latest U.S. submarine-launched strategic nuclear missile, successor to Polaris/Poseidon, and carried by immense Trident nuclear submarines.

triggerfish. A small colorful tropical reef fish that can extend and lock its dorsal spine, thus securing itself into small holes in the reef to escape predators.

trim. *n* The difference in a ship's draft forward and draft aft, expressed in inches. *vb* 1. A ship may be trimmed by the head or by the stern which is the same as down by the head or stern. 2. To trim a sail is to adjust it for best efficiency. 3. To trim cargo is to distribute it evenly, sometimes done by trimmers who may use a trimming hatch for access to bulk cargo such as wheat and who will be paid a trimming charge.

trimaran. A vessel having a central hull with a smaller hull attached to each side. Now popular as a sailing yacht.

trim tabs. In the nautical sense, flat and movable surfaces on the stern of a planing power boat that achieve an optimum planing attitude. They are sometimes also attached to rudders to improve efficiency.

Trinity House. An association of mariners, established in 1517 by Henry VIII, now responsible for navigational aids and piloting in the British Isles.

trinket. The uppermost sail, topgallant or royal, in a square rigger.

trip. 1. To trip an anchor is to break it out of the bottom in which it is embedded by means of a special line. 2. To swing a mast or yard up or to an upright position prior to lowering. 3. A ship's strength member bent or strained out of shape is said to be tripped. 4. To trip something is to let it go, usually by means of a slip or a pelican hook.

tripping bracket. A flat bar or plate fitted on deck beams, girders or stiffeners as reinforecment.

trip shore. Shore used in supporting a ship on a slipways just before launching and designed to fall away as the ship starts to move. Also called a tumble shore.

tripton. A collective word for all dead, suspended particles in water.

trireme. A war galley or oared ship of the ancient Mediterranean having three sets or banks of oars.

Trisec. A new cargo carrying concept under development in which a ship has two or more submerged buoyancy pods supporting a hull above the water.

triton. A trumpet-shaped whelk or mollusk much sought after by shell collectors. Its decline in numbers has led to a rapid increase in the crown-of-thorns starfish, its natural prey, to the detriment of coral reefs upon which the latter feeds. Also a Greek god of the sea, son of Poseidon.

troll, trolling. A method of fishing in which lures or bait are towed or trolled astern, usually several trolls to a boat with some leading from outriggers. Trolling is sometimes called shooting or whiffing.

troller. Boat used for trolling.

tropic. A circle or parallel of latitude, 23 degrees and 27 minutes either north or south of the Equator, marking the limit of the tropic or torrid zones where the sun is directly overhead. The Tropic of Cancer is in the northern hemisphere while the Tropic of Capricorn is the southern counterpart.

tropic bird. A white pelagic seabird of the genus *Phaëthon* that is marked by two very long tail feathers.

tropic tide. Common in the tropics, a diurnal or one-a-day tide that occurs during the period of the moon's greatest declination.

tropopause. The dividing line between the troposphere and the stratosphere.

troposphere. The lowest layer of the atmosphere, about 10 miles thick at the Equator.

trot. A short line, leader, or snood to which each hook is attached in a trot or trawl line. Also, in the United Kingdom, a trot is a multiple mooring for small boats.

trotline. A southern U.S. term for a fishing longline. Also a word used by small boat sailors to describe a line of moorings.

trough. 1. The hollow between wave crests. 2. A long depression between ridges on the ocean floor; also sometimes called a trench. 3. A long low pressure area that is part of a weather system.

trout, saltwater. *See* sea trout.

trow. A type of barge, once ketch-rigged, used to carry freight in the rivers and coastal waters of the United Kingdom.

truck. A fitting at the top of a flagstaff or mast, particularly the highest mast. It may contain a halyard block and a light. Also called a cap.

trumpet fish. A small colorful tropical reef fish of the family Aulostomidae that has a slender stiff body and a very long head and snout.

trundlehead. An old word for the lower drumhead of a double capstan that worked on a single shaft on two decks. Now, if used, it refers to the drumhead or capstan head.

trunk. Aboard ship, an enclosure or casing for a ladder between decks; an escape trunk. Also an enclosed passage, crawl space, or an air passage such as a ventilating trunk.

trunk buoy. A cylindrical mooring buoy with a central trunk through which the end of the mooring pendant is brought up.

trunk cabin. *See* cabin top.

trunk deck. An enclosed structure, about two-thirds the width of the ship, that joins the islands of such ships as coastal traders.

trunkfish. A small colorful tropical reef fish of the family Ostraciontidae that is so called because it is encased in a box of fused scales.

trunk, mast. Another word for tabernacle.

trunnions. The main supports of a gun on the axis about which the gun elevates and depresses.

truss. A strong iron pivoting device by which the lower yard of a square-rigger is held to the mast while allowing the yard to be braced or topped up. It is fastened to the yard by truss bands or truss hoops.

truss bow. *See* yard span.

truss yoke. *See* yard span.

trust-in-God. A light sail carried aloft in a square-rigger. *See* kites.

try. 1. An archaic word meaning to lie to in heavy weather with storm canvas set. 2. To try out whale blubber was to boil out the oil.

try cocks. Small faucets or valves on a steam drum used to verify the water level if the gauge glass fails.

try net. A small trawl net used to test the fishing before shooting the main trawl.

trysail. 1. In modern sailing yachts, a small yet strong sail that is used in heavy weather and often called a storm trysail. 2. On fishing craft, a sail is sometimes set to steady the boat and reduce rolling. 3. In olden days, the fore-and-aft sail used on square-riggers; also called spencer or spanker, depending on its location.

tsunami. Japanese word for tidal wave and is similarly used to describe a seismic sea wave. *See* tidal wave, seismic sea wave.

Tsushima Current. *See* Kuroshio.

tub. 1. A section of trawl line as well as the wooden tub in which the line and its hooks are coiled. 2. A derogatory word for an old, ugly, poorly maintained or uncomfortable ship or boat.

tube. *See* boiler, sounding tube, stern tube, voice tube.

tuck. The part of a ship where the after ends of the outside planking finish at a ship's counter or transom at the tuck rail or tuck timber. British word for reef and for making a reef or a splice.

tuck plate. An oxter plate.

tuck seine. Another name for a purse seine.

Tufnol. A plastic now often used in making blocks.

tugboat. A relatively small, sturdy, high-powered, sea-worthy vessel used for towing and pushing, salvage, fighting fires as well as berthing large ships. Called a tug for short and sometimes a towboat. There are small river and harbor tugs and large sea-going salvage tugs capable of rescue and salvage in any weather. A quarter-wheel tug is one having a paddle wheel on each quarter; still used on the White Nile.

tugmaster. A small vehicle used around the docks for pulling trailers.

tug, pusher. Tug specially designed with a high flat bow for barge cluster push-towing. Also called a pushboat.

tumblehome. The inward inclination of a ship's side; a convex curve in the ship's hull; opposite of flare.

tumbler. A device for tripping or casting loose an old-fashioned anchor by releasing the securing chains. Also called an anchor-tripper or a trigger-boat.

tumble shore. Same as trip shore.

tun. A large cask once used in shipping wine that when filled weighed 2000 pounds; the origin of the long ton.

tuna. A member of the mackerel family, Scombridae, that includes albacore, bonito, yellowfin, skipjack and the great bluefin tuna or horse mackerel that weighs over 1000 pounds. All tuna are fast, ocean-roaming, excellent food and game fish that are heavily fished everywhere by commercial fishermen and are thus declining sharply in number. Also called tunny. *See* mackerel.

tuna clipper. A long range U.S. Pacific tuna fisherman using both hook and line and purse seine fishing.

tuna tower. A lightweight elevated structure built on a fishing boat to obtain better visibility when fishing.

tunnel boat. A fishing and pleasure boat whose propeller revolves in a tunnel to protect it from debris and from the effects of grounding.

tunny. Another name for tuna.

turbidity current. A rapid, large-volume, down-slope movement of sediment on the continental slope, usually triggered by a seaquake.

turbine. A multi-bladed rotor, driven by combustion gases or steam, that drives a ship's propeller through a reduction gear. Turbine drive is the most common ship propulsion system.

turbler. A kind of fishing lure with a three gang hook at the end of a body that resembles a fishing plug.

turbot. A large flounder or flat bottom fish of European waters that is highly prized for food.

turks head. An ornamental collar of small line or white cord braided around, for example, a deck stanchion, boat's tiller, or boat hook.

turn. 1. A ship turns as it changes course and follows a turning circle, achieving both advance and transfer. 2. A sailor turns to when he starts work and he turns in when he retires to bed. 3. A sailor takes a turn of a line around a cleat. 4. A ship will take turns moving into an assigned berth in a harbor. British term: stem. 5. The tide turns when it changes from flood to ebb or vice versa. 6. A ship that capsizes is said to turn turtle. *See* round turn, all standing.

turnbuckle. A mechanical device, a link, which by turning a moving part in the center can screw in or out the two ends; used for tightening or setting up shrouds or other gear. Also called a rigging screw. British sometimes use the term bottle-screw instead of turnbuckle. The ends of a turnbuckle may be fitted with either an eye or a shackle (clevis). If both ends have shackles, it is a jaw-and-jaw turnbuckle; with both ends eyes, it is an eye-and-eye turnbuckle; and if mixed, it is a jaw-and-eye turnbuckle.

turning basin. The part of a port or harbor where ships have room to turn around. Also called a swinging basin.

turning block. Block used to change the direction of upper spinnaker and jib sheets; usually mounted aft in a sailboat.

turn of the bilge. *See* bilge.

turnpike sailor. Sailor who begs for assistance on the pretext that he has been shipwrecked.

turntable. A revolving platform on the stern of a fishing vessel to facilitate net handling.

turret. The revolving armored casing for a warship's heavy guns. Now rare.

turtle. A special container that holds the folded spinnaker on deck prior to hoisting. Also called spinnaker bag, and by the British, a spinnaker chute.

turtle, sea. Turtle that lives at sea and has paddle-like flippers instead of feet. There are green, loggerhead, hawkbill, and Ridley sea turtles all of the family Cryptodirea. Sea turtles crawl ashore to lay their eggs which are then left to hatch. Most are considered endangered species and are protected by law.

turtleback. The convex curved shape of the deck of a ship or boat where the center is higher than the scuppers. Also called a turtle deck or whaleback.

tweaker. A line secured to a sheet and used for fine adjustment of tension.

tweaker block. A single block on a tag line that is led to a block on the rail amidships and used for a spinnaker guy.

tweendecks. Contraction of between decks; also describes a tank, a hatch or a deck.

Twenty-foot Equivalent Units (TEU). A measure of container capacity of a ship since containers are either 20 or 40 feet long.

twiddling line. A small line used to steady the wheel or tiller. Also a line once used by the helmsman to stir a sluggish magnetic compass. Also called a twigging line.

twice laid rope or stuff. Rope or stuff made from old junk or used yarns.

twing line. A relatively short, light line used, when attached to a sail or a sheet, to adjust and improve the trim of a sail, particularly the spinnaker. Sometimes called twings or twing.

twilight. The period after sunset and before sunrise when there is enough daylight to see the horizon. Civil twilight is that period ending or starting with the sun 6 degrees below the horizon. Observational twilight is eight degrees, nautical twilight is 12 degrees and astronomical twilight is defined in terms of 18 degrees below the horizon.

twin-sheet lead block. Block designed to lead two sheets close to the deck, usually the genoa and staysail sheets that run through the block together.

two blocked. Said of a tackle in which the blocks have been brought together block-and-block or chock-a-block. In the U.S. Navy it once described a signal flag or hoist run all the way up but has been replaced by close up.

typhon. A sound signaling device that uses compressed air and is sounded as a warning to ships in low visibility.

typhoon. A very violent tropical storm of the western Pacific and Indian Oceans with winds over 64 knots. Same as a cyclone, hurricane, or Baguio.

tye. *See* tie.

tyer. *See* tier.

U

U. International signal code alphabet flag. When hoisted singly means: "You are running into danger." Spoken: "uniform."

UBA. Underwater Breathing Apparatus.

ULCC. Ultra Large Crude Carrier; a supertanker larger than a VLCC, now over 500,000 tons with larger ones still being built.

ullage. The amount of liquid that a tank or cask requires to be full. Taking ullage is often done through an ullage hole and measured with an ullage stick, rod, or gauge. *See* sounding.

ultimate wave. *See* rogue wave.

umbilical cord. Slang for the strength-power-communication-cable leading from the surface to the deep diving capsule.

umbrella. A bonnet, shield, or metal hood fitted around a funnel or stack to keep out the weather.

umiak. The Eskimo name for a hunting skin boat larger than a kayak and open; not decked over.

unbend. To detach, untie or remove from a secured position, such as to unbend an anchor from its cable, a sail from its boom, or a rope made fast to a cleat.

unbitt. To remove the turns of a line around a bitt.

unda. The part of the ocean floor that lies under the surf where the bottom sediment is always being stirred.

under. A ship may be undermanned, under-canvassed or under-masted. Also means below as in underdeck tonnage and an underset is a subsurface current.

under bowing. Sailing close to the wind with the set of the current against the lee bow, thus almost going directly into the wind.

underfoot. Said of an anchor when it is directly under the ship's stem or forefoot.

under hack. *See* hack, under.

underhauled. Said of an anchored ship lying at an angle to its normal heading as a result of a subsurface current.

underrun. 1. To haul a boat or float under and along a hawser, cable chain, or trawl for examination, repair, or in the case of the trawl, to remove fish. 2. To underrun a tackle is to separate its parts so that it is ready for use.

under the lee. Sheltered from the wind.

under the weather. Referring to a ship, affected, impeded or damaged by the weather. Now used ashore and at sea to mean mildly sick.

undertow. The brief downward thrust of a collapsing wave as it breaks on a beach. It can drive a swimmer down and under water for a few seconds but a rip current can carry him out to sea for a short distance. The two forces should not be confused.

underway. According to the Rules of the Road a ship is underway when she is not at anchor, made fast to the shore, or aground.

underway replenishment. The logistic supply of warships at sea while underway, using for example, stores ships, oilers or ammunition ships, either by going alongside or by helicopter. A highly developed U.S. Navy specialty.

underwriter. In marine insurance, the person who writes his name on an insurance policy, thus guaranteeing payment in case of loss and earning the premium. In the U.S. an underwriter is normally a corporation, while in the United Kingdom underwriters may be individual members of Lloyds.

Unigan. Trade name for a popular pivoted gantry designed for fishing with a stern trawl.

union. The emblem on a national flag or ensign, signifying the union of two or more sovereignties, located in the upper inside corner. In the U.S. flag, the stars represent states on a blue field. A flag flown with the union down is a distress signal.

union gear. A cargo moving system. *See* burton rig. British term: union purchase.

union jack. A flag consisting of the union or canton alone of the national flag if there is one; otherwise it is a small national flag. It is flown at a jack staff in the bow of a ship at anchor and was once flown aloft as a request for a pilot. In warships the union jack or jack goes up and down ceremoniously with the national flag at morning and evening colors when not underway and is flown at the yardarm when a Court Martial or Court of Inquiry is sitting. The union jack of the U.S. is a blue flag with 50 white stars and for the United Kingdom it is a small national flag, whose proper name is the great union, also called the union flag and, less accurately, the union jack.

union purchase. British term for burton rig.

unireme. An ancient galley of the Mediterranean having a single bank or tier of oars.

univalve. Any mollusk or shellfish having a single shell, such as an abalone.

universal time. As a refinement of mean time, Coordinated Universal Time (UTC) is established by the International Time Bureau using the atomic vibrations of cesium beam oscillators. This is the time broadcast on radio time signals.

unlay. To untwist the strands of a rope.

unloading charge. *See* wharfage.

unship. To remove from stowage aboard ship, as a rudder is unshipped; or to take apart.

unstuff. *See* stuff.

up and down. Describes the anchor and anchor chain when the anchor is directly underfoot. *See* anchor's aweigh. British equivalent, now uncommon, is apeak.

up behind. An order to men hauling in something after a stopper has been clapped on, to slack the line smartly so that a turn may be taken and the line made fast. The full term, rarely heard, is come up behind.

uphaul. A line on the mast of a windsurfer that pulls the sail up.

uphill. A yachtsman's word meaning to windward or upwind.

uphroe. *See* euphroe.

upper works. An old term for that part of a ship's hull above the waterline.

upset shackle. Shackle in which the curved end or bow is fixed, such as in a block or at the lower end of a shroud.

upsetting. The process of heating and hammering so that the part worked upon becomes thicker.

uptakes. Large enclosed trucks or passages for the exhaust gases to pass from the firerooms to the stack or funnel.

upwelling. The rise of cold sea water from the depths of the ocean, bringing important nutrients vital to sea life.

urchin, sea. A round echinoderm with sharp spines that are sometimes poisonous. It lives on the bottom, feeds on the roots of kelp and is considered a food delicacy by Japanese, Europeans as well as sea otters, and lobsters.

Ursa Major, Minor. A constellation of the northern hemisphere composed of bright stars in the shape of a dipper, the Big Dipper or Big Bear whose end bowl stars point to Polaris, the North Star. Polaris is at the end of the handle of a similar arrangement of less bright stars known as Ursa Minor, the Little Bear, or the Little Dipper.

U.S. Coast and Geodetic Survey. Now known as the National Ocean Survey, part of the National Oceanic and Atmospheric Administration.

U.S. Navy Hydrographic Office. Now known as the Hydrographic Center of the Defense Mapping Agency.

U.S. Power Squadron. A nonprofit organization of power boat owners devoted to promoting the interests of boat owners, boat safety, and the teaching of navigation and seamanship.

USS. A prefix before the name of a U.S. warship meaning United States Ship.

UTC. *See* universal time.

USYRU. U.S. Yacht Racing Union. *See* NAYRU.

V

V. International signal code alphabet flag. When hoisted singly means: "I require assistance." Spoken: "victor."

vail. An old seafaring word that means to lower sails as a salute or token of submission to a warship. Modern practice is to dip colors.

valve. A mechanical device used to control the flow of liquid or gas in a line or pipe. Common examples aboard ship include: safety valve (opens at a set pressure to prevent an explosion as on a steam boiler), check valve (permits the flow only in one way as in a boiler feed line), sea valve (brings in salt water from the sea for the sanitary system and firemains), and reducing valve (reduces the pressure of liquid or gas).

van. The leading ships in a formation of warships.

vane. A device made of sheet metal or cloth that is free to rotate on a masthead in order to indicate the relative wind direction to someone sailing a boat. *See* dog-vane.

vane propeller. A special propeller that is only half immersed and sometimes used in shallow draft vessels.

vane steering gear. *See* wind vane.

vanes, vertical sight. Sight vanes of an azimuth or bearing circle that are used by the observer to line up something on which the bearing is being taken.

vang. A rope or wire used to support or hold in place a spar, boom, or derrick. In a cargo ship, it holds a cargo boom in place. If rigged with a block, it is a vang purchase. In a sailboat, it is the tackle used to keep the boom from lifting and is known as a boom vang, boom jack, kicking strap, kicker, or martingale. British term: martingale.

vanship. British word for containership.

variable pitch propeller. Propeller whose blades can rotate to change pitch. *See* propeller.

variation. The angle between the bearing of the magnetic north pole and the actual north pole, measured east or west. Sometimes but inaccurately called magnetic declination. Together with deviation, it forms the magnetic compass error. Variation changes with the geographical position of the ship and with time, and is indicated on most charts.

vee-bottom hull. Describes the hull of a power boat that is relatively beamy with hard (straight) chines from bow to transom and has a relatively flat bottom. This hull is faster than a displacement hull because it can plane. There are also modified vee-bottoms and deep vee-bottoms. *See* hydroplane, displacement hull, hull.

veer. 1. To pay out or slack off, as the anchor cable is veered to allow a greater scope of chain. Most lines are veered but sheets are slacked or checked. 2. Sometimes used as a synonym for haul in describing a clockwise shift of wind direction. *See* back. 3. Once used instead of wear (changing tack).

"veer and haul." An old sailing ship expression meaning to alternately slack and haul on a line to establish rhythm for greater power.

vendaval. A strong southwest wind off Gibraltar in winter.

vent. An outlet or pipe from a tank or compartment aboard ship to the topside that releases gas and permits overflow. British term: vapour pipe or air pipe.

ventilation. Air being sucked into a ship's propellers, often causing heavy cavitation.

ventilators, ship's. Formerly used to direct air by natural pressure below decks. Ventilators were cowl or bell shaped or gooseneck, mushroom, or trunk type. Modern ships now have a forced air system whose terminals below are louvers, cowls, or bell-mouths or slots for large supply to hot spaces. Air exhausts topside through spray-tight louvers are called airlifts.

ventral fin. *See* fin.

venus girdle. A variety of open sea zooplankton, a drifter about a foot long with ribbonlike appendages.

Verity skiff. A small, clinker-built work and fishing boat developed on the southwest shore of Long Island.

vertex. Part of a great circle of a sphere that is closest to a pole of that sphere. *See* composite sailing.

vertical axis propeller. *See* Voith-Schneider propeller.

vertical replenishment. The logistic support of warships, while underway at sea, by means of helicopters. *See* underway replenishment.

Very's pistol. A special device, a flare pistol used to fire off pyrotechnics, especially parachute flares as a distress signal. Commonly called a Very pistol and pronounced veery.

vessel. According to the International Rules of the Road, (vessel) "includes every description of water craft, including non-displacement craft such as surface effect ships and seaplanes, used, or capable of being used, as a means of transportation on water." A power-driven vessel is one propelled by machinery; a sailing vessel is one propelled by sail alone. A cargo vessel is one that carries freight and up to 12 passengers. *See* not-under-command, give-way vessel, stand-on vessel.

Vessel Traffic System (VTS). System operated by the Coast Guard to control the movement of ships in such congested waters as Puget Sound or San Francisco Bay, by using radar and voice radio.

Vice Admiral. A senior Naval officer who flies a three-starred flag; a three star admiral, senior to a Rear Admiral and junior to an Admiral.

Victory Ship. A standard, 16 knot, single screw, turbine drive, 15,000 displacement ton cargo vessel built by the U.S. Maritime Commission in large numbers for World War II. Newer and larger than a Liberty Ship.

vigia. Once used on most charts to indicate a possible reef or pinnacle; now replaced for the most part by PD, position doubtful, or ED, existence doubtful.

Viking. A sea-going Norseman (Scandinavian) who ravaged the coasts and rivers of Europe in longboats during the 8th, 9th, and 10th centuries.

viol. A heavy rope, once used as a messenger to heave in an anchor hawser too large to go around a capstan. Also spelled violl and voyal.

viol block. 1. Any large block. 2. Block used in conjunction with a viol.

visibility. Degrees of visibility are indicated in the following generally accepted scale: 0–dense fog-objects not seen at 50 yards, 1–thick fog-objects not seen at 200 yards, 2–fog-not seen at 500 yards, 3–moderate fog-not seen at 0.5 mile, 4–thin fog-not seen at 1 mile, 5–poor visibility-not seen at 2 miles, 6–moderate visibility-not seen at 5 miles, 7–good visibility-not seen at 10 miles, 8–very good-not seen at 30 miles, 9–excellent-objects seen over 50 miles away.

visit and search. The traditional right under International Law of a belligerent warship to search any ship for contraband cargo in time of war or emergency.

VLCC. Very Large Crude Carrier; a supertanker smaller than an ultra large, up to about 200,000 tons. *See* ULCC.

voe. An uncommon word meaning an inlet, bay, or creek.

voice tube. A tube between such stations as the bridge and the engine room that is used for voice communication.

Voith-Schneider propeller. A vertical axis propeller having a number of blades rotating in a horizontal plane about a central vertical shaft. It has adjustable blades so that the direction and amount of thrust can be varied without changing the speed of rotation. *See* Kirsten-Boeing propeller.

volute. A single-shelled mollusk prized by shell collectors for its pattern of delicate red whorls.

Voss drogue. A patented folding cone-shaped drogue fitted with cross bars to maintain its shape when open.

voyage. 1. A journey by sea which includes both the outward and homeward trips. Each trip is called a passage. A longer trip, visiting several ports, is a cruise. **2.** In marine insurance, it covers the period from departure to arrival at destination.

voyage charter. A charter agreed upon to deliver a certain cargo to a specified port.

vulgar establishment. *See* lunitidal interval.

W

W. International signal code alphabet flag. When hoisted singly means: "I require medical assistance." Spoken: "whiskey."

waft. 1. Any flag or pennant stopped with small stuff around its middle. 2. The signal made by using such a flag. Also spelled weft and rarely heard today.

wager policy. In marine insurance, a policy under which the insured may collect without other proof of interest than possession of the policy. Also called an honor policy.

wahoo. *See* mackerel.

waif. In old whaling days, a shape or flag used to signal absent ship's boats or to mark a killed whale. A variant of waft.

waist. The central or middle part of a ship, between poop and forecastle above the main deck.

waiver clause. In marine insurance, the standard agreement that either party may take action to minimize a loss without prejudice to his interest or rights.

wake. The disturbed water alongside and astern of a moving ship. Because of skin friction, the water nearest to the hull is pulled forward creating a wake current that affects the efficiency of the propeller.

wake light. A dim, shielded light directed down on a ship's wake to assist the Naval ship astern in ship handling at night.

wake surfing. The sport of riding the wake waves of a moving boat on a surfboard.

wale. An obsolete word for the unusually heavy strakes of planking in old wooden ships; also called bends. The word survives in gunwale, the top strip of planking in a boat and in wale shore, another word for breast or side shore, a timber used to support a ship in drydock.

walk. 1. Men hauling on a rope walk away with it, meaning they pull steadily. 2. A ship underway in shallow water is said to be walking or taking a walk when she has steering difficulties.

walk back. A turnbuckle may walk back or loosen due to vibration or boat falls are walked back to be coiled after they have been made fast around a cleat. Walk back is now a general expression meaning to redo or reconsider.

walk out. A ship's anchor is walked out, meaning eased out slowly, before letting go when a ship anchors in deep water and letting go from the hawse would put a heavy strain on the anchor gear. This is also called backing out the anchor.

wall knot. Knot made at the end of a rope by back-splicing the ends, thus forming a knob.

wangle. British word for sculling over the stern of a boat with a single oar.

wardrobe. All the sets or suits of sails of a vessel.

wardroom. The officer's lounge and dining room on a naval ship.

warhead. The forward section of a torpedo containing the explosive. For training, an exercise head is used.

warp. *n* 1. A rope or hawser used in shifting a vessel from one berth to another or in securing a ship to a pier. In the latter case, it would more commonly be called a mooring line. 2. In trawl fishing, the warps connect the trawl to the trawler. 3. The name yachtsmen give to their anchor rode. *vb* To warp a ship is to move it by means of warps or warping lines.

warping bollard. *See* checking bollard.

warping winch. Winch used on deck for handling warps, mooring lines, and boat falls; may also be called a warping capstan. On a multipurpose winch or windlass, one of the drums may be called a warping head.

warship. A naval ship designed and commissioned for use in war; may be a combatant ship, such as a destroyer, or a support ship such as a stores ship or tender.

warshipvoy. A standard voyage charter form, originally prescribed by the War Shipping Administration (WSA). *See* charter party.

wash. *n* 1. Disturbed and agitated water caused by, for example, moving propellers, oars, paddles, or breaking waves on rocks. Also called swash. 2. The sound of the agitated water. 3. A flat area of a bay or inlet that is sometimes exposed or a marshy place. *vb* A man may be washed overboard or the deck may be washed down. *See* swash.

washboard. 1. A strake of thin planking above the gunwales of an open boat to keep out spray and water. Also called a wash strake, weather board, and waste board. 2. Any removable board or barrier that keeps out water such as one that might fit across a companionway.

washover. A small delta built up by sediment washing over a bar into a lagoon by storm waves. Also called a wave delta.

washplate. A divider in a ship's tank that reduces free surface. *See* swashplate.

wash port. Same as freeing port, a more common term in the United Kingdom.

wash strake. *See* strake, wash board.

waste board. *See* wash board.

watch. *n* **1.** Most duties aboard ship are performed in watches of four hours but lookout and helmsmen watches are usually two hours in length. A watch in three is standard but watch on, watch off or watch and watch are likely in cases of emergency. **2.** A team of men such as the anchor watch. *vb* To watch, in reference to a floating object, is to be visible, such as the anchor buoy is reported as watching.

watch buoy. A marker buoy moored near a lightship by which she can verify her position.

watch cap. 1. A canvas or metal cover for a stack or funnel. Also called a stack cover. **2.** The black band around the top of the stack. **3.** A blue knitted cap worn by Naval enlisted men, fishermen, and other mariners.

watch coat. A heavy, dark blue, knee length bridge coat or reefer that is worn at sea in cold weather.

watch-ho watch. The traditional call of the mate in charge as he released the deep-sea lead forward; repeated by each sailor along the rail as he felt for the bottom and then released his coil of line until someone felt the bottom and called out the fathoms.

watch mark. A narrow stripe on the sleeve of a Naval enlisted man's uniform; once showing his watch-port or starboard, now shows rating group.

watch officer. Officer in charge of a Naval watch such as the Engineer Officer of the Watch below or the Officer of the Deck on the bridge.

Watch Quarter & Station Bill. In a Naval ship, the posted list of the crew's assignments, such as during emergencies, battle, or watches at sea and in port.

watch routine. The middle or mid watch 0-4, the morning watch 4-8, the forenoon watch 8-12, the afternoon watch 12-16, the first dog watch 16-18, the second dog 18-20, the first or evening watch 20-24. Dog watches ensure that the same people do not stand the same watches every day.

watch tackle. A small purchase once used for various purposes by the watch on deck of a sailing ship, usually either a luff or guntackle.

water cannon. A special pedestal-mounted nozzle for the very high pressure pumps of a fireboat. Also called a monitor.

water deck iron. An iron collar or flange to keep water out where the stovepipe enters the boat.

water gall. Same as wind dog.

water jet. A propulsion system for boats in which the propeller is replaced by a pump-driven stream of water expelled aft at high velocity. Also called jet drive.

water-laid rope. Rope made up of natural fibers using water instead of oil. Not common today with the increased use of synthetic fibers.

waterline (w.l.) The level of water on the outside of the hull of a floating ship. *See* load waterline.

waterlogged. Saturated or filled with water; lacking buoyancy.

water marks. The numerals on a ship's stern and her stem indicating draft. Also the numerals on a tide gauge.

water monkey. A clay pot for keeping drinking water cool aboard ship in the tropics; also called a chatty. Now replaced by mechanical coolers or scuttlebutts in modern ships.

waterplane. Plane parallel to the surface of the water in which the ship is floating or will float. The horizontal, equally spaced waterplanes are used to compute the ship's displacement up to a desired level or waterplane.

water sail. A small sail set below the usual sails of a square-rigger in light winds. Also called a save-all.

water sky. Dark streaks on the clouds in polar regions caused by the reflection of open spaces or leads in large areas of sea ice.

waterspout. A small rotary wind storm over water, similar to a tornado ashore, marked by a funnel-shaped cloud that picks up water where it touches the sea. This water is called a bush and can endanger a ship.

water taxi. Same as a shore boat; a commercial harbor passenger boat.

watertube boiler. Boiler in which steam is generated in tubes by the surrounding hot gases of combustion in contrast to firetube boilers in which tubes carry the hot gases through a container of water. All modern steamships use watertube boilers.

waterway. The narrow gutter along the outboard edge of the deck topside into which water drains and then goes overboard through scuppers. Also a body or passage of navigable water such as the Inland Waterway along the U.S. east coast.

wave. A moving ridge or swell of water caused mainly by wind and moving at about half the wind's speed. The particles of water in each wave move vertically in a rough circle and thus remain more or less stationary except for the tops of breaking waves. *See* tidal wave, blind rollers, surf, swell, sea state, ground wave, seismic sea wave.

wave, bow. Wave formed by the pressure of a ship's moving bow.

wave length. The distance between crests of adjacent waves, separated by troughs.

wave delta. *See* washover.

wave direction. Direction from which the wave comes.

wave drag. The resistance or water drag of an object, such as a ship, moving in water due to the energy used in making waves.

wave height. Vertical distance in feet between the trough and the crest of a wave. Significant height is the average of the highest third of the waves measured. *See* rogue wave, sea state.

wave refraction. The change in direction of a wave train caused by the reduced speed in shallow water.

wave, rogue. *See* rogue wave.

WAVES. Women Accepted for Voluntary Emergency Service; the women in the U. S. Navy.

wave, standing or stationary. Wave in which the surface of the water oscillates vertically between fixed levels or nodes without forward movement. The points of maximum rise and fall are called loops. Standing waves are characteristic of a seiche or of clapotis (reflected waves).

wave train. A series of waves, a wave system, all moving in the same direction.

way. Motion through the water. A ship is legally underway although she may have no way on, when she is not attached to the shore, at anchor, or moored. A ship has headway when going forward and sternway when going astern. Not to be confused with weigh.

way enough. A command by the coxswain of a pulling boat to his oarsmen to stop pulling.

ways. Short for slipway, ground way, or launching way. *See* slipway.

weakfish. A small but popular food and game fish of the genus *Cynoscion,* found on the North Atlantic coast. Also called a sea trout.

wear. Same as jibe, although the latter may be accidental while a sailboat wears deliberately. *See* jibe. In the United Kingdom a ship wears a personal flag such as an admiral's flag while in the U.S. a ship flies such a flag. Both fly their national flag.

weather. *n* **1.** The side facing the wind, the windward side; opposite to the lee side. **2.** To make heavy weather of it is to struggle and suffer stress in bad weather; also used to describe a sailor ashore who is drunk. *vb* **1.** To weather a cape is to pass it safely. **2.** To weather bitt a line is to take an extra turn.

weather beaten. Worn and damaged by bad weather.

weatherboard. *See* washboard.

weather cloth. A piece of canvas rigged to protect someone from the elements such as spray, wind, or rain. Also called a dodger.

weathercocks. Said of a ship that comes up into the wind easily.

weather deck. Uncovered deck.

weather facsimile or Weatherfax. A system used for sending and receiving by high frequency radio, for example, weather maps, satellite cloud photos, and sea state diagrams. Ships receiving these data can make their own weather forecasts.

weather gauge. Position to windward of another ship; eagerly sought by racing yachtsmen today and fighting sailors of the past.

weather glass. A barometer. *See* glass.

weatherly. Describes a sailing ship or boat that can make good speed in a strong breeze and can thus point high and sail fast.

weather ship. Ship assigned to a particular ocean area where it reports, for example, pressure, temperature, wind, and sea state. Also called an ocean station ship.

weather symbols. A simple code of single letters used for recording the state of the weather in the ship's log; b is blue sky, c is cloudy, h is hail, and so on as found in the instructions for keeping the log.

weather working days. Those days on which, weather permitting, cargo may be loaded or unloaded under terms of a charter party.

weaverfish. A small aggressive fish that sometimes attacks divers inflicting painful and even fatal wounds.

web. In shipbuilding, the central or main portion of a steel beam, girder, frame, or other major component or member as distinct from, for example, an attached angle bar or flange.

web framing. A special system of shipbuilding involving web stringers and web plates.

web sling. A cargo handling device made of rope netting, similar to a cargo net, that is used for handling items requiring special care such as animals. Also called an animal sling.

wedge cleat. *See* cleat.

wedge rider. *See* launching cradle.

weedline. A line fastened along the top of the mesh of a gillnet that allows the net to be suspended a few feet below the corkline.

weep. A slight leak, as from a cask or along a seam.

weeping joint. Joint that permits a slow oozing of the liquid confined within.

weft. 1. In canvas, the cross threads or woof that are woven through the warp or threads running lengthwise. 2. The width measurement of sail cloth. 3. A variant of waft. *See* waif, waft.

weigh. To raise or lift a ship's anchor, especially before getting underway. Not to be confused with way.

weir. A sort of fence set in a stream or along the shore to catch fish. Often lighted at night if in navigable waters. Also called a fish weir or pound. Also the dam near a lock in a canal or river.

welin davit. Old name for quadrantal davit. *See* davit.

well. 1. Any area or space in a ship where bilge water collects. 2. In a fishing vessel, a tank filled with salt water to keep fish or bait alive. *See* drain well.

welldeck. Any deck area topside that has superstructure both forward and aft of it.

well-found. Said of a ship that is well-equipped and in good material condition.

westerlies. The prevailing winds from the west found in the temperate zones especially above $30°$ latitude.

Western Ocean. The ancient name for the Atlantic, still used by some European mariners.

West Wind Drift. Same as the Antarctic Circumpolar Current.

wet dock. Part of a port or harbor, a basin enclosed by gates in order to maintain an adequate level of water when there is considerable tidal range. Also called a wet basin. *See* dock.

wet suit. A close fitting flexible plastic (rubber) suit that permits a thin layer of water next to the diver's skin, thus keeping the wearer warm. Also worn by surfers, water skiers and others.

wetted surface. The area of a ship's hull or skin below the waterline, including bilge keels and rudder.

whack. *n* The old sailor's word for his daily ration of food as legally prescribed. *vb* To whack up is to divide into equal shares.

whale. A sea-going, breathing mammal whose tail is horizontal rather than vertical like a fish's. The Cetacea order comprises two suborders: Odontoceti, the toothed whales such as porpoise and sperm whales, and Mystacoceti, the baleen whales such as the blue and the gray whale. Whales are friendly, highly intelligent and, for the most part, being killed to extinction.

whaleback. Same as turtleback.

whaleboat. Originally a double-ended, seaworthy, pulling boat used for whaling. Now usually fitted with a diesel engine and used by warships as a lifeboat and small general utility boat. Also called a whaler.

whaleboat chock. A grooved fairlead over the bow of a whaleboat so designed as to take the strain of a harpooned whale without listing the boat.

whalebone. The strong, flexible strips of bone used by the baleen whales to strain out their food from sea water. Also called baleen.

whale-catcher. Small, sea worthy and fast ships from which whales are killed with explosive harpoons. They often operate from a factory ship.

whale factory. A ship equipped to cut up and render whales, collecting and storing the meat and the oil.

whaler. *See* whaleboat.

wharf. A structure parallel to the shore to which ships moor for loading and unloading or for minor repairs. Sometimes called a dock or quay but the latter is usually a solid structure whereas a wharf is supported by pilings. *See* pier, dock.

wharfage. A charge made to a cargo vessel for the use of a wharf, pier or dock.

wharfinger. A wharfmaster, a person in charge or owner of a wharf or waterfront warehouse or the space adjacent to a wharf. In the United Kingdom it is a person who directs the checking, loading and unloading of cargo as representative of the shipowner or charterer.

wharf rat. A vagrant petty thief who loiters near the waterfront.

wheel. *n* Nautical word for propeller, paddle wheel or steering wheel. *vb* Ships in convoy wheel when they change course by simultaneous turn.

wheel grating. Grating on which the helmsman stands to improve his vision and to keep his feet dry in bad weather.

wheelhouse. Same as pilothouse.

wheelsman. A helmsman or steersman.

wheel rope. Rope that connects the wheel to the rudder.

whelk. A marine snail having a turreted pointed shell, common to Europe and North America and used for food and bait. *See* conch.

whelps. The ribs or ridges on the drum of a capstan, winch, or windlass that provide friction for the rope being hauled in. Those on a wildcat, fit the links of the anchor chain.

where away. The proper inquiry of a lookout who has reported something, asking for its bearing.

wherry. Once a sailing craft of British waters, now a light pulling boat with a transom stern. Also a narrow racing or exercise boat for one man.

whiffing. Another word for trolling.

whip. *n* A rope or wire used as part of a tackle to handle, for example, cargo. *See* cargo whip. *vb* To whip a rope's end is to wrap it with small stuff to prevent fagging. *See* mooring whip.

whipstaff. A hinged wooden vertical lever once used to move the tiller of a sailing ship from a position above the tiller so that the helmsman could see; disappeared early in the 18th century with the introduction of the wheel.

whisker pole. A spar used to hold out the clew of a jib when sailing before the wind. In square-riggers, long spars or whiskers were once used at right angles to, and at the end of, the bowsprit for spreading the jib-boom guys.

whistle. A required ship's noise-making device that must be audible at two miles and that must, by U.S. law, be at least six feet above the pilot house; used for making the signals specified by the Rules of the Road, including fog signals. Also the old name for the boatswain's pipe.

whitecaps. The broken water at the top of a wave that is breaking at sea due to wind pressure. They generally start to form with winds of 12 knots. Also called white horses and Neptune's sheep.

whitefish. A British word for groundfish.

white horse. The tough, hard substance in the head of a sperm whale that usually resisted the thrust of a harpoon thrown by hand.

whiteout. An optical phenomenon encountered in low visibility in polar regions when clouds, shadows and the horizon are not visible, resulting in disorientation.

whoodings. The planks in a wooden ship that are fitted into the stem.

wide berth. Staying at a considerable distance such as a prudent mariner may give a hazard to navigation a wide berth.

wildcat. The chain grab or cable holder drum on an anchor windlass that is fitted with whelps shaped to engage the links of the chain. Also called a cable lifter or cable wheel. British term: gipsy or gypsy.

williwaw. A violent, sudden wind blowing off a mountainous coast, particularly in the Aleutians and in the Straits of Magellan.

willy-willy. Australian word for a tropical cyclone with winds over 64 knots.

winch. A mechanical device driven by steam, electricity, or hydraulic power that is used to handle lines, such as a cargo winch or a boat winch as well as fishing trawls and nets. In ship winches, the lines are usually passed around revolving horizontal drums. Sometimes called a capstan or windlass although the latter is normally used to haul in anchors and is known as an anchor windlass. In sailing yachts, winches are man-powered, geared, multi-speed, and expensive and are used to quickly haul in sheets and halyards when racing. Slang word is coffee grinder.

winch, towing. *See* towing machine.

wind. Air movement across the earth's surface; largely the result of differences in atmospheric pressure in adjacent air masses. Wind is identified by the direction from which it blows or by local names. Winds may be semi-permanent (trade winds), seasonal (monsoon), daily (solar winds, land and sea breezes), sometimes very violent (typhoons), or irregular and changeable due to the movement of high and low pressure systems. For wind shift definitions, *see* back.

wind dog. A broken or partial rainbow that is supposed to predict wind. Also called a wind gall or water gall.

wind drift. Same as drift current.

wind gall. Same as wind dog.

windjammer. A sailing ship, usually square-rigged. Also the sailor who goes to sea in such a ship.

windlass, anchor. A mechanical device on the forecastle used to haul in the anchor and to handle various lines such as mooring lines. The anchor chain feeds over a revolving steel drum called a wildcat and then passes below. One or two horizontal drums or heads are used to handle lines. They are known as gipsy or warping heads, warping ends, or whipping drums.

windlop. An old word for a short and choppy sea such as that produced by wind opposing a current.

wind-rode. Said of a ship at anchor lying bow to the wind as different from lying bow to tide or tide-rode.

wind rose. A diagram, usually on a pilot chart, showing the strength and direction of the prevailing winds in a certain area at a particular time of year.

wind sail. A canvas tube with an open mouth rigged to send fresh air below. Also called a galley staysail.

windscoop. A portable metal scoop fitted into a porthole to direct fresh air into the ship.

windseeker. A sailing yachtsman's word for any headsail he may use to improve his speed in very light airs. *See* drifter.

windship. Any vessel propelled mainly by wind, in contrast to a steamship.

windsurfing. The sport of sailing a surfboard by standing on the board while holding a sail rigged on a fully articulated mast, that is, a mast stepped on the surfboard with a ball and socket connection; called boardsailing outside the U.S. and also called surfsailing.

wind, to. To bring a ship around, end for end, while alongside a pier; usually done with warps. Also to turn a ship sharply in port with lines and tugs is to wind her. Pronounced wynd.

windtuft. Same as tell tale.

wind vane. A self-steering device for sailboats that connects to the rudder and is actuated by wind pressure on the vane. Also called a vane steering gear.

windward. The side from which the wind blows; opposite to leeward.

wing. Part of a ship's interior that is outboard, next to the skin of the ship.

wing and wing. Describes a sailboat running before the wind with sails rigged out on both sides. Also sometimes referred to as goose-winged.

winging. Stowing cargo so that most of it is in the wings of the hold, the outboard sections.

wing mast. Mast shaped like an airfoil to reduce turbulence and drag; increasingly popular for racing sailboats.

wing tanks. Tanks that are the farthest outboard.

winkle. *See* conch.

wipe out. Loss of a surfboard in a breaking wave. The surfer must then recover his board and paddle out again.

wiper. Traditional name for a relatively unskilled man in the engine room of a merchant ship whose major duties are cleaning and simple maintenance.

wire drag. To establish with certainty a safe depth of water by dragging a weighted wire between two boats at a fixed depth.

wire rope. Rope made from steel wire galvanized, uncoated or stainless, sometimes twisted around a fiber core to ensure flexibility.

wishbone. A sail rig for yachts having a double gaff in a similar shape to a wishbone. Also in U.S. Navy ships, the supporting rods or stays for the upper accomodation ladder platform.

witching. A procedure in sailing to windward through a narrow cut or canal by using bank cushion to reduce leeway.

withe. *See* crance.

w.l. Waterline.

WMO. The World Meteorological Organization; part of the United Nations. *See* Douglas Scale.

WNA. Winter North Atlantic; designates the highest permissible waterline a ship may be loaded to when operating there in winter.

wolf-eel. Similar to the moray eel, this snake-like fish grows to six feet and is found in the North Pacific.

wolf pack. Coordinated submarine attack group.

woodlock. A close-fitting piece of hard wood fitted and secured below a rudder pintle that prevents the rudder from unshipping.

woof. *See* weft.

woold. To wind a rope or chain around a spar at a place where it is being fished to hold the joint in place.

woolder. A stick made of hardwood used to tighten the woold by twisting the rope. Also called a woolder stick.

wooly. Same as telltale.

work. 1. To strain or labor, as a ship's hull creaks and groans under stress. 2. A sailing ship works to windward to clear a point of land and a stevedore works cargo.

working canvas. Canvas normally used; different from racing or storm canvas.

World Port Index. DMAHC publication 150, a companion volume to the new Sailing Directions, giving detailed information about the ports of the world.

worm, parcel, and serve. To worm a rope is to fill the grooves between strands with tarred small stuff. Parceling is wrapping the rope with strips of canvas. The rope is then served or wrapped with tight turns of marline.

worms. Marine worms or annelids, usually bloodworms or sandworms, are harvested on tidal flats in large numbers and are then sold as fishing bait. Not to be confused with shipworms which are marine borers.

wrack. Seaweed cast ashore and collected for fertilizer. Also a variant of rack, a thin mass of wind-driven clouds.

wrasse. Small and bony, shallow water fish of the family Labridae that is found along rocky coasts and tropical reefs. Most are brightly patterned and colored. Some feed on parasites of larger fish such as groupers.

wreck. A ship or parts of a ship that is no longer navigable and cast ashore or sinking.

wreckage. Cargo or parts of a wreck cast ashore.

wrecking. Same as shipbreaking. Also the ancient practice of showing false lights, such as tying a light to a horse's head, or otherwise deceiving ships into running aground so they could be looted.

wrecking blocks. Heavy duty, extra strong, large blocks used for salvage work and heavy lifts.

wriggle. Same as an eyebrow or rigol.

wring. To bend or twist a spar out of line as when stays are set up too tight.

wrister. A woolen wrist and arm covering worn by fishermen when working at sea in cold wind and water.

wye. A metal band around a mast or spar having one or more eyes welded to it.

X

X. International signal code alphabet flag. When hoisted singly, it means: "Stop carrying out your intentions and watch for my signals." Spoken: "X ray."

XBT. An expendable bathythermograph or BT whose data are transmitted by radio.

xebec. A three-masted sailing ship rigged with square, fore-and-aft and lateen sails and weighing up to 400 tons. Once common in the Mediterranean (used by North African pirates), now a rare sight.

xiphias. Another word for swordfish, as well as for the small constellation dorado.

Y

Y. International signal code alphabet flag. When hoisted singly, it means: "I am dragging my anchor." Spoken: "yankee."

yacht. Any vessel used for pleasure. Lloyds classifies any pleasure boat over 30 feet as a yacht. The owner is a yachtsman who may keep his boat at a yacht club when not yachting. The word connotes a certain pretension and an owner never refers to his boat as a yacht unless he is a landlubber.

yacht ensign. A flag adopted by the U.S. Congress for yachts only. It shows only 13 stars in the union, together with a fouled anchor.

yachtsman's anchor. *See* old-fashioned anchor.

yankee. A light foresail, similar to a genoa and a ghoster but not overlapping the main as much as a genoa; used in light winds by sailing yachts.

yard. A large round spar, tapering towards the ends that is used for supporting and extending sails and signal flags. Also short for shipyard or Navy Yard.

yard-arm. Either extremity of a yard that is rigged perpendicular to a mast. Signal flags are usually displayed from a halyard rigged on a yard-arm.

yard-arm blinker. A system of communication between Naval ships at night at anchor or when in formation using lights at the yard-arm keyed from the signal bridge below.

yard span. A metal forging, part of the truss fitted on the afterside of the lower yards of a square-rigger at the slings. Also called a truss bow or truss yoke.

yarn. One of the fiber threads which, when twisted together, form a strand. Also a telltale.

yaw. A temporary change from a ship's course, usually caused by a following sea which if very heavy could result in a broach. A ship is said to yaw or be yawing when it rotates about a vertical axis. *See* ship motion.

yawl. A small two-masted sailing vessel, a fore-and-aft rigged yacht with a smaller mizzenmast or jigger mast located abaft the waterline or, more obviously, the tiller. *See* ketch. Also a small, double-ended pulling boat.

yawl boat. A small powerboat used to tow a vessel.

yellowtail. A member of the crevalle family, *Seriola dorsalis,* a popular Pacific food and game fish, up to 100 pounds, found in deep water and often just outside the kelp beds.

yoke. Commonly found in a ship or boat, a crosspiece fitted to the rudderhead. Connecting wire or chain at the ends of the yoke are controlled by the steering gear.

York-Antwerp Rules. The most recent, 1974, international agreement for the adjustment of a general average loss. A common reference in most bills of lading and charter parties.

yuloh. Chinese word used by the British for a long, flexible, usually crooked oar used in sculling with a single oar over the stern of a boat.

Z

Z. International signal code alphabet flag. When flown singly, it means: "I require a tug"; when shown by a fishing vessel near the fishing grounds, means "I am shooting nets." Spoken: "zulu."

Z drive. Same as stern drive.

zebec. Same as xebec.

zenith. The point in the celestial sphere directly overhead.

zenith distance. The angular distance of an object from the observer's zenith that is found by subtracting its altitude from 90 degrees.

zincs. Pieces of zinc fastened near a propeller or other bronze or brass fitting that absorb the corrosive effect of electrolysis in sea water, thus protecting the bronze as well as the steel hull.

zone. *See* foreign trade zone.

zone description (zd). The correction, plus or minus 1 to 12, that is applied to local time to obtain Greenwich Mean Time.

zone time (zt). An international system of relating local time to Greenwich Mean Time and thus relating different local times to each other. The world is divided into zones 15 degrees wide over which the sun passes in one hour. The zones start at longitude zero, Greenwich near London with 7½ degrees on each side and are numbered plus or minus 1 to 12. A ship at longitude 50°W, for example, will keep +3 time.

zooanthellae. Tiny algae that live within a coral polyp in symbiotic or mutually beneficial relationship.

zooplankton. Small sea animal plankton that feeds on the phytoplankton or plants. They, in turn, are fed upon by other sea life and thus the food chain of the sea is sustained.

zulu time. Another term for Greenwich Mean Time, which, when used in communications, is followed by "z" to confirm that it is GMT and not local time.

623.8   N67v   71679a

Noel, John

The VNR Dictionary of Ships & The
                                  Sea

DATE DUE

MR 31 '87			
AP 29 '87			
NO 19 '88			
MY 15 '90			

HURON PUBLIC LIBRARY

333 Williams Street

Huron, Ohio 44839

DEMCO